# Life Sentence:
# Memoirs of a Ukrainian Political Prisoner

# Life Sentence:
## Memoirs of a
## Ukrainian Political Prisoner

## By Danylo Shumuk

Edited by Ivan Jaworsky

Translated by Ivan Jaworsky and Halya Kowalska

Canadian Institute of Ukrainian Studies
University of Alberta
Edmonton                    1984

# THE CANADIAN LIBRARY IN UKRAINIAN STUDIES

A series of original works and reprints relating to Ukraine, issued under the editorial supervision of the Canadian Institute of Ukrainian Studies, University of Alberta, Edmonton.

Copyright © 1984     Canadian Institute of Ukrainian Studies
                     University of Alberta
                     Edmonton, Alberta, Canada

**Canadian Cataloguing in Publication Data**
Shumuk, Danylo, 1914–
    Life sentence

    (The Canadian library in Ukrainian studies)
    Translation of: Za skhidnim obriiem.
    ISBN 0-920862-17-9 (bound).
    ISBN 0-920862-19-5 (pbk.)

1. Shumuk, Danylo, 1914–  2. Political  prisoners—Ukraine—Biography.
3. Ukraine—Politics and government—1917–
I. Jaworsky, Ivan, 1953–  II. Canadian Institute of Ukrainian Studies. III. Title.
IV. Series.
DK508.83.S48A3913 1984      947–.71084'0924      C84–091485–7

Cover design: Sherryl Petterson

Printed in Canada by Printing Services, University of Alberta
Distributed by the    University of Toronto Press
                      5201 Dufferin St.
                      Downsview, Ontario
                      Canada M3H 5T8

# Contents

# Foreword
by Nadia Svitlychna

Danylo Shumuk is Amnesty International's most "senior" political prisoner, having been incarcerated in various prisons and labour camps for almost thirty-seven years. He is now serving a five-year term of internal exile in Kazakhstan. The story of Danylo Shumuk's life is most fully depicted in his autobiography, the second part of which, under the title *Za skhidnim obriiem* [Beyond the Eastern Horizon] was published in the United States by "Smoloskyp" publishers in 1974. At the request of the author, I edited the manuscript of the first part of Danylo Shumuk's memoirs, entitled "The Story of My Experiences," and this was the main "crime" with which I was charged after my arrest in 1972.

During my trial, in March 1973, Denysenko, the lawyer assigned to me by the court, told me: "All you have to do is admit that this is an anti-Soviet document—nothing more—and this trial will immediately take a different course." The terms "Soviet" and "anti-Soviet," as well as "nationalism," "communism" and "fascism," have become so hackneyed that everyone imbues them with his/her own, often contradictory, content. But my interpretation of the term "anti-Soviet" did not allow me to accept the court's tempting proposition.

Danylo Shumuk was one of the three witnesses designated by the investigating authorities to testify at my trial. However, for some reason he did not appear (the explanation that transportation problems were involved is not very convincing). At the time Shumuk was already serving his sentence (for writing his memoirs) in a Mordovian special-regime camp.

Actually, I heard about Shumuk's trial in July 1972, very soon after he had been sentenced. When I asked the investigator in charge of my case what sentence Shumuk had received he told me, with a great deal of solicitude, that it was a long sentence—three years. I agreed: yes, after everything that Shumuk had gone through this was truly a severe punishment. Some time later, however, I learned, from the documents concerning Shumuk's case, that Captain Siryk had "humanely abbreviated" the sentence which Shumuk had received by a factor of five, for he had actually been sentenced to fifteen years' imprisonment.

In issue no. 22 of the Russian-language journal *Kontinent*, Edward Kuznetsov describes his former cellmate Danylo Shumuk as an uncommon lover of the truth.

> Shumuk is a Ukrainian not only by birth, but also by virtue of his passionate love for all that is Ukrainian. But even if you were a Martian of some kind, just tell Danylo that one of his countrymen—even his own brother—had done you an injustice.... Then you'll discover that when Danylo states that he prizes truth and justice above all, that it is truly so.

Danylo Lavrentiiovych Shumuk was born on 30 December 1914 in the village of Boremshchyna, Volhynia oblast. An unwanted child in a large peasant family, Danylo's childhood was full of grief and injustice, and even as a boy he sympathized with those who had been wronged in some way. "At the age of twelve I began to prepare myself spiritually for... a life of torment and suffering. It was even sweet to think about suffering for the truth."

Shumuk's thoughts became harsh reality when he was eighteen years old: he was arrested several times and eventually incarcerated in a Polish prison as a result of his underground communist activity. Shumuk was imprisoned for five years and four months (he was released in 1939 as the result of an amnesty); this was his first, shortest and most lenient period of incarceration. And although prison life is always harsh, in Poland, at least, political prisoners were treated with a certain respect. Food was not withheld as a form of punishment, and the prisoners were allowed visits from relatives, not forced to work, and allowed to receive books of various kinds.

For Shumuk the communist ideal was the "star of Bethlehem," and he continued to believe in this ideal even after the Soviet occupation of Volhynia in 1939. Even when his brother Antin Shumuk was arrested, and Danylo was forced to join a "work camp" on 15 May 1941 as the brother of an "enemy of the people," he did not lose faith in the benevolence of the communists.

When the Germans attacked the Soviet Union these work camps were transformed into penal battalions. Without military training, and without proper arms, they were sent to the front lines to fight tanks with their bare hands—"For the Fatherland! For Stalin!"—while "brave" Chekists in the rear used machine guns to keep up the spirits of the penal battalions. Two months after the war began some 600,000 soldiers on the Kiev front alone ended up as German prisoners of war. Among them was Danylo Shumuk.

"In August and September 1941 I was imprisoned in a German prisoner of war camp in Khorol near Poltava. People died like flies in this pit of death, from hunger, exposure and various epidemics. Faced with certain death I, together with three other companions, decided to make a break for freedom. One cold, rainy night three of us managed to escape.

"Passing village after village as I made my way by foot westward, through the oblasts of Poltava, Kiev and Zhytomyr, I learned from the villagers about the unbelievable horrors they had suffered between 1933 and 1937. The ruins of villages whose inhabitants had died during the artificially imposed famine and the terrible stories which I heard from the survivors of this tragedy now fully opened my eyes and cleared my mind of the opium of communist ideology. At this point, losing my faith in communism meant that my life lost its meaning, for that which had once been so precious to me turned out to be an abomination."

In March 1943 Danylo Shumuk joined the Ukrainian Insurgent Army (UPA) and was appointed a political instructor in an officer training school. But it became clear to Danylo that the UPA's struggle for an independent Ukraine was doomed, for the forces involved were highly unequal and it was necessary to fight on two fronts—against both the German and Soviet armies. Yet he considered it his duty to stay on till the end.

In February 1945 Danylo Shumuk was captured by the NKVD, a military tribunal sentenced him to be shot, and he spent forty-five days and nights waiting for the death sentence to be carried out. The death sentence was eventually commuted to twenty years of hard labour, and together with hundreds of thousands of other political prisoners, Shumuk, prodded by hunger and bayonets, helped build one of the gigantic industrial complexes in Norilsk which Soviet historians claim was the product of enthusiastic work by Komsomol volunteers. Shumuk was active in the underground movement in the labour camps, and in 1953 he was one of the leaders of the prisoners' strike in Norilsk, which lasted for two months.

During the so-called "thaw" Danylo Shumuk's case was re-examined and he was freed in August 1956. One year later, however, he was rearrested and charged with "anti-Soviet agitation and propaganda." Major Sverdlov of the republican KGB admitted cynically that there were no grounds for bringing this charge against him, and informed Shumuk that he would be freed immediately if he agreed to become a secret agent for the KGB. Shumuk, of course, refused, and was thus sentenced to an additional ten years' imprisonment. He was released in 1967, having served this sentence in full.

Danylo Shumuk writes that he feels "an obligation to inform the public about what drove me to follow the path I have taken, the path of a search and struggle for the truth." He has fulfilled this obligation, despite the horrendous barriers in his way. He began writing his memoirs several times. I remember from our conversations that on two different occasions several manuscript notebooks were confiscated from him when he was imprisoned in the Iavas camp in Mordovia, but he simply began writing all over again. In 1969, after he had been released and had written part of the new version of his memoirs, six manuscript notebooks which I was then editing were secretly confiscated from me.

When I was editing the second version of Shumuk's memoirs I rewrote the text, in my own hand, in a thick notebook which included only the beginning of the first section of the memoirs. A copy of this notebook eventually reached the West, but I don't know if the remainder of the first section was saved. Although I did not edit or read the second section of Shumuk's memoirs, I know that at the beginning of 1972 four full copies of the memoirs were in existence, and that they were all confiscated in January 1972. The most complete version, which included photographs, was confiscated from my brother Ivan Svitlychny, and the other versions were confiscated from various friends of Shumuk. The materials taken from my quarters included a typewritten version of the first section which I had not yet returned to the author, and a copy of the handwritten manuscript of the second section, on film, which I had made for myself in 1971.

In the winter of 1975, when Iryna Kalynets and I were returning to Iavas from Barashevo after our latest incarceration in a "cooler" (punishment cell), we accidentally (or maybe it wasn't an accident?) met Danylo Shumuk, who was being taken to the camp hospital, and he managed to inform us that a copy of his memoirs had remained undiscovered during the searches in 1972 and had already been published in the West. This was a pleasant surprise. Was it one of the confiscated copies which reached the West? I have no idea.

According to recent information which has reached the West, some three hundred pages of handwritten manuscript, prepared by Danylo Shumuk during his latest imprisonment, were confiscated from him when he was sent into exile late in 1981. But perhaps this manuscript will also be saved from destruction.

In 1973 Shumuk sent a statement to the Presidium of the Supreme Soviet of the USSR in which he renounced his Soviet citizenship and gave his reasons for doing so. He said that he would like to join his family in Canada, and for several successive years the Canadian government has intervened with the Soviet authorities on his behalf. In 1979, in response to the Canadian government's humanitarian request that this feeble and aging prisoner be released, the Soviet government resorted to its favourite tactic—slander and misinformation. It informed the Canadian government that Shumuk was a "war criminal" and thus did not deserve clemency. In turn, the Group for the Implementation of the Helsinki Accords in Places of Detention in the USSR appealed to all peoples, parliaments and governments of the signatory countries of the Helsinki Agreement in defence of the good name of Shumuk, a member of this group, recommending that they acquaint themselves with his open letter "To All Those Who Inspire and Direct the Repressive Organs of the USSR."

In his open letter Danylo Shumuk states: "During the war I became absolutely convinced of the harmfulness and danger of totalitarianism and authoritarian ideas, whatever their orientation.

And even when I was involved myself with authoritarian organizations during the war, words were my only weapon, words of humanism.

"I cannot help but admire the political systems of the United States, England and Canada, for they are based on humanism and democracy, and the cornerstone of their policies is human rights. In this respect President Carter's policies deserve special recognition. I support SALT II negotiations, but I believe that at the same time steps should be taken to establish a similar parity as far as the means of ideological struggle are concerned; that is, the volume of ideological literature of a free, democratic character published in the countries of the Warsaw Pact should equal the volume of communist literature of a pro-Moscow orientation published in the countries of the free world. For how can one talk of equality and justice when for a long time now the ideological battle has been waged on the territory of the countries of the free world, while in the USSR people continue to be persecuted for expressing their convictions and are forbidden to leave their country?

"It is hardly appropriate for you, the leaders of the USSR, to speak of war crimes or other such crimes, for during the period 1933–7 the Soviet regime destroyed more people than died at the hands of the fascists during the entire Second World War. And you were hardly farm hands at the time; you were active instruments of Stalin's bloody regime at the raion and oblast level.

"I know that I am in your hands and realize what awaits me; however, I will continue exposing you, no matter what the consequences, as long as I am among the living."

# Introduction

Danylo Shumuk was born and raised in Volhynia, a region of Western Ukraine which had been part of the Russian Empire before the First World War, but was assigned to Poland by the Treaty of Riga in 1921. Volhynia was one of the most economically backward provinces of interwar Poland, and the situation of the Ukrainians there was difficult, worse than in Eastern Galicia (part of the Habsburg Empire before the war), the other region included in Poland where Ukrainians predominated. The small but developing Ukrainian middle class and intelligentsia were almost wholly concentrated in Galicia, and the overwhelming majority of Ukrainians in Volhynia lived in rural areas.

Further, the Ukrainians in Galicia had benefited from certain constitutional guarantees under Habsburg rule and had passed through the stages of modern nation-building by 1918. In contrast, restrictions imposed by the tsarist government had severely hampered the development of Ukrainian schools, national-cultural institutions, and legal political parties in Volhynia and the other Ukrainian territories of the Russian Empire. In fact, during the inter-war period, the Polish government endeavoured to limit contacts between the Ukrainians in Galicia and Volhynia in an attempt to retard the development of a national consciousness in the latter region. The situation of the Ukrainians in interwar Volhynia was further aggravated by the Poles' heavy-handed persecution of the Orthodox Church (most Ukrainians in Volhynia were Orthodox) and government-sponsored colonization of certain areas by settlers: former Polish soldiers, officials and others trusted by the authorities.

During the twenties the radical left had much more political success in Volhynia than in Galicia. The Communist Party of Poland, which operated in Poland's Ukrainian territories through one of its territorial organizations, the Communist Party of Western Ukraine (CPWU), was illegal, but it stood behind several front organizations such as Selrob. Selrob Right became the strongest Ukrainian party in Volhynia after the 1928 general election and was followed by the radical-socialist bloc, whereas a large majority of Ukrainian voters in Galicia supported the political middle and moderate democratic left.

The popularity in Volhynia of the CPWU's front parties declined during the thirties, but many idealistic youths such as Danylo Shumuk were still drawn to the CPWU. Given the harsh poverty of the Ukrainian peasantry in the area of northern Volhynia (also known as Polissia) where the Shumuk family lived and widespread discrimination by the Polish authorities against the Ukrainian population, it was easy to fall prey to propaganda about the "paradise" which was being built in Soviet Ukraine.

For many other youths, however, an alternative was provided by the OUN (Orhanizatsiia Ukrainskykh Natsionalistiv—Organization of Ukrainian Nationalists), an authoritarian proponent of integral nationalism which grew steadily in strength during the thirties, although it was organizationally much weaker in Volhynia than in Galicia. The OUN, which placed the attainment of statehood above all other goals, and engaged in various terrorist actions in interwar Poland, suffered a debilitating split into two factions (OUN-B[andera] and OUN-M[elnyk]) in 1940. In addition, many prominent members were arrested and liquidated during the Soviet occupation of Western Ukraine in 1939–41. Nonetheless, during the German occupation which followed, the OUN was the only viable political force in Western Ukraine with widespread support among the Ukrainian population.

Germany was the only major revisionist power in interwar Europe and the OUN adopted a pro-German orientation during the thirties, hoping that a conflict between Germany and the Soviet Union would allow it to come to power in an independent Ukrainian state. Thus, on 30 June 1941, shortly after the outbreak of war between Germany and the Soviet Union, the OUN-B (the stronger of the two factions) proclaimed Ukrainian "independence" in Lviv, and in the autumn of 1941 the OUN-M attempted to establish itself in the civic administration of Kiev. However, the Nazi leadership had no sympathy for Ukrainian nationalist aspirations, and immediately commenced a series of reprisals against the OUN.

The situation in Volhynia under German occupation differed considerably from that in Galicia, which became part, together with most Polish territories, of the *Generalgouvernement*. For the Ukrainians the occupation regime in Galicia was much milder than in Volhynia, which was included in the *Reichskommissariat Ukraine*, the fiefdom of Erich Koch. An exceptionally brutal administrator of Nazi racial and economic policies, Koch considered Ukrainians to be subhumans, and his name became a symbol of German barbarity in the East.

The discontent of the population of the *Reichskommissariat Ukraine* grew rapidly as a result of the arrogant behaviour of the Nazi administration, the requisitioning of massive amounts of agricultural products and other goods for transport to Germany, and the forcible conscription of youths for labour in Germany. However, all of this area except for Volhynia had been part of the Soviet Union before the Second World War, and the spirit of the population of this former Soviet territory had been broken by the terrible man-made famine which devastated Soviet Ukraine in 1932–3, and the massive purges which followed.

Thus Volhynia was the site of the first armed conflicts between the local Ukrainian population and the German administration. The first paramilitary units bearing the name UPA (Ukrainska Povstanska Armiia—Ukrainian Insurgent Army) were established by Taras "Bulba" Borovets in 1942, and by the autumn of that year these units and small village self-defence groups had engaged in a number of skirmishes with the Germans.

It appears that throughout most of 1942 the OUN-B leaders in Galicia were against OUN-B participation in such actions, for they felt that premature armed conflict with the Germans would lead to massive reprisals against the Ukrainian population, expose the OUN-B's underground network, and threaten its important organizational and recruitment base in Galicia. However, as the situation in Volhynia continued to deteriorate, late in 1942 the OUN-B command in Galicia decided to begin a large-scale partisan movement in Volhynia, and by the spring of 1943, the activity of partisan groups sponsored by the OUN-B was considerable.

One of the first priorities of the OUN-B was to establish a single command for all Ukrainian partisan groups fighting under the nationalist banner, and considerable controversy surrounds the methods used by the OUN-B to gain control of the various groups in the nationalist resistance movement. However, by the fall of 1943 most of the units associated with Borovets or the OUN-M, as well as other independent groups, had been subordinated to the OUN-B, and the UPA title used earlier by Borovets was adopted by these "unified" forces.

By the end of 1943 approximately forty thousand men were in the UPA, and it controlled much of the Volhynian countryside. The UPA, which felt a severe lack of trained officers and proper equipment, avoided pitched battles with larger German units and engaged primarily in small-scale, guerrilla-type actions. German anti-partisan experts were transferred to Volhynia in 1943 in an attempt to eliminate the UPA, and the favourite tactic of the authorities was to punish the local population severely after every anti-German action by partisan groups. But other factors, including the bitter Ukrainian-Polish conflict, complicated the situation in Volhynia.

The roots of Polish-Ukrainian antagonism in this region were deep, and were based on historical stereotypes and animosities, bitter memories of conflict during the First World War and the interwar period, and Polish plans to reassert their claim to the old Riga frontier once German forces began their retreat from Western Ukraine. The result was a seemingly endless cycle of mutual reprisals during the Second World War which inflicted terrible suffering on the civilian population. Given the lack of reliable sources concerning this conflict, and the fact that the German administration as well as Soviet partisan groups attempted to inflame an already difficult situation, it may never be possible to provide a clear, objective account of Ukrainian-Polish relations during the Second World War. Certainly, however, neither Ukrainians nor Poles can take any pride in the tragic mutual slaughter and atrocities which affected Volhynia more than any other region of Western Ukraine.

Another problem facing the UPA was the presence of Soviet partisan units in the forest-swamp areas of Volhynia, especially in the north (Polissia). The Soviet authorities devoted considerable resources to installing and maintaining these units, and one of their aims was to undermine the Ukrainian nationalist movement in Western Ukraine. Many (if not most) of the leading cadres (and even the rank and file) of these units were non-indigenous, and the Soviet partisans attracted little popular support from the Ukrainians in Volhynia. Still, they demoralized the local population by reminding it of the imminent return of the Soviet forces to this territory and engaged in a number of provocative actions which resulted in brutal German reprisals against the local population or exacerbated the Ukrainian-Polish conflict.

It is also important to note that the OUN-B never succeeded in fully dominating all Ukrainian nationalist partisan forces in Volhynia, and there was a certain element of "warlordism" (*otamanshchyna*) in the activities of some of these forces. Additional complicating factors were the questionable reliability of some of the former Red Army personnel who joined the UPA after being trapped behind the German-Soviet front or escaping from German prisoner-of-war camps, and deliberate Soviet attempts to infiltrate the OUN and UPA.

Danylo Shumuk became involved in the Ukrainian nationalist movement in early 1943, after a period of gradual disillusionment with communism following the Soviet occupation of Western Ukraine in 1939. Shumuk was deeply affected by his experiences with both movements, but in his memoirs he is particularly critical of certain aspects of the OUN-B's activity during the war. However, Shumuk does not criticize the Ukrainian nationalist movement in gloating or vindictive fashion. On the contrary, it is clear that he shared some of this movement's ideals, and this is why he was so deeply pained by the narrow-minded intolerance of many of its adherents.

Shumuk was well aware of the very difficult circumstances in which the OUN-B and the UPA found themselves during the Second World War, and the ruthless nature of all partisan warfare. Still, he believed in a noble, humane form of nationalism, and was therefore repelled by the authoritarianism of the OUN-B and, in particular, the harsh methods used by its security service (the SB, or Sluzhba Bepeky). True, the OUN-B underwent an ideological reorientation in the course of the war, and introduced a number of democratic elements into its platform, but in Shumuk's opinion this was "too little, too late." Thus his memoirs often reflect the bitter disillusionment of an idealist who loses his faith in one set of ideals, turns to another, and finds it seriously flawed as well.

Nonetheless, after Shumuk was captured and imprisoned by the Soviet authorities in 1945 he firmly resisted all the pressure exerted on him to denounce the nationalist movement. To do so was against his principles, but he also had a profound respect for the courage and dedication of the rank and file of the UPA and the cause they were fighting for—an independent Ukraine. One indication of their determination is the fact that small UPA units continued to oppose Soviet rule in Western Ukraine until the late forties; in fact, the UPA provides one of the most important examples of prolonged, forceful resistance to the imposition of communist rule within the entire Soviet bloc.

Much has been written about the system of Soviet forced-labour camps in which Shumuk was imprisoned for more than thirty years after the Second World War. Nonetheless, Shumuk's memoirs make an important contribution to this literature, for relatively little is known about the activities of non-Russian prisoners in these camps. Shumuk not only underlines the important role which Ukrainians played in the Norilsk camp strikes of 1953, but portrays the strike in Hard-Labour Camp No. 3 from the unique perspective of the leader of a secret "self-help" organization which was in effective command of this strike. He also describes certain negative elements among the Ukrainian prisoners who undermined the generally positive reputation of the Ukrainians in the camps, although his evaluations of certain persons may be somewhat jaundiced.

Shumuk was thoroughly embittered by the harassment to which he was subjected after his release from the camps in August 1956, and its seems that he withdrew into himself during his second term of imprisonment (1957–67). But during the brief period of freedom which followed (1967–71) he became involved with a new, younger generation of Ukrainians who began to defend their native language and culture and the right to express their opinions. Shumuk was imprisoned for a third time in 1972 (and is now serving the remainder of his sentence in internal exile) for associating with these activists and writing his memoirs.

Throughout this entire period he has shown that he continues to despise all forms of hypocrisy and conformity to the powers that be. As Edward Kuznetsov, one of Shumuk's cellmates during the seventies, has written in an article dedicated to Shumuk:

> Many lofty phrases are bandied about—the good of the people, honesty, the search for truth, etc.... But how often does one meet a person for whom the truth means the truth and nothing else, honesty—honesty, and conscience—conscience? If you should happen to find yourself in a special-regime camp, then do your best to end up in the same cell as Danylo. He'll share his food with you, and the shirt off his back, and when you can't bear the latest indignity of the administration and declare a hunger strike, Danylo will join in, although he may already be tottering on his feet and his ribs may be sticking out from his sides....

Danylo Shumuk, whose formal education was very limited, is not a polished writer. In addition, almost all the segments of his autobiography which have reached the West were part of the first draft of a manuscript which Shumuk hoped to rewrite and edit thoroughly. In his letters to his nephew Ivan Shumuk, who lives in Canada, Danylo has expressed his dissatisfaction with the rough, unfinished nature of the manuscript. But what struck me, and many other readers of the Ukrainian original, is the passionate sincerity of Shumuk's memoirs.

> I [Kuznetsov] didn't always agree with Danylo. He has one very characteristic fault—he places far too much emphasis on the power of words, and feels that a few honest words, which may help to open the eyes of the world, are worth fifteen years of imprisonment. But is it all that strange, in a country where one may be imprisoned for ten-fifteen years because of a few words, to believe in the destructive and constructive power of the word? But what happened? He cried out, adding to this cry all his strength and his soul...and people continued to walk by without giving a damn, and attend to their everyday business. It's very important that there be people who are always ready to tell the truth.... But is this not too much—fifteen years of imprisonment, added to a preceding twenty-seven?... I'm not asking him, I'm not asking the prison guards—I'm asking myself, I'm asking you. Is this not too much for one person to bear? And can we, knowing of this case, remain passive and silent?

*Danylo Shumuk*

This is a slightly abbreviated version of the memoris of Danylo Shumuk. The full version, edited by Wasyl Hryshko, was recently published under the title *Perezhyte i peredumane* (Detroit 1983). I would like to thank the following individuals for their assistance at various stages of the preparation of the English-language version of the memoirs: Dr. Bohdan Bociurkiw, Dr. John-Paul Himka, Wasyl Hryshko, Halya Kowalska, Evhen Shtendera, Ivan Shumuk, Yaroslav Shumuk and Myroslav Yurkevich. I am very grateful to Dr. Manoly Lupul, Director of the Canadian Institute of Ukrainian Studies, for his patience during the lengthy preparation of the manuscript, and to Dr. David Marples, also of the Canadian Institute of Ukrainian Studies, for his assistance in preparing the manuscript for publication. Last but not least, I would like to thank my parents for their invaluable help and moral support.

Ivan Jaworsky
Ottawa
August 1984

# Glossary

| | |
|---|---|
| krai | homeland, territory |
| krai provid | territorial leadership |
| oblast | administrative division of USSR, province |
| okruh | region |
| provid | leadership |
| raion | district |

# PART I

# Chapter One

I was born into a peasant family in the village of Boremshchyna, Volodymyr-Volynskyi district, Volhynia, on 30 December 1914. My parents brought nine children into this world, but only four survived. I was the youngest; my father was fifty years old when I was born, and my mother was forty-three. My eldest brother and sister, Antin and Fedora, were both more than twenty years my senior; in fact, both married before I was even born. My sister Anna was eight years older than I. As a somewhat unwanted member of the family, I was a lonely child, and found little warmth in my family surroundings.

My father initially owned four desiatynas[1] of land, but through hard work he managed to buy four more, and thus became a farmer of average means in our village (which was relatively poor). My father was extremely industrious and loved the land, which he would work on until exhausted. He was especially fond of his garden and horses, and had a true passion for bee-keeping. But he was very stern toward his wife and children, especially myself. My mother was weak and sickly, but she was a good, sensitive woman who loved her children and did everything she could for them.

When I was a child I loved immersing myself in a world of fantasy. The everyday life of my elders struck me as drab and colourless, and when I was tending cows in the beautiful Polissian countryside I used to let my thoughts wander into my own, secret, imaginary world. Then, as now, it was difficult for me to understand why people caused each other so much grief, pain and sadness, and my greatest desire was to grow up as quickly as possible, to leave home, and to plunge into a search for truth and happiness.

In 1926 our house became an unofficial "reading room"[2] in the village, and the most radical villagers gathered there and would spend the long autumn evenings reading newspapers, journals and books aloud to one another. The initiator and organizer of this cultural, educational, social and political activity was my brother Antin, who was introduced to communist ideas when he worked at a railway station in Moscow during the First World War. Although only eleven years old, I absorbed everything I heard in the house with a child's naive, happy eagerness; no one was more attentive than I, for it seemed to me that a new "truth" was being born.

Our house served as both a reading room and the centre of social and political life in our village for two years. In fact, my brother Antin even organized a branch of the Selrob party in the village, which he headed for two years.[3] However, in 1928 this party, which served as a legal front for the Communist Party of Western Ukraine (CPWU), followed the CPWU's example and split into left- and right-wing factions. Bitter arguments between these factions filled the pages of their newspapers and disillusioned many rank-and-file members of Selrob, including my brother.

As a result of the split in the CPWU, and because my brother, under pressure from the police, abandoned his political activities, all this heady activity in our village completely died down. I was still only fourteen, but I was very upset by this development. However, in the 1928 elections to the Polish Sejm (Parliament) and Senate, four of the five deputies who were elected to the Sejm from Volhynia were communists who had run for office under the banner of Selrob.

Two years after these elections, I met Mykola Khymchyn,[4] who had been a candidate from our electoral region to the Senate. I considered myself virtually an adult, and therefore initiated a conversation with him. Khymchyn took down my name and address, and soon I began to receive various Selrob newspapers and the journal *Vikna*.[5] I also began distributing some of these periodicals, and thus became involved in political and community activities at a very early age.

In 1931 Petro Okseniuk, the head of the Kovel regional committee of Selrob, came to visit me, and told me that the Central

Committee of Selrob had made him responsible for organizing a Selrob committee in Liuboml district and had given him my address. I was very impressed that I had been approached to help out with this project, and that people twice my age were talking to me about such serious matters as if I was their equal. In fact, I was so inspired by this attention that I spent my free time and holidays visiting all the villages of Liuboml district. I knew the readers of the left-wing pro-communist press in each village, and they were the first people I turned to with the idea of setting up a Selrob committee. They had also been waiting impatiently to get involved in some concrete activity, and responded eagerly to my proposals.

The first meeting of Selrob sympathizers in our district was held in the village of Nudyzhe. During this (illegal) meeting, we discussed the political situation, elected a Selrob committee for the district, and prepared a plan of action. Sklianchuk, who was the oldest among us, was elected head of the committee, Krylas was elected secretary, and I was elected head of the committee's propaganda section. Fedir Romaniuk and Andrii Satsiuk were also included in the committee. In accordance with our adopted plan, over the next two months we set up Selrob committees in all the villages of the district. I was committed to the ideal of the Selrob movement, which became my overwhelming passion.

Our work was not always easy. The police, for example, began to harass us persistently by breaking up our meetings and finding all kinds of excuses to fine us. Sometimes fines were imposed merely for subscribing to the left-wing press. This often led to conflicts in my family, for although my parents complained about the behaviour of the Polish government and police, they bitterly resented paying heavy fines for my misdemeanours.

My situation was further complicated by the declining health of my father. He had suffered from varicose veins for some time and his legs were covered with sores. Then, on top of this, he developed diabetes in the spring of 1931. He had to be hospitalized in Shatsk, and my sister and I used to walk over thirty-five kilometres to visit him. After a month in the hospital, however, there was almost no improvement in his condition and he requested that he be allowed to go home. At the beginning of July, when he left the hospital, he was in critical condition.

One day in the fall, everyone went to work in the fields and I was left alone to take care of my father. He gave me such a sorrowful look that I could feel my heart ache, and it was difficult for me to believe that his stern gaze had once sent shivers down my spine. My father asked me to help him get up and, marshalling all his strength, he finally managed to stand on his unsteady feet. He looked like a helpless child first learning to walk.

After catching his breath my father asked me to lead him into the garden, where he parted tenderly with his beloved fruit trees and beehive. When he began to breathe heavily I led him back to the house, but before he left the garden my father fell devoutly to his knees, bowed three times, and kissed the soil.

Having returned to the house and rested for a while, my father, with great difficulty, thanked me for helping him to take a last look at his garden and beehive.

"I worked very hard my entire life," he said, "and I loved the soil, the garden, my bees and my horses. I never spared my children, and especially you. But don't think ill of me; after all, I managed to add four desiatynas of land to our property, and I'm leaving a fine garden and beehive behind for my family. Please take good care of all this; if you do so I'll rest easier in the next world."

It was very painful for me to look at my father and to listen to his deathbed confession. Two weeks later he died. He was unconscious for the last few days prior to his death, and spoke only of his beloved bees.

On the morning of the first Sunday of June 1932 a messenger from the village of Khvorostiv brought me a note from Tymish Kavetsky asking me to meet him at 10am at the church in Khvorostiv. This unexpected summons intrigued me, for although it was only five kilometres to Khvorostiv, this village belonged to Volodymyr rather than Liuboml district. I had no official organizational ties with Volodymyr district, and the only people whom I knew in Khvorostiv were Kavetsky himself and Samiilo Rud. Both were about four years my senior, and directed an amateur drama group in Khvorostiv, occasionally inviting me to attend their plays.

Kavetsky met me punctually at the church (which was celebrating its patron saint's day). With him was a young, pleasant fellow who turned out to be Stepan Zaholiuk, a member of the

Central Committee of the CPWU from Khvorostiv who was living in Lviv (he died in 1936 in the Spanish Civil War). After we had been introduced, Zaholiuk told Tymish to check whether everything was in order at Trokhym's house.

I realized that there must be an important reason for this meeting and listened attentively to Zaholiuk, who asked me about my family, the life of young people in Boremshchyna, and the state of cultural and educational activities in the village. Upon our arrival at Trokhym's house a festive table was awaiting us: a bottle of vodka, some headcheese, scrambled eggs and a deck of cards. The vodka and cards were there as a "cover" for our discussions, but we attacked the headcheese and the eggs with relish.

Finally Zaholiuk moved to the main objective of our meeting.

"I've been aware of you and your activity for quite a while now," he told me, "and everyone I've spoken to trusts you and thinks highly of your work. You should pass your Selrob duties to someone else now, because you're needed for underground work."

"What exactly do you have in mind?" I asked timidly.

"We have to organize underground CPWU and Komsomol[6] raion committees in Liuboml district," Zaholiuk replied. I was thrilled that I was being entrusted with such important and responsible work, but told Zaholiuk that I would have to learn the programme and statutes of the Communist Party and be officially accepted into its ranks before I could start organizing any raion committees.

"You're right," Zaholiuk replied, "but I don't have a copy of the party programme with me right now, and we have something which is much more valuable than a printed programme. We have the example of the Soviet Union—the first state in the world without exploiters and exploited, where everyone lives in one large happy family. From this day on you're already a member of the Communist Party, and you can best justify our faith in you by working conscientiously for our cause."

Two weeks later, on 22 June, I organized the first Komsomol conference in Liuboml district, in the Skyby forest. It was an informal, unpretentious affair and all those who attended were accepted into the Komsomol. When we elected an underground Komsomol raion committee, I was chosen as secretary, and was delighted at the confidence shown in me.

In July I began to organize a CPWU raion committee. I devoted all my energy and free time to this work, and at the beginning of August the communist underground began a propaganda campaign for peace. Since our propaganda accused the Polish government of militarizing the country, the police made a number of arrests and I was detained for two days in the local police station. When I was questioned I behaved in an aggressive, unrepentant fashion, and told the police that the social question was not my primary concern. For me the most important issue was freedom: freedom of conviction, freedom of speech, and freedom for my people. Thus I did not emphasize social inequalities, but rather the state's restrictions on the right to free speech, and its oppression of national minorities.

Soon afterward my brother was summoned to the district police commissariat. A senior investigator named Angelski informed my brother that if I did not cease my subversive activities, I would be prevented from continuing my studies, and would eventually be imprisoned. He informed my brother that if he did not share my political views he should divide the property our father had passed on to us, and let me go my own way in life.

"Do as you think best," I told my brother when he informed me about this meeting. "But I refuse to change my convictions at your demand or the demand of the police."

"My six children are my first concern," my brother replied. "Everything else is secondary."

"Fine, but don't interfere with the life I've chosen for myself."

In the fall of 1932 my brother divided the family property in accordance with my father's will. My mother remained with me and I found myself in a very difficult situation, for she was old, quite helpless, and suffering from asthma, neuralgia and frequent headaches. There was no one to do the woman's work in the field and garden, and often my mother was unable even to cook meals or wash my shirt. My older sister and two of my cousins helped us, but I could not expect them to do this indefinitely. Thus my mother started to insist that I find myself a wife. But the very idea of getting married was alien to me, for I was still young. Although I felt myself an adult when it came to politics, I was so shy that I never dared to start a conversation with a girl.

On the eve of 7 November 1932, I was again arrested and detained for two days. But the arrests of myself and others failed to curb the activity of the communist underground, and the next day red flags celebrating the anniversary of the October Revolution were flying from all the tallest poplars in the district.

# Chapter Two

In 1933 the world economic crisis reached its peak, and unemployed workers from central Poland were wandering through the villages of Western Ukraine. At the same time, however, refugees from the Soviet Union were talking about a terrible artificial famine in Soviet Ukraine which had driven people to commit acts of cannibalism.[1] In Western Ukraine the Ukrainian community basically split into two camps during the 1930s: the pro-communist press portrayed life in the Soviet Union in glowing colours, while the nationalist press wrote all kinds of terrible things about the Soviet Union, and Soviet Ukraine in particular. Both these antagonistic camps were active in Western Ukraine; in Galicia there was a strong Germanophile, pro-fascist orientation, whereas in Volhynia there was a pro-Soviet, pro-communist orientation.

Naturally, I ignored everything I read in the nationalist press. I simply could not believe that the Soviet government, the "government of workers and peasants," the government of the communists, whom I worshipped, could deliberately and systematically destroy, by means of starvation, the same workers and peasants who had fought to establish this government. I was an emotional youth, totally incapable of thinking in a critical, independent fashion, and devoted myself blindly to the doctrine which had captured my soul.

One day my Uncle Iakiv, who had just returned from a pilgrimage to Pochaiv,[2] came to our house and brought a small piece of bread which a refugee from the Soviet Union had given to him.

"Take a look at the bread which is fed to people in the communist paradise you're fighting for," he said to me as he took from his pocket a piece of bread as black as earth and made from grass.

"No, uncle," I replied. "I could never believe that anyone would want to flee Soviet Ukraine for Poland. This bread was not baked in the Soviet Union but here, to divert attention from the world economic crisis, from the dangers of unemployment, and from the destitution of the workers in the capitalist world."

"You've learned how to give a good speech, Danylo, but you're still very young and impressionable. You've never been to the Soviet Union; how can you tell what's going on there now?"

"You've never been there either, and yet you were given a piece of bread by some scoundrel and you're absolutely convinced that it's from the Soviet Union. Just think—how could anyone believe that a peasants' and workers' state could use hunger to destroy the labourers who feed the entire country?"

"It may be as you say. But if everything is so fine then why are people from Soviet Ukraine forbidden to visit their relatives here?"

This question threw me off for a few seconds, but I soon found a suitable response.

"I have my doubts about who is actually responsible for these restrictions; the Soviet Union or Poland," I replied and ended the conversation.

At the end of April 1933, the police arrested me for the fourth time. On the first three occasions I had been detained for a mere two days in the local police station in the village of Horodne. But this time I was sent to the district jail in Liuboml and detained for two months by order of the Office of the Prosecutor. I was imprisoned in a dirty, damp basement cell with one small window high on the wall near the ceiling. It had a depressing effect upon me. For the first time, I saw what a prison was really like and realized the value of freedom.

The Polish *defensywa*[3] always interrogated prisoners at night in the building of the police commissariat, which was located in a lonely spot on the outskirts of Liuboml. Three weeks after my detention I was awoken at midnight and asked to dress. When I entered the prison corridor I was handcuffed and ordered to walk in front of the guards. Upon arrival at the commissariat, we were told to wait, and I was placed in a corner with my face to the wall. Someone was being beaten in a neighbouring office, and I heard such terrible screams and groans that every cell in my body quivered with fear.

Fifteen minutes later a policeman told me to enter the office in which senior investigator Julian Angelski was seated.

"Well, what have you been up to?" Angelski asked and gave me a searching look.

"What do you mean?" I replied.

"Don't play games with me; you know very well what I'm talking about. Instead of coming to your senses and abandoning your subversive activity you've become even more active. Tell me," Angelski asked suddenly, "when was the last time you visited Khvorostiv?"

For a minute I was struck dumb by this question, but then I regained my composure.

"I was there during the patron saint's day celebration in the local church," I replied.

"Fine. Now tell my why you went there—to pray?" Angelski was sarcastic.

"No, simply out of tradition. We always attend patron saint's day celebrations in nearby villages."

"Just remember that your attendance at these 'patron saint's day celebrations' could land you in jail, and that you could spend your entire youth behind bars. You know what I mean. Go and think this over; it's not too late yet. I could force you to tell me everything, although I already know what you've been up to. Still, it would be better for you if you came here and talked to me of your own free will."

I wanted to say something, but a policeman told me to move and I returned to the prison.

My first prolonged detention was very trying, and I soon began to hate all manner of locks and warders. The worst days were when my mother, sick with grief, brought parcels to prison for me and tried to catch a glimpse of me through cracks in the gate when I was taken out of my cell for exercise. However, I was actually treated quite reasonably and after serving my two-month sentence I was freed, although the prison director warned me that if I ever came into their hands again I would never leave the prison.

On the Sunday after my release, several members of the underground raion committee of the Komsomol came to visit me. They told me that there was a police informer in our raion committee and that they suspected Ivan Krylas of being the culprit. I had realized that we had an informer in our committee after Angelski had questioned me, but I had no idea who it could be. Nonetheless, something had to be done. Therefore, after consulting with Zaholiuk, I informed all the committee members that since our contacts with the next level of the organization had been disrupted during my imprisonment, I was forced to liquidate the raion committee for an indefinite period of time.

After the raión committee had been (artificially) dissolved, I immediately called a meeting of all its members except Krylas, and we elected Havrylo Vlasiuk as the new secretary. I decided to transfer to the Pochapy raion committee, where I also served as committee secretary. Krylas, however, did not believe that the committee had truly dissolved itself, somehow found out that we suspected him of being an informer, and demanded that an internal court judge his case. But when I talked with Krylas, I found out that he knew a great deal more about the communist underground than was warranted by his position in the raion committee. The constant smell of vodka on his breath and the pistol with which he never parted only heightened my suspicions, and the communist underground decided to keep him under constant surveillance. Thus, Chyhryn, a member of our organization, "befriended" Krylas in order to watch his activities. However, after transferring to the Pochapy raion committee I had nothing more to do with this case, and Andrii Satsiuk took care of the investigation.

Throughout the summer of 1933 my mother and other members of my family continued to urge me to find a wife. I sensed that it would be a great mistake to marry at this point in my life, but it was very difficult to ignore such pressure, especially my mother's entreaties. However, not only was I extremely shy; my perception of women was based largely on a romanticized ideal derived from the literature I had read, and none of the village girls whom I knew even approached this ideal.

Finally I decided to confide in one of my friends from the underground, Havrysh Vlasiuk. Concerned about my dilemma, he offered to introduce me to a young woman who at least would not hinder my political work, since her parents and brothers were sympathetic to our cause and even allowed us to use their house for our meetings. On that same day Havrysh introduced me to Mariika Maslianka, who seemed a modest, good-natured young woman. However, I was not really attracted to her, and the period of courtship and the actual wedding were a great ordeal for me.

After I married my everyday life became more comfortable, but I had little in common with my wife. The routine of everyday domestic life continued to repel me, and I became even more involved in political activity. In fact I had lived with my wife for only two months when I was again arrested.

The Polish police arrested me for the fifth time on the evening of the Feast of the Epiphany (19 January 1934) and spent a long time searching our house, although they found nothing. This time I was handcuffed even before I was led out of the house. Four policemen, including Melas, the district investigator, led me away, while a large crowd of angry villagers gathered in the street.

"Don't worry," I told the crowd. "They may have put handcuffs on me, but no one can chain ideas and prevent us from fighting for the truth."

"Polish occupiers—off our land! Let's get them!" the crowd yelled. A fence was torn down, and pieces of the fence and bricks were hurled at the police. Melas turned pale and moved closer to me, while the other policemen also lost their bearings. They might even have fired shots at the crowd had they dared. Once we had left the village behind I thanked the villagers for their support and told them to return home. (Many of the villagers were later fined for taking part in this demonstration).

I was immediately taken to the district police station in Liuboml. All the members of the Liuboml Komsomol raion committee had been arrested and were standing in a large room in the police station, facing the wall. I was told to take a seat in the duty officer's bureau.

The first person to be summoned to the police commissariat for interrogation, at 11pm, was Fedir Romaniuk, and the next day, at 10pm, Andrii Satsiuk was summoned. At approximately 1am it was my turn, and the citizens of Liuboml were fast asleep as I walked silently through the town's streets, two steps ahead of my police escort.

When we reached the commissariat I was taken into a large, empty hall. A ladder was leaning against one of the walls, and Andrii Satsiuk was tied to it. He was as still as a corpse, and blood was dripping into a large bowl beneath the ladder. I was nauseated by this terrible scene, but managed to hide my distress from the policeman accompanying me.

Some twenty minutes later I was called into a small, empty room where four policemen, without saying a word, immediately began pummelling me. I flew, like a football, from one policeman to the other, until I finally collapsed. Then Angelski, the senior investigator, ran into the room. "What are you doing?" he yelled at his "boxers" and began cursing them. They left the room silently, while Angelski helped me to my feet and led me to his office. Here he sat down behind his desk, asked me to be seated, and started leafing through some papers.

"Well, Shumuk, shall we be open with each other now?" he asked after a brief pause.

"I didn't come here to chat with you," I replied. "If you have charges to lay against me, then tell me what they are."

"Those who end up here tell us what we want to know, and not vice-versa."

"I have nothing to tell you."

"No, there's a great deal you can tell us. And if you don't co-operate with us then we'll force it out of you. We've known for quite a while now about your underground activity, Comrade Lishchynsky."

Angelski's unexpected use of the term "comrade" and my pseudonym "Lishchynsky" was a great shock to me, and he clearly enjoyed my discomfiture.

"What's the matter?" he asked. "Cat got your tongue?"

"But you were addressing a friend of yours called Lishchynsky," I replied once I had gathered my wits.

"So, you s.o.b., you're going to play the idiot with me?!" Angelski bellowed and pressed a button on his desk. "Fine, then there's another, more productive way of talking with you. Take him away and tickle the soles of his feet for me," Angelski told the men who had just entered the room.

I was taken to a torture chamber which had rubber truncheons, pincers, pins and other equipment hanging on the walls. I was told to undress, did so as though hypnotized, and a few minutes later I was on my back. The "boxers" deftly bent my legs, roughly pushed my handcuffed hands over my knees, and stuck a strong pole through the spaces between my knees and my arms. Then, totally helpless, I was placed on my back with the soles of my feet facing upward.

"Now we'll loosen your tongue. When you feel like talking, move your fingers," I was told. One policeman stood over my head with a kettle full of water in his hands, while a second took a rubber truncheon off the wall and began beating the soles of my feet.[4] A terrible pain exploded in my brain each time he struck me, but I maintained consciousness, for water was continuously poured on my head. I moved my fingers three times, and each time I was freed from my bonds, but once the policemen found out that I was doing this only to take a rest I was flogged even more fiercely.

Finally Angelski came in with a file from which he read out the confessions of Fedir Romaniuk and Andrii Satsiuk. At this point I admitted that I was a communist and that I had disseminated communist literature, had strung up flags throughout the district, and had been behind one of the village strikes. Angelski let the "boxers" go and sent me to his office.

"So you've finally come to your senses," he said. "Now you can be frank with me."

"What do you mean?" I asked. "I told you that I was responsible for everything."

"We know that you were in charge, but I want you to tell me about your subordinates."

"I told you that I did everything myself. I have nothing more to say." Then Angelski read out, from the minutes of Romaniuk's and Satsiuk's interrogations, the dates and places of our conferences, as well as the names of the people who were in attendance, and demanded that I confirm this information.

"They've given evidence against you—why don't you do the same?" he asked.

"Bring them here and let them repeat, to my face, what you've read out to me. And if you don't believe their confessions, then that's your problem, not mine."

# Chapter Three

Soon we were all transferred to Kovel, where the prosecutor passed our case on to Stefan Lorenz, a court investigator. Most of us were placed in Cell No. 18 of the Kovel prison, where we were treated much more humanely than in Liuboml. We could receive an unlimited number of parcels from friends and relatives, and twice a month we were allowed to meet with members of our family for fifteen minutes. We were also allowed to receive a wide range of newspapers, journals and books of various ideological orientation, and thus had an excellent opportunity to improve ourselves. However, we did not take full advantage of this. In my own case, I stubbornly viewed all intellectual currents through a prism of communist ideology, devoured all the literature on Marxism-Leninism I could find in the prison, and fervently believed everything I read.

Our relatives visited us on Mondays and we all eagerly awaited these brief meetings, although I was simply paralyzed by the limited period of time available. My most frequent visitor was my wife, although my feeble mother also came. Approximately one month after I had been arrested my wife told me that she was pregnant. This news thoroughly depressed me, for only then did I fully understand that fate had bound me irrevocably to a woman with whom I had little in common. Our cell usually contained twenty-five men, of whom approximately twenty were political prisoners. It was quite peaceful, and although we were occasionally summoned for questioning, we soon became used to these interruptions, and spent most of our time reading or holding discussions.

The investigation into our case dragged on. We demanded that it be brought to an end, but to no avail. Thus we decided to start a hunger strike. Fourteen of the seventeen prisoners who began the strike refused to eat for a full six days, and the prosecutor eventually promised that our case would be brought to trial in April. We decided to boycott the three political prisoners who had broken their fast on the third day of the hunger strike, and for an entire month no one spoke to them. This is a drastic punishment and not always appropriate, for it leads to a great deal of resentment among the prisoners which is difficult to overcome once the boycott has been called off.

Shortly after the hunger strike had ended, the bleak routine of prison life was interrupted by a small riot. It began when someone in the corridor near our cell yelled out that prisoners were being beaten. We immediately took up his cry, others joined in, and soon the entire prison was shaken by our loud protests. A number of windows were broken, the residents of Kovel became perturbed by our cries, and those who sympathized with the prisoners began to mill around the prison building. In response the police and firemen drove up to the prison, and as the police shot at the windows fire hoses were used to put down the riot.

We never found out who was involved in the incident which led to the riot, but after this disturbance we were deprived of our meetings with our relatives and an investigation was initiated. All the prisoners in Cell No. 18 were transferred to other cells and I was moved to Cell No. 7, on the third floor of the prison. Eight men (all political prisoners who had been detained for communist activity) were kept in this cell, which was only nine square metres in area.

At this time, there were some 200 political prisoners in Kovel prison. Four of them, led by Andrii Marchenko,[1] were Ukrainian nationalists, and the rest were communists or communist sympathizers. Only five of the political prisoners had a secondary education, and none had a higher education, but in general they behaved in a civilized fashion. There was no fighting or cursing among them, and the senior figures among the communists were held in great respect. This "seniority" was determined by their organizational rank, their level of general and political education, and their behaviour during the court investigation. Discipline was exemplary, and all parcels were shared equally among the political prisoners. We had no conflicts with the ordinary criminals in the prison, but we kept them at a distance, for we were very proud that we were *political* prisoners rather than common criminals.

The communists kept in touch with one another in the prison by passing on notes or rapping out messages in Morse code. The notes were circulated in a variety of ways: often they were tied to a string (which was called a "horse") and then lowered through the window or thrown up (or even sideways) into another cell; prisoners agreed on hiding places in the washrooms where notes could be left or retrieved; and sometimes notes were simply thrown out of a window so that they would land near prisoners who were in the exercise yard. The administration, however, kept a close watch on our activities, tried to confiscate our messages, and punished those who were caught.

One day, in the second half of March 1935, Andrii Satsiuk, who was sitting on the window-sill of our cell, threw a note into the exercise yard, where prisoners from another cell were strolling at the time. However, a warder had seen him, and confiscated the note. Soon three warders and an officer named Szczepański entered our cell. Szczepański told Satsiuk to leave the cell but he refused. Thus the warders dragged him out into the corridor, where he cried out that they were beating him. We immediately informed the other cells of this and soon the entire prison was again in an uproar. To quell this disturbance the administration had to shoot through the prison windows and spy-holes in the doors to the cells, and firemen used their hoses to fill our cells with water. In the meantime an entire unit of mounted police patrolled the streets surrounding the prison and used their whips to disperse those townspeople who had begun to gather near the prison.

Suddenly a group of furious warders broke into our cell, dragged us into the corridor, and after our hands and feet had been shackled, we were thrown into the cooler in the basement. The disturbance, however, continued. Political prisoners in three cells took apart the small stoves which connected their cells and, congregating in one large room, started showering the administration with bricks.

Soon the prosecutor Robak arrived. He guaranteed the prisoners that no further beatings would take place and that he would look into this incident. The political prisoners, who trusted the prosecutor, started to negotiate with him, and the riot died down. During the investigation into the riot we were released from the cooler.

After being interrogated we were taken to Monopol Street. Here an old tobacco factory had been transformed into a prison, and its cellar had been reconstructed in such a way that it contained three tiny cells on both sides of a short corridor. We were taken into this corridor one at a time. Then we were stripped of our clothes, beaten and thrown into the cells.

Of all the coolers I have known these were the most terrible. The door at the end of the corridor was kept hermetically sealed, and the doors to the cells were also tightly closed. The partitions between the cells had just been completed, and the plaster was so fresh that I could easily sink my fingers into it. A small wooden platform covered most of the cement floor, which was hollowed out and filled with water.

For four hours we shouted to one another, but upon becoming aware of the lack of air in the cells, we fell silent. I tried walking, but there was no room to take even two full steps and water splashed up through the platform, which kept moving under my feet. Later I managed to lean one end of the platform against a wall of the cell in such a way that it did not move and I could lie down on it. But even the slightest movement on my part caused the platform to slip down the wall, and I would fall into the water covering the floor.

We were kept in these coolers for two days and then transferred to an ordinary cell for one day, after which we were returned to the coolers. I spent four days in these infamous basement cells, which were kept in absolute darkness, and each time that I emerged into the light I was blinded by sharp pains in my eyes. In addition, since I could only sit down in the cell by leaning against the damp, cold partition between the cells, my back became thoroughly chilled. For the next seven years, my spine felt frozen.

But we were not intimidated and declared a hunger strike on the second day of our incarceration to protest our brutal treatment. In response, the administration confiscated our clothes and linen, and withheld our water, but we proudly refused to give in. This was a total hunger strike, and I cannot begin to describe our suffering. By the fifth day of the strike we were running high temperatures and our mouths gave off a foul odour. It rained that day, and we rushed to the windows of our cells to catch a few raindrops on our hands, but we were too weak to drag ourselves up to the windows, and looked on helplessly as these precious drops fell to the ground.

On the morning of the eighth day of the hunger strike we were taken away to be force-fed. This is a very unpleasant procedure, but we were too feeble to resist. However, in the afternoon of the same day the prosecutor arrived, promised to send our demands to Warsaw by government courier, and we ended the hunger strike. Five days later we had prepared a petition to the League of Human Rights and the minister of internal affairs, and the prosecutor sealed the petition in the presence of Satsiuk and myself.

The investigation into our case ended in April 1935 and we were presented with an official list of the charges which would be brought against us. We refused to accept this document since it was written in Polish, and ten days later we were given two copies: one in Polish and one in Ukrainian. The date of the trial was set for 24 May 1935, and on the morning of this day seventeen young prisoners were removed from their cells, handcuffed, and led out in pairs through the prison gates. Guarded by a police escort, we made our way from the prison to the regional court like a funeral procession. Friends and relatives accompanied us; my wife, for example, walked alongside the column a few metres to my right, and in her arms she was carrying our daughter Vira, who had been born in the fall of the previous year. It was painful for me to look at my daughter, for I knew that the path upon which I had embarked would be a long and difficult one. I had no idea when it would end, and although I was ready to sacrifice myself for my ideals, my conscience greatly troubled me when I thought of my new-born daughter.

Finally we entered the court building, and were followed by the guards, our lawyers, our friends and relatives, and others interested in the trial. Soon the hall was packed. There were three lawyers for the defence. Dr. Volodymyr Starosolsky,[2] who was in charge of our defence, was a well-known orator and legal expert from Lviv and former head of the Ukrainian Social Democratic Labour Party. The other two lawyers (both Poles) were Jarosz (from Kovel), who was a member of the Polish Socialist Party, and Prus (also from Kovel), who was not affiliated with any particular party. They took their places next to us behind a barrier and, after consulting with us, improvised a plan for our defence. Soon the prosecutor, a self-confident young fellow named Kaczerowski, appeared and took his place opposite us. Fifteen minutes later the bailiff rang a small bell, announcing that the judge was approaching and that we were to rise. Three judges entered the courtroom from the side door to our left, and the presiding judge took the middle seat on a raised platform.

The presiding judge read out the long and monotonous documents listing the charges against us. Then he began to question us, but at this point Angelski and Melas entered the courtroom and all the defendants jumped to their feet. "Get those murderers out of here!" we yelled. The audience supported us, and shouted that these two were the ones who should be on trial. Then the presiding judge stood up and called the court to order, but we began to sing the "Internationale"[3] and the police guards responded by pointing their rifles, tipped with bayonets, at us. The prosecutor turned pale and appeared to be thoroughly bewildered; Melas and Angelski were also stunned by this commotion and looked imploringly at the presiding judge; while the judges and prosecutor looked helplessly at the *defensywa* officers just as a master would look at a watchdog who has broken his chain and been caught in a trap. We demanded that the court refuse to hear Angelski and Melas as witnesses, but the court denied our request. As a result we refused to answer the questions put to us and submitted a written protest concerning the torture to which we had been subjected during the investigation.

After all the witnesses had been questioned, Kaczerowski, who was an effective orator, made his presentation, and then it was the turn of the lawyers for the defence. Prus simply drew the court's attention to our youthful age and asked that the extenuating circumstances surrounding the case be taken into account. In short, his defence lacked any real substance. Jarosz, a more energetic fellow, criticized the Polish government's policies in Galicia and Volhynia which, he declared, had been adopted because Ukrainians were considered second-class citizens.

Starosolsky was the last defence lawyer to speak. It was clear that he knew the power of his words, and the entire courtroom listened attentively to his presentation. Even the judges were impressed by his eloquence. Starosolsky emphasized that society, and the government in particular, were to blame for our behaviour, since they were responsible for the injustices which had provoked our actions. He concluded his defence by stating that "There can be no talk of justice in Western Ukraine until the Ukrainians are allowed to assume responsibility for the fate of their own people." We were allowed to make a final statement and used the opportunity to protest the Polish occupation of Western Ukraine and the trials conducted by Polish pro-fascist officials on Ukrainian territory.

When the court adjourned we prepared ourselves to accept the court's verdicts in a dignified fashion, but tension grew in the courtroom, which was full of our friends and relatives. After the recess, the presiding judge read the verdicts: Tymish Kavetsky was sentenced to nine years of imprisonment, I received an eight-year sentence, and the other prisoners received sentences ranging from three to seven years. In addition, I was to spend six months in solitary confinement because of my behaviour in the courtroom.

After the reading of the verdict we shouted "Shame on the court and the occupiers!" and sang two verses of the "Internationale." There was some crying at this point in the courtroom, but the bailiff ordered all observers to leave and we were driven back to the prison. The next day our hands and feet were shackled and we were sent by train to Łomża.

# Chapter Four

Eventually we reached the four-storey prison in Łomża, which was built in the shape of a cross. We were taken immediately to the prison chapel, and using a hammer, anvil and chisel the prison warders began to hack through the shackles on our feet. This was a rather strange spectacle, but by this time we were used to all kinds of horrors.

We were assigned to the first floor of the building in which Ukrainian nationalists were imprisoned (on the second floor), and our solitary confinement cells were one-and-a-half metres wide, four metres long and three metres high. In these cells it always seemed as if the walls were pressing in on us, and sometimes I felt as if we were deep underground. I was in solitary confinement when the OUN (Organization of Ukrainian Nationalists) krai provid, headed by Bandera, was tried in Warsaw for complicity in the assassination of Pieracki, the Polish minister of internal affairs.[1] The OUN members in the prison were greatly shaken by this trial, and spread news about its progress by shouting to one another through the prison windows.

After six months of solitary confinement I was allowed to join the political prisoner commune, and after my long period of isolation it was almost like regaining freedom. The commune was a well-organized, disciplined community which encompassed all those political prisoners sentenced for communist activities.

In theory, an executive headed by a chairman was in charge of the entire commune, which consisted of several groups (one for each floor). There were forty-eight men in each group, and each group's executive was headed by a group delegate. The chairman kept in touch with the prison director, while group delegates kept in touch with the head warder of their prison block. The remainder of the communist political prisoners avoided conversations with members of the prison administration.

This is how the commune appeared to the prison administration, but in reality its structure was more complicated. There were three sections in the commune executive: cultural-educational; economic; and investigatory.

The cultural-educational section had a well-formulated plan for the general political education of the prisoners. All members of the commune were assigned to discussion groups in accordance with their previous educational background. A lecturer was assigned to each discussion group, and followed a general work-plan. Every three months a cultural-educational commission checked the progress of these groups, and we were all required to participate in their activities. I belonged to a senior group and our lecturers were party members who had recently completed their studies at the Comintern's "Institute of Red Professors" in Moscow.[2] Later we went on to lecture to other groups.

First we had a "short course" in politics, which consisted basically of elementary sociology taught from a party perspective. Then we went on to study political economy, historical and dialectical materialism, and the history of the workers' movement. In addition, we were supposed to read certain scholarly and literary works. In the case of the latter, we were asked to define the main themes of each book and the way in which they were presented; in fact, we set up literary "trials" for individual works and wrote critical reviews of them. All this was carried out conscientiously, and with a sense of responsibility for what we were doing. Our progress was examined during our exercise periods, while the literature we had read was discussed in the rooms leading to the washrooms, where we spent an hour each morning and evening. In addition, each month we also conducted a press survey, and provided a box for inquiries for our monthly question period.

For the press survey each group member took turns following certain topics in the press over a period of a month: one person kept an eye on world politics, and especially political developments in Poland; a second surveyed economic and fiscal policies; and a third followed developments in the revolutionary movement. On the first day of each month they reported on these topics while we waited to get to the washrooms. After the reports, people would ask questions and make comments or corrections (everyone read the same newspapers and journals). The last person to speak was the director of the group's cultural-educational activities, who would make some concluding remarks and evaluate the lecturer as well as those who took part in the discussion. If one disagreed with this "authoritative" evaluation, the consequences could be serious, and included expulsion from the commune, for all final decisions had to receive unanimous approval.

The notes deposited in the question box were discussed, in similar fashion, every month. All those present could comment on a given question, but the cultural-educational director again had the last word and closed the discussion. In short, all members of the commune were busily trying to improve themselves.

The economic section was in charge of all communal "housekeeping." For example, all money which commune members received from friends and relatives or from agencies such as the Red Cross, the International Organization for Aid to Revolutionaries,[3] etc., was placed under the control of this section and was used to buy food for the entire commune. All the food, whether it was purchased through this fund or came in parcels for individual prisoners, was divided equally among members of the commune. Those who had tuberculosis or ulcers, however, were given white instead of black bread, butter instead of back fat, and a double sugar ration. All this was done in a businesslike manner. Every month the economic sections made a report to their groups, informing them how much money and how many parcels had been received by the group and by the commune as a whole, and the average amount received by each member of the commune.

The food in Polish prisons was poor; we received only 400 grams of coarse bread per day. In the morning we were given black coffee and 20 grams of sugar; for lunch we received 750 grams of soup, 200 grams of gruel, mashed potatoes or mashed peas, and 50 grams of pork; and supper consisted of 750 grams of soup. The bread was worse (and there was less of it) than that I was to receive later in Soviet camps and prisons, but the other items in our "menu" were of better quality. In addition, there were no restrictions on the number of parcels and the amount of money we could receive. In this respect Poland, after all, was a "European" country and did not use hunger as a means to "reform" us.

The commune's investigation section studied all pre-trial investigations and court cases to determine how each political prisoner had conducted himself under pressure. The section tried to find out who had revealed organizational secrets or informed on others and how this had occurred. If it was found that party interests had been compromised then the guilty party was punished according to the degree of the offence committed. For the most serious offences, prisoners were expelled from the commune and boycotted along with their families. If less serious offences were involved, then prisoners were simply deprived of their right to vote in the commune, and were expelled from the party for a certain (and sometimes indefinite) period. Those who lost the right to vote had no say in the selection of the commune or group executive, and no longer participated in the daily decision-making process.

Those prisoners who had no "blemishes" on their record were considered to be part of the communist fraction which was the nucleus of the commune. For party matters, the chairman and all sections of the commune were directly subordinated to the head of this fraction. Thus the "election" of the chairman was democratic in form only, but this manipulation was handled in a refined, sophisticated fashion. Everyone respected the commune executive and carried out its instructions conscientiously.

The commune executive always tried to stay a step ahead of the prison administration and instructed the prisoners how to behave in various situations. This was to prevent the administration from provoking the prisoners into creating an incident in which it had the upper hand, and in order to extract concessions from the administration. For example, it was easier for the commune to put pressure on the administration when the Polish workers' movement was involved in strikes or demonstrations, or when members of the Human Rights League of the League of Nations were visiting Poland. The administration tried to provoke us when the workers were quiescent, but we carefully avoided direct confrontations.

The political prisoners demanded several concessions from the administration:

1. The right to wear civilian clothes instead of prison uniforms.

2. Access to writing materials.

3. A library for the commune.

4. The commune's representatives (the chairman and group delegates) were to be recognized by the administration.

There was a continuous dispute between the commune and the prison administration concerning these privileges. Initially the prisoners' most effective form of protest was the hunger strike, but later it was acknowledged that hunger strikes were inappropriate, for they seriously harmed the prisoners' health. Thus a new, more diversified form of protest was adopted, and conducted in several stages.

On the first day of a typical protest campaign, one prisoner in each cell spoke on behalf of his cellmates during the morning inspection, demanding that the prison administration return the writing materials which had been confiscated and that the commune be allowed to open its own private library. This spokesman stated that at lunchtime we would all start pressing the buzzers in our cells, and that in the evening we would refuse to eat supper.

On the second day of our campaign we all climbed to the windows of our cells when the workers in Łomża were leaving for work and informed them that we had been deprived of our rights as political prisoners, that we were being treated like ordinary criminals, etc. The workers, of course, had been informed about our campaign in advance and they immediately began to demonstrate in front of the prison. In addition, the workers took every opportunity to harass the families of the prison administrators and exerted a great deal of moral pressure on them.

Thus every day we used a new tactic in our campaign. The commune executive prepared well in advance and kept the plan secret, because its effectiveness depended on keeping the administration off balance. This was a war of nerves, and self-confidence as well as a sense of humour were essential. Our calm and cheerfulness infuriated the administration, and this in itself was a victory for the prisoners. Campaigns of this kind could last as long as two months. While I was in the Łomża prison there were two such campaigns, both of which were successful.

In form the commune was a democratic organization, for its executive was elected by the prisoners and various issues could be discussed and debated at commune meetings. In essence, however, it was a totalitarian organization, for the executive of the secret communist fraction indicated in advance who was to be chosen for each position so that the "elections" were a formality. The same was true of all our discussions and debates. We could discuss issues to our heart's content, but only from a communist perspective. All doubts concerning the pronouncements of our seniors were considered heretical.

I had the good fortune to be imprisoned on the fourth floor of the prison along with Zenon Nowak, the head of the communist fraction. At that time he was a member of the Central Committee of the Communist Party of Poland (CPP) and a member of its Politburo; later, in postwar Poland, he became a first deputy prime minister.[4] He was a calm, sensible person who was well liked because of his simple, honest style. Nonetheless, there was always a certain distance between Nowak and the other prisoners, and even the other members of the Central Committee respected him. Despite the secrecy surrounding the party hierarchy in the prison, in our group we all knew that even Dr. Pinas, the commune chairman, had to report to Nowak.

Two members of the Central Committee of the CPWU were imprisoned on our floor: Ivan Syvokhip from the village of Dobrivliany, Drohobych district, and Tsimmer from Lviv. Syvokhip was an unexceptional person and not particularly intelligent, but he had organizational experience. Tsimmer, however, was second only to Nowak as far as his knowledge of the social sciences was concerned. This young, talented and handsome Jew from Lviv was well versed in political economy, historical and dialectical materialism, and the history of the workers' movement.

Two members of the Central Committee of the Communist Party of Western Belorussia (CPWB) were also imprisoned on our floor.[5] Both were Jews, and one had just returned from the Comintern's "Institute of Red Professors" in Moscow. They were secondary figures compared to Nowak, but we viewed all these Central Committee members as eminent authorities and eagerly absorbed everything they had to say.

If one categorized the prisoners sentenced for their communist activities according to nationality, then the largest group consisted of Ukrainians and the second largest of Jews, while the Belorussians were also greatly overrepresented considering the size of the Belorussian population in interwar Poland. The smallest group was the Poles, who were generally Central Committee members or members of provincial committees. There were many changes in world politics during my period of imprisonment. Hitler began to implement his political plans, and there were important developments in the communist movement as well. In 1934, for example, another "nationalist deviation" was "discovered" in the Central Committee of the CPWU and the Comintern entrusted the Central Committee of the CPP to carry out a purge of its ranks. Rwal, a member of the latter body, directed this purge, as a result of which "Kosar" (Myron Zaiachkivsky) and "Baraba" (Hryhorii Ivanenko), both members of the Central Committee of the CPWU, were purged. They later died in Soviet labour camps.[6]

In 1938 the Comintern "dissolved" the CPP, the CPWU and the CPWB. Leński, the General Secretary of the CPP and a member of the Presidium of the Comintern, as well as his deputies Henrykowski and Rwal (the same person who had carried out the purge of the CPWU) were shot in Moscow as "agents of Polish intelligence organs."[7] We were greatly depressed by the news that these communist parties had ceased to exist, and henceforth considered ourselves to be "non-party communists."

All these events were accompanied by the growth of chauvinist tendencies in Polish society following the seizure of Zaolzie in Czechoslovakia by Poland.[8] On 13 December 1938 the prison administration decided to confiscate our civilian clothing. Early in the morning, before we had been awoken, warders broke into the cells, took away our civilian clothes, and threw us some grey prison uniforms.

Although this challenge came at a bad time for us we had no choice but to retaliate. We threw the prison uniforms into the corridor, after which our linen was taken from us. It was cold in the cells, and chilly draughts tormented us, but although we were in our underclothes, we declared a hunger strike. This was the cruellest test I experienced while imprisoned in Łomża, for I became very ill during the hunger strike. I began to cough up blood and became so weak that I could not even talk. I was sure that I would die. Our suffering, however, did not sway our resolve.

On 23 December all the political prisoners in Łomza were transferred to other prisons. I was included in a small group in Białystok, one of the harshest prisons in Poland. When we arrived, we were taken to the bathhouse, and while we were washing the administration took our clothes and left prison uniforms behind in their stead. We protested, but had to go to the cells in our underclothes. The next day we met with the political prisoner commune, but found that its members had been forced to wear the prison uniforms two months before we arrived in Białystok. They instructed us to follow suit.

In 1936 a partial amnesty was declared for political prisoners. Those with sentences of up to five years of imprisonment had their sentences reduced by half, while those serving more than five years had their sentences reduced by one-third. I was the last prisoner in our group to be freed—on 24 May 1939. My last companion from oma had been freed on 15 April, and for more than a month I was alone in my cell and during the exercise period.

My five years and four months of imprisonment now seemed like an eternity. It was as if freedom was something I could only dream about, or read about in a fairy tale. The prison, with its harsh grey walls and monotonous surroundings, represented concrete reality. For some reason I could not believe that I would be freed.

Finally the day of my release arrived. I was told to gather my belongings, summoned to the main prison office, and there I was given a document authorizing my release. The warder on duty checked this document, opened the prison gates, and I timidly crossed the last prison threshold.

# PART II

*The section of Danylo Shumuk's memoirs which covers the period between May 1939 and March 1943 has not reached the west. However, some information about this period is available in samvydav [samizdat] documents written by Danylo Shumuk and in his letters to his nephew Ivan Shumuk, who lives in Canada. The biographical sketches in this chapter are based on this material. In addition, in 1979 Danylo Shumuk managed to send an autobiographical essay to his family in Canada describing the circumstances under which he was captured and imprisoned by the Germans in 1941. Danylo Shumuk wrote this description in the third person, and used the pseudonym "Davyd Shostak" (Shostak was his mother's maiden name). The translation in Chapter 5, has been modified to read in the first person.*

*[Editor]*

# Chapter Five

*After his release on 24 May 1939 Danylo Shumuk returned to his
family and native village. On 1 September, less than four months
later, and shortly after Molotov and Ribbentrop had signed the
German-Soviet Treaty of Non-Aggression, Germany invaded
Poland. On 17 September, when Poland had already lost the war
against Germany, the Red Army invaded Eastern Poland (Western
Ukraine and Western Belorussia), on the pretext that it was
"liberating" the population of this area. Danylo Shumuk, who had
remained a committed communist throughout the period of his
imprisonment in Poland, welcomed this development, especially
since it meant not only a change in political regimes, but also an
end to Polish domination of Western Ukraine.*

*Under the new regime the Polish government's restrictions on
Ukrainian-language educational facilities were lifted and there was
a severe lack of qualified teachers, especially in the villages.
Danylo Shumuk immediately volunteered to teach in the local
primary school, and also used this opportunity to continue his own
studies. He taught until the summer of 1940 and became close
friends with Nina Zelynska, a fellow teacher (and daughter of the
former village priest) whom he had known as a young girl before
his imprisonment.*

*Ideologically the two were far apart, since Nina's brother Iurko
had belonged to the OUN underground before the Soviet invasion,
and she also had connections with the OUN. Because of her
"unreliable" background, Nina Zelynska soon began to encounter
difficulties at work, but Danylo was able to help her because of his*

*reputation as a well-known activist of the prewar pro-Soviet communist movement. This strengthened their friendship and they soon discovered that, despite their different backgrounds, they had a great deal in common. As a result of their frank discussions, in which Nina often criticized the new regime, and as a result of his own natural curiosity, Danylo Shumuk slowly became disillusioned with certain aspects of the Soviet regime.*

*For example, it was obvious that despite the publicity accorded the hastily organized plebiscite held by the occupying authorities on 22 October 1939, these were not elections in the true sense of the word but a meaningless ritual. Shumuk was also struck by the artificiality of the propaganda claiming that the "people" demanded that Galicia and Volhynia be included within the Ukrainian SSR. He noted also that the petition "humbly requesting" this measure was addressed to Moscow rather than Kiev, the capital of the Ukrainian SSR, and the excesses which accompanied the start of enforced collectivization of agriculture in 1940. In addition, many of Shumuk's former friends and associates from the communist underground complained to him about the behaviour of the new authorities, many of whom had been sent to the occupied territories from Eastern Ukraine or other regions of the Soviet Union. However, Shumuk tried to quell their complaints (and his own growing doubts) about the new regime by arguing that various problems were bound to occur during a certain unstable transition period, especially in view of the hostile environment in which the new authorities were operating.*

*In 1940 Shumuk decided to rejoin the Communist Party and turned to the raion party committee in Liuboml to inquire about the procedure to be followed. He was told, however, that he still had to undergo a certain period of "re-education" before he could be accepted back into the party ranks, and later he was informed that he could best demonstrate his loyalty to the party by helping combat "anti-Soviet elements" in Western Ukraine, especially among Ukrainian intellectuals who were connected with the nationalist underground and former members of the CPWU.*

*This was in effect a proposition to collaborate with the NKVD,[1] which by 1940 was stepping up its activities in Western Ukraine, and this greatly disturbed Shumuk, who had grown to loathe all secret police activity and all forms of political repression. Thus he let it be known that he was not interested in this proposition and ceased his efforts to rejoin the party.*

*In the meantime Shumuk had decided to give up his teaching job, because teachers from Eastern Ukraine were now taking over many positions in the local schools. Working conditions for those teachers (like Shumuk) who had no formal pedagogical education deteriorated, and since Shumuk was now the father of two children (a son, Volodymyr, was born in 1940), in the fall of 1940 he found a better-paying job as a loans officer in the state bank in Liuboml.*

*Nonetheless, Shumuk's doubts about the system continued to grow, and were exacerbated by the negative impressions of those who returned to Western Ukraine after visiting or working in Eastern Ukraine. Among them was Danylo's nephew Ivan Shumuk, who had been recruited to work on construction projects in Kiev in December 1939 and who returned home in December 1940. Ivan, the son of Danylo's brother Antin, was only five years younger than Danylo and in their youth they had been close friends. They shared many interests, and although their views on many issues varied considerably they respected each other's opinions. Ivan left for Kiev with an open mind and his account of working class life in the capital of the Ukrainian SSR made a deep impression on Danylo, for many of Ivan's comments were highly critical of certain aspects of the Soviet system that Danylo had idealized.*

*From the beginning of the "liberation" of Western Ukraine, the NKVD arrested or persecuted various "hostile" or "unreliable" elements among the population. This persecution soon acquired a mass character and a large number of families, including women, children and the aged, were uprooted and deported to Siberia or other far-flung corners of the Soviet Union.[2]*

*In January 1941 Danylo Shumuk's family was affected by this persecution, when his brother Antin was arrested. There had been various disagreements between the two brothers, and Danylo had bitterly criticized Antin for dropping out of the Selrob movement in 1928, but Danylo knew that his brother could not possibly be an enemy of the new Soviet regime. Soon, however, Danylo was summoned to the local NKVD office, where the investigator in charge of Antin Shumuk's case demanded that Danylo testify against his brother. It soon became clear that the investigator was well informed about the old differences between the two brothers,* and that the case against Antin was based on the "treason" he had allegedly committed by abandoning his pro-Soviet activities in the Selrob movement in 1928. The investigator demanded that Danylo confirm this accusation and condemn his brother's past. When Danylo tried to explain the circumstances surrounding his brother's "betrayal," the investigator hinted that his refusal to co-operate with the NKVD could have unpleasant consequences.

In the meantime, there were rumours afoot about a possible war between Germany and the Soviet Union. Thus the Soviet authorities stepped up conscription and the construction of fortifications on their side of the border. Since Danylo Shumuk had received no previous military training, and was the father of two small children, he had received a deferment, but on 15 May 1941 he was finally called up for military service.

To Shumuk's surprise he was not assigned to undergo military training but to a special "construction battalion" which was sent to build border fortifications along the Buh River. These construction battalions were made up of persons who, for various reasons, were considered by the NKVD to be "unreliable" and "politically suspect."

On 22 June the German forces attacked the Soviet Union and the construction battalion in which Danylo Shumuk was serving was transferred to Zhytomyr oblast. Here the battalion was armed and transformed into a so-called "special" penal battalion, which was sent to the most dangerous section of the front. In a matter of days two-thirds of the soldiers in the battalion had been killed.

In August 1941, in accordance with an order from the higher command, almost 150 men in the penal battalion, including Shumuk, were deprived of the right to bear arms because of their political unreliability. On the outskirts of Pyriatyn, Poltava oblast, these soldiers were assembled into two battalions and were to be transferred deep into the rear, to work in factories in Novosibirsk. By this time, however, the German forces had broken through the front and surrounded the five Soviet armies assembled to defend Kiev. The unarmed battalion to which Danylo Shumuk belonged was included in this encirclement.[3]

[Editor]

The battalion of disarmed soldiers assembled in the village of Maiorshchyna, near Pyriatyn. The soldiers bivouacked near the village in a large old orchard which had once belonged to a landowner, while rumours circulated that they were to be sent to work in war factories in Novosibirsk. A captain was in charge of this special battalion, but evidently he was not trusted because there was no gun in his holster.

On our third day in this orchard the officers in charge of the battalion and companies disappeared, and the soldiers began to form small groups according to their place of origin. There were seventeen men from Liuboml raion in the battalion and they gathered around me spontaneously, since I had found myself a good pair of binoculars, a map board with topographic maps and a compass in the orchard. These military paraphernalia gave me the air of an officer.

Early in the morning, on the second day after the commanding officers had disappeared, I boiled some pea soup in my mess tin. After this "breakfast," I walked to a pond on the other side of the road. It was quiet here, and there were no soldiers nearby. There was a swing near the pond, so I began to rock myself. Suddenly a mortar shell exploded about ten metres away. Then another mortar shell exploded on the other side and a shell fragment shattered the swing's support. As I ran to the battalion's bivouac the Germans began to fire mortar rounds into the entire orchard.

"Where the devil have you been!" the men from Liuboml shouted when I ran up to them. "We've been running around looking for you and shouting away, and you run out on us! We have to do something—we can't sit here with folded arms waiting for the Germans to deafen us with their mortars."

"We should go in the direction of the least shooting and then we'll see where it's best to turn," I replied. "I think we should go through the orchard down into the gully, and along the gully into the steppe. I don't hear any gunfire in that direction."

"Just get us out of here," everyone cried out.

In the steppe, on both sides of the gully, people were running feverishly from one stack of wheat to another and setting them on fire. We felt uneasy watching this strange scene, for it is difficult for those who till the soil to watch a crop being burnt. Each grain of wheat is sacred to a peasant, for bread is life.

By hurrying through gullies and ravines we finally arrived at

Korovai. The village was full of people in military uniforms, but this was no army; it was a rabble. Villages were burning all around us, crops were afire in the fields, and stray horses, cows, sheep and pigs roamed the steppes near Korovai. The ring of rifle and machine-gun fire came closer and closer, and the noise was deafening.

Soldiers had occupied almost all the buildings in the village and it was some time before we found an empty house. But finally we approached a small building almost hidden in an orchard on the outskirts of the village. The woman of the house greeted us in a friendly fashion.

"You may be hungry, lads," she told us, "but I have nothing but potatoes. Get me something to go with the potatoes and I'll prepare anything you want, as much as you can eat. There's plenty of meat running around."

Everyone looked at me and I understood at once her meaning.

"Well, who's a cowboy here?" I asked. "We have to catch one of the strays wandering about in the steppe." Several butchers from Liuboml immediately went to work. They deftly lassoed and killed a small pig and dressed it expertly. Thus there was a tasty and nourishing dish to go with the potatoes and there would be some meat left for our hostess. In the meantime she prepared some mashed potatoes and even set out some dill pickles for us. Everyone had his fill of home-cooked food and went to sleep in the orchard under the open sky.

The woman woke us early in the morning.

"Hurry up, lads, and get up for breakfast," she said. "The Germans are approaching the village from all directions."

"Where are they?" everyone cried.

"They're already shooting at the village from three sides. On the fourth they've set up machine guns behind the haystacks and that's where the soldiers are surrendering to them." We quickly washed ourselves and were sitting down to breakfast when a girl from a neighbouring house came in.

"You're still here?" she asked. "All the soldiers who stayed in our house have already gone to surrender."

"But why? They're armed and they gave themselves up of their own free will?" I asked.

"They threw down their arms, tore the stars off their caps, and turned themselves in, for the Germans say that those who surrender before noon will be given some documents and sent home, while those who don't surrender by noon will be killed."

"Whom have the Germans been speaking to? They're not in the village yet," I noted.

"That's true, but some strangers have been passing through the village and talking to the villagers and soldiers."

"Is she really your neighbour?" I asked the woman of the house when the girl had left.

"Yes, and she's also a Komsomol activist, although her father is of German origin."

"What do you think about what the girl said?" I asked the men in my group.

"She was telling the truth. If even those whom the Communist Party entrusted with weapons are surrendering, then what about us, who were disarmed and held in contempt by the Soviet authorities? If the Germans are issuing documents then surely we'll receive them as well and be sent home. After all, we were considered to be politically unreliable, and we're all from Western Ukraine," everyone piped in, interrupting one another. Those who had voluntarily left their fate in my hands, and gladly followed my lead, were transformed after my conversation with the girl. They now had a concrete hope—that the Germans would issue them documents and send them home—and this expectation was etched on their faces.

I was in a difficult situation. I had to make an immediate decision. My expression betrayed my concern, and the men kept their eyes fixed on me.

"For the time being there's no need to hurry," I said after a few minutes. "Those who can't wait can go to the other side of the village and see what's going on there. When you come back we'll talk things over and then decide what to do."

Everyone remained silent for a few minutes and seemed to be confused.

"Why should we wander around?" one of the men asked.

"Let's go to the other side of the village, see what's going on, make a few inquiries and there, on the spot, we can decide what to do."

"We don't have any choice," someone else noted. "We're surrounded, we have no arms, and our officers have abandoned us.

There's no way we can avoid being taken prisoner now, for where else can we go?"

The situation was indeed hopeless, for the mortar fire of the Germans was closing in from all sides. Together with my compatriots, I went to the other side of the village. Some three hundred metres beyond the edge of the village there were two large stacks of wheat, and two or three German soldiers occasionally stepped out from behind them. Wave after wave of Soviet soldiers came out from all corners of the village and, leaving their weapons behind, approached the Germans with their arms raised. I found this entire spectacle repugnant and humiliating.

A young German soldier with rolled-up sleeves pointed to the soldiers who still had stars on their caps and demanded grumpily that they remove these stars and hand them to him. The prisoners promptly carried out this command while the German, a smirk on his face, took the five-sided stars and put them in his pocket, swearing at those who approached him without their insignia. I remained silent when ordered to take my star off, so the German yelled at me, grabbed the cap off my head, tore the star off and angrily threw the cap in my face. Then the Germans herded us to a small railroad station and later two more columns of prisoners were brought here. We were tired, depressed and hungry, but no one even thought of feeding us.

The next day, hungry and sleepless, we were herded further to the east, following the front. Toward evening we approached the city of Lubny and were chased into the courtyard of a demolished factory. Another large unit of prisoners was brought in shortly. Our hunger and fatigue became more and more unbearable, but the Germans did not even allow us to pick up the food which the kind and generous women of the Poltava region threw in our direction. And thus the prisoners slowly began to lose hope that the Germans would issue them documents and send them home.

Three German officers drove to the factory, bringing along two wooden boxes and a large camera, and after examining the surroundings they set up their equipment on a small hillock. All the prisoners congregated around the hillock, and some began to speculate that these boxes contained the documents that the Germans were going to hand out to us.

As the Germans began to unpack the "valuables," we anxiously held our breath. Suddenly, however, the two officers began to take pastries and cigarettes out of the boxes and started throwing them into the crowd of prisoners. They did this intentionally, for they took great delight at the sight of these starved and exhausted unfortunates throwing themselves at the pastries and cigarettes, pushing one another aside. In the meantime the third officer hastily took photographs of this nightmare. I merely looked on from the sidelines.

In the evening we were forced to march further to the east. We were taken along side-roads, through villages and hamlets, and the villagers looked at us with great sympathy, thinking that perhaps some of their own relatives were wearily trudging along in the column. These bystanders threw melons, canteloupes, apples, pears, carrots, bread and crusts in our direction, but if a prisoner broke the ranks of the columns to pick up a carrot or a crust two or three steps away, the guards shot at him or used their rifle butts to beat him.

Thirst soon began to torment us more than hunger, but the guards did not take us near any water. However, as soon as darkness fell the prisoners began to run to nearby wells, one at a time, to gulp down at least a small mouthful of water. The guards shot at them, but thirst had overcome their fear of death, and even I could not restrain myself. First, however, I considered carefully in which direction and at what moment I could best dash out to a well. Suddenly I saw a woman drawing water from a well near a house behind some lilac bushes. At that same moment, the guard at the rear of the column ran after another prisoner. I sprinted toward the well and drank my fill of fresh water, but for some reason I did not dare to try to escape. Afterward  I could not forgive myself for this lost opportunity.

We were driven along roads which had been broken up by heavy traffic, and as we passed along one such road after a rainfall the prisoners simply fell down and drank from the puddles of rainwater, gulping the water down together with all kinds of filth. The guards directed long bursts of fire at these laggards, and thus several corpses were left near every puddle, and sometimes in the puddle itself. The guards fired at the prisoners in a random fashion, without the least feeling of remorse, as though scoring goals at a soccer match.

Early in the morning we arrived in Romodan and were again taken to a demolished factory. Within a few days almost forty thousand prisoners were brought here. The officers were housed in barracks while the other prisoners stayed among the ruins of the factory, under the open sky. We remained here for three days without food, but on the fourth day eight field kitchens and several German cooks arrived. However, a large crowd of prisoners from Georgia came to the kitchens, forming three tight circles around them and holding each other's arms to prevent anyone from getting to the kettles before they had eaten their fill. No one could prevent them from doing this, for the Russians and Ukrainians did not attempt to form organized groups. The Germans had their own plans, and led a column of Soviet officers out of the barracks, telling them to stop near the kettles.

"First of all we'll feed your officers," a German officer said in broken Russian, "and then we'll feed the rank and file. So make some room and let the officers get to the kettles."

But the Georgians who had encircled the field kitchens did not move, and did not even consider letting anyone through to the kettles. The hungry crowd hissed and there was a feeble commotion. Apparently the Germans wanted to provoke such a reaction, for they immediately began to photograph this scene. As a result of the ensuing disorder I became separated from my few remaining compatriots. I had no intention of approaching the kitchen, and when I heard that the soup consisted of horse meat gathered at the front, the thought of eating repelled me.

Early on the morning of the fifth day the Germans began to lead us from the factory grounds. At the gates each person received three raw carrots and from Romodan to Khorol we were herded along a paved road. In every village the people again threw bread, biscuits and all kinds of fruit in our direction, while the Germans continued to shoot at anyone who dared to take one step to the side of the column. I lost my strength and began to lag behind, passing from one row of prisoners to another until I found myself at the tail end of the column. Three German soldiers armed with machine guns and two large German shepherd dogs were marching behind us. If anyone lagged behind, the soldiers first set the dogs on him and then shot him and left him behind on the road. When I realized that I was only three to five metres from death, I summoned all my remaining strength to avoid this fate, and managed to make my way to Khorol.

The prisoners were detained near some buildings in front of the large gates of an empty prison camp near Khorol. Towers equipped with projectors were located at the four corners of the camp, and German soldiers armed with machine guns, pistols and hand grenades with long wooden handles manned the towers. The Germans frisked us and confiscated all knives, razors, compasses and topographic maps. Unfortunately they found my compass and topographic map, and as a result I was beaten up on the spot. Then the prisoners were chased into the camp—the most terrible death camp in Ukraine.[4] Few managed to escape from here, and they were predominantly from villages near Khorol for whom wives and village elders could vouch before the German authorities.

Barbed wire divided the camp into two sections which were linked by a gate; one section consisted of a clay pit about two-and-a-half metres deep and the other section had an even earth surface. At first the prisoners were all released into the latter section; then the gate was opened and they descended into the clay pit. As soon as they got into the pit the prisoners immediately lay on the dry clay surface and fell asleep.

Early next morning we were awoken by the furious cries of German soldiers who used cudgels to chase us into the other section of the camp. Tubs of soup and boxes of bread were placed near the gate which linked the two sections of the camp, and two Germans in white smocks ladled out the soup while two others handed out the bread. Every day we received half a litre of soup (the soup was always thick but contained no salt) and once every three days we received two hundred grams of black bread. The prisoners had no dishes, and not all had spoons, so the miserable soup was often poured into their caps, the flaps of their overcoats, or the folds of their tunics.

Every day the feeding was accompanied by beatings. Four German soldiers with cudgels stood alongside the cooks and beat everyone in turn for moving too slowly, for everything had to be grabbed on the run. The soldiers were rotated every two hours, so that they were not too tired to administer a proper beating, while the cooks were rotated every four hours. Before nightfall we were all chased back into the clay pit and beaten one more time. We were "fed" in this fashion every day. During the first few days I walked from one end of the pit to the other looking for someone I knew, but my search was in vain; it was as if all my companions had disappeared into the ground. Without some companionship it became harder and harder to while away the time. Friends, acquaintances and those from the same village or region could at least huddle together at night, warm themselves, and eventually fall asleep.

Autumn was slowly approaching and the nights were becoming colder. Then the rains came, the clay became soggy, and the prisoners' strength ebbed with every passing day. Risking their lives, women occasionally approached the camp and threw biscuits, canteloupes, carrots, pears and other food across the two barbed-wire fences. Thousands of starving prisoners then threw themselves at the food, knocking each other off their feet, and snatched the food out of each other's hands, or sometimes even out of each other's mouths. As a result of these skirmishes several prisoners were trampled into the clay which had been softened by the rains and stirred up by the prisoners' feet.

Thirst still plagued us more than hunger, but there was only one neglected well, with stale and stagnant water, in the entire camp. In despair, and overcome by thirst, the prisoners started to drink this stale water, after which dysentery began to spread. Since there were no sanitary facilities in the camp, the prisoners began to die like flies. The corpses accumulated faster than they could be moved, and thus some of them were simply trampled into the clay and a horrible stench soon permeated the camp. The prisoners began to throw themselves onto the barbed wire fence, in full view of the Germans, so that they would be shot, and the Germans cold-bloodedly obliged.

I grew so weak that in my thoughts I calculated the time left to me in this world in days rather than weeks. The prisoners looked like skeletons and, smeared with clay, could barely move and almost stopped talking to one another. The camp was quietly dying. Some prisoners resorted to cannibalism, and one could recognize the cannibals by the look in their eyes. Everyone avoided them like the plague. But even in these conditions there were people who spent all their time praying, and the spark of eternal love burnt in their eyes. Among themselves they said that this suffering was God's punishment for our sins, and they awaited death calmly, with prayers on their lips. I was not a believer in the religious sense of the word, but in my heart I was also preparing myself to die by trying to come to terms with my conscience. One day when I was in this gloomy frame of mind I suddenly and unexpectedly met three old friends from neighbouring villages. Two (Skybets and Borkivsky) were in better shape than me while the third (Kusnytsky) could barely stand. They were very happy to see me and I was overjoyed. After we had each described how we had ended up in this death hole, we started discussing how we could save ourselves.

"Escape and only escape," I said. "We either get out of the camp tonight or the guards shoot us; anything is better than waiting to die of starvation in this hole." My countrymen agreed.

"Fine, then let's discuss what we have to do first, and how and where it would be easiest to break out," I proposed.

"I have a razor," Skybets said.

"And I have a small pair of scissors," Borkivsky added.

"Good. First of all we have to shave, cut our hair, and then decide where it would be easiest to break through the camp perimeter," I said. Carefully, so the Germans would not see us, we quickly shaved ourselves and cut each other's hair. "Now all we need is some civilian clothing, but those who remain alive can worry about this when they find themselves on the other side of the fence. The important thing is that whatever happens, our suffering in this hole will be over tonight."

The camp was enclosed by two three-metres high barbed-wire fences, and in order to reach the lowest strand of barbed wire from the pit one had to stand on the shoulders of someone who was fairly tall. Near one of the towers there was a space of some thirty metres where there was only one fence. Here it was easier to dig our way out at night, using our hands, and to crawl under the lowest strand of wire.

The sky was covered by dark autumn clouds as though a huge cabbage leaf was hanging over this terrible pit of death. Night fell and the drizzle increased, eventually turning into a thick autumn rain while the prisoners, living skeletons, were lying motionless in the wet clay. Under these conditions we began our work, while from the tower a guard alertly followed the beam of the projector.

We dug small trenches under the wires, using our hands, working whenever the guard focused his projector on the opposite end of the fence. He illuminated both the right and left sides of the fence with the projector and carefully examined them in a fairly regular pattern. But for some reason he suddenly changed his rhythm, and quickly turned in our direction. He focused the projector directly on us, gave us a shout and then, grabbing a long-handled grenade, started to swing it in our direction. Seeing that our plan had failed we ran back toward the centre of the camp. When the guard actually threw the grenade, we threw ourselves to the ground. It exploded some five metres away. A cloud of smoke rose, a second grenade exploded, and under the cover of this smoke screen we ran to the centre of the camp, leaving muffled cries and groans behind. Suddenly everything grew quiet. The cloud cover became even heavier, and the rain began to fall more strongly than before.

It was about 500 metres from one tower to the other, and on a dark and rainy night the projectors could not penetrate this distance. At such times the Germans reinforced the guards with two additional soldiers. Their task was to walk from tower to tower alongside the barbed wire, and check whether the prisoners were trying to escape from the pit. They divided the section between the towers into two equal halves, so that each soldier was responsible for keeping an eye on about 250 metres of fence. The soldiers would start from each tower simultaneously, and meet in the middle, in the area that the light of the projectors could not penetrate. The rain continued to fall and the two German soldiers raised the hoods of their black capes. The first three times they met they exchanged a few words and then turned back toward their respective towers. Observing this procedure, we decided to cut the wire at the place where the two guards met. Skybets was the tallest and strongest fellow in our group, so he served as the "scaffolding" for this job. The first to stand on his shoulders was Borkivsky, who began to snip away at the lower strand of wire with the small pair of scissors, and then I and then Kusnyshchsky took over. As soon as the guards separated and started to return to their towers, we continued, one after the other, to snip away stubbornly at the wire until the guards again approached their rendezvous.

We worked away for what seemed more than an hour while the prisoners who were lying around us anxiously watched our efforts.

That's it," Borkivsky finally noted. "Now we have to see what we can do with the second fence." The tension mounted. Our hearts were pounding, for we knew that only minutes remained before we would either be free or killed while escaping.

When Borkivsky returned he lowered himself to the bottom of the pit.

"I've cut through the lowest strand of wire in the first fence," he told us, "I slithered through the gap and crawled on my stomach to the second fence. But fortunately it won't be necessary to cut through the wire there. I simply stretched the bottom strand and hooked its barbs onto the upper strand, so everything now is ready."

We heard the footsteps of the guards and fell silent. They were only about five metres from us, behind the two barbed-wire fences, and we all pricked up our ears. But the guards, as before, simply exchanged a few words and then went their separate ways.

"I think we should let Kusnytsky go first, for he's in the worst shape," I told the others.

"Fine, but you'll follow him," Skybets added. "Your health isn't much better than Kusnytsky's."

First we lifted Kusnytsky out of the pit, and then I was given a boost. I pressed myself to the ground as I slowly crawled under the wire, afraid that I might snag my overcoat on the upper strand. I overcame the first obstacle and slithered to the second fence with a tremor in my heart, but here the gap was larger, and I crawled through it quite easily.

I advanced another seventy metres, saw a sharp slope some fifty metres long in front of me, and since it was impossible to crawl any further I turned on my side, threw myself forward, and rolled down to the bottom. At this point I heard a commotion in the camp. The Germans began to fire flares, and once the camp and the area around it were lit up they started firing from machine guns.

I jumped up and began to run, but it was not really running, for I was totally exhausted. When I came to a creek I heard someone jump into the water ahead of me; I thought it was Kusnytsky and thus followed suit. The machine guns started to rattle again, and gathering my remaining strength I ran to a row of trees along the side of a road. In the meantime flares continued to burst overhead, lighting up the entire area around the camp, and from time to time I could hear the desperate cries of the prisoners among the bursts of machine-gun and rifle fire. When I reached the trees I stopped, looked around, then continued carefully through the grove, away from the camp.

Gardens stretched out beyond the trees, and a tendril upon which grew a large canteloupe reached into the grove. When I stumbled onto this "treasure" I was overjoyed, for the thousands of hungry prisoners in the camp would have thrown themselves upon such a find. But I could not simply bite into the canteloupe; first I had to break it open or cut it apart. I started to kick it, but lacked the strength to break it open. I could not bear to leave it behind, so after a rest I found a sharp rock and finally managed to open the canteloupe. Biting into the soft flesh, I felt its sweet juices flow into my mouth, and then into my gullet and stomach. I managed to swallow some ten morsels of canteloupe flesh and probably would have continued gnawing at it, but the yelps of dogs approaching from the direction of the camp forced me to move on. Crossing the road, I found some more gardens, containing sugar beets, and thought that I might try these as well. But I lacked the strength to tug them from the ground and had to dig one out with my hands. After wiping the soil off with some leaves I bit into it a few times, but a wave of nausea soon came over me.

There was a second line of trees ahead of me, behind the gardens, and throwing the beet aside I made for them. After crossing a railroad track I came out into the steppe, where many horses were grazing, and felt very peaceful walking among them. Soon I came across a small village and was overjoyed that finally I would meet some people who were at liberty and would tell me what was happening in the area. I knocked on the door of the first house I came to and heard a rustle inside. After a few minutes I saw a woman's face in the window. It disappeared immediately, but a few seconds later I heard the door leading to the vestibule creak.

"Are you from the camp?" a young woman asked through the front door, opening it slightly.

"Yes, I've just escaped," I replied.

"The Germans check all the houses in our village every two hours, both day and night, so take these meat pies and go into the corn field. When you go through the field you'll come out into an alder-wood grove which stretches along the river. You can turn right there and when you come out onto the road you'll see a village as soon as you cross a bridge. You can rest in that village, for the Germans don't visit it very often."

"Thank you very much for the meat pies and the advice," I said and bowed to the woman. I went into the corn field, and sighing with relief, immediately bit into the pies.

Passing village after village as I made my way by foot westward through the oblasts of Poltava, Kiev and Zhytomyr, I learned from the villagers about the unbelievable horrors which they had suffered from 1933 to 1937. The ruins of villages whose inhabitants had died during the artificially imposed famine and the terrible stories which I heard from the survivors of this tragedy now fully opened my eyes and cleared my mind of the opium of communist ideology.

Losing my faith in communism meant that my life lost its meaning. I had fought and suffered in Polish prisons for this ideology, for I believed that its ideals were the most noble and most enlightened ideals of mankind. From this time on, however, Stalin's regime became just as repugnant to me as Hitler's. The war and everything else around me no longer made any sense, and I felt terribly isolated and defenceless.... I continued, however, walking toward my native village in my beloved Volhynia.

When I finally reached the village late one evening I looked around and then entered my house quietly.

"O God! Why did you come here?" my wife cried in anguish. "All the German henchmen in the auxiliary police have been on the lookout for you, and are gloating at the thought of the tortures they'll put you through if you fall into their hands."

I had to leave my house before dawn and decided to visit the teachers with whom I had worked in the same school in 1940. Nina Zelynska was now director of the school (she was later executed by the Germans for her activity in the national liberation movement) and Emilia Shvedova was a teacher. They were also worried when I appeared before them, but they were sympathetic when I told them about my plight.

"I'm sure you know, Danylo," Nina told me, "that I have contacts with the national-liberation movement, and I'd like to help you, because you helped me once. Unfortunately, I can't really do all that much, because the police chief in Pidhorodne and the police chief in Liuboml don't cooperate with the OUN. They're fully controlled by the Gestapo and they've been itching for quite a while now to get their hands on you. But I'll get you some documents."

Nina managed to provide me with an identity card and with a diploma from a teachers' college, which were both made out in someone else's name. I spent a long time wandering back and forth between the Buh and Dnieper rivers, but finally, in March 1942, a farmer in a hamlet in Ostrih raion took me in as a farmhand.

The Germans had advanced deep into the Soviet Union but in 1942 the strength of their drive weakened. The occupation forces began to requisition all remaining grain and cattle from the villagers, young people were deported to Germany to work as forced labourers, and since I was also threatened by these deportations I again turned to Nina for help.

In the spring of 1943 the people of Ostrih raion took up arms and challenged the German occupation forces, repossessing the grain and cattle which had been confiscated by the Germans. This is when I became an active participant in the national-liberation movement, for at this difficult time all the Ukrainians in Volhynia were united around those who challenged the German occupiers.

Maps produced by:
Stephanie Kucharyshyn
Cartographic Section, Department of Geography
University of Alberta

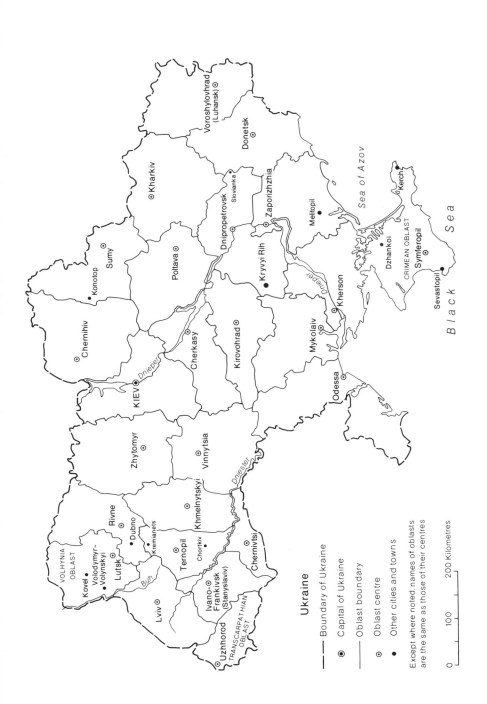

Ukraine

— Boundary of Ukraine
⊙ Capital of Ukraine
— Oblast boundary
⊙ Oblast centre
• Other cities and towns

Except where noted, names of oblasts
are the same as those of their centres

0        100       200 Kilometres

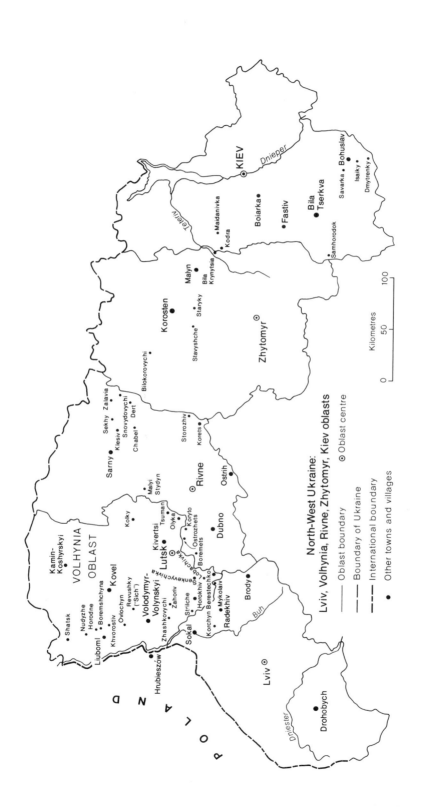

North-West Ukraine:
Lviv, Volhynia, Rivne, Zhytomyr, Kiev oblasts

⊙ Oblast centre

——— Oblast boundary

— — Boundary of Ukraine

—·—·— International boundary

• Other towns and villages

Kilometres
0    50    100

POLAND

VOLHYNIA OBLAST

KIEV ⊙

Dnieper

Teteriv

Dniester

Buh

Drohobych

Lviv ⊙

Hrubieszów

Shatsk
Liuboml
Nudyzhe
Horodne
Boremshchyna
Khvorostiv
Ovlochyn
Revushky ("Sich")
Kamin-Koshyrskyi
Kovel
Volodymyr-Volynskyi
Zhashkovychi
Sokal
Striliche
Horokhiv
Korchyn Berestechko
Mykolaiv
Radekhiv
Brody
Zahoriv
Senkevychivka
Lobachivka
Lutsk
Kivertsi
Kolky
Malyi Stydyn
Tsuman
Olyka
Koryto
Ostrozhets
Boremets
Dubno
Rivne ⊙
Ostrih
Storozhiv
Korets
Sarny
Kliesiv
Sekhy Zalavia
Snovydovychi
Chabel
Dert
Bilokorovychi
Korosten
Stavyshche
Starxky
Zhytomyr ⊙
Malyn
Bila Krymytsia
Maidanivka
Kodra
Samhorodok
Boiarka
Fastiv
Bila Tserkva
Savarka
Isaiky
Dmytrenky
Bohuslav

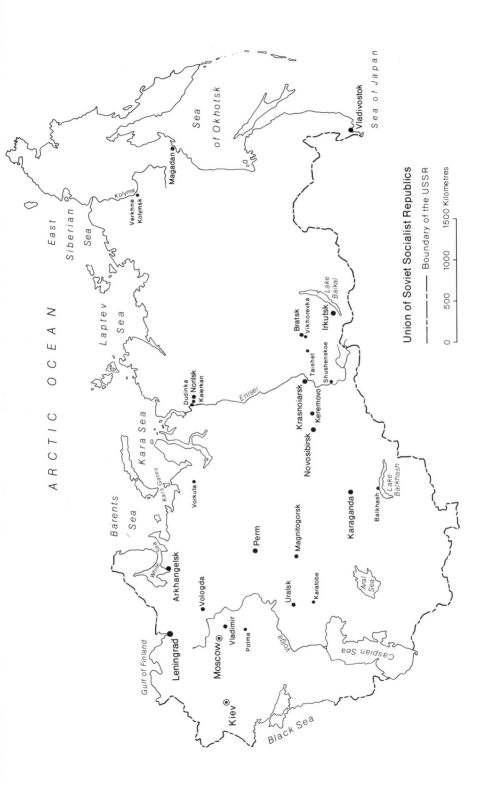

ARCTIC OCEAN

East Siberian Sea

Laptev Sea

Kara Sea

Barents Sea

Sea of Okhotsk

Sea of Japan

Vladivostok

Magadan

Kolyma
Verkhne Kolymsk

Enisei

Dudinka
Norilsk
Kaierkan

Bratsk
Vikhorevka
Irkutsk
Lake Baikal
Taishet
Shushenskoe

Krasnoiarsk
Keremovo
Novosibirsk

Balkhash
Lake Balkhash

Karaganda

Vorkuta

Perm
Magnitogorsk

Kara Gates

White Sea

Arkhangelsk
Vologda

Uralsk
Karatobe

Aral Sea

Gulf of Finland

Leningrad

Moscow
Vladimir
Potma

Volga

Kiev

Caspian Sea

Black Sea

Union of Soviet Socialist Republics

- - - Boundary of the USSR

0    500    1000    1500 Kilometres

# PART III

# Chapter Six

On a beautiful day in the latter half of March 1943, with the scent of spring in the air, I was on my way to meet a representative of the OUN. I was accompanied by two youths from the nationalist underground, who spoke freely about their dreams of a new Cossack era in which they could finally prove themselves.

"You know, Vasyl, as soon as we meet Lysy I'll ask to be sent away for military training. I didn't escape from the convoy and slip out of the clutches of the Germans just to avoid hard labour in Germany. I want to fight for our national independence," boasted the taller of the two.

"I'll join you, Petro. I also want to get some training and join a company."

"But where are these companies?" I asked.

"All our military detachments are in the Polissia area. Just last week almost the entire police force of Volhynia took to the forest with their guns."

"Why only last week, why not earlier? The Germans have been plundering our country, robbing our people and deporting our youth to Germany for hard labour for a long time."

"Everything is done at the command of the OUN. There were no orders—they stayed where they were. The command came—they went."

"How could the OUN give orders to the police? The police have been serving the Germans!"

"The OUN had underground cells inside the police force, and most of the police were OUN members," replied Petro, looking at me closely. "Today we'll arrive at the rendezvous, where you'll meet someone from the raion provid. You can put all your questions to him—we're not allowed to talk to you about these matters."

The rendezvous was in the village of Boremets, Ostrozhets raion, which lay at the edge of a majestic forest along the Styr River. We were taken to a large house near the forest where a man of about thirty met us and looked us over in an authoritative fashion.

"Where have you lads come from?" he asked.

"From Pysytyn," replied Petro.

They exchanged passwords and Petro handed the stranger a sealed message which he carefully opened and read. He then gave me a stern, questioning look. After he had dismissed the youths, the stranger asked me to enter his room. The two young men sitting there rose to their feet, shook my hand, and declared: "Glory to Ukraine!"

"Glory to our heroes!" I replied hesitantly, feeling ill at ease with this greeting.

The elder of the two introduced himself as Makar, and the younger, blonde-haired with striking blue eyes and a pleasant smile, introduced himself as Slavko. Their supervisor, who used the pseudonym Lisovyk and was the senior member of an instructors' team, explained:

"This is where you'll receive your ideological and political training, and these are our instructors, who'll help you study the ideology of the OUN, politics, international affairs, and other subjects." Then, showing me the door into yet another room, Lisovyk told me to meet the others who had come, like myself, to attend the training course.

"Glory to Ukraine!" I greeted the twenty or so young men assembled in the room as I entered.

"Glory to our heroes!" they replied in a friendly chorus, springing to their feet. I soon learned that they were all former officers and NCOs of the Soviet army from Eastern Ukraine, with a secondary or higher education, who had escaped from German imprisonment and had begun to work for local farmers or widows in order to survive. The OUN brought them together from all over Volhynia (there were a few in every village), gave them some ideological training, and then drew them into its own network or, more frequently, into the UPA. In all, twenty-seven men were being trained here, and it was evident that the purpose of the course was to "cleanse" us of Marxist-Leninist influences and to imbue us with nationalist ideology.

At dusk the head of the instructors' team, Lisovyk, came to our room to make an announcement.

"The Organization of Ukrainian Nationalists is a political organization, fighting for national independence, which arose out of military and semi-military sporting organizations such as the Ukrainian Military Organization, the Union of Ukrainian Nationalist Youth and Plast.[1] The OUN observes military discipline, which will be enforced during the course, and I'm appointing Iakiv commanding officer of your group. His responsibilities are to prepare a roster for sentry duty, to wake all of you for morning assembly, to muster everyone in the evening and to prepare you for your classes. Iakiv knows his duties as an officer, so remember that his command is an order from the OUN and should not be questioned. Those who don't submit to our discipline are unworthy of the struggle for independence, since our sacred cause demands single-minded, selfless dedication: above all from OUN members and, eventually, from the entire nation," Lisovyk concluded rather ostentatiously.

Everyone listened attentively, but without much enthusiasm. Everything that he said, however, was new to me and I followed his words closely. My opinions about nationalism had been influenced by membership in the Communist Party of Western Ukraine (CPWU), but in the CPWU I had had no opportunity to elaborate a position of my own based on direct contact with Ukrainian nationalists. I therefore began to study carefully both theoretical and practical aspects of this movement.

The next morning reveille was at 6am. Scrambling quickly to our feet, we faced a tall young man, who was standing at attention. Iakiv, a teacher of physics and mathematics from Kharkiv oblast, told us to wash and tidy up, and ten minutes later he returned and prepared us for morning inspection. Lisovyk entered the room and Iakiv marched up to him to report that the group was ready for the day's lectures.

"Glory to Ukraine!" Lisovyk proclaimed loudly.

"Glory to our heroes!" we replied enthusiastically. Lisovyk slowly and deliberately began to recite the "Decalogue,"[2] which we repeated after him, and then we sang "O God Almighty and Unique."

During Lisovyk's first lesson we wrote out the "Decalogue," the forty-four rules of a Ukrainian nationalist,[3] and the hymn "O God Almighty and Unique." The "Decalogue" embodied the most important dogmas of the OUN variety of Ukrainian nationalism, while the forty-four rules were its canons.

Makar was our instructor for the session on politics, but I learned nothing new from his lectures since I already knew this subject very well. Slavko gave the third lecture, on Ukrainian literature and the Ukrainian national spirit. His lectures did not follow a set pattern but were fascinating, and dealt with the main themes of a book he was planning to write. He was so enthralling when he spoke that I could have listened to him for hours.

In the afternoon Lisovyk spoke about various events and prominent personalities of Ukrainian history, while Makar lectured on international affairs and Slavko on literature. After supper the instructors usually organized informal talks and discussions as well as literary evenings, and our first such discussion was chaired by Lisovyk, the head of the instructors' team.

"Let's talk about the first few lessons. What are your impressions, what comments or suggestions do you have, and what do you think of the 'Decalogue'?"

No one spoke. Such silences always irritate me and Lisovyk also began to lose his composure.

"Did you memorize the 'Decalogue' and understand everything in it?" he demanded suddenly.

"I memorized it," I replied, "but to be honest I don't agree with everything in it."

"I'd be interested to hear what you accept and what specifically you found so disagreeable," Lisovyk asked.

"Well, let's start with the introduction. Listen carefully: 'I am the spirit of the eternal natural force which protected you from the Tatar hordes and placed you on the frontier of two worlds to create a new life.' This sounds like a shaman's incantation. It may appeal to the imagination of youths and stir their emotions, but it doesn't suit intelligent adults."

This immediately put everyone in the class on the alert.

"What about the 'Decalogue's' first clause? In fact, what do you think of the text as a whole?" asked Lisovyk, controlling his indignation.

"I agree with the first clause of the 'Decalogue,' for it's true that only a nation whose people are ready to die for independence will be able to achieve it. This clause is especially appropriate today, when the fascists are pillaging our countryside and deporting our youth to Germany for hard labour. This is precisely how every citizen and the whole nation should be confronted with the issue: 'Win a Ukrainian state or die fighting for it.'

"The second clause—'Allow no one to besmirch the honour and glory of your nation'—is clearly open to discussion, for one would first have to establish what a slur on the nation is.

"The third clause—'Be proud that you have inherited Volodymyr's trident'[4]—is, in my opinion, just pompous verbiage.

"The fourth clause—'Avenge the deaths of the great knights'—is simply ridiculous. Who knows who was given the title of knight and for what reasons? Whom is one expected to avenge, and why?

"The fifth clause—'Don't hesitate to perform the most dangerous act if the good of the cause demands it'—sounds all right, but it's not clear what is considered to be good and what bad for the cause.

"The sixth clause—'Don't discuss the cause indiscriminately, but only when absolutely necessary'—and the seventh—'Neither pleas nor threats nor torture nor death itself will force you to betray secrets'—are important, relevant, and do not require discussion.

"The eighth clause—'You will fight the enemies of your nations by all ways and means'—clearly implies an amoral outlook which, when put into practice, discredits the OUN and the whole nation. It negates the very essence of the second clause. (Previously, the eighth clause had sounded even worse: 'You will fight the enemies of your nation with treachery and intrigue.')

"The ninth clause—'You will preserve organizational secrets as you would your most precious possession'—is essential, especially for younger members of the OUN.

"The tenth clause—'You will struggle to extend the strength, wealth and territory of the Ukrainian state.' This talk of 'extending territory' smacks of greed; it's a disgraceful clause to which I could never agree. A nation which is struggling for independence cannot pursue expansionist plans."

"We've violated a basic OUN principle by allowing a discussion of the 'Decalogue'," replied Lisovyk. "We're not supposed to discuss it, just memorize it and implement it in our day-to-day activities. Still, we'll forgive you this. You've come to us from another environment and with a different background. The most important thing is that you approve of the 'Decalogue's' first clause. This will be the common platform of our struggle and everything else will sort itself out." Lisovyk examined the assembled group. Everyone remained silent; no one even stirred.

"Can one fight for the independence of Ukraine without knowing the 'Decalogue'?" asked a former naval officer who was surprised by Lisovyk's statement.

"Of course. But the OUN has taken upon itself the role of organizer and vanguard of this struggle. Have you read any contemporary Ukrainian nationalist literature?"

There was no response. Everyone tried to look as small as possible.

"How about you?" Lisovyk nodded in my direction.

"I've only read the newspapers published in Lutsk and Rivne."

"And what did you think of them?"

"I find those newspapers that lavish praise on Hitler and his army in a servile fashion repugnant. As for their literary content, I'd single out the articles of Ulas Samchuk[5] in Rivne and Iaroslav Mova in Lutsk. But Ulas Samchuk uses his pen to grovel before the 'Führer' of the Reich like everyone else. Only Iaroslav Mova stands out amid this rubbish."

Lisovyk glanced at Slavko, who blushed and lowered his eyes. Lisovyk came up to me, took me by the elbow, and led me over to him. "Here is Iaroslav Mova," he said, as Slavko looked at me gratefully and thanked me for my praise.

Mova and I soon became inseparable friends, and throughout my entire lifetime I never met anyone to compare with Iaroslav Harasymenko (Mova was his pen-name), a good-looking man with striking eyes, who was modest, and possessed a kind nature and a gift for public speaking. Slavko's poetry was fresh and lively, but in it he also demanded social justice and a relentless struggle against evil, while his essays, written with a light touch and in a measured, calm style, disconcerted his opponents by their honesty.

For me Slavko was the embodiment of physical grace and spiritual virtue. Everyone liked him, especially women, and I was overjoyed that I had the good fortune to meet such a person. Slavko was a poet of the highest order not only in the literary sense but also in his actions. There was not the slightest discrepancy between his daily life and personal relationships on the one hand, and his creative activity on the other. He was a person of exceptional integrity.

Makar had been the principal of a high school in the village of Pizne, Ostrozhets raion. We thought highly of him as a person, but were not impressed by his lectures.

Lisovyk, whose real name was Andrii Lutsyk, had completed his studies at the minor seminary in Lviv, was an old member of the Ukrainian Military Organization, and had previously been involved with the OUN's SB (Security Service).[6] He repelled people with his smugness and his habit of laughing in a strained, self-righteous manner, and we soon learned to ignore or make fun of him and his quirks.

Lisovyk never gave his instructors a chance to express themselves during the literary evenings and informal discussions; radiating self-satisfaction, he would always read to us from *Literaturno-naukovyi vistnyk*[7] as if he had written the text himself. The *Vistnyk*'s publication of Khvylovy's "Woodsnipes"[8] especially drew our attention, and made a great impression on me. I had my own "Aglaia"[9] who drew me away from communism and toward nationalism. But no! My Aglaia only taught me to observe life and people more clearly, removing the blinkers of fanaticism from my eyes, while life itself was my teacher.

But did the nationalist movement show us a way out of our general impasse? If the OUN had consisted entirely of people like Slavko, then it certainly would have provided a way out. But unfortunately there were probably many people like Lisovyk, or maybe even worse than him, in the OUN. People who are full of themselves and lust after power, shove their way into positions of leadership more quickly than people like Slavko. There probably never has been and never will be an idea or doctrine which cannot be sullied in this fashion, for ultimately human beings and their frailties play the decisive role in society, and the only function of political systems is to impede or encourage evil. But can a

*Danylo Shumuk*

totalitarian system combat evil? For the OUN was a bearer of totalitarianism, and here Andrii Lutsyk represented the OUN, not Iaroslav Harasymenko.

A marine cadet started off the discussion on "The Woodsnipes."

"The same questions that concerned Khvylovy also disturbed me, but he emphasized their social rather than their national implications. I was outraged that in the spring of 1933 people were dying of hunger in Ukraine while Moscow horses were being fed Ukrainian bread, and sugar from Ukraine could be bought only in Moscow and Leningrad. This nightmare in Ukraine was perpetrated consciously and methodically, from beginning to end. I was accepted into the navy, for example, only because my parents had not died in 1933. Those whose parents had died during that terrible year were unable to gain entry into the navy, the air force or the border forces, and those who concealed their parents' death and were later exposed were immediately transferred to the infantry."

"We're all primarily concerned with the social question; land and bread are the most important issues," said Khoma, formerly an MTS book-keeper.[10] "But for some reason the nationalists don't even mention the social question, as if it didn't exist."

"Isn't it enough that the Bolsheviks always and everywhere speak and write about nothing but the social question, yet at the same time they starved the very people who tilled the land and fed them?" asked a village teacher from the Uman region.

"The national question is at the root of all these problems—it's the key issue. An unfettered language and culture—these are our greatest spiritual achievements, and the ideal expression of our nation's soul," added Slavko.

"Without freedom in the social sphere, which creates the foundations for a nation's cultural and spiritual life," rejoined Khoma, "national independence is impossible."

"You're almost parroting Marx, treating social issues as a base and the national culture and spirit as a superstructure," said Makar.

"But Marx's base and superstructure formula is still valid," insisted the cadet.

"At first glance this 'formula' seems to be correct, but in essence it's a vulgar simplification," Slavko replied. "For every individual and every nation, the quest for spiritual expression and consolidation is an end in itself. Social conditions provide only a means of achieving this spiritual strength."

"Okay, that's enough for today. Otherwise we'll turn our course into a debating club: the OUN is an organization of action, not discussion," said Lisovyk.

# Chapter Seven

In mid-April, on the day before the course ended, the okruh OUN leader visited us and, after reading a lecture on the Soviet Constitution, gave us our assignments. Iakiv was appointed senior organizer of former residents of Eastern Ukraine, and took Zhuk along as an SB commander. Everyone else was assigned to various raions to do similar organizational work with the "Easterners,"[1] while I was sent on another propaganda course in the village of Teremne, near Lutsk. All the raion leaders and socio-political directors of our okruh attended this course. Dubchak, the Lutsk OUN leader, was also there, together with a priest from Senkevychivka raion. Except for the priest and myself, all were armed with revolvers and sub-machine guns. All were senior members of the OUN—I was the only non-party member among them.

The house where the course was held was located near the road linking Lutsk and Rivne, and the Germans were continually driving or marching along this route. In his spare time the priest, his lips trembling with fear, prayed that the Germans would not enter the house, but the others were well prepared for this eventuality. Instructors from the krai provid gave the lectures. They were all well-educated and their presentations were fairly sophisticated, but there were no informal discussions at this course; those who attended had unquestioning faith in the OUN and its leaders. I completed the course with excellent results and the okruh leader assigned me as an instructor to Lisovyk's inspection team.

Lisovyk gladly accepted me, happy that the number of his subordinates was growing. I was also pleased by this appointment, primarily because it would enable me to be with Slavko. In addition, my new duties allowed me to include some of my own ideas, which I had mulled over and tested by experience, in my lectures. Lisovyk gave me the official outlines for the courses on politics and the OUN, and I began to prepare myself by modifying these outlines and having them typed up anew.

Soon afterward we were assigned to give a course for women in Koryto. This was the first course that I attended as an instructor, but I quickly mastered the job. The women hardly ever asked any questions, trying instead to write down everything, and our evening discussions were not very successful since the beauty of springtime in Volhynia drew their attention away from politics, toward love and romance. They would spend all their time gazing at Slavko, and it seemed that some could hardly tear their eyes from his face.

After the course we were sent to the village of Pianne, and had an unforgettable journey, by horsecart, through the Pianne forest. The birds, exercising their voices as the forest awoke from its sleep, seemed to be calling to each other, and my companions, immersed in this beautiful forest music, grew silent. Pianne itself was swimming in milk-white cherry blossoms, and was drenched in their fragrance.

Two groups, one of women and the other of men, were already waiting for us, and among the men were two youths who had come from an UPA detachment in the forests of Polissia to attend the course. They gave their friends a vivid description of the formation of the first Ukrainian military units in that area and of their skirmishes with the Germans. At the time this all sounded very romantic, even legendary, and these youths, whom everyone envied, were the centre of attention.

The informal discussions at this course differed from our previous discussions, since this group was not interested in the socio-political aspects of the nationalist movement, but in the history of the Cossack era. This pleased Lisovyk tremendously, and in the evenings he would launch enthusiastic discussions about the time of Khmelnytsky[2] and draw parallels with our movement. He cantered about on this hobby horse with a smug, conceited air.

"Polissia, with its impenetrable forests, swamps and lakes is the contemporary Sich, it's our great Khortytsia[3] which is drawing all those youths who have Cossack blood flowing through their veins.

Today our whole nation looks to the forest, and in the forests of Polissia an army is being formed which has been chosen by God Himself to defend our native land and our people from German plunderers and Muscovites," declared Lisovyk, intoxicated by his own rhetoric.

Lisovyk's listeners sometimes reacted to his first speech of this kind with enthusiasm, but by the second or third time around they were usually disenchanted by his constant repetition and the artificial laugh with which he emphasized his statements.

"What armed forces is he talking about?" I asked Slavko. "Where did they come from and where did they get their weapons?"

"When the Germans occupied our territory," Slavko replied, "military schools were organized in all the towns of Volhynia with the permission of the Germans and under their control. They were for Ukrainians only, their commanding officers and instructors were also mainly Ukrainians, and the OUN operated within these schools on a clandestine basis.[4] In the autumn of 1942 the Germans decided to transfer these schools to the West, to France and Holland, and the OUN responded by ordering the school personnel and the auxiliary police to seize as many weapons and as much ammunition as possible and to take to the forests. Over 4,000 men obeyed, and they became the founding nucleus of our UPA units. This happened just when the Germans began the mass deportations of our youth to Germany for hard labour, and the senseless behaviour of the Germans propelled all the young people of Volhynia into the ranks of the UPA."

"And who is in charge of these forces?"

"The head of the movement in Volhynia is Krai Leader Klym Savur—his real name is Kliachkivsky—but direct command of the UPA units is in the hands of Honcharenko (Stupnytsky), a former colonel in Petliura's army.[5] He was the commanding officer of the military school in Rivne and now he's the military commander at UPA headquarters."

"Did all the commanding officers of these schools subordinate themselves to the OUN?" I asked.

"No," Slavko replied, "Borovets, who later assumed the name Bulba,[6] broke with the Germans earlier and took his school from Sarny into the forest. Initially he attracted many young people and managed to form quite a large detachment. He fought against both the Germans and the Soviet partisans and also harassed the OUN members in his own ranks. Lisovyk, by the way, was one of Bulba's bodyguards. But when the OUN ordered all the schools to take to the forests and form the UPA, almost all Bulba's men, in whole companies, joined UPA units."

"Have you belonged to the OUN for a long time?"

"I'm not sure, even now, whether I really belong or not. I was a writer by profession until a short while ago, when I was summoned here to work as an instructor. If everything goes well and an independent Ukrainian state is finally established, I'll return to my literary work, for politicians can change regimes but can't improve human character. Everything depends on ordinary human beings, and only art and literature are capable of changing them for the better."

"And do you believe in the success of our struggle?"

"Success or failure depends on a number of factors beyond our control. If the West opens a second front in Greece and forces a wedge through the Balkans, toward the Baltic, then we'll succeed and an independent Ukrainian state will be established. If the West opens a second front in Italy and France then everything is lost and we'll be crushed. However, we're not allowed to speculate aloud like this."

"But the West signed a military pact with the Soviet Union which discusses joint, co-ordinated military action. And the OUN itself was created 'in the form and image' of the fascist parties, with an ideology based on the philosophies of Nietzsche, Schopenhauer and Machiavelli. What will the West think of this?" I inquired.

"It's not so bad now that there are some non-party people like us in the OUN. Independence is the fundamental issue. The question of a desirable socio-political order is secondary, and will be determined later, when our state is being established. I personally have no objection to the resolution of important socio-political issues by means of a referendum, and favour a democratic system based on the British model."

Only three hundred metres separated the women's camp from the men's; they both studied and lived together. For some reason the women taking the course, teachers and nurses from Eastern Ukraine, thought that I was also an Easterner, and perhaps that is why they were so friendly toward me. I once tried to explain that this was not so, but they just laughed.

"Don't try to fool us. How else would you know Eastern Ukraine and everything that has happened there before the war so well? And you have a better grasp of Marxism than any of us. But take Lisovyk and Makar, for example. It's obvious that they're from Western Ukraine," one girl said.

"Isn't it obvious that Slavko's a Westerner too?" I asked, smiling.

"Ah, Slavko!" they laughed. "Slavko's unique; you won't find anyone else like him in all Ukraine."

On the third day of the course Alla and Zina joined the women's group. Fedir, the regional leader who accompanied them, warned us:

"Keep a close eye on Alla—she's a Soviet agent who's trying to recruit people from the OUN into her intelligence network. It should be interesting to see who she'll go for here."

Alla certainly stood out from the rest of the women, for she always had a sensible, business-like look about her. All the women occasionally tried to look serious, but always ended up looking a bit ridiculous. Alla, however, was different. She tried hard to be cheerful, to appear as if she didn't have a care in the world, but she was unconvincing. Besides, she gave herself away by always trying to gather as much information as possible. She asked her fellow students about members of the OUN at every opportunity, and showed particular interest in the surnames, pseudonyms, and ranks of everyone in the underground. This put us all on our guard, because it was taken for granted within the OUN never to make such inquiries.

When the course ended, everyone left to assume their new responsibilities. We were ordered to move to Ostrozhets, and as we made our way through the village of Svyshchiv I was struck by the unexpected sight of a group of girls engaged in military drill. Nearby, in the village square, a group of boys with wooden rifles was also being drilled, by a youth aged about sixteen. All this was being done in a conscientious fashion; both the boys and the girls had an earnest, responsible look about them, as if the fate of the Ukrainian nation depended on their training.

"I've never seen anything like this before!" I exclaimed.

"This is nothing," boasted Lisovyk. "We'll turn every farmstead into a fortress, and all our youth and every woman will bear arms. Not a single Ukrainian family in Volhynia would refuse to help the UPA now, and at least one person from every family is in an UPA detachment or involved in our organizational network. The whole nation has joined our struggle, and we're sure to succeed."

"But Volhynia isn't the entire nation. It's only a small part of it."

"Why only Volhynia? What about Galicia and Eastern Ukraine?" retorted Lisovyk.

"We haven't seen the situation there for ourselves, so we can't be sure about those regions."

"Even among Christ's disciples there was a doubting Thomas," sighed Lisovyk. "If the backward and browbeaten people of Polissia have rebelled, then we can be sure about the Galicians, who have a strong sense of national identity. The OUN became entrenched in Galicia a long time ago, whereas until recently your Polissia was a Communist stronghold."

"Is there an UPA in Galicia?"

"When it's needed, an UPA will be formed there," Lisosvyk replied in a dissatisfied tone of voice.

"It's true that the Communists were entrenched in Volhynia and especially Polissia before the war. The nationalists should thank the brutal policies of the Bolsheviks in 1939–41 for their success in these areas."

"What are you two arguing about?" Makar interrupted. "The Soviet army is a long way off, and for the time being we're fighting the Germans, not the Bolsheviks."

"It's true that the Soviet army is a long way off, but the Soviet partisans are close by," said Lisovyk.

"Where do you see these Soviet partisans?" Makar remarked skeptically. "They're holed up somewhere in the forests past Sarny and only occasionally make sorties into the territory under our control to blow up the railway line and get supplies from our villages."

"You've forgotten Medvedev," noted Lisovyk. "He's sitting in the Tsuman forests, right under our noses."[7]

"True, Medvedev isn't far off, but he just stays put, and controls only a few dozen square kilometres."

"But he's living off territory which we control, and is robbing our mills and peasants. Worst of all, his partisans are blowing up railway lines near the most patriotic Ukrainian villages, and the Germans retaliate by destroying those villages and executing innocent people. Medvedev is trying to destroy us by using the Germans as a proxy," said Lisovyk, ending the discussion.

In the evening we reached the farmstead assigned to us, and rested there for two weeks. The owner, a serious, upright man with two grown-up sons and a daughter, was a Baptist and immediately started to tell us about God's word. The sons eagerly eyed our weapons—we were all armed—but their religious beliefs forbade them to even touch our guns. The daughter could not take her eyes off Slavko and kept giving him winning smiles. But Slavko was just his usual friendly self; he had a fiancée in Lutsk and was faithful to her.

Slavko, Makar and I were reluctant to get involved in serious discussions with our hosts, but Lisovyk did nothing but argue with him.

"You say that to kill someone is the greatest sin against God and humanity. But just imagine the situation if the Germans were to burst into your yard. As they confiscate your last cow and your wife begins to protest, they beat her and point a gun at her. What would you do? Wait till the Germans shot your beloved wife, the mother of your children? Or would you grab this sub-machine gun and shoot them?" Lisovyk asked, anticipating a moral "victory" over the Baptist.

"This situation which you've so cleverly dreamed up could never occur, if only because my wife would never risk her neck for a cow."

"In the Holy Scriptures it is written," stated Lisovyk pompously, "that whoever lives by the sword shall die by the sword. The Germans entered our land arms in hand, and they shall die by force of arms."

"God often punishes such sinners," our host replied quietly.

"Do you call those who defend their land and their nations sinners?"

"No, that's not what I said! I can understand that you've taken up arms against the Germans, who are armed to the teeth. But what you're doing to the Poles is inexcusable. For example, not long ago in Lizhyn a Polish teacher was murdered and thrown into a well by some of her former pupils! And this wasn't an isolated incident—a number of Poles have been killed in this area in the last month. There's nothing honourable about suddenly attacking and murdering innocent, unarmed people," our host answered, agitated.

"But look at what the Poles did to our Ukrainian peasants in the Kholm region! Do you know that in 1942, during March and April alone, the Poles burned down about 40 Ukrainian villages and 130 churches, and killed 34,000 people! They rode horseback on our priests and then brutally murdered them; they raped girls in front of their parents and then killed both the girls and their parents," Lisovyk replied in a fury.

"I don't know. Perhaps what you describe did take place. But these horrible murders of innocent Poles are a great sin before God and humanity. You haven't been killing the Poles who burned your villages, destroyed your churches and committed murders in the Kholm area. The people you're killing are peaceful and completely defenceless."

"You shouldn't talk as if we were responsible," interrupted Slavko, "for we weren't involved in these actions. Our only weapon is the power of literature and the printed word, and we haven't been calling for anyone's death. Our main task is to awaken a sense of pride and self-awareness among our people."

"I'm sorry, I apologize," replied our host, bowing his head.

The okruh leader sent us from this farmstead to the village of Iaroslavychi, where an OUN krai conference was being held. At this conference the leader of the Lutsk okruh was transferred to the post of deputy director of the krai socio-political directorate, and the leader of the Horokhiv-Volodymyr okruh, Krylach, was named oblast leader. All the other okruh leaders were also promoted. Slavko was selected to serve on the editorial board of the krai socio-political directorate, Makar was assigned to the Kovel-Liuboml organizational okruh, and Lisovyk and I were assigned to the same directorate as instructors.

As the conference began, a detachment of Soviet partisans from the Tsuman forests raided the village of Malyn and seized all the flour from the local mill. The Germans, misled by the Poles in their service, retaliated by using about two thousand Polish *Volksdeutsche*[8] to form a ring around the entire Ostrozhets raion, and after combing this area they entered Malyn, detained raion leader Lysy, and shot him on the spot together with his closest colleagues. The Germans and the *Volksdeutsche* then rounded up all the Ukrainians from the Ukrainian section of Malyn and herded them into a church, while all the Czechs[9] from the village were chased into a school. Both buildings were set on fire, and those who tried to escape were shot. The Germans carried out this massacre quite calmly, looking on in much the same way as Spaniards watch a bull-fight, and about eight hundred people died in Malyn that day.[10]

"Medvedev's partisans in the Tsuman forests knew about the German offensive in Ostrozhets raion," the okruh leader explained, "but they had no intention of opposing this operation. Their only concern was to seize some flour."

"Why didn't UPA units go to the rescue?" I asked.

"Our units are based near Kolky, almost seventy kilometres from here."

Early in June we crossed the Styr River and, together with all the participants in the krai conference, we moved in the direction of Volodymyr. We passed through the luxuriant orchards, the lush wheatfields and the drowsy forests of the Volhynian countryside, and only occasionally did we hear bursts of enemy gunfire cutting through the air. Toward evening we entered Sadiv. We decided to spend the night here, on farmsteads near the forest, and the village head allocated two or three of us to each house. The village women, especially the younger ones, begged him to billet us in their houses, and Lisovyk, myself and a fellow called Diatel stayed with a woman about forty years old and her unmarried daughter, who was just blossoming into womanhood. Both mother and daughter treated us as members of the family, and carefully washed and ironed our clothes. Diatel was a slim, good-looking lad, and the girl kept looking his way. But, like all nationalists, Diatel behaved in a restrained manner.

"What do you think about the work of the SB?" Diatel asked me unexpectedly later that evening.

"I'm not sure what you mean."

"You know, the work of the Security Service. The Germans, the Poles and the Bolsheviks are infiltrating the ranks of the UPA and the OUN with their agents, so we have to expose and neutralize them."

"I know nothing about these matters. Not only have I never worked for such a service, police forces of all kinds have hounded me all my life."

"But we're fighting against the very forces that used to persecute you."

"What about Alla, the woman who attended our course and was rumoured to be a Soviet spy? Only God knows who she really was."

"After I pretended to fall in love with her she 'recruited' me into the Soviet intelligence network and gave me various assignments—that's what our work is like."

"If you had made Alla fall in love with you, and had her spy against the Bolsheviks, I'd value your work. But if you simply did away with her, then I find it obnoxious."

"Someone has to do this dirty work," replied Diatel sadly, and he did not pursue the conversation further.

The next morning the Sadiv village head brought us four horsecarts and the newly appointed oblast leader, Krylach, invited me to ride with him. Iashchur, the Kovel-Liuboml okruh leader who was being transferred to a new assignment in Rivne oblast, also joined us.

"You don't approve of the work of our Security Service, but how else can we operate?" Krylach asked. "In my opinion we should always fight fire with fire, and deal with the Bolsheviks using their own methods."

"If we do what you suggest, we'll increasingly come to resemble the Bolsheviks, and the people will turn against us just as they turned against them," I replied. "You can't fight evil with evil."

# Chapter Eight

At dusk we reached Mychulky, which lay at the edge of the great Svynaryn forest, and saw an UPA company for the first time. Its presence in Mychulky seemed to give the villagers more confidence, and one could sense an unusual animation here.

Sentries had already reported our arrival to the company's commanding officer, and when we stopped at the company headquarters he quickly came out, stood to attention, and reported to Krylach on the current activities of the company. Then he ordered that his table be set for supper.

"Don't trouble yourself on our account," Krylach said. "It would be better if you arranged for us to be fed at the field kitchen. We're also soldiers, and we should eat the same food as the rank and file."

The soldiers who were standing nearby beamed when they heard this from such a high-ranking leader, and in no time at all his comment was known to the whole company. With trembling hand the cook tried to fish something better for us out of the pot, but Iashchur put a hand on his shoulder and told him to feed us just as he would feed everyone else. The soldiers looked at us with devotion in their eyes, and I was very impressed by Krylach's and Iashchur's attitude.

The rest of our road led through a forest, and five kilometres further on I was intrigued by the sight of a sawmill just to the side of the road. The sawmill was working at full blast, and I asked who was responsible for its operation.

"The sawmill and watermill on the Turiia River belong to the UPA detachment permanently based in this raion" Iashchur replied, "and we've already built a large hospital, a tannery and a bakery here in the forest. Several Czech craftsmen work in the tannery; they're very good at their work, and can process all kinds of leather."

Three kilometres from the sawmill we came across three recently built large buildings, which served as a hospital, and two others which housed a school for NCOs. Near these buildings we were stopped by guards manning a large machine gun who demanded the password.

"Turiia!"

"Turiisk!" the officer in charge of the guard post replied.

The commanding officer of the NCO school, Honta, came out to meet us and stood to attention as he reported to Krylach that all the recruits were involved in military drill in the clearing. We examined their barracks and found everything in perfect order; the beds were made up, for example, in neat military style.

Next we walked over to the hospital, where we were met by the head doctor, a young, handsome and dignified man who was a skilled surgeon and a graduate of the Odessa Medical Institute. Three other doctors, all Jews who had been rescued from the ghetto, also worked at the hospital, and were extremely conscientious about their duties. In the wards the morale of the soldiers who had been wounded by the Germans and of the patients suffering from various illnesses was high, and they praised their doctors.

The staff headquarters of the UPA forces in this area, guarded by an entire UPA battalion, were in the village of Vovchak, which consisted of a few dozen houses in the forest surrounded by marshes. A bakery had been built in Vovchak to bake bread for the battalion, and a tannery and various workshops provided everyone with footwear and clothing. All the guard posts were linked by telephone, the communications centre was always staffed by a senior officer, and the entire village looked like a large military camp.

Sosenko, the battalion's commanding officer, met us near the headquarters, reported to Krylach, and invited us inside. Then he described the latest German attack on the Sich (the Styzhoriv forest, as well as the villages of Mychulky, Vovchak and Revushky, together comprised the area known as the "Sich"). According to Sosenko, about four hundred Germans participated in the attack.

"Three planes strafed Vovchak, while two tanks and about two hundred Germans attacked Mychulky and three tanks and two companies of Germans advanced on Revushky. They failed to destroy the Sich; only five houses were destroyed and fourteen of our men were killed, while we knocked out one tank and three trucks," Sosenko told us excitedly.

"How many Germans did you kill?" asked Krylach.

"I don't know. The Germans managed to retrieve their dead and wounded."

"They were probably seeking revenge for the SD colonel who was ambushed on the highway.[1] Are you still making sorties onto the same road?"

"Our men are very anxious to continue them. They all want German sub-machine guns and pistols, and the highway linking Lutsk with Volodymyr is the easiest place to get them," replied Sosenko.

Krylach changed the subject and nodded in our direction.

"The krai provid has sent us two ideology and politics instructors, Lisovyk and Boremsky.[2] We'll give them their assignment after you organize a course for the former officers of the Red Army."

"Should the former major of the general staff be included?" asked Sosenko.

"Send everyone, including the major."

"And what should we do with the Polish staff group?"

"We'll discuss this some other time," Krylach said, but later he asked how the local Poles had been behaving in general.

"Everything appears to be calm for the moment, but you can sense their anxiety. Quite a few families have packed their belongings," Sosenko said.

Krylach asked that we be assigned our quarters, and the course began shortly afterward. Seventeen former officers of the Soviet army attended our lectures, and Lisovyk appointed the former major of the general staff as leader of the group. But no one attending the course took our lectures seriously. They simply ignored Lisovyk and Brova (the political instructor permanently attached to the battalion), and did not show much interest in my lectures either. At the end of the day, however, they enjoyed discussing topics of their own choice with me, and posed questions which had nothing to do with the course programme. Like the group of former Soviet officers I had taught earlier, they were particularly interested in socio-economic issues.

On Sunday, at 11am, we were surprised to see a car stop near our new quarters. Sosenko entered our room and saluted.

"Glory!"

"To our heroes!" we replied.

"Let's go and visit our neighbours," said Sosenko, with a crafty smile on his face.

"What neighbours?" I asked.

"Oh, you'll see what fine neighbours we have," he replied.

Sosenko, Brova, Lisovyk and myself got into the car and drove along a poor road among the marshes for about two kilometres. Suddenly, at the edge of the forest, we came across an old house with the barrel of a machine gun staring coldly at us from one corner and were ordered to stop. Sosenko opened the car door, gave the password, and after driving another hundred metres we drew up before a fine new house.

Much to my surprise a Polish lieutenant in full regalia emerged from the house and, in the elegant manner characteristic of the Poles, he clicked his heels, saluted, and greeted Sosenko. Sosenko stood to attention, shook hands with him, and after we had all exchanged greetings the lieutenant invited us into the Polish staff headquarters.

Inside the headquarters a captain rose from the table and formally greeted us. Then he politely invited us to sit down and resumed his place behind the table. Near him was a very pretty Polish woman, sitting before a typewriter.

"Now that we've agreed to help each other in defending ourselves against the Germans," said Sosenko, "you should contribute at least one company from your forces."

"We have neither arms nor soldiers on this side of the Buh River," the captain replied.

"Then how can you help us?"

"We can give you bread."

"We have our own bread. At least you could give us some arms and ammunition."

"Unfortunately we have neither one nor the other. But we'll discuss your demands with our superiors."

On our way back to headquarters, Sosenko told me that there were about 150 Polish and two Ukrainian families in this Polish village, Dominopol.

"The Poles have always regarded us as inferior. They even have the nerve to establish their 'headquarters' here, supposedly as a mission to carry on negotiations with us. In reality, it's a Polish intelligence centre to gather information about our activities, and they're especially interested in the location of our storage depots. Maybe it's time to end this cat-and-mouse game."

When the course ended, Lisovyk and Sosenko set off to inspect the UPA units billeted in the Volodymyr area, while Brova and I left to do the same in the Horokhiv area. It was my first trip to this beautiful forest and steppe region of Volhynia. The weather was wonderful, and the sun shone warmly on the fields of ripening grain.

After we had inspected the UPA company stationed in a forest near Lobachivka, we left for the village of Strilche, where an UPA company was quartered on local farmsteads. The family we visited evidently knew Brova quite well, for they ran out of the house to greet us as soon as we arrived. The Kovalchuks had a rich farmstead and were well known in Strilche as an educated family. We were given a warm and affectionate welcome, and Iulko Kovalchuk's wife treated us like her own sons.

Our next stop was in the Zavydiv forest, where another UPA company was stationed, and where oblast-level courses in ideology were being offered in a forestry building. Brova visited the company while I helped Zina, a young woman who was oblast youth leader, to supervise the course examinations. The young soldiers taking the courses were very conscientious about their studies, and always attained high marks. They may not have had a profound grasp of the material under study, but they always memorized it, and were convinced of its sanctity. They recited the "Decalogue," for example, with great feeling and emotional fervour. After closely observing these youths and listening to their answers during the oral examinations, I was reminded of an observation by Leibnitz[3] back in the seventeenth century: "Let me control education and I will change the world."

"This is where true power lies," I thought to myself, "in discipline and control of information." And therein lies the secret of totalitarian regimes. These young men had much greater faith in the ideals being discussed, and a greater devotion to them, than the entire Provid of the OUN.

On our way back to the Sich, we heard the sounds of a battle near the Korytnytsia forest. We stopped near the camp of an UPA company quartered in the forest, and went to find out what was happening. From the edge of the woods we could see that a major conflict was taking place. Three German planes were circling over Zahoriv, strafing the village's old monastery, and tanks and artillery were raining a steady stream of shells on its walls. After returning to the camp we sent out a reconnaissance patrol, which later reported that the monastery was surrounded by Germans who had come in tanks and trucks from Kovel, Lutsk and Volodymyr. About 1,500 Germans were involved, but we had no idea with whom they were fighting.

"If we knew that it was our boys who were in the monastery then we could attack the Germans from the rear," the company's commanding officer said. "But if they're Bolsheviks, who've been staging provocations to incite the Germans to destroy our villages, why should we intervene?"

Later we found out that the defender of the monastery was an UPA platoon from the Sich which had begun to dig trenches around the monastery when it was attacked from all sides by German tanks and armoured cars. The nerves of the platoon's commanding officer gave way, he shot himself, and a squad leader took over command. Although the men in the platoon fought like wildcats, they soon began to run out of ammunition, and by morning only eleven of the original forty-four men were still alive.

In the meantime a thick fog had descended on the village, and the survivors managed to steal into the trenches which had been occupied by the Germans. The Germans did not realize what was happening and mistook them for their own men. The UPA soldiers, however, not knowing German, were afraid of being exposed and began to flee. The confused Germans began to run along with them, but when they heard our boys speaking Ukrainian they began to shoot at them.... Four hundred Germans and thirty-three of our men died in this unequal battle.[4]

As I describe these events I cannot help thinking that if those who died fighting the Germans in this battle had been Soviet partisans, Soviet journalists would have hailed them as heroes, and numerous articles, maybe even books, would have been written about them. But they were UPA soldiers who may have ended up doing hard labour in the Arctic region of Norilsk branded as fascists and German lackeys.

Once we crossed the Turiia River we were back on the territory of the Sich, which was totally controlled by the OUN and the UPA. As we rode through Dominopol we noted that the village seemed to have been abandoned. Although all windows and doors were open, there was no one to be seen, the guard posts at the edge of the forest were no longer manned, and a feeling of gloom and foreboding came over me. In Vovchak, however, there was the usual hustle and bustle. Everyone was going about his or her business, and here and there one could hear the tapping of typewriters.

We stopped at headquarters but came across neither the commanding officer nor his chief of staff. Then we entered the office of the quartermaster, who met us with a weary and dejected look. He was an older man, who had previously taught at the Horokhiv secondary school.

"What happened in Dominopol?" I asked.

The quartermaster stared at me in surprise. "And where have you been the last few days?" he asked.

"Enjoying our trip to the Horokhiv area."

"So you don't know anything about Dominopol yet," said the quartermaster as if he was speaking to himself. "Three days ago Dominopol was liquidated," he added.

"What do you mean? The people were liquidated?"

"Yes," he replied with a deep sigh. I said no more and walked out, followed silently by Brova.

The commanding officer's aide-de-camp, Voron, was standing near the headquarters with two youths. Although the youths were armed, they were in civilian clothes, and all three were chatting cheerfully until they saw us, whereupon they stopped their conversation and turned in our direction.

Voron stood to attention, gave the usual greeting, and reported that the commanding officer was away until the next morning.

"And what were you lads discussing in such a lively fashion?" asked Brova.

"We were just describing how we handled the Polacks[5] in Dominopol," replied Voron.

"Who are these armed civilians?" I asked.

"These lads are from the SB, and they're better than anyone else at taking care of the Poles. This one here," Voron nodded at one of the youths, who stood to attention, "drowned twenty-seven."

"Tell us what happened."

"At about twelve o'clock we surrounded the whole village of Dominopol. Then myself, the commanding officer, and the entire command went up to the Polish staff headquarters and knocked on the door. The lieutenant looked out of the window and immediately saw what was going on, but he had no alternative and opened the door. I shot him right on the threshold, and then shot the captain in his bed. The typist jumped out of the window and was shot outside by our boys. In the meantime the commanding officer fired a flare to indicate that the headquarters had been taken and that we could begin. Then our lads from the SB went on a spree in the village, and by morning not a single Polack was left alive," Voron ended, evidently expecting praise.

"Not only do your 'exploits' fail to impress me," I informed him, "I find them repulsive. Forty-four UPA soldiers in the Zahoriv monastery took on one-and-a-half-thousand Germans, and the battle that followed lasted some eighteen hours, even though the German attack was supported by three planes and five tanks. About four hundred Germans were killed, to our thirty-three dead—that's our pride and glory! But no one should boast about killing defenceless people in their sleep. This is a black stain on our liberation movement, when compared to the heroism of the men who died at Zahoriv."

"A black stain?" one of the SBists repeated, offended by my remarks. "And what if the Poles had pulled your mother out of your house by her braids, murdered her before your very eyes, and thrown her into the Buh River, as happened in 1942? If your father had been shot in front of you? If your sixteen-year-old sister had been raped, bayoneted, and then thrown into the Buh? Would you still say that this was a 'black stain'?" the SBist asked with tears in his eyes.

"You can't fight evil with evil," I replied. "The terrible crimes committed by the Poles in 1942 have disgraced them in the eyes of all humanity, but by committing the same kinds of crimes you have simply obscured their brutal excesses."

Soon afterward we were assigned to lecture to two groups of young men and women from Eastern Ukraine. There were about twenty-five students in each group; most of the women were young teachers, while the occupations of the men varied. Neither of the groups showed much interest in our lectures, and it was impossible to get them involved in political discussions, since the women and the men soon paired off and waited impatiently to get together in the evenings. Our daily routine and our efforts to prevent them from meeting only heightened their desire, and added a romantic, at times even adventurous, thrill to their encounters. Sometimes we sounded the alarm in the middle of the night in both the men's and women's camps, and would find about half a dozen men spending the night with the women.

Just before the end of the course Krylach arrived with the oblast SB director. They greeted us in a friendly manner, talked about the course and our students, and then Krylach asked me to join him for a walk.

"Try not to get so upset in public about the recent events in Dominopol," said Krylach. "The classic age of chivalry ended a long time ago. In the past our ancestors used to make an official announcement before they went into battle, but no one does this any more. We can't behave like lambs; when we fight the Bolsheviks or Poles we have to use their own tactics."

"I hadn't intended to express my feelings about the tragedy in Dominopol so openly, and I wouldn't have done so if I hadn't seen how some people relished talking about their actions there. This kind of enthusiasm is a sign of sadism, it's a psychological aberration of the worst kind, and I don't think it's in our interest to be training sadists. Every sadist is by nature a coward, and we don't need cowards."

"All right then, as long as you understand our point of view," said Krylach and we parted.

# Chapter Nine

When the courses ended Sosenko introduced Lisovyk and myself to the former principal of the secondary school in Volodymyr and to a physics and mathematics teacher.

"Our oblast provid sent letters to all the Ukrainian intelligentsia in the cities of Volhynia," said Sosenko, "telling them to join us to avoid deportation to Germany for hard labour. The reaction so far has been poor. These two came from Volodymyr, and some have come from Horokhiv and Lutsk, but the rest refused. The editor of the oblast newspaper in Lutsk, Postryhach, read our appeal and remarked disdainfully that he would never take to the forest and live in our primitive shelters."

When Sosenko left, we took the new arrivals to our quarters, and since they felt ill at ease in their new surroundings, we gradually explained everything to them. The principal asked why we weren't bringing the people who had escaped from the German deportation convoys to our camp. Two men and a woman from Eastern Ukraine were staying with his sister in the village of Verbychne, and we agreed to go together and pick them up on Sunday.

The three persons in question were a locksmith from Poltava oblast, a student from the city of Kiev, and a nurse from Kiev oblast. After a long discussion they agreed to go with me to the Sich, and the men joined an UPA unit while I took the nurse to meet the head doctor. She was an attractive young woman of about twenty, and was soon the centre of attention at the NCO school. Everyone was drawn by her child-like naiveté, freshness, and spontaneity.

The OUN krai provid was preparing to call a conference of Soviet "captive nations," and Lisovyk and myself were assigned to accompany three Georgians, three Armenians and three Azerbaidzhanis to the town of Kolky.[1] We knew little about the traditional enmity of these people, but along the way we saw that the three groups kept strictly to themselves, and that there was no love lost between them. In Kolky they were joined by representatives of the Central Asian peoples, and continued on to Mali Stydni in one large group.

Our superior ordered Lisovyk and myself to stay in Kolky, a raion centre which had been under German control. In the spring of 1943, however, UPA units forced the Germans out of Kolky, and by the summer of that year, the town was a major centre of UPA and OUN activity. A number of UPA units were stationed here, and all mills and workshops in the area were under the control of the OUN's economic directorate. The local school system was supervised by an oblast educational directorate, and courses were offered at one of the secondary schools in Kolky. The teachers selected to work there all had a higher education and were very capable, while less qualified teachers were sent to teach in primary and incomplete secondary schools in nearby villages. Local performing ensembles included an amateur drama group, an acrobatics group (organized by a woman from Eastern Ukraine), a choir and an orchestra. In addition, our writers gave regular lectures at the local club.

The publications department of the krai socio-political directorate was located in the village of Starosillia, two kilometres from Kolky. Fedir, who headed this department, proposed that we go there to help edit articles and pamphlets which were being prepared for publication. The best writer among the seven who worked here was Dnipro, an historian from Eastern Ukraine.

My superior sometimes authorized me to visit local UPA detachments, and I would meet and talk with the rank and file and with the commanding officers of these units. Their overall morale was satisfactory, but the former members of the Soviet armed forces who had ended up in the UPA after escaping from the Germans were unhappy for some reason. All Easterners in these UPA units knew me, and I asked Masliany (a former Soviet army lieutenant), why they were so down in the mouth.

"You really don't know why? You don't know what happened to Solovii, the former major of the general staff, to his friend Captain Krasnov, to the mechanic and to the Sich doctor?" he asked.

"No, I have no idea."

"Well, tigers will fight to the death rather than be captured alive. And we're all awaiting the same fate."

"I can't believe this. Someone must be spreading rumours to create panic."

"You may not believe this, but we do," Masliany replied firmly.

The following day I went to the military okruh headquarters. The okruh commander was out but Klym, the chief of staff, was there together with Khmury, the military okruh's political instructor. I told them what I had heard about the major and his friends.

"I don't know where the major and his comrades are just right now," Klym replied. "But I'd recommend that you don't concern yourself too much with this case."

"I'd also advise you not to get too involved in these matters," added Khmury.

Their attitude and their comments convinced me that what Masliany had told me was true.

Shortly after this incident Lisovyk and I began to prepare ourselves for a large oblast-level course which was to be held at the Sich. All of a sudden, however, I was informed that I should report immediately to the military okruh headquarters, since I was to be sent into Eastern Ukraine with an UPA company.

When I reported to the headquarters, Klym and Khmury both treated me in a friendly manner, and I stayed with Khmury for two days before the company I was to travel with arrived from Berestia. Our route, from Kolky eastward, at one point crossed the route used by Soviet partisans travelling from the north to Medvedev's forces in Tsuman. Thus it was dangerous to travel to our destination in small numbers. Our group consisted of the UPA company from Berestia, two doctors, two young women and two young men on their way to an officers' school. It was a two-day trip to Mali Stydni, and on the second day I rode with the company's commanding officer and asked him about the situation in the Berestia region.

"It was fairly rough, and we got into a number of skirmishes. But we only fought against the Germans, and usually we initiated the skirmishes; it was worse near Kovel."

"Why? I would have expected the opposite—the closer to here, the better."

"In the Kovel area the Soviet partisans kept harassing us. The Germans don't venture into the forests or marshes, but those bastards were everywhere. One of our military hospitals was being transferred from the vicinity of Kamin-Koshyrskyi to the village of Chornoplesy when the partisans unexpectedly attacked it. They bayoneted every single person in the transport who was wounded or sick with typhus."

I was shocked that the Soviet partisans would finish off men who had been wounded fighting the Germans. Although the Soviet authorities accuse the UPA of collaborating with the Germans, by fighting the UPA they themselves were only aiding the Germans, I thought to myself.

We parted with the company in Mali Stydni and each of us was given separate quarters. Three days after we arrived I was summoned to meet a middle-aged man who introduced himself as Horbenko and told me that he was temporarily replacing Halyna.[2]

"Will I be sent into Eastern Ukraine?" I asked.

"No. The decision about your next assignment will be made here, in Mali Stydni. Tell me about your work, but first of all how is your health, and how is your family?"

After I told Horbenko about my personal affairs, and described my work, he asked about the state of personal hygiene in the UPA units I had visited. Horbenko was interested in all matters which affected the well-being of the rank and file in the UPA, and was very concerned about their morale. He also asked how I got along with the Easterners.

"They're in despair," I told him.

"Why?"

"They claim that the officers among them are being taken away to be executed, and that soon they'll all be shot. They're especially concerned about the fate of Major Solovii, Captain Krasnov and the Sich head doctor."

"It's true that there's a darker side to our activities and that not everything is as it should be. But you shouldn't get upset in public and show your feelings. Is that understood?"

On my way back to Kolky I spent a great deal of time thinking about Horbenko and what he said. He impressed me as an intelligent and thoughtful person, although at the time I knew little about him. Later I learned that he was actually Rostyslav Voloshyn, a member of the Bureau of the OUN Provid.[3] He was the representative of the Provid for Volhynia and Polissia, and supervised the activity of the OUN krai provid. I also learned that the Provid was forced to establish this form of supervision because Okhrym, who was the commander of the UPA-North forces (in this capacity he used the pseudonym Klym Savur), refused to accept the authority of Maksym Ruban (Mykola Lebed)[4] and had stopped reporting to him and to Horbenko. But all members of the provid reported to Horbenko and respected him as a decent, intelligent person. Colonel Stupnytsky was the first to tell me all this, for although he was not a member of the OUN, he had a great deal of respect for Voloshyn.

I received no further assignments when I returned to Kolky. The military okruh headquarters had been transferred to another location, and both Fedir and Halyna were away, so I hoped to keep a low profile and get some rest. A few days later, however, a strongly built young man, armed with a pistol and a German sub-machine gun, came to my quarters and said that Volodymyr wanted to see me.

"But who are you? And what's your name?" I asked.

"I'm Kuk, the raion SB director," he replied proudly.

"Fine. Where are we going?"

"Just come along with me."

As I left, my landlady and her daughter glanced at me with alarm and sympathy in their eyes.

When I met Volodymyr,[5] the first deputy of the krai SB director, he shook my hand and took me into a large room. "I invited you here so that you could examine the materials in this dossier," he said, pointing to a folder lying on a desk. The dossier contained the transcripts of the interrogations of a group of seven people from Eastern Ukraine, led by the head doctor of the UPA detachment quartered in Kolky. All the transcripts, which described a secret communist organization within the UPA unit and its plans to conduct espionage and sabotage, had been typed up except for the doctor's own handwritten statement. The doctor had provided most of the evidence exposing this organization, while the others confirmed his testimony and added to it when confronted with him. The doctor's statement made revolting reading, and I felt disgusted at the very thought of this man.

Volodymyr returned a few hours later, asked if I had finished reading the materials, and then went to fetch the doctor so that I could question him myself about his statement. A few minutes later Volodymyr came back and left me alone with the elderly doctor, whose face was like a mask hiding a man frightened of his own shadow.

"I'm not from the SB, but from the socio-political directorate. I'd like to know about the circumstances in which you wrote down your testimony," I asked.

"Is there anything wrong with my statement?"

"I want to know if you were beaten, or if any other methods were used to make you talk and to prepare this statement. What you've written down is the most important evidence in this case."

"I have a wife and two children here in Kolky, and I want to live!" he blurted. I had no desire to continue the conversation further and when Volodymyr returned he told the doctor to leave.

"Now you can see what our work is like. I summoned you here so that you could convince yourself how unreliable the people we arrest really are," Volodymyr said.

"From what you've shown me I can see that he's a thorough scoundrel, but I m not so sure about the other people he's been denouncing."

"The others are even worse. One tells you the truth, while another denounces one or two genuine agents and then drags in three or four of our best people. Just try to discover who's guilty and who isn't in this mess! That's why innocent people sometimes suffer."

"How did you find out about them?"

"A member of the group, who used the pseudonym Nul, tried to recruit one of our women from Eastern Ukraine into this network. But the woman's father, a scholar, had been shot by the Chekists[6] in 1937, so she immediately reported the agent's attempt to her superior. She was told to agree to co-operate with the communist network, and was asked to find out where Nul spent his nights. We nabbed Nul, he exposed the doctor, and the doctor exposed the others. They had orders to kidnap our leaders and deliver them to

Medvedev's headquarters, or, if necessary, to kill them. Contacts with Medvedev were maintained through a Kolky resident who had been a Communist in Poland before the war. He managed to escape."

"This is depressing, very depressing."

"Someone has to take care of these matters," Volodymyr said as though trying to justify himself.

"True enough! Every country has criminals and police. But although we don't have a country yet, and it's uncertain when we'll have one, we already have a police force," I said.

"Well, I still have work to do, but I'll come back later and we'll continue the discussion. So stay here tonight and you can leave in the morning, since you don't have an assignment right now."

I stretched myself out on the bed and for a long time all kinds of thoughts passed through my head. It didn't even cross my mind, however, that at this moment, in that very same building, my fate was being decided.

Volodymyr returned late, and I was already asleep. In the morning, over breakfast, he asked me what I had been doing recently.

"I'm finishing Nietzsche's book *The Will to Power.*"

"I've heard that it's quite a good book. Although I haven't read it yet, it's caught everyone's fancy."

"I don't see why everyone is so enthusiastic about this book; Nietzsche's philosophy doesn't suit me at all."

"Why?"

"The Nietzschean superman is essentially an anti-human, and all those who respect themselves and their fellow human beings have to treat such a being with disgust. The fascists based their ideology on Nietzsche's anti-human philosophy, and its practical implementation is a crime. Nietzsche's philosophy, as applied by these 'supermen,' has resulted in mountains of people shot and incinerated."

"What about the thousands who were shot without an investigation and trial in the Lutsk prison?[7] Wasn't this also the work of anti-humans?" Volodymyr asked reproachfully.

"Yes, it was. And those who shot the Poles in Dominopol are in the same category. Ordinary human beings would be incapable of doing this."

"If a person is surrounded on all sides by anti-humans, then in order to survive he also has to become an anti-human."

"To legitimize the Nietzschean superman, whatever the motives, means starting out on a path leading to the degradation of humanity, which is a sign of a sick mind."

"Well, it seems I'll have to read this Nietzsche myself."

"Yes, there's no substitute for reading and thinking for oneself," I said as we parted.

When I returned to my quarters the landlady cried out and wrung her hands: "Dear God, I'm so glad you're here! We didn't think you would come back."

"Why shouldn't I come back? I left my belongings here." I replied.

The landlady shook her head sadly. "When the man who came for you makes his rounds, the people he summons never return home. They're terrible people, even worse than the Gestapo and the Cheka."

"Are you also afraid of the UPA?"

"No, they're fine lads. We billeted some of them and they were as good as gold. But they also don't like these SB-ists or whatever they're called."

A few days later, early in the morning, a stranger armed with a pistol entered my room and asked me to come out to the road. When I went out I saw Volodymyr and Zalisny sitting in a horsecart.

"Throw your things together; we're evacuating Kolky and leaving for the Sich," said Volodymyr. Ten minutes later I was in the horsecart, sitting next to Volodymyr and opposite Zalisny.

"The Germans have transferred a large number of troops to Tsuman and have brought in planes and tanks. We've been forced to evacuate Kolky because we'd be unable to hold our ground against the Germans in the open," said Volodymyr.

"Why don't they attack Medvedev's camp in the Tsuman forest?" I asked.

"His camp is closer to the Germans than we are, but the Soviet partisans are just as hungry and poorly clothed as the Germans. We have storage depots, and supplies of bread, back fat, butter and meat—that's why they're bypassing the Reds and attacking us."

"If the Germans attack Kolky, maybe the Reds will hit them from the rear and take Tsuman at the same time," I said.

"No, they won't do that. On the contrary, they'd attack us together with the Germans if it was to their benefit to do so."

It was already dark when we came to the Kovel-Lutsk railway line, and I dozed off along the way. Once we crossed the tracks however, I suddenly realized that the briefcase with my documents and teaching materials was missing. I was very concerned, for I was on my way to teach a course, and my notes were among the missing materials. At the time I was convinced that my briefcase had fallen off the horsecart during the evening, when we had been dozing. But a few months later, when Zalisny quoted a phrase from a draft of one of my personal letters, I finally realized that Volodymyr and Zalisny had stolen the briefcase, hoping to discover something to use against me. But they were disappointed; there was nothing subversive in the briefcase.

When we reached our new destination I had to prepare quickly a new set of notes. This course was unique in that it was a special course for raion SB directors, and five instructors who were complete strangers to me gave special lectures which the regular group of instructors were forbidden to attend. Fifty-six big, handsome young men, all well dressed and with a self-righteous air about them, attended the course. Every day for a month I lectured for two hours on politics and international affairs, and I had a good opportunity to observe the men empowered by the OUN to make life-or-death decisions about individual human beings. It seemed to me that the most dull-witted youths had been chosen for this work; I had not come across such dolts among any of the men or women attending the previous courses. Of the fifty-six students, only five managed to learn and understand the course material; for the remainder the course was a total loss. It was very boring to lecture to these men, and it was impossible to carry on any discussions with them—they were simply incapable of using their heads. This did not, however, prevent them from thinking that they knew all there was to know, and that they were experts in their own line of work. Lecturing to this group was a true ordeal.

One day I happened to meet Iashchur and sensed that I could confide in him.

"Why is it that everyone in the SB seems to have been deliberately selected to be strong, handsome and stupid?" I asked.

"And where have you ever seen a police force made up of intelligent, thoughtful people? They're not needed in the police," Iashchur replied frankly. "At one time I insisted that members of the OUN receive some instruction in Marxist-Leninist ideology, arguing that you have to know your enemy in order to fight him effectively. I was threatened with expulsion from the OUN for advocating this, although ultimately I was simply removed from my position as okruh leader and now I'm being assigned to work somewhere out in the Kremianets area. That's the state of affairs here!"

# Chapter Ten

When the course ended Lisovyk was sent to Rivne oblast and I was told to organize study sessions to discuss the "Resolutions of the Third Extraordinary Congress of the OUN."[1] A few days later Krylach arrived and we drew up a schedule of meetings in each raion for the Easterners at which I was to present and make appropriate comments about these "Resolutions." It was important that the Easterners have a clear idea of what the OUN was fighting for, and Krylach sent directives to all the raion leaders to prepare enough provisions for these meetings, to find appropriate meeting halls, and to ensure that all the Easterners attended. The raion leaders always carried out their superior's orders impeccably, and everything was prepared as we requested.

All the Easterners in Volodymyr raion were summoned to a school in the village of Vladynopol, and about seventy-five people including teachers, agronomists, doctors, and former soldiers and officers of the Soviet army attended a meeting there. On the whole they seemed to be interested in the "Resolutions," although everyone knew that they were not destined to be realized. Naturally, when I was discussing the OUN "Resolutions" I interpreted them in my own fashion, and the opportunity to squeeze some of my own ideas into my course lectures and into my speeches, discussions and articles made me feel that my work had some real meaning.

I devoted six hours a day, for two days, to reading and discussing the OUN Resolutions. On my second day in Vladynopol, when I was returning from dinner, I was surprised to see the nurse whom I had brought from the village of Verbychne to work in the Sich hospital.

"What brings you here, Katia?"

"I have to talk with you," she said with a sad look in her eyes.

"Fine, let's go to the teachers' staff room and chat for a while," I suggested, showing her the way.

"Do you know that I'm getting married on Sunday?" Katia asked.

"How could I have known? Have you come to invite me to the wedding?" I replied cheerfully.

Katia buried her face in her hands and began to sob.

"Tashkent, the Uzbek commander,[2] wants to force me to marry him," she said through her tears.

"Have you told Sosenko?"

"No. He and Tashkent work together very closely and, in any case, Sosenko is away at present."

"But how can I help you?"

"Whom else can I turn to? You're the one who brought me to the Sich from Verbychne and found me a job. I have neither father nor brother here, so you're the only one who can help me!"

"All right, I'll try to think of something before I leave tomorrow evening."

We went outside and Katia climbed into her horsecart. As she set off, however, Tashkent and three of his men rode up, grabbed Katia, and put her in Tashkent's wagon. This scene greatly upset me, and turned my attention away from the resolutions, which I hadn't finished presenting, to the problem of rescuing Katia. Speed was essential; I had to leave the next evening, and there was no one on hand to help me.

I quickly finished dealing with the resolutions and asked headquarters to provide me with a few men to help me cross the Kovel-Volodymyr railway line, which was guarded by the Germans. The secretary at headquarters recommended that I join Oles, who was leaving for the Sich the next day with his guards and would wait for me near the hospital in the village of Ovlochyn. This complicated matters, but when I went outside I came across Pavlenko (who was from a Kuban Cossack family)[3] with one of his companions and decided to enlist their help.

"What are you doing here, Hrysha?" I asked.

"I'm helping to steal Ukrainians out of the hands of the Germans in Volodymyr."

"Could you both go with me to the Sich tomorrow evening?"

"We'll do anything you say," Pavlenko replied.

Oles and his unit were stationed in Olesk, not far from Vladynopol. I was on good terms with Oles and sent him a note asking him to assign two men armed with a machine gun to escort me.

Pavlenko and his friends were ready by the time the two men chosen by Oles arrived; I set out in one cart with the two men from the Kuban and one driver while the other two men followed us. Near the hospital in Ovlochyn we were stopped and surrounded by Uzbeks, who were part of the Uzbek legion of the UPA and were responsible for guarding the local hospitals, mills, dairies and bridges. Tashkent and three carts full of Uzbeks were ready to leave and wanted to follow us, but I did not agree to this and they had to lead the way.

As we drove along I gave Pavlenko and his friends their instructions: they were to slip quietly off the cart, stay behind without raising any suspicions, and quickly find Katia. They were to obtain a horsecart from the village head and take Katia immediately to Revushky; I would be waiting for them in Iaroslav's room. All this had to be done very carefully and quietly.

After my friends had slipped away, we approached the railway line and stopped to check whether we could safely cross the tracks. When we left our carts and went into a nearby house, Tashkent came up to us.

"Where is Pavlenko and his partner?" he demanded.

"They stayed behind in Ovlochyn," I replied. Tashkent immediately realized what was happening, but although his expression gave him away he silently went back to his troops.

Around midnight my two friends and Katia came to Iaroslav's room in Revushky, where I told the men to take Katia to a certain farmstead near the village and ordered her not to move from there. In the morning, Tashkent accosted Pavlenko:

"What have you done with Katia?!" he shouted.

"Boremsky took her away, but I have no idea where they went," Pavlenko replied.

The next morning I visited the editorial office, which was run by Kuzmenko. Everyone greeted me with mysterious smiles and Kuzmenko's wife was beaming with joy. I seemed to be the cause of their high spirits, and I asked why everyone was so happy.

"Oh, you're the hero of the day," Kuzmenko's wife replied playfully.

"What do you mean?"

"You don't know? Tashkent has just been here and was shaking with anger and frustration because you stole his fiancée away from him," she explained.

"He's been running around to see everyone in Revushky," Kuzmenko added.

"You've done a good deed, and I'm very happy for you," Mrs. Kuzmenko said. "Our soulless politicos will of course be furious, but that's not important. They think they're very wise, but they have no idea how important and all-powerful love can be."

"Maybe you're right, but in my case there's no romantic involvement," I said and explained the whole situation to them.

"What you've said sounds logical," said Mrs. Kuzmenko, "but Katia went to tell you her story only because she loves you. And you rescued her from under Tashkent's very nose, on the eve of their wedding, only because you love her as well."

"If so, it's a surprise to me. My motives were quite different," I laughed.

"Like a shy girl, you're using these 'motives' to hide your true love," Mrs. Kuzmenko retorted.

"Save your breath and give up, my friend," Kuzmenko suggested and laughed.

Later that day a messenger came to my quarters with a dinner invitation from Volodymyr.

"Fine, tell him I'll come," I said.

"I was told to come along with you."

"All right, we'll go together," I replied calmly. This sturdy lad had obviously been taught how to accompany prisoners; he walked closely behind me, on my left-hand side, the whole way.

When we came to Volodymyr's quarters my escort opened the door, clicked his heels, and reported that he had carried out his order. Volodymyr and Zalisny both welcomed me warmly, and shortly afterward we were served a hearty, delicious meal of dumplings filled with cheese and smothered in sour cream. Although Volodymyr and Zalisny seemed to be in a casual, happy mood, I was on my guard since I knew that the SB never summoned anyone without a good reason, and probably wanted something from me.

During the meal Volodymyr asked me in an offhand manner about my work and whether anyone was creating any difficulties for me.

"I've just started my assignment dealing with the 'Resolutions of the Third Extraordinary Congress of the OUN,' and everything seems to be going well," I replied.

"But what happened between you and Tashkent?" Volodymyr asked in a more serious fashion, and I gave him a detailed account of the whole affair.

"I'm afraid this scandal doesn't reflect on you very well. We need Tashkent—he's been doing a good job and I wouldn't even begrudge him my own sister."

"I can't agree with you," I replied. "We don't have the right to dispose of our own sisters, much less other people's sisters."

"I used to think that you had some political sense, but you're simply a sentimental humanist and romantic. You can't mix your sentiments with politics."

"It all depends on who you're dealing with. If ne'er-do-wells are given even the most noble task, the filth on their hands will still leave a black stain on their work. Parties and governments come and go, but society won't change until the individual becomes a better person."

"You'd be better off giving university lectures on aesthetics rather then getting involved in politics, especially in these harsh times," Volodymyr commented. "Why do you have such a low opinion of politics?"

"Because of my experience in this area. The higher the level of politics, the dirtier the political games. In general the political standards of each country are determined by the cultural level of its people. Politicians, statesmen, ministers and presidents are usually no better than the people they govern, and vice-versa."

"Do you discuss topics like these during your lectures?" Volodymyr asked.

"No. I give my lectures and interpret ambiguous issues in the spirit of the official material which I've studied."

"Good. Do as you think best—it's not for me to teach you. But it would be a good idea if you didn't interfere in matters which don't concern you," Volodymyr concluded.

It was impossible to leave the territory of the Sich without a pass, for outposts from the UPA's Uzbek legion were guarding all the roads and bridges. But I got a pass for Katia, dressed her up as an old woman, and drove her in a cart to the Horokhiv area in the evening. The Uzbeks on the bridge let me go on after checking the pass, and didn't even notice Katia.

Soon afterward I was transferred to another raion to help with a new training course for instructors where, as usual, I lectured on politics and international affairs. The course was held in Strilche and I stayed with the Kovalchuks, who always kept a room free for me when I was in the area. They and the Bratuns[4] always enjoyed chatting with me, or, rather, complaining to me about all the problems in their raion.

One day Andrii Bratun and his wife visited the Kovalchuks for dinner and I sat as usual in the place of honour, with Bratun's wife on my left. After we had drunk some cider Bratun gave me a quizzical glance.

"Tell me, do you believe in the success of the movement in which you're involved?"

"No, I don't," I replied without hesitation. "As soon as the Americans and the British landed in North Africa, heading for Sicily and the rest of Italy, it became clear that our struggle was doomed."

"What's the sense of continuing to fight if you know that defeat is inevitable?" Bratun asked as if speaking to himself.

"I see sense in this struggle because I consider the cause of independence to be a just cause. If I adopted a utilitarian, philistine point of view, my first question would be: what will I gain? A laurel wreath, fame, riches, power, or perhaps jail and death? But I'm not a philistine, and I don't ask myself these questions. For me the guiding beacons of my life have been truth, kindness and love."

"And do you believe that the OUN embodies these values?" Bratun asked, a reproachful look on his face.

"No, I don't believe this and never did. In essence the OUN is an anti-democratic, totalitarian organization which doesn't satisfy my spiritual needs and suit my tastes in the least. But what can one do when nothing better is available?"

"Wasn't it possible, for example, to find someone more suitable than Khmara to be raion leader? He's a lazy oaf who barely passed in school and only finished seven grades!" Kovalchuk complained.

"I don't have the right to remove or appoint raion leaders. But if you approve I could arrange for Khmara to be replaced by your Stefko."

"O no, no!... My son has a job. He's the school inspector here, you know."

"It would be better if you, Mr. Bratun, took the position of school inspector. Stefko's young, and would make an excellent raion leader."

"But it's not in our national interest to expose our intelligentsia to open danger. Our intelligentsia is very small and should keep a low profile until it can assume its proper role when our independent state is being established," Bratun explained pompously.

"Our nation's greatest tragedy is precisely our intelligentsia's failure to think of our national interest and to teach its children to do the same," I replied, raising my voice. "Instead they only worry about how best to adapt to each new conqueror's regime, and when it begins to weaken they shy away from it and wait patiently for a new overlord. Just look, for example, at all our intellectuals who faithfully served the Germans in 1941–2, and then deserted them in 1943. Only the OUN movement prevented the Germans from deporting them to Germany. These dolts, however, play at being patriots and in their cheap souls are already preparing to serve new masters, no matter who they are and where they come from."

Kovalchuk and the Bratuns sadly bowed their heads and did not say a word, but Kovalchuk's wife Afanasiia was beaming with satisfaction.

"You really gave it to them," she said after the Bratuns had left. "They were among those who warmly welcomed the Germans and served them in every way possible. Andrii, for example, immediately became the director of the high school in Horokhiv. But now he's turned against the Germans, looks askance at the OUN, and will join the Bolsheviks as soon as they arrive. If they were Englishmen or even Turks he'd adapt to them just as readily, as long as he had a foot in the food trough. Their Rostia is no better; the Bratuns excel at being toadies and careerists."

"Then why did Bratun run the risk of becoming a founding member of 'Selsoiuz' in his youth?"

"He risked nothing by doing this, and was drawn by the very real prospect of becoming a deputy to the Polish Sejm. He didn't join the CPWU, for example; that would have been dangerous and could have landed him in jail."

When I finished my work near Horokhiv I left for the Berestechko region, and presented the "Resolutions of the Third Extraordinary Congress of the OUN" for the last time in a village school in Smoliava. Later I stopped at a farmstead in the forest near Lobachivka. It was impossible to return to the Sich, for it had been seized by Soviet partisans who were now moving toward Horokhiv and Berestechko. The UPA had retreated in considerable disarray and the Soviet partisans had occupied the entire Volodymyr and Horokhiv regions.

During this campaign, the Berestechko raion provid, in the guise of an underground communist organization, had managed to rescue twenty-seven Kazan Tatars and fourteen Georgians from the Germans, who had recruited them from among Soviet prisoners-of-war to guard the border between Volhynia and Galicia. The raion provid asked me to help disarm these troops, who were stationed on a farmstead near Lobachivka.

When I came to look them over, the Tatars—who were young, healthy and well-disciplined—impressed me as good soldiers. A sentry armed with a machine gun was stationed near their lodgings, allowed no one to approach, and kept us waiting a hundred metres away while he called his commander. The latter came out to meet us and then took the raion leader, the socio-political director and myself into his quarters for negotiations. The Tatars assumed that I was an important official in a communist detachment and, probably because of this, warmly declared their loyalty to the Soviet Union.

Then we moved on to the Georgians, who, although slightly older, were completely lacking in discipline since they had come to loathe the war and dreamed only of returning to Georgia. I realized that it would be easy to disarm them. But the Tatars were a different matter, since they clearly would not lay down their arms voluntarily.

I wrote to the nearest UPA commander, Sosenko, asking him to place a well-armed platoon with a heavy machine gun under my command for a day. Sosenko replied that although he was no longer a commanding officer, and was being kept under surveillance,[5] he would try to meet my request.

The next day the heavily armed platoon arrived and we arranged the men in such a way that they could easily pour a heavy stream of fire into the vale where we planned to lead the Tatars. When everything was ready the raion leader went to the Tatars and told them to march in full battle order, with all their weapons, to this vale. Once their commander had mustered them in this spot he was to report to us at the farmstead.

I stayed at the farmstead with the socio-political director and we anxiously watched as the Tatars, briskly marching in neat double files, moved out into the vale and halted. Their commander gave them some instructions and then ran to the house where we were waiting. He marched up to the table, stood to attention and reported to me that his soldiers were awaiting further orders.

"In the name of the Ukrainian Insurgent Army," I declared, "I order you to return to your men and tell them to lay down their arms immediately. Otherwise we'll have to use force, and we've made sure that any resistance on your part will be useless."

The lieutenant turned pale. His hand went for his holster but he immediately lowered it, clicked his heels, and said that my order would be obeyed. Then he turned, quickly left the house, and ran back to his troops. Holding my breath, I carefully watched the lieutenant and his Tatars who, rigid with nervous tension, had remained motionless. The lieutenant spoke to them for five minutes, then gave them an order and the two columns of Tatars turned right. Marching to the front of his troops, the lieutenant was the first to take off his pistol and lay it on the ground. The first two Tatars behind him did the same, went to the back of the column, and all the others, in strict order, followed suit. When the lieutenant came to the house to inform us that the order had been followed, we went back with him to the Tatar unit and gave our troops a signal to come forward. As soon as the Tatars saw the heavy machine gun and the well-armed platoon they understood their situation.

In this way we gained some new German pistols, sub-machine guns and two light machine guns. We allowed the lieutenant to keep his pistol and billeted the Tatars in the village, but soon afterward Soviet partisans occupied the area. According to what we later heard from local villagers, the partisans shot the Tatar lieutenant and incorporated the other Tatar soldiers into their own ranks.

A few days after we had disarmed the Tatars and Georgians, I again met Colonel Honcharenko (Stupnytsky), with whom I was temporarily sharing my lodgings. He turned out to be a cheerful person with a good sense of humour, and told me a great deal about the Caucasus region and the people who lived there. I was particularly interested, however, in hearing about his past and how he and his associates had reacted to the February Revolution of 1917 and the overthrow of the Tsar.

"That's a very broad topic," Stupnytsky began, "and I can't begin to cover it in detail. I heard about the events of February 1917 in Odessa, where we were forming regiments of the Tsarist army to be sent to the front. Eighty per cent of the officer corps there was Ukrainian; most of them spoke Ukrainian quite well and were conscious of their national identity. In the rank and file the proportion of Ukrainians was even higher. All the officers felt that the time had finally arrived for us to decide our nation's destiny, but no one knew exactly what had to be done. At one unofficial meeting of Ukrainian officers we decided to send a fact-finding delegation to Kiev, and it returned to inform us that a Central Rada[6] had been established in Kiev and was acting as a Ukrainian provisional government. The Rada had begun to organize a Ukrainian army and we, in Odessa, were also supposed to organize Ukrainian military units.

"One officer suggested that we muster our regiments and simply order all the Ukrainian soldiers to step forward and turn to the right. We decided to try out this naive proposal, but our attempt was unsuccessful. Only thirty-three soldiers out of an entire regiment responded to the colonel's order; the others looked at each other anxiously, but didn't move. The officers were very discouraged by this first failure, and everyone was silent until a captain joined our group and snapped to attention. 'Let me separate the

Ukrainians from the rest of the soldiers,' he requested. 'I know these men better than you do.'

'Only colonels should address a regiment,' one of us told him. 'It would be better if you told us what you would do.'

'It's very simple. I'd use the term 'Little Russians'[7] instead of Ukrainians, and then almost everyone would respond.' We initially took this proposal to be a joke, but eventually we did try it. And, believe it or not, almost all the men in the regiment, without even pausing, stepped forward and only a handful of soldiers was left behind. This immediately boosted our morale and from this point on everything went quite smoothly. We managed to set up a number of Ukrainian regiments, and the remaining soldiers were demobilized."

"So you have to admit that now the level of national consciousness among Ukrainians is considerably higher than it used to be."

"That's true, but our chances of victory are much smaller," Stupnytsky noted sadly. "In 1917 the Bolsheviks were starting from scratch, just like ourselves, and they were much weaker in Ukraine than we were. Abroad we were recognized just as the Bolsheviks were, the Central Rada was installed in the capital, Kiev, and we controlled almost all Ukraine. By comparison we're nothing today, and no one recognizes or pays much attention to us. At our peak we controlled Volhynia and partially controlled Galicia. Even there, apart from raion centres such as Kolky and Kamin-Koshyrskyi, we dominated only the rural areas. Russia has strong allies, and many more Ukrainians are fighting in the Soviet army than in UPA units. Although now they know that they're Ukrainians, and not Little Russians of some kind, this doesn't prevent them from destroying us as accomplices of the German fascists. The fact that at one time the OUN naively regarded Germany as its ally has remained a stain on the entire nationalist movement."

"If initially the Bolsheviks were quite weak in Ukraine and started from nothing, like the Central Rada, how was it that the Rada was unable to defeat them?"

"First of all because Muravev's Russian forces entered our territory,[8] and second because our nation isn't ready for statehood. We haven't learned to think in terms of a state, and we don't know how to combine our social interests with those of the state. The Rada, for example, didn't consider itself legally competent to resolve long-standing social problems such as the question of land reform, and in a legal sense it was correct, since such questions are usually decided by democratically elected parliaments. But our people didn't understand the importance of having an independent state, and didn't understand that all other problems are internal issues which should be decided, in times of peace, by the nation within the framework of its own state.

"Lenin skilfully took advantage of this situation and formulated slogans dealing with the burning issues of the day. Thus he used the slogan 'steal what has been stolen from you' to mobilize all sorts of rabble, and the slogan 'land to the peasants, factories and enterprises to the workers' to mobilize the workers and peasants. He was quite straightforward: 'Go ahead, it's all yours, just help us to take power!' The poor peasants fought for the Bolsheviks to get free land, and the workers fought to gain control over factories and profits. But the struggle for a Ukrainian state was an abstract concept for most citizens, who didn't know what they would gain and whether anything would improve if Ukraine achieved independence. Long centuries of bondage had smothered our aspirations for independence, replacing them with narrow utilitarian concerns, and the Central Rada, preoccupied with questions of state sovereignty, was unable to establish close contacts with the people. Lenin was also interested in state power, but managed to link his ambitions to the interests not only of Russian workers and peasants, but of all people of the Russian empire. After gaining power, however, the Bolsheviks decided the fate of the peasants and workers as they saw fit. After the civil war 'it's all yours' was changed to 'it's all ours,' and all the 'genius' of Lenin and his party lies in such trickery. Mykhailo Hrushevsky,[9] on the other hand, was incapable of such manipulation, and his plan failed," Stupnytsky concluded.

"If the strength of evil lies in cunning and deceit, wasn't the OUN justified in advocating the use of Bolshevik methods against the Bolsheviks?"

"No, I don't agree with such slogans, which make us lose sight of our aims and resemble our enemies. The Japanese philosopher Uchimura[10] once said that 'Truth is divine, and is not proclaimed to serve the interests of the state. Lacking the strength to save the state, we must exert all our efforts to save the truth. If we can preserve the truth then even if the state perishes it can always be reborn. If we renounce the truth the state may revive, but in the long run it will be doomed. So, if one loves one's homeland, loyalty to the truth is far more important than loyalty to the state'."

I was enchanted by this quotation and immediately wrote it down.

"I'm very glad that you think this way," I told Stupnytsky, "but the OUN has its own totalitarian tendencies."

"That's true, but at the moment it's the only organization capable of fighting against the occupying powers and that's why we're obliged to co-operate with it. Moreover, by working for the OUN we're simultaneously changing it, and someday these new influences will bear fruit," Stupnytsky stated firmly.

# Chapter Eleven

The next day I left Lobachivka to retrieve my typewriter, which I had left behind in the village of Skobelka. Kovpak's Soviet partisans[1] were already taking over the neighbouring village of Smoliava, but I managed to stay ahead of them and saved the typewriter. On my way back, I discovered that the road in the forest near Lobachivka had been blocked by trees, felled deliberately to impede the progress of the Soviet partisans. This is where I first met these partisans, who had been riding toward Smoliava and were forced to halt at the barricade. I quickly recognized who they were by their curses, made a rapid turn, and rode off in the direction of Mykolaiv, on the Galician side of the Volhynia-Galicia border.

From my previous trips I knew the owners of a small house near the Pototsky estate and decided to call on them. I was met by Stymyd, the Volodymyr-Horokhiv okruh leader who was accompanied by his bodyguards, and Danylo, the Berestechko raion leader. They had also been squeezed out of their territory by the Soviet partisans.

"We've picked up three people here," said Stymyd, "two men and a woman who don't know each other but claim that they know many of our people in the provid and have mentioned your pseudonym. One, about your age, is called Styr, the other, younger fellow is called Voron, and the girl is called Bystra."

"I know them," I replied. "Styr is one of our writers from Polissia, Voron is the director of a travelling drama group which reports to the oblast socio-political directorate, and Bystra worked as a nurse in Sosenko's detachment."

Stymyd arranged for the three detainees to be brought to us; soon they were wildly hugging and kissing me, and the pistols and papers belonging to Styr and Voron were returned to them.

Stymyd was afraid to assume responsibility for our safety and advised us not to stay in his okruh but to make our way to Galicia. We agreed, and the next day we were already in Mykolaiv. The Soviet partisans, however, were usually only one day behind us as we moved from one village to another in the Radekhiv raion. In fact, in one village we were surrounded by Soviet partisans, but we abandoned our horsecart and escaped, under cover of darkness, toward Radekhiv. After this incident Styr and Voron tried to convince me to go to the Carpathian mountains, for Voron was from this region and Styr, whose wife was from Prague, wanted to reach Czechoslovakia. They suggested that I also go abroad, but I had no desire to do so and decided to return to Volhynia. At one point my companions actually left me and started off for the Carpathians, but later they returned.

By the end of January 1944, the Germans had positioned an entire army along the border between Galicia and Volhynia. Five to seven hundred Germans were stationed in every village within ten miles of the border, but although it was difficult to get through this zone it was essential that we do so. We left the nurse behind to cross the border during the daytime, and made our way to a remote village not yet occupied by the Germans. Here we located the village liaison person, who took us to a nearby village which was under German control, and although guards in white capes were stationed around the village, we managed to evade them.

The liaison person in this village was reluctant to let us into his house, but relented when pressed by our guide. However, after we had let our old guide go, the new one refused to take us any further, and his procrastination in such a difficult situation was so infuriating that I finally drew my pistol.

"You and your wife get dressed and lead us to the next village on the way to Volhynia now," I ordered. His attitude changed immediately and five minutes later we left his house, avoided the German outposts, and set off for the next village. We stopped about three hundred metres before our destination and I told our guide to enter the village on his own.

"Think of a way to bring the next liaison person out here; in the meantime your wife will stay with us. If you don't succeed you and your wife will have to remain as our guides, and if you're too much of a coward to come back here your wife will have to take us all the way to Volhynia herself."

While we waited we trampled out a path in the snow and walked back and forth to keep warm, but soon our guide returned and turned us over to a bold, cheerful young fellow; it was a pleasure to have him show us the way.

When we reached the next village, which was very close to the Galicia-Volhynia border, our guide immediately took us to see the village head, an older, well-dressed man of about forty-five. He was playing chess with his neighbour when we came in, and after replying reluctantly to our greeting he returned to the chessboard without even asking us who we were or where we were going. For five minutes we patiently watched the chess game and the village head, who calmly studied the pieces on the chessboard and seemed to have completely forgotten us. My patience quickly evaporated, for my nerves were stretched to the breaking point, and finally I drew my pistol, walked up to the table, and ordered the village head to stand up.

When he saw the gun the village head quickly jumped to his feet.

"What do you want?" he asked in a frightened voice. "I'll help you at once."

"Harness your horses and drive us to Volhynia," I demanded. "Understand!?"

Styr and Voron, who were standing by silently, also pulled out their pistols, and ten minutes later everything was ready. It was only five kilometres to the border, and one hour later we were in Volhynia. I had no desire to talk with our guide, who kept quiet throughout most of the trip, and when we parted I told him that he had been treated very leniently; if a village head in Volhynia had behaved in the same manner he would have paid dearly for his actions.

The next day we visited the Kovalchuks in Strilche and then I left for the village of Buzhkovychi, where I decided to rest while Styr and Voron went their separate ways. A few days later, however, a courier from the krai SB brought me an urgent message. I was to go immediately to the village of Kolona and meet with Mitla (the krai SB director)[2] and Volodymyr, his first deputy.

"Where on earth were you during the Soviet offensive?" Mitla asked me when I arrived. "And what happened to your typist?" I described everything that had occurred, and explained that my typist had never returned from her assignment to deliver a parcel to Halyna.

"Your parcel and the typist never reached Halyna, and ended up at Soviet partisan headquarters. Now the typist says that you sent her there yourself. Would you like to see her?"

"Yes," I replied calmly. Mitla asked that the typist be brought in and a few minutes later she was knocking at the door. When she entered and saw me she fainted, fell to the ground, and after coming to she simply bowed her head and did not say a word. It was painful to look at this unfortunate woman but there was nothing I could do to help her. She was told to go to her quarters and she slowly left the room without even raising her eyes.

"We haven't questioned her yet," Mitla explained. "We know only what she told us herself, and were waiting for an opportunity to confront her with you. She's originally from Voroshylovhrad oblast, but her father worked as a machinist on the railways in Lviv during 1939–41 and when the Germans attacked the Soviet Union she was a fourth-year student in a pedagogical institute. She was evacuated to Eastern Ukraine and tended pigs there until the communist underground sent her to Lviv and then to Volhynia. This is how she described her activities after we told her that you had been blown up by a mine; she assumed that you were dead and that's probably why she made these accusations against you."

"I still feel sorry for her and the thousands of other young women who are victims of this senseless war," I said.

"So what should we do with people like her?" Mitla asked.

"Let her go. If we release her those who sent her here won't believe anything she says and will take care of her themselves."

"We won't get very far with your brand of sentimentalism," Mitla noted. "The Bolsheviks aren't so forgiving with our people."

"But we're not Bolsheviks," I replied.

"Well, we'll still have a chat with her," Volodymyr added, and Mitla told me that I was now free to go and do as I please.

Katrusia ["Bystra"], the cheerful, vivacious nurse who had travelled with us in Galicia, was waiting for me when I returned to Buzhkovychi.

"Did you have a hard time getting here from Galicia?" I asked.

"Oh, it was quite an experience. Near the border I was stopped by three soldiers who searched me and found some pistol cartridges in my pocket. When the soldier who was in charge saw the cartridges he stiffened with surprise and began to search me again, but the other two lifted my spirits by giving me a friendly smile. After the search I was taken to a bunker where an entire squad of soldiers was stationed, and when the soldier who had carried out the search left, I found out that he was the only German in the unit; all the others were Ukrainians from Galicia who started asking me who I was, where I was from and where I was going. I told them everything, and even mentioned you."

"What exactly did you say about us?"

"I told them that if they tried to attack my friends not one of them would survive," Katrusia replied proudly.

"And how did they respond?"

"They just laughed. 'I like your spirit,' one of them said, 'but we have no reason to go after your friends. We're Ukrainians just as you are, and we share the same goals.' 'Who knows what you really want?' I replied. 'We're fighting the Germans: you serve them, and wear the uniforms.' 'The Germans don't pose a threat to us any longer,' the same soldier retorted. 'There's no good reason to fight them now; we have to resist the Soviet onslaught from the east.'

"When I told them that we have to fight both enemies the soldiers laughed and one of them hugged me and kissed me on the forehead. 'With women like you,' he said, 'especially from Eastern Ukraine, independence will be ours for sure.' Tears rolled down his cheeks, I also started to cry, and the other men smiled through their tears as they embraced me. Then two of them escorted me back to Volhynia," Katrusia concluded.

"Is that why you're so happy?"

"Maybe. Isn't it good to know that others also share our goals?"

"Of course. But many people have good intentions and would like the world to be a better place. Unfortunately, many of them end up, despite themselves, doing harm both to themselves and to others," I replied as if I was speaking to myself.

"And you've done the same?" Katrusia inquired, not taking her large tear-filled eyes off my face.

"I'm not sure," I replied. "Maybe I have."

"You know what you want and what you're doing better than anyone else," Katrusia reproached me, "and yet you're talking like this!"

I looked through the window with a heavy heart and thought about our destiny. It was as if a bottomless abyss surrounded us, and no one knew when one of us might suddenly fall into it.

"What's happened? Why are you so quiet, and why do you have such a vacant look in your eyes?" Katrusia asked and touched my shoulder as if to reassure herself that I was all right.

"Something's happened to you, and I'm scared. Tell me what's wrong, or at least where you've been!"

"The krai SB called me in."

"So that's it! Are you under a threat of some kind?"

"They're always threatening people, and trying to convince themselves and everyone else that their omnipotent role as 'guardians' is absolutely essential."

"And are they really so important?"

"It seems that no nation can get by without it's own 'SB,' but this organization and its activities are leaving a very dark stain on the whole liberation movement."

"But, you see, most of us rely on faith, and when we're told that something is necessary and has to be done for the good of the cause we believe what we're told. It's easier this way, for then we're relieved of responsibility for what happens. It's more difficult for people like you, who weigh everything on your analytical scales, take enormous responsibilities on your shoulders, and suffer. But who needs your suffering if nothing better exists to replace what we already have?"

"That's the tragedy of it all," I replied, "we have nothing better. We were incapable, because of our inexperience, of creating anything better, and the OUN represents the best we could come up with. Foreigners say that we're the most democratically minded of all the Slavic nations. But our democracy isn't a constructive, state-building form of democracy, and it rapidly degenerates into anarchism, which is the psychological product of centuries of oppression. This vulgarized protest against slavery quickly becomes a destructive force which works against our best efforts to build a state."

"Why are you talking to me so seriously? I'm just a nurse, and I'm only twenty years old. I don't want to be overwhelmed with ideas, I want to *believe* in something! You're very good at speaking to audiences and you often inspire people with enthusiasm for our struggle, but now for some reason you're sowing pessimism and despair. Why? We can't live without faith—without faith we're nothing!"

"Katrusia, you haven't understood me at all. I'm not a pessimist and I'm not spreading despair. On the contrary, I'm trying to stress that first of all you have to believe in yourself and teach others to believe in themselves. Once you're sure of your own spiritual strength, it won't be so terrible if you become disillusioned in some-one like myself, and you'll be able to hold your own no matter what the circumstances. We shouldn't compare ourselves with those nations which, like herds of sheep, need strong rulers. We need a nation of individuals like the English, not a nation of leaders and 'masses.' You've seen for yourself how intelligent human beings have been transformed into 'masses,' how the word 'masses' has been turned into an idol for those very same masses, and how it has been used as a shield behind which the 'leaders' can hide whenever someone dares to accuse them of anything. You should learn to love your nation as it really is—a nation of 'cripples,' a nation which other nations treat like dirt. I want you to see things as they really are to *protect* you from disillusionment and self-destructive feelings of inferiority. The nationalists idealize the "people" in their speeches, but if you so much as mention the word democracy they all shout: 'What? Democracy for our people? Oh no, nothing will come of that! Our people won't respect democracy, they respect only brute force and the whip'!"

From Buzhkovychi I moved on to the village of Zamlychi, Lokachi raion, where I spent most of my time reading and writing. Twice I was disturbed by groups of Soviet partisans who were passing though Zamlychi on their way to blow up the Kovel-Lviv railway line, and once I had to escape across the river onto the farmsteads of a neighbouring village. It was clear that I wasn't welcome here, for the entire family in the house where I took shelter was sullen and no one wanted to talk. This unexpected hostility disturbed me, so I decided to move next door and asked who lived there. The farmer's wife shuddered, gave me a frightened look, and told me that the house was deserted.

"Did Poles live there?" I asked.

"No, Ukrainians. But some two weeks ago they just disappeared."

"What do you mean?"

"Just what I said. They were there one evening and at night they simply vanished, with all their children," she replied with a clear tone of reproach in her voice. I felt that something very distasteful was being hidden from me, and shivers ran down my back.

"Did only one family in your village disappear?"

"No, sixteen families vanished on that one night alone," the farmer replied.

"Who were the people who disappeared so mysteriously?"

"Just ordinary people like you and me."

I decided to speak with the village head, and asked that he be brought to the house. The farmer sent his son to fetch him, and one hour later a young man with a broad peasant face arrived and wanted to know what was wrong.

"Please tell me what happened to the people next door," I asked.

"You should ask the raion SB director, Chumak."

"But you're the village head, and should know what's going on here," I insisted.

"That's true, but I wasn't involved in what happened here on that night, and I can't tell you anything more."

"Didn't you take the SB-ists from one farmstead to another?"

"No, they have their own network of agents in every village who help them with this work."

The next day, in the village of Dorohynychi, I located Chumak, a tall, handsome young man. He greeted me politely and asked what brought me here.

"Yesterday I visited the farmsteads on the other side of the river and discovered that sixteen whole families, including old men and children, have simply disappeared! I'd like to know why such horrors are taking place and who's responsible for them!"

"I'm surprised that you've come to me with such questions. You occasionally meet with our top leaders—you can ask them," Chumak replied.

"They didn't order you to exterminate sixteen families! That was your own work."

"I carry out my orders and that's all! Understand?"

"You're making life and death decisions and murdering children—do you know what that means?!" I shouted and stormed out without saying another word. I couldn't stop thinking about this tragedy, which weighed heavily on my soul. I kept imagining the last minutes of the distraught mothers and their young children, and I could almost hear their last cries and reproaches.

A few days later a courier on horseback brought me a letter from Mitla asking me to meet him in the village where he was quartered, about five or six kilometres from Zamlychi, at 8am the next day.

When I reached Mitla's lodgings at the appointed time, oblast leader Krylach, socio-political director Arsen, editor Kuzmenko and several others of lower rank were already there, and I was given a warm reception.

"Kuzmenko," Mitla said, "is going to read an article which he wrote in reply to an article by Khrushchev.³ Listen to it carefully and make whatever comments you wish." When Kuzmenko finished he accepted all our suggestions and corrections in a friendly spirit, and afterward Mitla invited Krylach and myself into a separate room.

"What happened between you and the raion SB director?" Mitla asked. I told them that sixteen families, including small children, had been liquidated without a trial or investigation, and described my conversation with Chumak. Mitla frowned throughout my account, kept cracking his knuckles, and it was obvious that Krylach was also displeased by what I had to say.

"Soon the Soviet forces will occupy all Volhynia. Do you want us to leave a network of Soviet agents behind to await their arrival?" Krylach asked.

"We should root out everyone the Soviet authorities can rely on while we still can," added Mitla.

"My impressions from my stay in that village are quite different," I noted. "The campaign to exterminate 'potential Soviet agents' has antagonized people who were once sympathetic to our cause and is forcing them to turn to the Soviet authorities. The actions of the SB have provided our enemies with a powerful weapon which they'll use to attack us and to justify their own brutality. Only they will be grateful to us."

"Do you know what the Bolsheviks did in the prisons when they retreated before the German advance?" Krylach asked. "Were you in Lutsk, and did you see how many young people were shot there without any investigation or trial?"

"I know what happened in Lutsk, but do we want to outdo the Bolsheviks in evil deeds? If so, then everyone will stop talking about *their* crimes, and will talk about the crimes committed by the SB," I replied.

"You should apply your logic and casuistry elsewhere and stop interfering with the work of the SB," Mitla retorted. "If you have comments to make about the SB, then come and see me, not the raion director."

Suddenly, Ostrizky, the battalion commander, entered and snapped to attention in front of Mitla.

"Two tanks of Germans have arrived," he reported, "They want to negotiate with us. Should we hold talks with them or not?"

"They didn't want to talk with us in 1941 and we won't be bothered with them now," Mitla replied. "Politically they're finished."

# Chapter Twelve

At the beginning of April we moved with the battalion to the village of Zhashkovychi and here we buried Oleksii Shum [Vovchak], the deputy commander of a military okruh who had been killed in a skirmish with Soviet partisans.[1] By this time Lutsk and Kovel had already been occupied by Soviet forces under the command of General Vatutin.[2] The Germans still held Horokhiv and Volodymyr, and Ostrizky's battalion, to which we were attached, was also stationed in that small area of Volhynia which had not yet been occupied by the Soviet forces. One day two carloads of Germans drove into the yard of Mykhailo Mysechko, a priest who lived in Zhashkovychi, and several of them walked into his house. I was there with Krylach and one of the Germans turned to my companion, whom he mistook for Ostrizky.

"Tomorrow the Fourth German Panzer Army will be passing through this territory, destroying every armed group in its path. We'd advise you to retreat past Volodymyr and to stay near Liuboml—the troops won't be heading in that direction," he informed us.

After the Germans had left the room, Krylach called Ostrizky, Kuzmenko and the battalion staff together to discuss the situation and they decided to move the battalion to the Kholm region. That evening the rest of us headed toward the village of Korytnytsia, which was very close to the front, to stay ahead of the German Fourth Army. I stayed with Kuzmenko in Korytnytsia for two days before moving on to Strilche where I stayed, as usual, with the Kovalchuks. Iulko was rather cool toward me, but his wife treated me as warmly as ever.

By now it was the end of May 1944, and it was clear that a Soviet victory was inevitable. Many people began to treat us coldly, primarily because of the hopelessness of our struggle, but also because of the widespread summary justice meted out by the SB to those whom they considered to be potentially "unreliable," and support for the nationalist movement dwindled with every passing day. Many of those who had once politely invited us to visit them were now clearly reluctant to open their doors to us, and refused to let us in after dark. One day I asked a young woman, a liaison person, why so many people had become rude and hostile.

"You see, no one believes you any more. Everyone is afraid of you, and we've begun to fear one another as well. I'm not scared because I've known you for such a long time, but even I'm afraid of strangers. Recently, for example, three members of the OUN came to our village, walked into one house, and asked the woman living there to serve as a guide. She went with them and disappeared into thin air—we haven't seen her since. And this isn't the only such case. In short, the situation has rapidly changed for the worse, and the villagers are again preparing for Bolshevik rule."

In June, Okhrym, the new krai leader, visited Strilche along with his escort and Krylach, our oblast leader. Krylach, on orders from Okhrym, summoned me and told me to select a few "Easterners" who could help me to set up an OUN network in Eastern Ukraine. For this assignment I selected five men, all former officers in the Soviet army who were in Horokhiv-Volodymyr okruh and, heading for the Hrubeshiv area, we crossed the Buh River near Sokal.

We ended up in a village which was crawling with Germans, and found ourselves in a very awkward situation—our arms were hidden in the seats of our carts, and underneath my seat were two pistols, a typewriter, and various printed materials. At one point a German soldier stopped us and, carrying a kettle, jumped into our cart. My heart was beating very quickly, for I was afraid that if he sat down he would immediately notice that something hard was hidden underneath the seat. But to our great relief the soldier simply stood at the back of the cart. After riding some two hundred metres with us he ran off to his kitchen, and we managed to continue on our way through the village without further problems.

The next day we reached Korchyn, where Ostrizky (a former lieutenant in the Polish army), whose battalion was stationed here, welcomed me warmly. He knew about my orders, immediately asked me to submit a list of the people I needed, and two days later assigned seven more men to my group, bringing the number to twelve. They were all former officers of the Soviet army who, after being captured by the Germans, had escaped and ended up in UPA units. Although they had fought magnificently against the Germans, once the Soviet army began to draw near, these officers were no longer fully trusted. This distrust greatly perturbed them, and they were expecting to be shot any day. We settled down in a separate house on the edge of the forest, although we still received our food from the military kitchen, and I lectured to them on Ukrainian history for two hours every day.

One day the battalion's sentries on the outskirts of the village stopped two German armoured cars and refused to allow them into the village. The German officers in the cars then gave the sentries an ultimatum—by morning everyone would have to leave the village, for the German army would be passing through and would destroy every armed group in its path. Ostrizky responded by ordering his company commanders to take their men into the forest, and appointed one of the company commanders, Nerozluchny, to take his place since he and his deputies had to leave on official business. We also took to the forest, where both we and the UPA companies continued with our normal schedules.

A field kitchen arrived at lunchtime and each platoon went to receive its food in the usual order. We ate our share on the spot and then returned to our camp. Nerozluchny, however, soon caught up with us and asked sternly if we had been eating in the kitchen.

"Yes," I replied.

"Then go back right now and clean up your mess!" he ordered.

"We didn't leave any mess behind," I replied.

"I'm ordering you to go and clean up immediately! Understand!?" Nerozluchny shouted.

"I refuse to clean up after your company. In fact, I'm not even under your command."

"You won't forget this!" Nerozluchny threatened and stalked away.

My men were frightened out of their wits.

"When Ostrizky comes back we'll be in big trouble for refusing to carry out Nerozluchny's order—after all, he left Nerozluchny in charge," said Daman, a former lieutenant in the Soviet army.

"Don't worry, no one will bother you. This isn't your problem, it's mine," I replied.

That evening the battalion returned to its quarters in the village, we returned to ours, and early the next morning a courier brought me a note from Ostrizky's headquarters asking me to join him for breakfast. I left immediately and, when I reached headquarters, Ostrizky greeted me in a very genteel fashion, as only a Polish officer could. The table was already laid and we were joined by Ostrizky's second-in-command Verkhovyna (a lieutenant from Transcarpathia), the chief of staff, the political instructor, and the escort commander. They greeted me amicably, and when we sat down to a tasty meal of dumplings with cheese everyone behaved in a cheerful, carefree fashion. Ostrizky did not mention the previous day's incident in the forest with Nerozluchny, but after breakfast he made a signal of some kind that prompted everyone to leave and turned to me.

"What happened yesterday? What was behind your misunderstanding with Nerozluchny?" Ostrizky asked.

I described everything that had happened and when I finished Ostrizky called in and told him to apologize to me for his tactlessness. Nerozluchny reluctantly did so and left.

"I'm at fault for failing to inform him about the independent status of your group," Ostrizky explained, "but you're at fault for failing to find an intelligent solution to this problem and allowing it to turn into such a spectacle. Any act of disobedience in an army sets a very bad precedent, and you should have settled this matter on the spot."

I parted with Ostrizky and set off for my lodgings when, about two hundred metres from the headquarters, I was surprised to see my men crawling out of a field in full battle dress. When I asked them what they were doing here they looked at each other and Khoma told me that they would explain everything when we returned to our quarters.

"We know that Ostrizky is a very strict commander," Khoma later told me, "and in the present situation we could be shot for practically any reason at all. When he selected us from our units and followed us on our way here, we were preparing for the worst and were ready to fight for our lives. Although we breathed more easily after we arrived here safely and met you, yesterday's conflict with Nerozluchny again put us on our guard, for Ostrizky never forgives anyone for disobeying an order. Not knowing this, you were quite calm when you went to see him, but we were sure that he would quickly finish you off and decided to take care of him before he did so. When we saw you parting in such a friendly fashion, however, we quietly left our positions, for we see that he respects you, and doesn't treat you the same way that he treats us."

One day I happened to enter the hospital and I met my old friend Katrusia, who gave me an aloof, measured glance and behaved as if she didn't even know me. Puzzled, I asked her to meet me outside.

"What's wrong?" I inquired. "What have I done to offend you?"

Katrusia gave me a cold look, then turned around and went back into the hospital without saying a word. This intrigued me even more, and I summoned her to come and see me on official business. When Katrusia finally came she asked me, in a businesslike tone of voice, what I wanted from her.

"I have to know why you're acting so strangely," I gently inquired.

"I was very fond of you and wanted to stay with you, to help you, to share your happiness and your misfortunes. But you didn't want to bother with me, you sent me off to this unit without even consulting me, and after you arrived here a whole week went before you came by to see me. In the meantime I, stupid fool that I am, boasted about you to all my friends. Now I'm devoting myself only to this unit, the hospital and the wounded. Understand?"

"Fine. Just don't be angry with me, for I didn't mean to hurt you. You're a nurse and you should be in the hospital caring for the wounded—this is where you can do the most good for our cause."

"Now you're again trying to inspire me with faith in something which you don't even believe in yourself. You told me a long time ago that we'll be wiped out, and now I can see this myself. So why talk so piously about a struggle which is already doomed to fail?"

"Anyone can fight with a belief in victory and in anticipation of the laurels and privileges that accompany it. But only those who have faith in themselves and their cause, and don't need a leader to tell them what to do, will continue fighting to the very end even when they realize that defeat is inevitable and they know that suffering and humiliation will follow."

"From what you told me before I know that you don't share the ideals of the OUN. Yet now, when even members of the OUN have given up hope and are deserting from UPA units, you insist on continuing the struggle."

"Those OUN members who are deserting, surrendering and asking the Soviet authorities for forgiveness weren't fighting for freedom and independence but for fame and power. I don't approve of the OUN's totalitarian and dictatorial ambitions, and strongly condemn the disgraceful activities of the SB, but I've always approved of the struggle for independence."

"I'm no longer sure that I know what you're looking for in your life."

"Freedom, Katrusia, freedom and nothing else."

When the Soviet army broke through the German defences and advanced toward Volodymyr, Sokal and Brody, Ostrizky assembled his six companies and, after my group had joined them, we moved north toward Berestia. Seven kilometres from Korchyn we came across a village which had been destroyed by fire. Not a single house was left standing, and only the remnants of a few chimneys were poking out of the tall weeds. An ominous, funereal silence hung over the ruins. It was a thoroughly depressing sight, and that day we passed through three more villages like this in a row, all burnt down by the Poles. After dinner we finally came across a village which had been spared, and stopped here to rest while the villagers described the horrors committed by the Poles during the destruction of these villages.

During the stop I went to see Ostrizky and asked him where we were going and about our further plans.

"When Okhrym, the krai leader, was here," Ostrizky replied, "he ordered me to move north and cross the front near Berestia. I'm simply following his orders."

"Well, Okhrym didn't give me any such instructions, and I refuse to accompany you to Berestia. That may have been the logical thing to do when he gave the order, but now it makes no sense at all. To stay parallel to the German front lines and to travel one hundred kilometres through the thick of the German army is crazy."

"A soldier carries out his orders without question," Ostrizky replied sadly. "When Okhrym gives me an order I'm obliged, whatever the circumstances, to obey it."

"Then I'm taking my men and today we'll head for the Volodymyr area."

"Go ahead! I have no right to force you to stay with me, and maybe you're doing the right thing," Ostrizky concluded.

When we were preparing to leave two young women—Katrusia and Mariika—came up to us and said that they also wanted to join our group.

"Did you come of your own free will?" I asked.

"Yes. We asked Ostrizky if we could go along with you and he gave us his permission," Mariika replied.

"Then it's fine with me. But can you handle the long marches?"

"We'll manage, as long as we're heading toward home," Katrusia replied.

We reached our first destination, a nearby village, by midnight, but in the meantime the Soviet army had approached the village from the opposite direction and was subjecting it to heavy artillery and machine-gun fire. We had reached the most advanced line of the front, so we decided to rest and consider our next step.

It was late June and the air was heavy with the smell of ripening grain. We made ourselves comfortable in a wheat field, but caught our breath when we suddenly heard a child begin to cry and realized that the surrounding fields were full of people. At this point the morale of my group was very low, for everyone was immersed in thought and brooding about the dangers the next day would bring. I was also downcast, but decided to go with Khoma to find out who was hiding in the fields.

We soon discovered that all the villagers had hidden there to escape the fighting. We found one of their shelters, heard some children's voices through the entrance, and when we lowered ourselves inside we discovered an entire family of seven. I asked one of the girls in the family to talk to the village head, and after she had spoken with him he quickly filled a basket with food for us. This cheered me up tremendously and immediately lifted the spirits of everyone in my group. The village leader then assigned one of his men to keep in touch with us.

When morning came and the sun began to rise the last German tanks holding back the advance of the Soviet army retreated and an ominous silence fell over the fields. Finally, when the sun rose higher in the sky, we spotted an endless line of soldiers, spaced seven to ten metres apart, slowly combing every square metre of swamp, meadow and forest in the area. As the line of soldiers approached us, I was petrified but mobilized all my strength to crush this fear before my men could notice it. Fortunately, however, our group went unnoticed by the soldiers.

The Germans had not mounted a very spirited defence; they were simply restraining the Soviet offensive to allow their own orderly withdrawal. Thus the next morning the Soviet military authorities ordered all the villagers to return to their homes; all who disobeyed were to be shot on the spot, and we prepared to continue on our way.

This, however, proved to be both difficult and dangerous, for all the roads were clogged with Soviet army units rushing west, whereas we were heading east. I asked the village head to prepare four carts piled up with hay, with a scythe and a rake on top, and after changing into peasant clothes we hid all our weapons and other belongings which might give us away in the hay. I was in the first cart, accompanied by a young woman with a baby, for I hoped that their presence would restrain any soldiers we met from requisitioning our horses. The second cart kept its distance, so that it could turn off the road if anything happened to me, and the other two carts also stayed quite far apart. The rest of my group—barefoot, with rolled-up sleeves and trousers and with scythes over their shoulders—walked behind the carts. We travelled like this all day, trying to move as far as possible from the front.

After a few kilometres we stopped at a farmstead, hid our weapons, and decided to wait there until nightfall, for all the roads were clogged with military vehicles and it was impossible to travel further with our carts. When darkness fell our guide led us toward the village of Turkovychi, but along the way it began to rain. At dawn, thoroughly drenched, we reached our destination, but there were Soviet soldiers everywhere. We hid in a sodden wheat field and sent our guide to meet and pass us on to the Turkovychi liaison person. Soon we heard a woman's voice calling out my pseudonym, but we were afraid to take any risks because of the soldiers who were nearby, and waited patiently in the field, soaked to the skin, the whole long summer day.

In the evening we left for a nearby forest where we started a fire to dry ourselves, and were pleasantly surprised when the Turkovychi liaison person found us here and brought us two baskets full of dumplings and other delicacies. After we had eaten, she found us some boats and we quickly crossed the Buh River. Then we made our way to the Lytovezh farmsteads, where we slept in a barn near a young pine forest.

In the morning the two women in our group went to an empty house near the barn to cook breakfast, but soon after I had joined them, a senior lieutenant and sergeant of the Soviet army entered the house. I sat quietly behind the kitchen table and carefully watched the expression on the lieutenant's face, but the two men didn't even glance at me and only asked the women where the owner of the house was. When one of the women replied that he had gone to the village they turned and left without another word.

In the meantime all my men in the barn, who were sure that the two strangers had come to take me away, had fully prepared themselves to rescue me. This made me realize that I should select someone who could, if necessary, take over from me, and I appointed Lieutenant Donetsky group commander.

From Lytovezh we set off for the Horokhiv area. I left my men at a farmstead near Strilche and went to visit the Kovalchuks, but when Afanasii spotted me he gave me a cold look and went into the house. His hostile attitude disturbed me so I went to see his neighbours instead, and although Afanasii's wife came running after me and begged me, with tears in her eyes, to visit their house, I refused to do so. When the Soviet army arrived in a given area two factions often arose in many households: some members of the family were still prepared, despite the hopeless situation, to continue the struggle no matter what the consequences, while others wanted to accommodate themselves immediately to the new regime.

From Strilche we went toward Berestechko. When we crossed the Lviv-Lutsk railway line we stopped in the forest that extended toward Lobachivka and Smoliava, and there we came across approximately thirty men from Ostrizky's battalion. I asked one of the platoon commanders what had happened to Ostrizky's unit.

"After you left us Ostrizky changed his plans and went in the same direction as your group," he replied. "Along the way, however, we were trapped in a small wood between the Germans and the Soviets, who both started shooting at us. We were in a hopeless situation and there was nowhere to hide, so our forces suffered quite badly."

"And where's Ostrizky—was he killed?"

"No, they say that he broke through the enemy lines and took the northern route to the east."

Zalisny, the oblast SB director and Stymyd, the OUN okruh leader, decided that the remnants of Ostrizky's unit should join my group and now I was in charge of forty-four people. We travelled only at night, resting during the day, and after crossing the Styr River near Smoliava we rested in a small wood on the banks of the Styr. One of our sentries climbed to the top of a tall oak tree at the edge of the wood and kept a close watch on the surrounding countryside with his telescope while we washed ourselves thoroughly in the Styr, ate breakfast, and relaxed. We did not sleep long; soon our sentries woke us and told us that sixteen armed horsemen were heading in our direction. We quickly roused ourselves and our riflemen, hiding in the undergrowth some ten-twenty metres from each other, took up defensive positions to the side of the road passing through the forest. If the "strybky"[3] gave even the slightest indication that they were about to attack us the plan was for each one of us to shoot the closest horseman upon receiving the given signal.

The "strybky" were moving quickly, but they halted at the edge of the forest, looked around carefully, and then quietly and cautiously rode into the trees. When they noticed the barrels of our sub-machine guns they fell silent and, without exchanging a word, simply continued on their way. The platoon commanders from Ostrizky's battalion advised us to leave immediately, before more "strybky" arrived. I was sure, however, that they would not tell anyone that they had seen us, for they would hardly be praised for their cowardice. And I was right; we rested here for the rest of the day and no one bothered us.

In the evening we moved on toward the village of Vovnychi, which we reached just before daybreak. The contact person here told us that a group of "strybky" was guarding the bridge across the

Ikva, but since we had to cross the river before dawn we hurried down to the bridge and simply ignored the men guarding it. We crossed the bridge without taking the slightest precautions and our bravado was so effective that the "strybky" left their posts and hid themselves nearby. They began to shoot at us, using tracer bullets, only after we left the bridge some three hundred metres behind. Out of "politeness" we refrained from returning their fire, for there was no point playing at war with them; we simply wanted to reach the forests of Polissia as soon as possible. After crossing the bridge we turned left in order to reach the Boremets forest, and fifteen minutes later we reached our destination. Now we were in Ostrozhets raion, which I knew quite well.

We stopped to rest, and after taking a nap my men brought out some food and began to eat their breakfast. Suddenly a bearded man carrying a basket and accompanied by a small boy came across our resting place and was brought to me by our sentry.

"Why are you wandering about so early in the morning?" I asked the stranger.

"It's the custom here to gather mushrooms just after the dew has fallen," he replied.

"Where are you from?" I asked.

"Horodnytsia."

"What villages in this area are still free of the Reds?"

"Where are you heading?"

"Toward Velyka Horodnytsia," I replied, concealing our true destination.

"Oh, then you'll have to go through Iaroslavychi."

"Fine," I replied and, turning to my men, added, "that's where we'll pick up our medicine."

"You know what I'd recommend," the stranger suggested. "Wait here for an hour until I go home, find out where the Reds are stationed, and bring you something to eat."

"That's a good idea—we're very grateful to you," I said as the bearded man turned and left us.

"Why did you talk with him so freely?" Khoma asked. "It's obvious that he's an NKVD agent."

"That's exactly why I chatted with him," I replied. "We can't let him realize that we know who he is and why he came here. People like him have to be neutralized and, if possible, turned to our advantage by being fed 'information' which will help rather than harm us. After I told him that we had to go to Velyka Horodnytsia I turned to you and mentioned, in an offhand manner, that we had to pick up some medicine on our way in order to convince him that we really are heading in that direction. If he mentions this detail to the Chekists, that will convince them that we were telling him the truth. They'll throw all their forces in that direction to ambush us, and we'll go right through the very villages where Soviet troops have been stationed."

"Maybe you're right," Khoma noted, "but we have to clear out of here as soon as possible. It's daylight now—where do we go?"

"Don't worry; I know this area well. Now, to confirm what I told the fellow we just met we'll ask for directions to Velyka Horodnytsia—that should finally convince the Chekists that we're going there. We're in the very midst of the enemy now and we have to rely on our brains rather than on our strength."

When we visited these farmsteads some people assume that we were "strybky" and others assume that we were Banderites, but everyone was too scared to show us either sympathy or hostility. We had something to eat here and, in accordance with our plan, everywhere we went we asked where Soviet troops were stationed and for directions to Velyka Horodnytsia. Then, after walking half a kilometre toward Horodnytsia, we made a sharp turn into an L-shaped forest near the Boromets farmsteads and rested here for a full day while the "strybky" searched for us in the area where the stranger had spotted us.

Posing as Soviet soldiers, we returned to the farmsteads early in the evening, requisitioned ten horsecarts, and rode off toward Koryto. In Svyshchiv, which we reached before sunset, Soviet soldiers were strolling in the streets, so we rode through this village and Piatka, which was also full of Soviet troops, loudly singing "Katiusha" and cursing in Russian. When we were about to enter the Piatka forest, however, a Soviet liaison officer stopped us and warned us that, because of the Banderites, it was dangerous to enter the forest at night.

"We're in a hurry to reach Olyka and we have to press ahead," Donetsky explained.

After driving more than half a kilometre into the forest we sent the carts back with their owners and headed for some farmsteads on the outskirts of Koryto, near the Viun forest. We stopped at a house here which served as a liaison point for the Ostrozhets raion and I walked in with three of my men. The occupants, whom we had awakened, seemed suspicious of us, but they did treat us to a meal of meat-pies and milk. I knew a young woman from the village of Posnykiv, Nina, who happened to be spending the night in this house, and asked her to help me locate the raion or okruh leader.

"We're afraid of everyone now," she told me, "and don't trust a soul. I can't even be sure of you—you may have gone over to the Reds a long time ago. But I'll try to link you up with the raion leader on my own personal responsibility."

"I'd be very grateful if you could help us. We've been on the other side of the front and have no idea what's happening here."

"What's happened is that many who were with us just a short while ago are now against us, and that's why we've become so distrustful," Nina explained.

"We'll go back to the forest now and we'll stay there the whole day. We'd be very grateful if you could round up some food for us."

Our host did a wonderful job. We received three good meals that day, and in the evening Nina took us to Posnykiv and then to Pitushkiv, where the Ostrozhets raion leader came to meet us together with the Olyka raion patrol leader.

"Where are you heading?" the raion leader asked, "and whom do you want to see?"

"We're heading for the Tsuman forest, and I need to speak with someone from the oblast or krai leadership."

"Fine. Tomorrow you'll go to Olyka raion, and from there you can head straight for the Tsuman forest."

# Chapter Thirteen

When we reached Olyka raion we stopped in the village of Zhornyshche and rested in a farmer's barn. On this very day, however, the Chekists, who were everywhere, were arresting everyone in the village who was suspected of being a nationalist. They arrested the owner of the house next to our barn, walked around the barnyard, and even approached our hiding place. But God spared them and us and they didn't check the barn. That evening we continued on our way, and as soon as we entered the shelter of the thick Tsuman forest we breathed a sigh of relief. Five kilometres on we finally reached the camp of Orlyk's detachment. Orlyk, a slim, handsome young man, greeted me and asked me where I was heading.

"We're heading east, and I have to see someone from the Provid," I replied.

"Whom would you like to see?"

"Preferably Halyna or one of his subordinates," I replied. Orlyk told me that Halyna was not there, and at this point Orlyk's superior, Oleh, whom I already knew quite well, and Volodymyr, from the SB, also greeted us. I informed them that in addition to the eleven men and two women who were to accompany me further east, my unit included those men who had been separated from Ostrizky's unit when it crossed the front. I was instructed to wait there with my original group until a company arrived which would be going past Sarny toward Stolin, and in the meantime Slavko Harasymenko and Andrii Mysechko appeared.

I was overjoyed to meet Slavko again, and he was as delighted as a child to see me. For a while we just looked at each other without speaking, for it was impossible for us to express our feelings, and then we started telling each other about our experiences. Slavko was the only person among all my friends with whom I could discuss my personal life as well as politics, for he had a kind, sensitive soul and I could always be perfectly frank with him.

After we had talked for some time, I asked Slavko how he had reacted to the decisions of the First Founding Assembly of the NVRO.[1]

"I'm afraid, Danylo, that this move toward greater democracy has come too late," he replied.

"It seems to me that we'll have these paper resolutions, but that in practice we'll remain just as we are. No one is going to carry out any programme of democratization," I agreed.

"Of course. Nothing will change, for we have no real idea what democracy is all about. The spiritual need for democratization must originate, develop and mature in our own consciousness; only then will it become part of our public life."

"And where will you be heading now?"

"We have to go to a new location and set up our editorial offices again. There's a great deal of work to be done, and although I'd like to work on some of my own ideas, I have no time for that now."

"I'm heading for Eastern Ukraine, but I have no idea what I'll be doing there."

"I would prefer, Danylo, that you return to the socio-political directorate. This is where you would be of the most use, although you're probably a good organizer as well."

"How does Mysechko feel now? Wasn't he with the Melnykites[2] before?"

"More important is how he behaves as a person. Mysechko is a splendid fellow and a very efficient editor," Slavko concluded.

Early the next morning Slavko came to say goodbye. He and Mysechko were leaving for Korets, and this was the last time I saw him. Later, in the camps, I was told that one of Slavko's friends was killed when they were both surrounded by Soviet troops. Slavko refused to leave his friend's body, and eventually shot himself to avoid being captured.

The UPA company, which we had been awaiting, arrived soon after Slavko left and we set off for Sarny. The forests along the way were very thick so we were able to travel in the daytime, but it still took us three days to reach our destination. The forest was burning near the railway line linking Sarny and Klesiv, and there were Soviet troops everywhere, so we found ourselves in a dangerous situation and decided to cross the railway line near the outskirts of Sarny, right next to the military barracks. When we met some soldiers we stopped and questioned them about the "Banderites" and then, cursing the nationalists, continued on our way to "track them down." We had a good laugh afterward when we thought about how easy it had been to trick the enemy and cross the railway line without firing a single shot.

After this incident we changed direction and headed north-east toward Sekhy, where Soviet partisans had maintained a strong presence throughout the German occupation. No Banderites had been active in this area during the occupation, so I was curious to see how we would be received. We stopped just before we reached Sekhy and the company commander, who ordered us to march briskly through the village, also forbade us to accept any food, or even milk, from the villagers. After a brief rest we marched into Sekhy and saw that all the inhabitants had left their houses to see the "Banderite army." Girls and women brought us eggs and pitchers of milk, and men tried to give us some home-grown tobacco, but the company followed its orders and did not even look aside. The company commander thanked the villagers for their kindness as he marched alongside his troops, and some of the women were so moved that they began to cry. Everyone was impressed by the company's order and discipline.

From Sekhy we made for the village of Zalavia, but it was already dark so we decided to stop for the night. The company posted men at three look-out points, while we were responsible for the fourth, and during the night a duty NCO, one of the platoon commanders, came up to me with the sentry we had posted and stated that he had been caught sleeping on duty.

"Is that true?" I asked Poltavsky.

"Yes," he replied.

"And you know how the UPA punishes those who neglect their duty?" the company commander asked.

"I know," Poltavsky said, an empty look in his eyes.

"Then I'll muster the company, we'll read out your sentence, and comrade Boremsky will shoot you in front of the entire company. Understand?"

"I refuse to shoot him and won't allow you to do so either," I stated.

"What do you mean! You won't execute him for sleeping on duty?" the company commander exclaimed.

"No, I won't. You can complain about my behaviour to anyone you wish, but I won't allow any of the people in my care to be executed. Do you understand?"

"If that's the case then you won't be going any further with my company. And you'll be called to account by Vereshchaka for violating regulations. He'll speak to you in a different fashion."

In accordance with its plans the company continued on its way north, and after a short march I decided that our group would stop near Zalavia. Here, on a wooded piece of land surrounded by marshes where Jews escaping from the Germans had once hidden, we built ourselves some crude shelters. We received plenty of food, including fresh meat, from contacts in Zalavia, and stayed here for two weeks while I waited for a reply to a letter I had sent to Vereshchaka. But as I received no reply, I grew impatient, and decided that we would continue on our way east. Upon reaching the old Soviet-Polish border we stopped at the village of Snovydovychi and in the evening we set off for Zhytomyr oblast.

There was no OUN organizational network in Eastern Ukraine at the time; in fact, our aim was to set up such a network, or at least determine whether it was feasible to do so. Thus we travelled through Zhytomyr oblast without the help of liaison people, and as soon as we entered a village its collective-farm chairmen and brigade leaders fled from us.

One evening we stopped to rest in a thick forest in Bilokorovychi raion, and being very tired we immediately fell sound asleep. At dawn, however, Odesky, who had been standing guard, fired a round from his rifle and we sprang up to find ourselves under heavy fire. We were pinned down in a "horseshoe" formed by a group of "strybky" and were forced to flee into a nearby clearing, where my men had already split into two separate groups. Katrusia and myself were some way behind them, but although I was only thirty metres away from the "strybky" they failed to shoot at me, perhaps because I was in civilian clothes and they assumed that I was just another "strybok." I was afraid, however, that when my men reached the forest all the gunfire would be directed at me, so I made a sharp turn to the right to reach the forest more quickly and was joined by Katrusia.

After we had spent the whole day in the forest, we came across a village and rested nearby until darkness fell. Then we carefully approached an isolated house. Three women welcomed us, gave us a meal and one of them agreed to take us to a house on the other side of the village. Here we woke three village youths and told them to lead us through the forest toward the village of Harty, but they offered instead to take us to some houses, just outside the forest, which had completely escaped the ravages of the war.

It was so dark when we entered the forest that I feared our guides might desert us, so I asked Katrusia to tear up her handkerchief and to sew a piece of it onto each of the youth's backs.

"You'll march in single file," I told them, "and if anyone tries to escape I'll shoot and aim just above the handkerchief."

"We wouldn't leave you stranded in the forest even if you were unarmed," they replied. "We wouldn't desert people who are in trouble."

"How do you know that we're in trouble?"

"We guessed right away that you're from the group that was broken up by our 'strybky' yesterday in the forest on the other side of the village. Didn't they attack you when you were sleeping?"

"And whom do you take us to be?"

"Why, you must be Banderites," the oldest youth replied. "Who else could you be?"

When we reached our destination, two small houses just beyond the forest, I sent two of our guides to one of the houses and we followed about a hundred metres behind. Suddenly, however, we heard an order to halt from the house, and quickly retreated to the shelter of some old oaks in the forest. Five minutes later we heard a group of people leave the house and head for the forest. This puzzled me, and we waited patiently to find out what was happening. As the strangers drew closer we became all ears, and suddenly I heard Khoma's familiar voice call out my name. I called back, and when I emerged from the forest I was immediately surrounded by all my missing men, who explained joyfully that everyone in our group was alive and that only Odesky had been wounded during the skirmish with the "strybky." I was very happy to find all my men here, and Katrusia, also overjoyed to see them, immediately made a dressing for Odesky's light wound.

We left at dawn, and after passing through the village of Harty we continued, through dense forest, on our way east. Around noon we stopped at the house of a forester who, we discovered, had been mobilized to help catch us.

"They took my husband away to track you down, and here you've come to me on your own," the forester's wife said and laughed. "I'll feed you, but in return at least promise not to shoot my husband."

"Don't worry," I replied, "we're not out to shoot anyone."

By evening we reached the village of Chmelivka, at the edge of the forest. We decided to rest here and eat, so we divided ourselves up among a number of houses.

"Could you possibly give us a bite to eat?" I asked a woman in the first house I entered.

"I can give you some food," she replied, "but first I should warn you that a whole truckload of 'strybky' is stationed in our village; they've been waiting for you all day." Suddenly I heard a commotion in the street, and we ran out to see that our men were already in battle order. In the distance we heard the sound of "strybky" shouting and firing their weapons.

"Let's show them what it means to tangle with us," Khoma suggested, half in fun.

"No, we have no reason to get into a fight, and who knows, we might be unlucky and shoot the forester whose wife fed us at lunchtime," I replied. So we slowly retreated, and when we took up defensive positions near the forest the "strybky" halted and stopped firing.

Soon it grew dark, and since it seemed that the "strybky" had no great desire to pursue us we quietly left our positions, entered the forest, and the "strybky" returned to the village. After this incident the "strybky," under Chekist supervision, tried to ambush us at every opportunity, but with the help of our maps we predicted where they would be waiting for us and always managed to outsmart them. It was more difficult when it came to crossing the highway and railway line between Korosten and Zhytomyr, for here the forests which we used for cover were interrupted for a distance of twenty-seven kilometres. It was not hard to guess that this would be where the Chekists would make their greatest effort to prevent us from crossing over to the Chopovychi and Malyn forests, which extended beyond the Teteriv River and were part of the heavily-wooded forest zone in the north of Kiev oblast.

We reached the village of Stavyshche, where the forests ended, early in the evening. We rested here for a while, looked over the surrounding terrain, and then went to some nearby houses for supper.

"We'll feed you," a farmer told us, "but you'll find the going very rough from here on. The 'strybky,' who have come here from all parts of the raion, have been waiting for you for two days now."

"Fine, let them wait. We're not so stupid as to leave the shelter of the forest and walk right into their hands. We'll cross at a location which they would never expect us to use," Khoma replied.

After supper, I took out my map, carefuly aligned it, and explained to my men, in a loud voice, how we would head north and cross the railway line and highway near Korosten. I showed them our entire route on the map and was so earnest that everyone believed what I told them. By now the Chekists were probably convinced that rather than take the easy routes, we always went where we would be least expected to go. So they believed the farmer's account of my plan, and, as the women in our group (who often acted as scouts) soon found out, they quickly transferred their troops to the north.

We crossed the gap between the two forest zones at its narrowest point, since we wanted to cross the Irsha River near the village of Staryky and hide in the forest while it was still dark. We reached Staryky before dawn but suddenly spotted some strangers emerging from a pine grove to our right. They stopped some fifty yards from us, and when they shouted "password!" we immediately took cover.

"There are quite a few of them," we heard the stranger say just before they turned and ran back to the pine grove, and we used this opportunity to get up and cross the river quickly. Once on the other side we came across some houses hidden in the forest and had some breakfast there before continuing.

We stopped at noon, having discovered that a long swathe about four hundred metres wide had been cleared out of the forest. It was obvious that an ambush was being prepared, and we were forced to wait until evening when, in small groups, we made our way to the other side of the cleared area and stopped at a forester's house. We were told that forty armed men had waited here all day for us, but had finally left for Staryky earlier the same evening.

The women in our group immediately began to peel some potatoes for supper, and several men helped them while six others went to fetch some bread from neighbouring farmsteads. Four returned with several loaves of bread and the other two came back guarding two older men who had cartridge belts slung across their shoulders. Vasyl walked behind the prisoners with his rifle cocked, ready to shoot, and Petro, a seventeen-year-old former "strybok," carried their rifles. One of the prisoners, about forty-five years old, was the local "Zahotsin"[3] director. The other, about thirty-five years old, was the "Zahotskot"[4] bookkeeper, and I was quite amused to see that my youngsters had managed to capture these two older, more experienced men.

"Where and how did you capture them?" I asked.

"We walked into a house to ask for some bread and found these two fellows sitting at a table drinking moonshine," Vasyl replied. "There was no need to ask them who they were—their cartridge belts spoke for themselves—and when I ordered them to put their hands up they obeyed quickly. It turned out that their rifles were in a corner near the stove, so Petia took the rifles and we brought the men here."

"Is that what happened?" I asked the prisoners.

"Yes," the older man replied.

"Who were you planning to track down?"

"We didn't leave for the front so we're occasionally called out to take part in operations against gangs of Banderites."

"What do you know about these 'gangs' and what have you been told by those who order you to go on these operations?" I asked.

"We don't really know anything about the Banderites because we haven't seen any yet," the younger man replied, "but we've been told that they murder people, cut off their tongues and ears, and gouge out their eyes."

"And what do you think such a 'gang' would do to those who, like you, are trying to track it down?" I asked.

"We know that we won't leave your hands alive," the older man, visibly shaken, replied.

"This is an interesting twist of fate: you were looking for us but have ended up in our hands. If you had captured me you would have killed me, released me, or sent me to jail. We have no jails, so in your case only the first two alternatives are open to us, although I've never had to resort to killing anyone before. This is the first time I've ever seen either of you, and you've never done me any harm, just as I've never harmed you. Why should we kill one another?

"We're not bandits. We're fighting for the independence of our country, our nation, and for everyone's freedom. You'll be released safe and sound, and will be living proof that the Chekist propaganda about our 'brutality' is a lie. When the Chekists find out that we released you and they accuse you of becoming our agents you'll quickly find out what kind of 'justice' prevails in this country. They won't listen to anything you say, for then their propaganda against us would be in ruins and no one would believe that we're murderers and bandits. But we can't protect you from the Chekists, and if the farmer's wife here tells anyone about our conversation then she'll also be arrested on the grounds that she is a Ukrainian nationalist.

"The Soviet authorities aren't afraid of those nationalists who kill and plunder, for such behaviour only strengthens their propaganda and helps them to mobilize the population against the nationalist movement. Their worst enemy is cultural humanism and a *noble* form of nationalism, for nothing in their arsenal can oppose these forces."

"So you're letting us go?" the older prisoner asked in wonder, as if he could hardly believe his ears.

"Yes, but you'll have to spend a few more hours with us," I replied.

"What would your comrades do," Khoma later asked me, "if the Chekists captured you and released you two days later? Would they believe in your honesty?"

"It's better not to pose such questions," I replied. But I knew that I probably would have been treated much more harshly than the people we had detained; I would have been killed. This train of thought frightened and repelled me. Life in the underground was nasty and brutish, with suspicion and death walking hand in hand, and it was impossible to know what awaited us.

After we had eaten a simple but filling meal, prepared by the farmer's wife, we spread some straw beneath us, assigned a sentry to guard the door, and immediately fell asleep. In the morning we took the rifles which belonged to the prisoners, broke them in half, and threw the pieces into the forest.

"You can go home now," I told our prisoners, who looked at each other and seemed afraid to move from the spot.

That day we pressed on more quickly than usual, for we were anxious to cross the Teteriv River and reach the dense forests on the other side as soon as possible. By evening we reached Bedryk, where we ate with some of the villagers, and after wading across the Teteriv and passing between the villages of Mykhalka and Bila Krynytsia we finally entered the depths of the forest.

We soon came upon a few houses belonging to some peat-diggers and decided to rest there. Our group had already split up among the houses when we suddenly heard the sound of gunfire nearby and ran out into the street. The shooting came from a house at the edge of the village and the three men who had gone there never returned. . . .

Although we were extremely tired we were forced to continue eastward, in the direction of Kiev, to a point south of the village of Maidanivka. We stayed in this area for more than a week, and this is where a courier from Vereshchaka reached us. His assignment was to establish contacts between our group and a nearby UPA company in order that it supply us with food for the winter, and the courier, whose pseudonym was Pohrebny, spent several days with us. In the meantime, however, I managed, quite accidentally, to find the company myself, without Pohrebny's help.

A rendezvous was established and one evening I set off with Letun to meet the company commander. After the meeting Letun and I went to an empty house where Khoma and Pohrebny were waiting for us, for I had to write a letter to Vereshchaka and send it to him via Pohrebny. But I was so tired that I barely reached our destination, where we ate some potatoes and then stretched out on the bare floor. I immediately fell sound asleep.

Around midnight I was awoken by an explosion. Realizing that a grenade had gone off I flattened myself against the floor and after a second, more powerful explosion, I heard Letun groan. Then a deathly silence fell over the house, and I realized that I was the only one left alive.

A weight of some kind had fallen on my stomach during the explosion, and when I grabbed it I found out it was yet another grenade. The trigger of the grenade was still on hold, so in a reflex action I pressed it down and kept the grenade in my left hand. Then I took my pistol in my other hand and rose to my feet amid the choking fumes left by the explosion.

"They must have surrounded us," I thought to myself as I quietly opened the door, "And are waiting to see if anyone is alive. My only chance is to break through before they throw another grenade or riddle the house with bullets."

As I left the silent house small clouds drifted across the sky, hiding, and then exposing, the secretive face of the moon. I spotted some tall pine trees, as straight as candles, about thirty metres from me, and as I slowly moved toward them I could not help thinking that this might be the last time I would ever see such a scene. There was a strange tickling feeling between my shoulders, as if I was expecting a burst of gunfire to strike me, but not a sound broke the nocturnal silence. When I reached the first pine tree I hid myself, looked back at the house, and thought about the friends whom I had left behind. It was difficult to believe that it was all over for them, and that people could die in such a senseless fashion. I began to move slowly from one tree to another, further and further from that house of death, and once I reached the forest I set off quickly toward our camp.

After walking quite a distance, I saw my men sitting around a bonfire. When they saw me with a grenade and a pistol in my hands they suddenly interrupted their light-hearted conversation, looked at me with alarm in their eyes, and asked what was wrong. I described everything to them, but we were all rather mystified by what had happened. It was clear that if the house had been surrounded I would never have emerged alive, but we had no idea who could have thrown the grenade.

I proposed that in the morning we go to retrieve the bodies of our comrades and my men readily agreed. If it had been an NKVD agent who had followed us and thrown the grenade, then he would soon return to the house with a whole gang of Chekists, so it was necessary to bury the dead and leave this area as soon as possible.

Early in the morning we surrounded the house and approached it in full battle order. To our surprise, however, in the house we found not three bodies but only two—those of Letun and Khoma. There was no watch or sub-machine gun on the body of Khoma, who had slept beside Pohrebny, so it became clear to us that Pohrebny had been sent to us not by Vereshchaka, but by the NKVD. We took the bodies, carried them to our camp, and buried them near a cross-roads in the forest. I made a short speech appropriate to the occasion, and after we had shed some bitter tears we bid our comrades farewell. After filling in the grave, I marked the gravesite on my map and we prepared to continue on our journey.

At this point I asked the two women in our group to come over and I showed them the road to Boiarka on the map.

"You should leave immediately for Boiarka," I told them. "Then you can make your way to Kiev, and from Kiev you can find your way home. You should say that when you were being deported to Germany you escaped from the convoy and lived in a village in the Kholm area. Do you understand?"

"Yes," the women replied and tearfully took their leave of us, leaving only eight in our group. We decided to retrace our steps, but it was too late and the Chekists managed to catch up with us from the south. We were in a very difficult situation, for we were surrounded on three sides and were being pushed back toward the Korosten-Kiev railway line, where a large number of guards had been stationed. As we retreated toward the railway line, where machine-gunners were already waiting for us, I thought to myself that it would be impossible to break out of this trap.

Fortunately we kept our nerve and prepared calmly for the worst. At one point we even considered crawling to one of the machine guns, blowing it up with a grenade and then immediately breaking through the enemy lines. But when we approached the railway tracks we changed our plans, for on our side of the tracks there was a peat bog, covered by thick undergrowth, and on the other side there was a large, dense forest. We decided to scatter, plunge into the bog, slowly make our way to the tracks, and then wait until we could slip across.

As evening approached the circle around us grew tighter and the men who had been herding us toward the railway line linked up with the machine-gunners on the tracks. They were only sixty or seventy metres from us and we could clearly hear them talking and swearing. They decided to rake the bog with their machine guns, and fired so low that we were forced to hold our breath and sink into the water. However, when the firing stopped they started walking along the track in the direction of Kiev, and after waiting another ten minutes we left the bog and headed south. Two kilometres further on we entered a house, dried our clothes and had some supper.

After crossing the Teteriv we moved west quite rapidly, since it was much easier to travel now that there were only eight of us. I was quite curious, however, to find out what had happened to the "Zahotsin" director and the "Zahotskot" bookkeeper, and when we passed through the area where we had detained them and I asked a woman we met about them she laughed and told me that they had been arrested. As we continued on our way we still came under fire from time to time, but we tried to ignore these incidents and returned to Rivne oblast without mishap.

# Chapter Fourteen

After crossing the old Soviet-Polish border, we entered the village of
Dert, located deep inside a forest which extended all the way to
Zhytomyr oblast, where the life of the villagers reminded us of old
stories about the Tatar raids. Day and night a sentry with a
telescope sat in a tall oak on the edge of the village and a man
waited below with his horse. As soon as any "strybky" appeared on
the horizon the sentry informed his companion who then galloped to
the village church and rang the church bells to sound the alarm.
When the villagers heard this signal they quickly gathered their
belongings, rushed into the forest with their families and cattle, and
stayed in shelters specially prepared for such occasions. We spent
two weeks in Dert before we could get in touch with Vereshchaka,
and during this time we were often forced to hide from the
"strybky," along with the peasants.

"What do the 'strybky' do when no one is left in the village?" I
asked one lady.

"They steal everything they can lay their hands on: back fat,
butter, moonshine, clothing, chickens—nothing is safe from
them—that's why they're called 'strybky'."

"But they don't plunder villages in Zhytomyr oblast, just two
kilometres away from here."

"What can you steal there? In Zhytomyr oblast everyone's a
'strybok,' for they're all hungry and there's nothing left to steal."

"Were there any communists here before the war, under Polish
rule?" I asked.

"No," the old woman's son replied. "We could see the 'paradise' which had been created just across the border with our own eyes, and that's why the people here detest communism."

"But those who live in that 'paradise' don't hate communism as strongly as you do," I noted.

"Their hatred is greater than ours, but the years of oppression have destroyed their faith in the possibility of any change for the better and they've resigned themselves to their fate," he replied.

At last I received a sealed letter by special courier from Vereshchaka, which proposed that the courier and myself should go to Chabel. Upon arrival at this village, I stayed at an UPA NCO school in the forest where more than one hundred students were attending lectures. The director of the school was a former Melnykite called Orel who had subsequently joined the Banderites. I asked him what had happened to his friends among the Melnykites who had joined the Banderites together with him.

"Didn't you know that they were shot?" Orel replied with tears in his eyes.

"Who shot them?" I asked angrily.

"This is a very painful subject, and I don't want to talk about it. But this mutual extermination will continue for a long time because of our intolerance of one another."

From Chabel we moved south until we reached the Storozhiv farmsteads, where I met with Vereshchaka, Daleky, and the socio-political director.

"Please tell us where you've been, what you saw, and your impressions of Eastern Ukraine," Vereshchaka asked me. After I described everything that had happened to us, and all we had heard and seen during our raid, Vereshchaka asked for my views about potential organizational work in Eastern Ukraine.

"It's ridiculous to send these groups out there to carry out this kind of work," I replied.

"If that's the way you feel, what do you think should be done?" Vereshchaka asked.

"In my opinion we have to switch to legal forms of activity, and should ensure that our most talented young people obtain the best possible secondary and higher education so that our people become specialists in all branches of industry, science and culture. We can promote and defend our socio-political programme only when we have a firm base of suport in all these sectors. And we'll have to start this large-scale, long-term project as soon as possible, for these clandestine groups that are wandering from one forest to another will achieve nothing. People who are hungry, cold, filthy and have no widespread support are incapable of carrying out any kind of organizational work, for they're looked upon as foolish, pitiful fanatics."

Vereshchaka was squirming with impatience throughout my presentation, although Daleky listened thoughtfully and the socio-political director was impressed with what I had to say.

"You're predicting a very long life for the Soviet regime, and you bore me," Vereshchak noted irritably when I had finished. Daleky, however, remained silent, while the socio-political director said that he shared my opinions.

"Nonetheless, you'll have to go back east," Vereshchaka told me, "for the krai provid has appointed you leader of region 'B,' which includes all Zhytomyr oblast and the northern section of Kiev oblast up to the Dnieper River. Tomorrow okruh leader Mykola arrives here and he'll start transferring his responsibilities to you."

"Why was I assigned to this position in my absence and without my consent?"

"You know what the situation is like now. If you hadn't gone east on your own then you would have been summoned and consulted, but you weren't here."

"I didn't go east on my own. I was given instructions to do so even before the front passed through this area."

"You were assigned to Eastern Ukraine, but no one defined your sector of operations or your functions," Vereshchaka replied.

The following day Vereshchaka introduced me to Mykola and told me that the krai provid was placing great hopes in me.

"This is quite a paradox," I replied, "since I never took the oath of membership and never officially joined the OUN. Yet suddenly I've been made the leader of such a large okruh."

"I'm not responsible for this. The krai provid knows what has to be done and who's to be assigned to what position," Vereshchaka retorted.

Mykola, a man of about thirty-five, was a calm, sensible fellow. A former student in a polytechnical school, in 1941 he had served as the police chief in Khorostkiv and had married a medical student from Malyn raion, Zhytomyr oblast.

"And where are you being transferred?" I asked him.

"I don't know. I escaped from a prison in Zhytomyr just two weeks ago, and my wife is still being held there."

"Were you and your wife arrested together?"

"Yes." I looked at Mykola and was filled with horror and pity for him.

"When did you join the OUN?" I asked.

"In 1937."

I was amazed that Mykola had not guessed what was going to happen to him, for it was obvious to me that no one believed that he had actually escaped from prison. He would probably be forced to confess that his escape had been arranged by the authorities and that he had been given an important assignment by the NKVD, while his wife, whom he obviously loved a great deal, was kept in prison as a hostage.

A few days later Daleky sent me two young women from Eastern Ukraine, a teacher and a medical assistant. Since I already knew what it was like to have women along during a forced march, I decided to send them straight home from Storozhiv.

Early one morning the women prepared some dumplings and we had just begun to indulge ourselves when a group of "strybky" suddenly attacked the farmstead, about three hundred metres away from us, where Vereshchaka had his quarters. When bullets began to fly about our ears we were forced to interrupt our meal, abandon the delicious dumplings and beat a hasty retreat. Oblast leader Voron was killed in this skirmish and we buried him in the cemetery of the village to which we retreated, erecting a large oak cross on his grave.

A few days later the "strybky" again attacked us, this time sneaking up quite close to us and striking when we were still drowsy. I survived only because I was again wearing civilian clothes, and the "strybky" were shooting at those who were fully armed and in uniform. Since one of our sentries was killed in this attack, I was left with only seven of my "old cadres," so Vereshchaka assigned seven of his men to my group.

In December 1944 I left Storozhiv and set off for Eastern Ukraine with a group of fourteen. On the second day of our trip, after we had crossed the Sluch River, all seven of the men from

Vereshchaka's unit fled back to Rivne oblast, but the rest of us pressed on. This time we no longer declared ourselves to be nationalists. We decided that it would be better to pose as deserters, and as a result we were not persecuted by the Chekists.

We reached the vicinity of Fastiv without mishap and decided to enter a house near the village of Vechory to warm up and sleep for a while. But when Pavlenko, the commander of my group, knocked on a window, three shots rang out, fatally wounding him. My men wanted to burn the house down and kill everyone in it but I categorically forbade this, and when Suchok prepared to throw a grenade through the window, I grabbed his arm just in time and took the grenade away from him. We carried Pavlenko into the forest, where he died, and after we had buried him I decided to let the members of my group go to their homes. I addressed my men the next morning:

> My dear and faithful friends! Neither we nor our cause will benefit from our wandering around in these forests. With the exception of Vasyl Prysiazhny and myself you are all from the eastern oblasts of Ukraine, so you should go home and, each in his own way, settle down to make a new life for yourselves. But never forget that you're Ukrainians. Love your country, love your native language, our nation's most valuable treasure, and try to discover and understand the roots of our misfortunes and the sources of our ancestors' strength. Don't engage in any special propaganda for the nationalist cause or set up any organizations, for your own behaviour will serve as your propaganda. When other people like yourself gravitate toward you, this will be the best form of organization, one that can never be exposed and for which you can never be sentenced. Make sure, however, that you never mention your involvement with the UPA.

I ended by wishing my men a safe journey back to their families, and as they thanked me and shook my hand, with tears in their eyes, I also cried. When they had quietly gone their separate ways, Vasyl and I set off for the south of Kiev oblast.

"There's no reason for us to return to Western Ukraine," I told Vasyl. "We should try to obtain some official documents and go to the Donbas[1] for a while. If we succeed in finding a job and in making a good name for ourselves, then we'll try to enrol somewhere to continue our education—that should be our goal."

"And what will the OUN make of this?"

"We're on our own now and we have to act in accordance with our own conscience. Everything else is irrelevant."

"But where will we get the documents we need?"

"That's a good question—I'll take care of that."

At Bila Tserkva we spent five days with a teacher whom at one point I had sent back home from Volhynia, and I spoke to her about our need for documents. She could not help me, however, and we moved west, to the village of Samhorodok, to visit a family with whom I had spent some time during the German occupation. They welcomed us quite hospitably, but the next day we received a visit from the head of the village council, accompanied by an official of some kind, who demanded that we go with them to the village council headquarters. This was not at all to my liking, but I put on my coat and told Vasyl to join me. Vasyl gave me a questioning glance and followed me into the street, where a cart awaited us. The official, who wore glasses and carried a briefcase, mounted first, Vasyl and I followed, and the head of the village council walked behind the cart. Instead of heading for the village council headquarters, however, the cart set off toward the state farm, where the militia were stationed.

"Where are you taking us? This isn't the right way!" I exclaimed.

"We know where we're going," the village council head replied arrogantly.

At this point I jumped off the cart and fled down the road. Vasyl hesitated for a second, but joined me when I shouted to him. The head of the village council stood in the middle of the road and started yelling for help, but he made no attempt to go after us. We ran past the village of Berezna, and then, with four people on our trail, we entered a small wood. Our pursuers started shooting at us, but by a stroke of luck a thick fog moved in, allowing us to slip through their fingers.

After this incident, we returned to the teacher who lived near Bila Tserkva, but she greeted us very cautiously.

"What happened, Mariika?" I asked.

"The very evening you left me some men came to search the house and examined every nook and cranny," she replied. We decided to spend only one night here, and stayed in a barn rather than in the house. Then we headed for Bohuslav, travelling mainly by night and resting during the day. Occasionally we met some friendly people and managed to get a proper rest, but at other times the going was very rough. We spent whole days in sub-zero weather (sometimes it reached thirty degrees below zero!), trudging back and forth in a small wood, and we continuously suffered from hunger and exhaustion through lack of sleep.

Once we spent a whole day in the Prusy forest, and after building a large fire and laying down some branches as a mattress we quickly sank into a deep slumber. Suddenly we were awoken by the sound of a gunshot and tried to jump to our feet, but discovered that we couldn't get up because the camp fire had melted the snow around us and when the fire died out we had simply frozen to the ground. We had to rip our coats out of the ice slowly, centimetre by centimetre, and when we got to our feet, my whole right side was frozen stiff. We decided to continue walking to prevent ourselves from turning completely numb, and after a three-kilometre trudge through the deep snow in the forest, I began to feel some warmth slowly seeping into my right side.

During the night we reached the village of Savarka, Bohuslav raion, and made our way to a house on a local farmstead hoping that we could rest there. It was daybreak when we entered the house, and a woman was already bustling about.

"Please let us rest here," I asked. "We've been travelling and are very tired."

"I'd gladly let you stay, but my son is here," she replied, just as we heard a threatening voice from the other room.

"Who are you, and where have you come from? I'm getting up to find out what's going on."

I looked through an open door to see a strong, healthy young man getting out of bed, and when I saw a military uniform and a gun lying on a chair we quickly left the house and hurried toward a small wood nearby. Although we heard shouts and gunfire from the direction of the house no one gave chase to us. We spent a miserable day hiding in the wood, however, for even if we had been able to build a fire here it would have given away our location.

We left Savarka for Mysailivka on the eve of the Epiphany, in January 1945. Emerging from the Mysailivka forest just before dawn, we entered the first house along our route that was lit up, and were given a friendly welcome by the occupants.

"Could your daughter possibly take a letter from me to my friends in Bohuslav?" I asked the man of the house. He readily agreed to this, and about an hour and a half later the girl returned with a good-looking young woman named Zina who boldly came up to me and greeted me as if we were old friends.

"My sister's not at home," she told me, "but I'll help you in her absence."

"Fine," I replied. "How long can I stay at your place?"

"As long as you wish," she said and smiled.

"Could my friend stay with you for four days until I return?" I asked our host.

"Of course; where else could he go? He'll be our guest for the feast of the Epiphany."

On the way to Bohuslav, Zina explained that her sister was now working in Lviv oblast as a teacher. Before she left, however, she had asked Zina, who lived at home with her parents, to meet me and give me shelter if I needed any help.

"What will your parents think?" I asked.

"Don't worry; I know what to tell them. Just try to talk with them, and especially my father, as little as possible. I'll take you through the kitchen into the attic room, and no one but myself will go in there."

Zina's mother greeted me warmly, but Zina didn't give her an opportunity to question me and quickly led me into a large, well-furnished attic room. After the terrible conditions I had recently experienced this was like paradise. Zina brought me a wash-tub, some warm water, and a clean set of clothes and underwear. After I had washed and shaved myself thoroughly I looked in a mirror: I looked refreshed and at least seven years younger. Zina then served me a very tasty, nourishing lunch, and told me to rest while she cleared the table.

When Zina returned she smiled and said that everything had been arranged. "You'll stay in our house as my sister's fiancé, okay? With my mother and father you should just talk about my sister, but with me you can discuss anything you want and I'll help you in any way I can."

"Zinochka, we need some documents so that we can settle down and find a job, even if it's in the Donbas."

"Fine. I'll do some thinking and we'll talk about this later."

I spent four wonderful days with this family. Zina and her mother were especially good to me, and prepared a special package of delicious food to take with me when I left.

I met Vasyl in Mysailivka, as we had arranged, and then we set off for Isaiky. As evening approached, we left the forest and approached a house where an old couple welcomed us warmly and gave us a large meal. After we had explained who we were and where we were from they told us their own story.

"We're originally from the village of Medvyn [Kiev oblast]," the husband explained, "but during the collectivization campaign we left our beautiful village and made for Zaporizhzhia oblast, where we were caught up in the famine of 1933. The famine left bodies lying everywhere in the villages and on the roads, and it's simply impossible to describe the horror of this tragedy. You know how we saved ourselves from starving to death? We walked through the fields, digging up mice and gopher holes, and stole the food reserves of these animals."

"Didn't the authorities try to confiscate their supplies as well?" I asked sarcastically.

"Oh no. The authorities treated and still treat human beings like dirt, but they're quite humane in their treatment of animals."

We spent a whole day with this couple and then moved on toward the village of Dmytrenky. On our way we stopped at a forester's residence. The woman of the house greeted us warmly, but asked us to visit also their neighbours and the forester so that no one would be tempted to denounce the others.

We knew how important their request was, for we had run into problems in similar situations, and did as they asked. We were received well in every house; in fact the forester treated us to a rabbit stew which, for us, was an exceptional delicacy. We rested here the entire day and then left for Dmytrenky, where we came under fire from a group of "strybky." Once again we were forced to sleep in the open with the temperature at thirty below zero, and our hunger and the cold bothered us far more than the Chekists.

The next morning we found an empty forester's hut in the Dmytrenky forest, lit a fire in it, and spent the day there. Then we returned to the house of the old couple in Isaiky and I left Vasyl there while I went to Bohuslav to see Zina. Although she and her mother were delighted to see me, they hadn't obtained the documents I wanted, and were just as depressed as I was.

"Stay and rest here for a few days," Zina proposed, "and I'll visit my relatives in Kiev to see if I have any luck there."

Three days later I again left for Isaiky and, together with Vasyl, we returned to the empty forester's hut near Dmytrenky. We had some food with us and stayed there for two days, but on the third day some youths showed up at the hut so we returned to Isaiky. This time, however, the old couple let us in with reluctance.

"They searched for you here and spent several nights watching the house," the woman told us. "If no one has spotted you, then go up to the loft, for it's dangerous to stay in the house now."

We spent one night in the loft and then left for Rozkopantsi, near Bohuslav. I left Vasyl with some people in Rozkopantsi and went on to Bohuslav to check whether our documents were ready. However, the moment I opened the door to the kitchen, Zina's mother clasped her hands and told me to flee.

"The room where you stayed is full of men—they're having a drink there now," she said.

"Is Zina home?" I asked.

"No, she's still in Kiev."

I quickly left and returned to Rozkopantsi, where I told Vasyl about my close call. After the woman of the house had put some bedclothes out for us near the warm stove, she left to visit some neighbours. We lay down and fell sound asleep.

Suddenly I felt someone give my leg a strong jerk and woke up to find seven armed men standing over us. One, with several medals on his chest, waved his sub-machine gun at us, another pointed a pistol at my head and told me to keep still, while a third rummaged under my pillow and pulled out my pistol and grenade. Then they searched our clothing. They were very pleased when they found my map-case, and were overjoyed when they pulled out my topographic maps, in various scales, covering all the oblasts of Ukraine.

"We've caught quite a big fish here!" the man with the medals exclaimed. Our captors showed little interest in the lists of the many groups which had left for Eastern Ukraine or in our leaflets, but were fascinated by these maps.

"Well, my pigeons, you can get up now," the medal-bearer declared in a self-satisfied manner, and we were taken to the headquarters of the Rozkopantsi village council.

"Go to Bohuslav and find Major Novikov," he instructed one of his men. "Tell him that we've captured an important spy. In the meantime I'll take care of these fellows myself."

Our captors placed Vasyl in a corner of the room, and ordered me to sit at the table. With a serious expression on his face the medal-bearer sat opposite me. took out a piece of paper, and with the haughty air of a victor tapped his pen on the table.

"Now tell us who you are, where you came from, and your mission!"

"We came here from Volhynia, from the NVRO," I replied.

"Is that the name of your espionage outfit?"

"No, it's the People's Liberation Revolutionary Organization."

"Don't play games with me. You're not the first fellow I've questioned, and I've heard all kinds of stories. These jokes of yours prove that you're a spy."

"I'm telling you the truth, so write down what I say."

"All right, tell me about this NVRO."

"Our group was made up of eight people, and we were broken up near Fastiv. Our commander, Pavlenko, was killed there, and from that point on the two of us travelled together." The medal-bearer, who was sweating heavily, carefully took everything down.

"And where were you heading?"

"We were wandering around quite aimlessly. We thought of leaving for the Donbas to look for jobs, but we don't have any documents. So we've been trying to get papers which would allow us to settle down and start working somewhere."

"Hold on," my interrogator interrupted, and brought out a second piece of paper. "I've begun to write down the protocol of the interrogation, but I don't even have your name and place of birth. What's your name and patronymic?" When I told him my name I added that he should also jot down my pseudonym—Vasylenko—and glanced at Vasyl to make sure that he understood what I was doing. My interrogator wrote everything down and was very pleased with himself.

Finally Major Novikov arrived, totally drunk.

"To hell with you! Did you have to catch this fellow on Red Army Day? Couldn't you pick another time to catch spies? You've dragged me away from the supper table," he complained in a half-joking, half-serious tone of voice.

"Look, he's already confessed," the medal-bearer proudly stated and showed Novikov the protocol of the interrogation. Novikov glanced at the protocol and glared at my interrogator.

"Who told you to question them here?" he demanded angrily.

"But look, he's admitted everything," the medal-bearer stammered, waving the protocol under the major's nose.

"Do you know what an idiot you are?" Novikov asked, and arranged for us to be transferred to the preliminary detention cells in Bohuslav.

It was five kilometres to the Bohuslav militia station and we travelled in sleighs escorted by "strybky." Our arms were tightly bound behind our backs and our hands immediately grew numb because of the biting cold. Once we left Rozkopantsi the senior "strybok" turned to his subordinate.

"Where's the ravine where the major told us to do them in?" he asked in a loud voice.

"It's to the left of the Ros River," his subordinate replied, nodding in the direction of the ravine. Vasyl suddenly turned white.

"Are they taking us to be shot?" he asked me quietly.

"Their heads would roll if they shot us," I replied loudly. "They need us alive, not dead."

"You see what an old fox he is. He thinks he knows everything," the senior "strybok" noted.

At the militia station we were untied and led to the detention cells. Twelve men were already sleeping on plank beds in our cell, and as newcomers we were forced to sleep on the floor.

"You heard how those idiots questioned me," I told Vasyl when everyone else had fallen asleep. "When you're questioned remember the following: my pseudonym is Vasylenko, not Boremsky; I wasn't in charge of our group, for I'm an ordinary UPA soldier who was assigned to defend Pavlenko, and the pistol and map-case are Pavlenko's—I took them from him when he was killed near Fastiv. We'll be split up in Kiev and you'll probably be told that I admitted to being the head of our group. But as long as they keep referring to me as Vasylenko, you'll know that I haven't confessed."

"Fine, I won't mention anything except what I heard you tell them," Vasyl assured me.

In the morning, as newcomers, we were questioned about who we were, where we were from, and how we had landed up in this cell.

"So you're 'politicals'!" a joker in the cell noted when I finished. "We've got another 'political' here," he said and laughed as he placed his meaty paw on the shoulder of an old man.

"And what kind of 'politics' were you involved in?" I asked, going along with the joke.

"I'm not here for political reasons—they're just making fun of me," the old man replied timidly.

"Tell him why you were imprisoned. He's not like us—he seems to be an intelligent fellow, and he can tell you what is or isn't 'political'," the joker mocked.

"Seriously, do tell me what happened to you," I gently urged the old man.

"Well, my wife woke up one morning and told me about a dream she had. In the dream a large rooster was perched on our chimney shouting that Hitler and his regime would disappear and that Stalin would follow. Then he crowed loudly and repeated the same thing. That's all the 'politics' that were involved. Stupid old fool that I am, I went and described that accursed dream to my neighbours, and that's why both my wife and I were imprisoned."

"That's quite an anti-Soviet dream, isn't it?" the joker laughed.

"Well, it's clear that it was just a dream, for if this had really happened then the rooster would already be on trial," another old man commented. Everyone laughed and began to make up their own stories about the rooster.

Major Novikov called me out to begin the investigation into my case at 10am, and after he had completed some biographical details on a form he began to question me. I repeated, word for word, everything I had stated in Rozkopantsi, and after Novikov wrote everything down he read it back to me.

"I'll sign this protocol," I told him.

"Oh, I know that you'll sign this," Novikov replied. "You see what happens when people interfere in something which is none of their business and make a mess of things. That idiot with the medals wanted to play at being an investigator and now he's ruined the whole case. Don't you agree?"

"I don't think that he's ruined anything. On the contrary—look how easy it is to question someone who's already been processed."

"Oh, I can see how easy it is," Novikov said and gave me a meaningful glance. When he finished with me he called in Vasyl, but my partner knew what to say and everything went just as we had planned.

After three days in the detention cell we were put in chains and taken twenty kilometres by sleigh to a station in Myronivka. Several militia officers came to the station and asked our guards who we were.

"The older fellow," the senior guard proudly explained and pointed at me, "is the political instructor of a Ukrainian nationalist division, and the younger one is his aide-de-camp."

"Ah, so you're 'freedom' fighters?" the militia lieutenant sneered.

"Yes, and we're proud of it. But why are you so proud of being the toady that you are?" I asked. The incensed lieutenant bared his teeth and kicked me before the head of our escort grabbed him by the arm and pulled him away.

"Those who are weak in the head always have strong feet," I called out after the lieutenant as he walked away.

# PART IV

# Chapter Fifteen

In Kiev we were taken to the oblast NKVD headquarters at 18 Korolenko Street and were escorted to the office of the deputy head of the oblast NKVD where two colonels, a major and a captain looked us over contemptuously and asked who we were, where we were from, and about the nature of our mission. Then they unsealed a packet and bent over a protocol.

"Well, comrade Vasylenko, we'll burn this protocol right now, before your very eyes," the colonel said and, glancing at Vasyl, suddenly ordered that he be led away.

"We'll release you," the colonel said when Vasyl had left, "if you act intelligently and co-operate with us. You have an excellent opportunity to do more for our Fatherland than all of us put together."

"What do you mean?" I asked.

"We need your help, Comrade Vasylenko," the colonel replied.

"I won't become an Azev![1] Don't insult me—is that clear?"

"Well, if you don't betray your gang then you'll end up betraying your children!" the colonel shouted angrily and immediately ordered that I be taken to the punishment cell.

I spent five days in a tiny box one-and-a-half by one-and-a-half metres square, in pitch darkness, and received only three hundred grams of bread and half a litre of water a day. Only a person who has actually experienced the agony of such confinement can imagine it. When the five days were up I was transferred to a general cell in the basement, where for three days I could walk only by supporting myself against the walls with my hands, for all my strength had left me and I could not stay on my feet. I was proud, however, that I had maintained my dignity, although at this point it was only my *personal* dignity that was at stake, for by now I was just as far removed in my convictions from OUN-style nationalism as I was from communism. But treachery is treachery, no matter who or what is betrayed.

Five days later we were transferred to 33 Korolenko Street, to the ministry of internal affairs, where I was kept in a relatively comfortable cell. Eight square metres in area, the cell had a small window high up near the ceiling, and by pressing against the wall I could even see a small piece of the sky. There was nothing in this cell except for a wooden grating on the asphalt floor which served as my "furniture," and a guard continuously watched me through a peep-hole to make sure that I did not fall asleep.

At 10pm, I was summoned for interrogation. I was escorted by two warders who held me under my arms while a third walked in front of us and loudly snapped his fingers as a signal to clear the corridor so that no one could see us pass. Finally I found myself in a large office. A folder and a pitcher of water were lying on a table in the middle of the room, and the colonel with whom I had spoken earlier was seated behind the table.

"Maybe you've mellowed and we can begin to talk?" the colonel asked.

"You have the protocol of the earlier interrogation," I replied. "I have nothing more to say."

"It's all the worse for you, and by the time you regret your decision it will be too late," the colonel said as he smiled venomously and left the office. I sat on a stool in the middle of the large room all night long, kept dozing off, and several times I fell asleep and keeled over. A warder kept guard over me all this time, and in the morning I was taken to my cell where again I was prevented from sleeping. At 10pm I was taken to the same office where the same colonel sat behind the same table smoking a cigarette. He asked me to sit down on the stool and for a long time he simply dragged on his cigarette and carefully scrutinized me. Then he rose, went up to a large map of the Zhytomyr, Kiev, Vinnytsia, Kamianets-Podilsky and Rivne oblasts, which was hanging on the wall, and beckoned to me.

"Do you want us to believe your testimony?" the colonel asked. "Then look—on this map we've traced the routes taken by your groups on their way east, and here's a notebook in which all their activities have been listed. A file has been started for every one of them, but your group isn't even mentioned."

"We went east not as a group of nationalists, but posed as deserters fleeing from a penal battalion," I told the colonel. "That's why our group wasn't marked on your map."

"So that's it!" the colonel exclaimed. Leaving me near the map he left quickly, and I used this opportunity to examine the map and the routes taken by the different OUN-UPA groups. Two hours later the colonel, who seemed to be very pleased, returned and offered me a cigarette.

"Thanks, but I don't smoke," I said.

"You should be helping us, Danylo Lavrentiiovych," the colonel declared benevolently, "for that would be as much in your own interests as in ours. You ended up in the nationalist camp by accident, for you remain a communist at heart."

"No, I'm not a communist. As a youth I looked to communism for my ideals, but later I became convinced that what I thought were ideals were only a mirage."

"What aspect of communism disturbs you so greatly?" the colonel asked.

"The communists have taken it upon themselves to do everyone 'good' forcibly and I want no part of this, for I believe in a system which would legally guarantee all citizens the right to help themselves. The law should only ensure that people don t help themselves at the expense of others," I replied.

"And did you find what you were looking for among the nationalists?"

"No."

"Then why search for something which may not even exist? Maybe your ideals are simply the fantasy of a dreamer?"

"Maybe. But I'm better off with my own dreams and hopes if I have to settle for a primitive 'reality' which is based on satisfying one's own base appetites."

"You're a difficult man, and you're especially difficult on yourself, your friends and your family," the colonel said and left the room. Once again I was left on the stool until morning: losing consciousness and falling; sitting down again and then falling as soon as I was upright. In the cell it was the same; a warder stood at the door to make sure I stayed awake, and I was prevented from sleeping for five full days. This form of torture, which is just as exhausting as physical violence, is incomprehensible to those who have not experienced it.

On the morning of the sixth day the same colonel, accompanied by a group of officers, came to my cell.

"You didn't want to tell us the truth about yourself," the colonel said, "so now you'll be sent to Rivne, where people who know you better will give us the information we need."

I was led out to a truck, where Vasyl joined me five minutes later, and seven guards (two officers and five soldiers) escorted us all the way to Rivne. We stopped only for one night, in Novohrad-Volynsky, where we stayed in a preliminary detention cell. Here I finally caught up on my sleep, which at this point was more important to me than anything else.

The next day we arrived at the oblast NKVD headquarters in Rivne, where an Armenian NKVD captain checked my documents and looked me over.

"If you behave here as you did in Kiev," he told me, "then we'll take you to your village and we'll hang you there. Understand?"

"Fine—I'd have a chance to see my native village again and bid it farewell," I replied cheerfully, as the captain gave me a dirty look and ground his teeth in anger. After the formal paperwork was over we were taken to the prison.

It was early 1945; the Rivne prison was crammed with people arrested on charges of Ukrainian nationalism, and every day the Military Tribunal[2] sentenced 20–25 prisoners for their alleged participation in the nationalist movement. The cells had no bedding, and everyone slept on the floor. The guards fed us soup which consisted of water with some sort of chaff floating in it, reminding me of the mash which my mother used to prepare for lambs, and often we had no bread for several days on end. The prisoners' bodies began to swell from hunger, but eventually their relatives were allowed to pass on food parcels and my cellmates revived, a spark of life returning to their eyes. No one brought me any parcels but my cellmates sometimes offered me treats from their packages. Later three young men from Korets raion took me into their group, and since we shared everything they received from their relatives I slowly began to regain my strength. Soon my investigation began. The man in charge of my case was a young fellow demobilized from the navy, and he always came to see me with a list of prepared questions. These dealt with various petty details concerning my case, and their purpose was to give it a semblance of authenticity. I was questioned three times, and each time three questions were put to me, but I simply ignored the ridiculous formalities of the investigation and prepared myself for execution. After Vatutin was killed by UPA troops in 1944, large number of prisoners were sentenced to be shot, and at any given time about 300 prisoners who had been sentenced to death were kept in the prison basement.

April arrived and the scent of spring was in the air. At the age of 31 I felt myself to be in the spring of life and started to review mentally its happiest moments. On the morning of 16 April I told my cellmates about a dream in which I imagined that I had entered a large room with a deep hole in the middle. My mother and sister-in-law were sitting in a corner behind a barrier, and carefully avoiding the hole, I made my way toward them. They rose to embrace me, but failed to reach me. Then, remembering even in my sleep that they were dead, I deliberately stepped back from them.

"You're facing a death sentence but it will pass you by," an old man in the cell told me. And at this very moment the cell door opened and I was summoned to appear before the tribunal.

I had devoted all my time to preparing myself for the death sentence, and during the investigation my only concern was that I should maintain my pride and accept death with the dignity of a person who is fighting for the truth. But although I mobilized all my reserves of strength to prevent myself from trembling, when my name was called out and I was told to gather my belongings a shiver of fear ran through my body. This fear, however, gripped me for only a few minutes and by the time I reached the courtyard I had regained my composure.

Vasyl and I were in a group of twenty-one prisoners who were being led away to be tried, and everyone was silent, alone with his own thoughts and hopes. The road to one's trial is always short, and I had had little time to think everything over when the convoy guard told us to halt before the building housing the Military Tribunal. We were led into this small, dingy building two at a time, and spent half an hour in a filthy, smelly side room before the convoy chief called out Vasyl's name and mine. We were taken to a small room where a major and two young women sat behind a table and a secretary sat on the right: this was the Military Tribunal which decided who was to live and who was to die.

After verifying our names and the dates and places of our birth the head of the Tribunal quickly got down to business. First he placed the concrete "proof" of our guilt—a pistol, grenade and large trident—on the table.

"Is this your pistol?" he asked, brandishing it in the air.

"No, it isn't," I replied.

"What do you mean? Wasn't a gun confiscated from you when you were arrested?" he asked angrily.

"My pistol was new—you're showing me a rusty old Browning."

"The sons of bitches swapped them," the head of the Tribunal mumbled to himself when he compared the pistol and its serial number with the description in the protocol. "It's irrelevant whether or not this is the gun which was confiscated" he said, raising his head. "The fact is, you did have a pistol."

"That may be irrelevant to you, but in a real court, trying to establish the truth, it would be of great significance," I replied.

The head of the Tribunal simply glared at me.

"And this grenade also doesn't belong to you?" he asked.

"It's mine."

"And the trident?"

"Why, it must weigh about two kilogrammes. No one ever carried anything of this sort; those tridents were used only to decorate the walls of offices."

The head of the Tribunal again checked the protocol.

"You're right. The trident isn't even mentioned here."

"The protocol mentions a watch and a compass, but your assistants, who wanted to keep them and have no use for a trident, simply made an exchange," I declared contemptuously.

"Defendant Danylo Lavrentiiovych Shumuk, tell the Tribunal when you joined the bandit gang and why," the head of the Tribunal demanded, changing the subject.

"I never joined any such gang. On the contrary; I've fought against banditry of all kinds throughout my life."

"Quiet!" my questioner yelled as he jumped to his feet and brought his fist down on the table, his jowls twitching nervously.

"I was just answering your question."

"Shut up!" The room fell silent. The head of the Tribunal was trembling with anger, as if he was the defendant rather than the judge, and the women who were sitting at the table exchanged frightened glances.

"Defendant Danylo Lavrentiiovych Shumuk, tell the Tribunal when and under what circumstances you joined the UPA."

"I joined an UPA unit in March 1943. At that time the Germans were plundering our land and people and deporting our youth to Germany for hard labour, and I decided that it would be better to join the ranks of the UPA and defend my people than to be deported."

"And why didn't you join the Soviet partisans?"

"First of all, I hadn't met any. In addition, my convictions had changed, and I was no longer a communist. For ten years communist ideals had obsessed me, and I was prepared to face proudly the most horrible of deaths for their sake. To a certain extent I even enjoyed suffering for my convictions in Polish jails. But during the almost two-year Soviet occupation of Western Ukraine you 'de-communized' me, and destroyed my faith in the ideals in which I had placed so much hope and for which I had fought and suffered. Your lies and cruelty repelled me and made me turn toward nationalism."

Throughout my speech the head of the Tribunal, incensed, kept yelling at me to shut up, and when I had finished a deathly silence reigned for several minutes.

"Defendant Danylo Lavrentiiovych Shumuk, did you shoot any Soviet partisans or soldiers when you were in the UPA?" the head of the Tribunal asked.

"No, I never shot anyone; words were my only weapon."

There were no more questions concerning my case and Vasyl Prysiazhny was next. He behaved naturally, for he had no reason to get into any arguments, and was also asked three questions. He answered them calmly, with dignity, and the court began to wind up its proceedings.

"Defendant Shumuk, do you have any request to make of the court in your final word?" the head of the Tribunal asked.

"This is no 'court'; it's a mockery of the very concept, and I refuse to make a final statement."

"Defendant Vasyl Prysiazhny, do you have any request to make of the court in your final word?"

"I ask the court to take my age and inexperience into account." Before the trial I had instructed Vasyl to make this request, since I hoped that he would stay alive and preserve the secret of our case and "trial" until he was freed. (In fact, the opposite happened, as Vasyl later died during an escape attempt.)

After a short break the head of the Tribunal read out our sentences.

"In the name of Soviet law, on the basis of Articles 54–1a and 54–2 this Military Tribunal sentences Danylo Lavrentiiovych Shumuk, born in 1914 in the village of Boremshchyna, Liuboml raion, Volhynia oblast, to the supreme penalty—execution by firing squad. The sentence of this Military Tribunal cannot be appealed. The Military Tribunal has sentenced Vasyl Prysiazhny to twenty years of hard labour, and orders the convoy to keep the prisoners under the strictest supervision!"

At this point the convoy guards noisily raised their rifles and pressed their bayonets into our backs. The parody of justice had been transformed into harsh reality. We were led out into the stench of the waiting room, where everyone began to ask us what had happened. After I had given a brief description of the "trial" the crowd demanded to know why I had not asked for mercy from the Tribunal. I waved off their inquiries.

"Leave me alone. I'm no longer part of your world, so don't try to tell me what I should have done. The norms by which I lived and will die are different from yours, and that's why I behaved the way I did during the trial."

I wanted to be completely alone, and wanted nothing to do with people who were clinging to life so pitifully that they were ready to throw their personal dignity at the feet of those inhuman creatures without the slightest hesitation. I wanted to collect my thoughts, reach some conclusions, and then leave this world aware of my goal in life. I withdrew so much into myself that I didn't even notice that the Tribunal had already processsed the prisoners who had been brought to the court with me. They were all preoccupied with their own sorrow and therefore left me in peace.

Soon afterward the convoy chief opened the door, read out my name, and ordered me to leave the waiting room.

"You three are fully responsible for this prisoner. He has received the death sentence," the convoy chief told his soldiers when I stepped outside. "You must bring him in safe and sound, and today we'll finish him off. Understand?"

"Yes, sir!" the soldiers replied and prodded me with their bayonets. Then the other prisoners were called out and lined up in front of me, and the column set off under strict supervision. No one said a word. Men, women and children were strolling along as usual on the sidewalks, with their own needs, concerns and desires, and from high above us we could hear the mournful cry of cranes. The passers-by, the cries of the crane, and the young buds on the trees together created a harmony. But I was longer part of this harmony. I felt estranged from everything around me, as if one foot was already in the grave and the other foot was pushing me away from this world.

The column was brought to a halt and the warder's key grated in the lock of an iron gate. Once inside I was told to face one corner of the enclosure while a second gate was opened. Then the column was led away to the prison and I was left between the two gates, certain that now I would finally be led away to be shot.

Ten minutes later I was taken to a small cell, two metres by three metres square, where I began to pace from one corner to another. I was upset about the long delay, for now that my fate had been sealed I wanted to leave this world without delay. All night long a warder, never lowering his eyes, carefully watched my every move through a peep-hole. I paced back and forth until dawn, when I heard a key in the lock and the door opened.

"Follow me," a lieutenant ordered sternly, and as I left the cell a warder carrying a pistol brought up the rear.

It was deathly quiet in the prison courtyard when I was taken to the bath-house beyond the wall, and not a soul was in sight. "So they'll kill me in the bath-house," I thought to myself, "and then wash away the blood." To my great surprise, however, the bath-house was full of prisoners who had just been brought in from work. They were being fed here and I also received half a bowl of potato dumplings, which I ate as if nothing at all was wrong. Soon the other prisoners were led out and I was told to undress. "This is it," I thought as I quickly took my clothes off.

"What are you standing around for; go and wash yourself!" the warder ordered. I complied quietly, certain that I would be shot there and then, but upset that the whole affair was being dragged out so unmercifully.

"Come on out," the warder ordered. When I stood in front of the warder he brusquely told me to get dressed, and then the lieutenant ordered me to follow him. When I entered the prison courtyard with the lieutenant the entire prison staff was lined up in two rows, forming a corridor for me from the bath-house to the prison, and it seemed to me that they were all probing me with cold ruthless stares as if to determine whether I was still alive. This time I was not taken upstairs but into the cellar, and I obediently followed the lieutenant into a dark, silent corridor with only a dim red light of some kind blinking in the distance.

All the prison staff silently entered this corridor, which reeked of death, and they stared at me sadistically. I was led through the darkness to a door where I was told to undress, and as I did so my imagination raced ahead of me. It seemed that I could already smell the stench of death which would hit me when the door was opened, and I imagined a damp windowless cell in which a cold, cruel death awaited me when the warder fired into the back of my head.

Finally the warder's key cranked into a padlock on the door and then into two other locks. As the door opened slightly I could see that the cell was illuminated, that it had whitewashed walls, and that there were living people inside. I immediately thought that the warder had opened the wrong cell, and, strangely, was upset by the mistake, for I was afraid that I would lack the strength to maintain my calm, and that my nerves would break. But then I was told to enter the cell, and when I walked in, completely naked, the door closed behind me.

The prisoners in the cell walked up to me and started asking me who I was and where I had come from.

"Leave me alone," I told them. "I've been sentenced to death and have nothing to say to you."

"If you've been sentenced to death then what are you doing here among the living?" a long-limbed prisoner asked derisively.

"Don't get excited," a younger prisoner said sympathetically, "All of us here have been sentenced to death." In the meantime the food hatch in the door had opened and my clothes were pushed through. I dressed myself and then took a good look at the other prisoners, who had been in this cell for a long time.

# Chapter Sixteen

The cell was compact, about thirteen square metres in size, and housed seventeen people. It contained only a latrine bucket, and all the prisoners slept on the floor in their daytime clothes.

"When and where were you arrested, and on what charges?" asked Fedir Bukhalo, one of my cellmates. Mykhailo Humenchuk, who had been sentenced together with Bukhalo, listened to my response, and afterward the two treated me to some white bread and sour cream. All this time Andrianov, the tall Russian who had first approached and mocked me when I was still naked in the doorway, walked confidently around the cell staring at me.

After the evening inspection the prisoners began to prepare themselves for sleep, withdrawing into themselves and lying down silently in their places.

"Hey you!" I heard behind my back. "Listen, you'll be sleeping and eating with these chaps here." I turned around and faced Andrianov.

"Who are you, and what gives you the right to tell me where I should sleep and who I should eat with?" I shouted angrily.

"Do as you're told if you want to live here peacefully," was the reply.

"I spit on you and your orders!" I retorted. The other prisoners watched us as if they were petrified. Suddenly Andrianov stuck out two of his fingers and whipped them up to my eyes, but I stepped back and hit him under the chin with all my strength as the other prisoners held their breath. Andrianov gave a yelp and fell to the ground, unconscious. I filled a pail with water and poured it over his face. He shuddered, rose slowly to his feet, and gave me such a pitiful look that even I felt sorry for him.

"Do you know who I am?" he asked. "I'm a 'repeater.' I've been sentenced three times, saw all the labour camps of Russia, and then was taken from the camps and transferred to Kovpak's detachment, behind German lines. I was with Kovpak until he reached the Carpathian mountains, and here you've dared to raise your hand against me!" he said in an aggrieved tone.

"You're lucky that I didn't know what you just told me," I replied. "Otherwise I would have hit you even harder."

"Well, now we'll be friends," Andrianov said and smiled. "You can lie down right here, beside me."

"I don't need your favours. I'll find my own place."

"Will you sleep with us, Danylo?" Bukhalo asked politely.

"Fine, thanks. Can you tell me why Andrianov was sentenced to death?"

"He says that he killed his commander in Kovpak's partisan detachment."

"And was he in this cell when you came here?"

"Yes. He was already in charge when we arrived. But he didn't bother us, and even tried to gain our favour," Bukhalo explained.

In the middle of the night mysterious noises and footsteps could be heard in the corridor. Everyone in the cell woke up and listened intently as these footsteps, moving from cell to cell, stopped at each door for about ten minutes.

"Someone's been taken out of number 13," my cellmates whispered to each other. Then the footsteps moved closer and closer, filling us with a deathly fear, until finally they stopped before our cell. We heard a key rattle, our food hatch was opened a fraction, and through this thin slit appeared a pair of malevolent eyes and then a mouth.

"The letter 'A'," the mouth ordered. Lowering their heads in terror, the prisoners whose surnames began with an "A" called them out, and in this fashion the mysterious voice went through the entire alphabet. That night, however, no one was taken from our cell. When the food hatch closed my cellmates gave a sigh of relief and became more cheerful.

"Now we'll have another day of peace," someone remarked. But suddenly the footsteps grew louder at the end of the corridor, we heard a scuffle of some kind, and the prisoners again were all ears.

"What you just heard," a prisoner explained, "was the sound of a gag being stuffed into someone's mouth to prevent him from screaming, and now they'll drag him past our cell." At this point all my preparations to meet my death bravely evaporated into thin air, and I began to feel as terrified as everyone else.

In the morning the prison bell rang and the duty officer entered the corridor to carry out the morning inspection.

"Lie face down on the ground!" the warder ordered through the food hatch. The locks rattled and when the door opened the duty officer walked in with a doctor. They stepped over us as if we were logs, counted us, and then asked if we had any requests to make. This procedure was repeated every morning and evening, and was designed to humiliate us.

After lunch the warder brought me a scrap of paper and a pencil and told me to prepare a request for a pardon. I hesitated, but my cellmates insisted that I do as he said, although I had no idea what I should write.

"You're the only person here capable of standing up for himself," Andrianov told me. "I respect people like you, but I advise you, as a friend, put in a strong request for a pardon! Only pleas for mercy will get through here." Andrianov's behaviour surprised me greatly, but he seemed to be quite sincere.

"I refuse to ask for mercy," I thought to myself. "I'll simply call this a 'statement,' and will write down what appears in the protocols of the interrogation." I based my statement to the chairman of the Presidium of the Supreme Soviet on the fact that I had not killed anyone or participated in armed combat, and that I had not occupied any position of leadership. Therefore I asked that the Military Tribunal's decision be reviewed and that my death sentence be repealed.

Andrianov read my statement and looked at me in surprise.

"So you've never killed anyone?" he asked.

"Never," I replied.

"Then where did you learn to fight so well?"

"If someone's asking for it then I can give him a good thrashing, but I would never kill anyone."

"I understand," Andrianov muttered. From this point on he never asked me another question.

I sat down next to Bukhalo and Humenchuk. These two lads, with whom I both slept and ate, had been friendly to me from the first, and told me all about each prisoner in the death cell. Most had behaved quite poorly during the investigation, denouncing everyone left and right, before implicating themselves and receiving the death sentence. Several, however, had been captured after being badly wounded in battle, and they had behaved quite well.

"And were you in an UPA company?" I asked my companions.

"No, we were in Omelko's group," Bukhalo replied.

"What kind of group was this?" I asked.

"It was an SB operational group."

"Where did it operate, and under whose supervision?"

"We were most active in the northern part of Rivne oblast, under Daleky's supervision."

"So you probably know Vereshchaka?"

"Of course."

"Do you by any chance know Mykola, who had been the leader of okruh 'B,' encompassing Zhytomyr oblast and the northern part of Kiev oblast?"

"Do you mean the fellow who escaped from the Zhytomyr prison?" Bukhalo asked.

"That's the one."

Bukhalo gave me a questioning look.

"His case was a great tragedy. Vereshchaka told Omelko, or in effect our group, to arrest Mykola and interrogate him so that he would admit to the assignment he was given when he was released from prison and ordered to make contact with our underground."

"And what did he tell you?"

"Nothing. We roasted his legs up to the knees on a bonfire and he didn't even say a word. He kept swearing his loyalty to the ideals of Ukrainian nationalism until he died, and at the end he said that one day we would find out who Vereshchaka really was."

"So you tortured him to death."

"Yes, but even more horrible tragedies took place," Bukhalo said sadly.

"What could be more horrible than being tortured to death for your ideals by your own comrades?" I asked.

"Do you know what was going on in Enei's okruh, and especially in my native village, Derman?" Bukhalo asked.

"No. I never visited the area."

"In Derman the SB or, to be more accurate, Smok, murdered the finest people in the entire village. He didn't liquidate entire families; he would select one person from each of the most patriotic families devoted to our national cause and liquidate that person after accusing him or her of being an NKVD informer. In this way he pushed our best friends, people who had been the backbone of our liberation movement, into the arms of our enemies. For example, when I was with the SB operational group in the north of Rivne oblast, Smok killed my brother for allegedly collaborating with the NKVD. And there was a system behind this. He crippled precisely those families in which at least one family member occupied an important post in the nationalist movement."

"But what were his motives?" I asked.

"Motives? I'll tell you what 'motives' he had," Bukhalo snorted. "Once a small group of Chekists entered a house on the outskirts of Derman to eat supper and the owners of the house fed them without asking who they were and where they had come from, for such is our custom. But someone quickly informed Smok's mistress, who posed as his wife in the underground, and she in turn told Smok. She insisted on accompanying the SB combat group, which was sent to give the insolent Chekists a scare and Smok, of course, agreed to this. The house was shot up and the Chekists ran away, but in his 'fright' one of the Chekists 'forgot' his map case. Smok's mistress picked the case up and, without even looking at it, took it to her lover. When Smok examined the papers in the map case he found exactly what he was looking for—a list of all the 'NKVD agents' in Derman. This list included the names of members of the best known nationalist families in our village, and even included their denunciations of other villagers. People were arrested, tortured and killed because they were on this list, and Smok's 'evidence' and his ensuing vendetta shocked the entire Kremianets and Rivne regions.

"Some time later Smok was informed that an NVRO conference would be held on some farmstead in Mizoch raion, and he was instructed to ensure that these farmsteads were kept under guard. Smok didn't know, however, that other secret sentries had been posted on all the local roads and trails who were to stop and search everyone who was on the way to Mizoch or Rivne. When these guards detained a girl who was on her way from Derman to Mizoch they found a note giving the place and time of the conference and the password to be used, and took her away for questioning. She immediately told them that Smok's 'wife' had given her the note. Immediately the two women were confronted with one another. Smok's mistress, cynically and without the slightest hesitation, in fact, even with a certain pride, then described her activity as an agent in our underground. Her testimony revealed that she was a trained NKVD agent who had been especially assigned to become Smok's mistress, and that for a long time Smok had been taken in. Recently, however, she had arranged for senior NKVD agents, using the OUN password, to meet with Smok at his quarters near Mizoch. Here they listed all the crimes which Smok had committed at the prompting of his mistress and on behalf of the NKVD, and proposed that he should now continue working for them. When Smok was confronted with his mistress he also confessed. That's the story behind the nightmare which took place in Derman."

"The NKVD manipulates the nationalists so that they destroy one another in the most horrible fashion imaginable," I said. "But it couldn't have done this without a certain precedent to follow. The Chekists simply imitated the SB, using it to destroy the very people it should have been defending, and now everything has become so complicated that no historian will probably ever be able to unravel this mess."

"I've heard that Vereshchaka also worked for the Reds," Bukhalo said.

"So when you roasted Mykola on the bonfire on Vereshchaka's instructions, you were also helping the NKVD," I replied. "The most terrible element in an underground movement is a 'fifth column,' and the Bolsheviks have set up such a fifth column at the very heart of the nationalist movement."

"That's true. Terrible things have been happening recently in Rivne oblast," Bukhalo noted. "Vereshchaka and his bodyguards have been chasing Daleky, claiming that he's an NKVD agent, and vice-versa. Lately a clear boundary has even been established between the two, marking their respective territories."

In the death cell the prisoners tended to associate with those who had similar interests, views and convictions, and all day long we discussed topics of mutual interest. In the evening, however, each prisoner concentrated on his own thoughts, for no one was sure whether he would survive the night.

One young fellow, about eighteen years old, hardly ever spoke to anyone, and regarded everyone and everything as if he was already in another world.

"For what did you receive the death sentence?" I asked him one day.

"For murder," he replied quietly.

"Whom did you kill?"

"No one. I was simply present when a person was killed."

"And was what you have just told me written down in the protocol of the interrogation?"

"No, the investigator wrote down that I was responsible."

"And you signed the protocol?"

"I had to, for they beat me very badly."

"Did you confess to anything else?"

"The authorities noted down that I participated in every single murder which had taken place in Mizoch raion," the young man replied. It was painful to look at him, for I would never have believed that this youth could kill anyone.

And so, listening every night to the ominous footsteps in the narrow, gloomy corridor of the Rivne prison cell, we awaited the Easter season. Knowing the great spiritual significance of this holiday, Bukhalo, Humenchuk and myself decided to celebrate it in the death cell. Everyone except Andrianov, an elderly Pole and myself had received parcels containing eggs and Easter bread, so we had ample tasty food for the occasion. Bukhalo and Humenchuk divided the eggs and Easter bread among the prisoners and the atmosphere was solemn. Someone had to say a few words of hope on this occasion, and since everyone's eyes turned toward me, former militant atheist, I stepped forward:

"My dear brothers, brothers in misfortune and sorrow! In the past, in times of peace, with joy in our hearts, we celebrated this Easter Sunday in our churches and broke the fast in our own homes, at our tables, together with our families. On this day, according to Christian morality, we forgive each other even the greatest offences. Let us also forgive our enemies all the evil they have done and are doing to us. They do this out of ignorance, not knowing that evil gives birth to more evil, and that one day it will turn against them. And may the Lord forgive us the evil which any of us have ever done.

"'Christ has vanquished death through His death, and bestowed life to those in their graves.' His praises are being sung in the churches today. Christ lives on in the hearts of all Christians, and likewise, those who have died in the search and struggle for truth are alive and will live eternally in the hearts of those who are destined to continue along their difficult path. May the Lord help all of you so that next year you will greet Easter Sunday together with your parents, sisters, brothers and children, in joy and happiness. May truth, goodness, happiness and love reign in this world of ours!"

After my speech the prisoners solemnly crossed themselves and said "Christ is risen!" The Pole rose to his feet, kissed me with tears in his eyes, and all the other prisoners began to kiss one another. Even Andrianov loosened up and hugged me, and the warders, who had been listening at the door, became more cheerful and treated us in a civil fashion.

During the Easter season the bearers of death no longer stalked the corridors. But they soon resumed their nocturnal rounds, and eventually it was our cell's turn. When the young man who had been accused of the murders in Mizoch raion called out his name one evening, he was told to gather his belongings and leave the cell, and he bid us a tearful farewell before the door closed quickly behind him. We all held our breath, and could hear the guards mumbling to each other as they quickly pushed a gag into their victim's mouth and dragged him away. We spent the next day in silent mourning. It was a long time before the sad expression on the youthful face faded from my memory.

One beautiful May night, as we were nervously awaiting the arrival of the messengers of death, we heard a flare being fired. The prison yard lit up brightly. There was more pistol, rifle and sub-machine gun fire, as well as more flares. As the shooting grew louder we heard some incomprehensible shouting above the din, thought that an UPA unit was trying to liberate the prison, and when we heard some running in the corridor we all fell to the floor, fearfully expecting a grenade or a burst of fire from a sub-machine gun. The shooting died down, however, and somewhere nearby we heard some women singing, which completely bewildered us. We did not find out what had happened until the morning inspection, when the deputy director of the prison opened our cell.

"Victory, boys!" he told us happily. "Now you'll be allowed to live." And from this moment on the treatment of prisoners improved, even in our death cell.

And so, my heart trembling with fear, I had awaited death for forty-six nights, each of which lasted an eternity. Finally, on the forty-sixth day, the door to our cell opened. The deputy director of the prison read out my name and asked me to step into the corridor. He took me to see the prison director, and although it was daytime my heart was beating frantically as if it would burst through my chest.

"Good day!" I said when I entered the director's office.

"Good day!" he replied and looked at me closely. Then he read a statement from a small sheet of paper: my death sentence had been repealed and commuted to twenty years of hard labour in the eastern regions of the Soviet Union.

"So I'll live," I thought to myself when I was taken upstairs to the cell for prisoners sentenced to hard labour. I even began to think about the future, and painted it in a relatively rosy hue.

As was always the case with new arrivals, when I entered the cell the other prisoners first asked me who I was, where I had come from, and the length of my sentence. Then I was assigned a table and a bunk. Now I had the right to receive parcels, although there was enough to eat in these cells and no one went hungry whether or not (as in my case) he received any parcels from home.

"Do you know anything about the hard-labour camps?" someone asked me.

"No, I don't," I replied.

"You'll be transported to the north, or to the Soviet Far East, where you'll be released in the taiga or tundra to fend for yourself as best you can," an old man sentenced to hard labour said.

"That's not so bad," someone else pointed out. "You can always escape through the taiga."

"Don't kid yourselves," a judge from Ostrih interjected. "This isn't tsarist Russia—you're in different hands now."

"That's true," another old man added. "In old Russia even Lenin, whose brother tried to assassinate the tsar, was deported to the village of Shushenskoe where he was given a house and was free to wander as he chose. He skated on the Enisei, went hunting, and used to meet with his friends there. And we're nothing in comparison with Lenin. No one in our families tried to kill Stalin."

"That's how it was in the days of the 'bloody' tsar," a distinguished-looking man noted angrily. "But Stalin, who is known for his 'humanity,' would never allow for such privileges. You'll work, hungry and cold, until you drop dead." Day after day passed in those endless discussions, but eventually we were transferred to the transit section of the Lukianivka prison in Kiev.

Here I met a group of nationalists sentenced in Bila Tserkva. They were from Kiev, Bila Tserkva and the surrounding area, and were all intellectuals who had been connected with the Banderite or Melnykite factions of the nationalist underground. At first I could only meet them during the exercise period, but later we all found ourselves in a large cell which contained more than a hundred people. Among them was a group of young, healthy men who had been transferred here from the Lutsk prison. Their leader was Kindzeliuk, a tall, strong fellow.

Shortly after our transfer Kindzeliuk waited until we had finished our morning wash and then unexpectedly ordered us to stand up. All the prisoners, and not only the men in his group, immediately jumped to their feet. After gazing at us sternly Kindzeliuk announced that now it was time for the morning prayer, and all the prisoners, crossing themselves when he did, began to pray aloud. The group from Bila Tserkva was quite impressed by Kindzeliuk's behaviour, and from then on he became the centre of attention and was honoured and respected by everyone in the cell.

"It's all well and good to hear and look at you now, but what will remain of this after two-three years of hard labour?" my neighbour mumbled as if he was speaking to himself.

"What do you mean?" I replied angrily. "Everything will remain just as it is."

My neighbour, who was from Eastern Ukraine, gave me a long, searching look.

"No it won't. You don't realize yet whose hands you've fallen into and where you're being taken. The system of camps in this country is such that the prisoners themselves force one another to work for the authorities. And your group will do the same, no matter how much you despise your enemies. You'll even fight among yourselves because someone isn't working as much as your common enemy demands. I've already gone through this system, the most refined system ever devised. It makes mincemeat of everyone, and people like you don't survive in the camps, for honesty and conscience are of no use there. The prisoners who survive are those who are capable of grabbing the last scrap of bread from a neighbour's mouth in order to survive just a single day longer."

"I don't believe you. I've been in both Polish jails and a German camp, and I've seen that a person retains his human qualities even in the most difficult circumstances. You can't convince me otherwise," I stated categorically. My companion was not convinced.

"But the Soviet labour camps are part of a permanent system. In its absence the regime couldn't survive, and that's why it breaks even the strongest people."

# Chapter Seventeen

In the middle of the summer we were transferred to a long echelon of red boxcars and our train left the capital of Ukraine for the far North. Sixty to seventy prisoners had been squeezed into each boxcar, and it was so cramped and stuffy that they often fainted. Every morning the convoy chief opened the boxcar with the help of three or four soldiers and, chasing us from one end to the other, counted us to make sure that no one had escaped. The convoy troops always carried wooden hammers which they used to bang at the walls and floors of the wagons to check whether anyone was preparing to escape. On many occasions, however, the hammers were used on the prisoners and someone's lungs or kidneys were always injured during these beatings. The Vologda convoy troops had a reputation for brutal treatment of prisoners, and were even proud of this.

Finally, our convoy arrived at its destination on the White Sea, thirty kilometres from Arkhangelsk. Our camp was built on a swamp, and we had to walk on raised wooden sidewalks. Nearby was a large camp for German prisoners-of-war. The Germans were relatively well treated: they were allowed to wear military uniforms and were well fed.

There were approximately twelve thousand prisoners in the camp. Our group was imprisoned together with ordinary criminals and "repeaters," who greatly outnumbered us, and soon widespread thieving and fighting broke out. The main instigators belonged to a gang called "The Black Cat," which was headed by a young Jewish fellow from Kiev. He was always dressed in fine clothes, said little and spoke in a calm, quiet voice, but he acted very decisively and all the criminal elements in the camp trembled before him.

The Balts, especially the Estonians, had the most goods and clothes, and were thus the first to be robbed. Kindzeliuk's group, however, occupied one corner of the barracks where it defended itself bravely against attacks from these criminal gangs. I stayed with this group (I knew some people in it from the underground), which also took in the people from Bila Tserkva. We were attacked only when we left the group; I was set upon, for example, by some thieves who wanted my jacket, and when I resisted, received a severe blow on the head.

Later the authorities began to chase us out to work. We were forced at gunpoint into cold water up to our waists, and were ordered to clear it of sea-weeds. The work was arduous and our only food consisted of greyish, sour bread and a kind of nettles. After two young men escaped, however, we were no longer taken out to work.

Two months later we were herded into the hold of a ship which set off through the White Sea. Initially, the going was smooth, but after reaching the Barents Sea, the ship started to pitch and roll and we developed diarrhoea and began to vomit. As we passed through the Kars Gates a violent storm hit us, forcing our ship to drop its anchors. We were tossed about so much that we would simply slide off our bunks onto the floors. Two days later, however, the storm died down and our ship moved out into the Arctic Ocean.

The food situation on the ship was deplorable. The guards gave all the prisoners' food to the criminals, who then confiscated the sugar and everything else worth taking. Like dogs, we would occasionally be thrown a biscuit and sometimes got some watery foul-smelling gruel, but unfortunately we could do nothing about this situation because we were all weak from sea-sickness and diarrhoea. Worst of all, we lacked unity and decisiveness.

Occasionally we were herded up to the deck for inspection, and this was the only time we saw the Arctic Ocean which, with its enormous icebergs, seemed to embody the cruelty of our suffering. This depressing sight only underlined our helplessness, for it was as if the elements had allied themselves with our tormentors, who were no less cold, cruel and merciless than the ocean around us.

After nine days of indescribable suffering, our ship, the *Dixon,* entered the mouth of the Enisei River and continued on its way until it docked at Dudinka, some three hundred kilometres from the ocean. Upon disembarking, we were taken to a nearby labour camp where we were met by the camp administration and trusties[1] (members of the camp crew), who greeted us with cudgels in their hands.

The head of the security section tore the wax seal off each prisoner's dossier, examined it, and then questioned the prisoner about personal details, making sure that all the answers coincided with the information before him. Then he ordered his subordinate, a trusty, to write each prisoner's case number on the back and front of his jacket, on his pants (just above the knees) and on his cap. My case number was D-288, and thenceforth my name ceased to exist for the administration; I was only a number.

"Take D-288 away," the head of the security section shouted.

"D-288, here on the double!" bellowed a plump trusty who had been appointed camp supervisor by the administration. When I approached him he glared at me, paused, and then stuck his cudgel under my nose.

"Take a good whiff—this is the only medicine you'll get for all your whims, illnesses, and malingering. Understand?" he shouted. I did not say a word. He yelled at me even more loudly, but I remained silent.

"Turn around!" he screamed, and when I did he pushed me in the small of my back with his cudgel and I fell face-first to the ground.

"Take him away to Barrack No. 5," the camp supervisor ordered his assistants, whom he had appointed as senior orderlies in the barracks.

"Over here!" a thug with ugly scars on his arms and chest yelled out. "You don't know Russian, is that it?" he asked and hit me in the face. "We'll teach you Russian, you fascist pig. Get a move on." I followed his orders silently and eventually arrived at Barrack No. 5.

"You've seen nothing yet," the orderly told me as he left. "The real fun comes later."

One-hundred-and-twenty hard-labour prisoners were to be quartered in my section of the barracks, which was quite large, and when I arrived thirty men were already there. All were lying quietly on the top bunks, and they raised their heads only when someone new was brought in. The section continued to fill up with new people from our transport, and when everyone had been processed we were given some clay-like bread and soup made of beet leaves. We found this very tasty, quickly emptied our bowls, and were then taken to the bath-house in the women's camp. The women looked us over, smiling and asking us where we came from, and their smiles and kind words immediately revived us. Our eyes lit up, our faces softened, becoming more human, and we began to talk to one another. Although the guards shouted at us, forbade us to talk and threatened us, the women paid no attention to them.

Then the medical commission began its work. The doctors prodded our stomachs, chests and backs as if they were buying cattle at a market, and then assigned us to one of the three categories listed in our medical records. Those in the first category were given very hard work regardless of the weather, and for all practical purposes the second category was equivalent to the first. Conditions were better only for those in the third category, for they were given lighter work and only went out when the temperature was above minus thirty-three degrees. (In the Arctic regions, the temperature often remained at minus 40 degrees for two or three weeks in the winter, and at these times those in the third category stayed in the barracks). By this time my bones were covered by nothing more than a thin layer of skin, so without the least hesitation I was placed in the third category and was assigned to the rehabilitation ward to recuperate.

The camp administration and representatives of the Norilsk mines and quarries were waiting alongside the medical commission, and immediately selected the prisoners to work as free labour in their enterprises. Here a human being counted for nothing; only his muscles and capacity for work were important, and those, like me, who were suffering from malnutrition were regarded as useless rubbish.

Evening finally came, and after roll-call in the barracks and the sounding of a bell to mark the end of the working day, everyone lay down on the bare bunks to rest. It took me a long time to fall asleep, for all sorts of thoughts crowded into my tired head. I could not help being bitter when I thought that it was communism and the Communist Party, which I had idolized and for which I had once fought and suffered, that had given birth to this system of boundless human suffering in which people senselessly destroyed one another.

The next morning, after breakfast, I was told to gather my belongings and go to the central medical office, where I was assigned to a rehabilitation ward. Here I was given some bedding and somewhat better food, and after a few days I was told to report for work to the yeast kitchen (in the Arctic regions prisoners were given a daily ration of 100 grams of boiled yeast to prevent scurvy).

The fellow in charge of the yeast kitchen was a non-political prisoner, but he was very good to me and each day he brought me something special from the kitchen. The month passed quickly. When the medical commission came to examine us, I remained in the third category but was transferred from the rehabilitation ward to a third-category work brigade. However, there was little work for us in Dudinka. Occasionally we were taken to the port to unload ships, but most often we were made to carry thirty-three-kilogramme cement blocks three hundred metres from one spot to another. This senseless work had been devised to torment us, and was well beyond the strength of those suffering from malnutrition.

Shortly afterward, I was transferred to Kaierkan, where three large coal mines were being opened and a new camp was being established. Labour was so scarce here that even third-category prisoners were put to work, and conditions were horrible. The barracks were so cold that ice formed on the walls, we received no bedding, and there was no running water. We would melt snow in our mess tins, but the resulting water only sufficed to spread the coal dust all over our faces. We were taken to the bath-house, which was outside the camp zone, once every ten days, and since the water here was also produced by melting snow we only received a small basin of water and thirty grams of greasy soup smeared on our shoulders. This resulted in our getting coal dust all over our bodies, and since we had a total of fifteen minutes to undress, "wash" and dress again we looked worse upon leaving the bath-house than when we had entered.

After two months I had lost so much strength that I could not even lift my feet to cross the railway tracks. My legs refused to carry me, and I had to be supported when I was returning from work. Those of us in this condition—and there were several—were called "goners," and the number of "goners" grew every day. I became totally indifferent to everything, and remembered only that in no circumstances would I act against my conscience and do anything I would be ashamed of. I kept this foremost in my mind even during the most difficult moments of my life.

When the medical commission reviewed our cases I was again assigned to the rehabilitation ward. This time I remained in the ward for two whole months before being transferred directly to Dudinka, where the prisoners were engaged in construction work. The work was difficult but it was easier than working in the mines, and living conditions were much better than in Kaierkan.

In the spring of 1946 we were transferred to the BOF camp² near Norilsk, about 120 kilometres from Dudinka and twenty-two kilometres from Kaierkan. This camp was located on the slope of a hill on which a dressing mill, the largest in Europe, was to be built to concentrate non-ferrous metals and especially copper, for there were large reserves of this metal in the Norilsk area. Our job was to dig into the hill, three hundred metres above our camp, using pickaxes and wheelbarrows, and to create a vertical face near the BOF camp. This was difficult work; we spent twelve hours a day, without a day off, hacking away at the frozen earth and carrying it a hundred metres or more in wheelbarrows. At times thick clouds, which smelt like a putrid swamp, would envelop us and occasionally clouds surrounded the lower part of the hill and created the impression that we were cut off from the earth below.

At the BOF camp the brigade leaders were no longer ordinary trusties but rather men who had served the Germans as auxiliary police commanders. These brigade leaders were like house dogs who served their masters no matter who they were and where they came from. When they served the fascists they beat up communists and now, serving the communists, they beat and tormented the prisoners whose work they were exploiting.

The leader of our brigade was Shostak, the former chief of the auxiliary police in Kharkiv, an obese and exceptionally strong ruffian. He used a crowbar to beat and often cripple the prisoners who worked under his command, for the camp administration gave people like him complete freedom to maltreat us. In the kitchen every brigade leader was fed to bursting, at the expense of the food allotment for his brigade, and the administration called this privilege the "gullet." "You have access to the 'gullet,' so bark, beat the prisoners, whatever, but make sure that you fulfill the plan," the camp administration would tell the brigade leaders.

In the spring of 1947 we were transferred, in groups of forty, to Camp No. 25, which was only five kilometres as the crow flies from the BOF camp. Our first encounter with this new camp was grim. Three cart-loads of dead bodies had been placed near the watch-tower of the camp, and we watched a sentry who emerged from the tower with a crowbar and climbed onto one of the carts. After he had examined the corpses, checking the tags tied to their feet, he took a crowbar and calmly smashed the skulls and chests of every single corpse.

"That's your only escape route to freedom," he said when he climbed down off the cart and came up to us. "Remember—there's no other way out. Understand?" Lowering our heads, we remained silent.

"I'm asking you whether you understand what I just said!" the sentry shouted. But again no one raised his head even to glance at this creature. In the meantime the camp duty officer arrived accompanied by two guards, took our dossiers from the convoy chief, and began to call out our names. He cross-checked the information in the dossiers, asking who had sentenced us, when and for how long, and after being searched we were released into the camp.

The next day we were split up into brigades and led out to work, and once again we used pickaxes and wheelbarrows to prepare the same kind of vertical face, although this time it was near a brick factory. Our brigade leader was Meleshko, from Korsun, who was also a strong, well-fed former auxiliary police chief. Although he shouted more and beat the prisoners less than Shostak, I arrived in Camp No. 25 suffering from third-degree malnutrition, and had no strength left for the difficult work assigned to us. Ten days after our arrival, when I was taken to the bath-house, I lost consciousness and fell. I was taken to the central medical office and from there to the hospital.

"What happened?" I asked the doctor.

"Your temperature has dropped and you almost died," he replied.

All the people in our ward were suffering from third-degree malnutrition, and food was the sole topic of conversation here.

"Today the cook was a good lad. When he brought the ladle out of the pot I saw a whole fish head in it. There was some fat on the fish head, and I had a wonderful meal," a Russian prisoner began.

"He's a fine chap," a Belorussian patient added. "He gave me a whole scoop of potatoes."

"He's a decent sort in general," an Uzbek added. "Not like the fellow with the pock-marks."

"Well, lads, who took the soap from the toilet?" a medical orderly asked as he walked into our ward.

"There are no Estonians or other Balts here, so there's no one here who would gobble up the soap," the Russian patient answered.

"What stupid people those Estonians are," the Belorussian commented. "When they work, one does the work of ten, but when they end up in the hospital they keep stuffing soap down their gullets until they croak."

"The Estonians use soap to cut short the suffering and humiliation to which they're subjected," the Uzbek said, "whereas the Russians and Belorussians chop their fingers off and become cripples for life."

"And what about the Ukes [*khokhly*]?"[3] the Russian asked.

"Well, one day a very polite, quiet Uke in our brigade climbed out of the pit and said that he refused to go back in. When the brigade leader came up to him and slapped him the Uke covered his face with his hands, walked away, and the brigade leader sat down by the pit to have a smoke. Then the Uke grabbed a pickaxe, quietly crept up behind the brigade leader and hit him so hard that he plunged into the pit and was dead when they pulled him out. That's what the Ukes do."

"That wasn't a Uke, that was a Westerner, a Banderite," the Russian noted.

"'Westerner,' 'Banderite'—that's not a nationality, is it?" the Uzbek asked.

"The devil knows who they are," the Russian replied. "But they're not Ukes, for the Ukes live in Poltava oblast."

I was in the hospital for a whole month, and every day I listened patiently to conversations like these. In the brigade the prisoners were always exhausted and hungry and therefore kept quiet, but after resting for a while in the hospital they immediately started chattering.

# Chapter Eighteen

When I left the hospital I returned to Meleshko's brigade and the same old routine began. There were more than four thousand hard-labour prisoners in Camp No. 25, and approximately 70 per cent were young men from Western Ukraine, most of whom had been soldiers, NCOs and officers in the UPA. It puzzled me that at one time they had fought, guns in hand, and sometimes defeated an enemy who was a thousand times stronger, yet now people like Meleshko, who had once served the Gestapo and were now working for the Chekists, would beat and abuse them without fear of retribution. I wondered what had happened to their courage and fearlessness, and where the trusties, who served anyone who fed them, drew their strength from.

I was determined to get to the root of this problem. Since I had been active in politics, and had considerable experience in organizational matters, I felt that I should be responsible for restoring the prisoners' physical and moral well-being. Therefore I began to observe the behaviour of the prisoners, to learn about their past, and to study their personalities, for I had to ascertain which of them would have the moral and physical strength to survive his predicament and help his friends to do the same.

First, I needed a nucleus of prisoners who would plan and direct the work of our self-help organization. Then, after careful consideration, and making use of our observations and insights, we could gradually approach former rank-and-file members of the UPA. I had known Mykhailo Diachyshyn quite well for a number of years, so I began to discuss my concept with him. He responded favourably, but lacked the intellectual depth to be included in the inner circle of the organization.

In the summer, however, Tarashchansky—a friend of mine from the Kiev transit prison—was transferred to our camp from Kaierkan. He was ten years older than I, had a higher education, and had been sentenced for belonging to the OUN. Tarashchansky's qualifications were suitable for my project, but he thought constantly of escaping from the camp and before discussing my plans with him I had to discourage his unrealistic hopes. In addition I had some preliminary discussions with a former student, seven years younger than I, who had been a member of an oblast OUN provid. He was very intelligent, but had less experience than Tarashchansky in dealing with people.*

After suitable preparations had been made, I introduced Tarashchansky to the student and we organized a meeting to discuss a detailed plan of action. This was held in Tarashchansky's cabin (because of his job in the camp he had separate quarters) and after a brief informal discussion, I gave the main presentation.

"Close to fourteen thousand prisoners sentenced to hard labour were brought to this camp. After only three years approximately eight thousand remain, many of whom have been partly or completely crippled; the other six thousand, broken by the cold, hunger, harsh work and constant brutality, are no longer with us. None of their relatives will ever know where their bodies are buried; no one will weep over their graves and pray for them. Every day the corpses of six or seven of our brothers are buried somewhere near Shmidt mountain, and the same end awaits all of us. No one will help us unless we help ourselves, and it's our duty to do this. First, we have to locate the most reliable Ukrainians in the camp and gather as much information as possible about their activities before they were arrested, their behaviour during the investigation into their cases and their trials, and finally their behaviour in the camps. If this information confirms their reliability then we should carefully prepare them for inclusion in our self-help organization, which will encompass all aspects of life in the camp and respond effectively to every single act of the authorities that aims at

---

*For reasons which I am sure the reader will understand, I have neither used the real names of these two people nor given any details about their background. (Author's note)

destroying us in body or spirit. But above all we have to revive the inner spiritual strength of the men we select and make them more aware of their personal and national dignity. Then we can begin to discuss a further plan of action with them.

"It's important for us to organize these discussions in such a fashion that they seem to arise spontaneously, and the person we're speaking with has to be encouraged to think creatively. Our job is simply to ensure that the original direction and purpose of the discussion is maintained, for we should never impose our ideas on people who can think for themselves. In fact, it's essential that they reach the correct conclusions on their own, for this is the only way to train people capable of thinking for themselves. These people will form the backbone of our organization, for they'll have the authority and capacity to lead those who require some sort of guidance.

"Both the communist and nationalist underground organizations in prewar Poland underestimated the importance of choosing the right people in their organizations. Ours will be a modest organization, for its goal is simply to defend itself against the encroachments of the MVD[1] and its lackeys. Nonetheless, it must be superior to all other forms of organization. The members of each cell must like and respect their superior, and consider him their closest friend in all situations. And the superior, in turn, must like and respect his subordinates as his best friends. Every person in our organization should create an organizational cell of his own, but before anyone is recruited into a cell we should use our own channels to determine whether the conditions for recruitment have been met.* Three to five people can be included in each cell, but they should not know of each other's involvement in the organization, each individual person will know only the identity of his superior.

"Everyone included in our self-help organization has to behave in a correct, civilized fashion, and must be sensitive to the suffering of others. We must find the courage to defend ourselves physically every time the administration acts in an arbitrary fashion, and especially in all cases where the trusties are involved. We should respond to their crude indignities with subtle but effective slights of our own, and when they use force we'll respond with an even

---

*Those in the inner circle of the organization had the right to veto the recruitment of a new member. (Author's note)

greater show of strength. We must stop their acts of brutality, for we have an obligation to ourselves, our fellow Ukrainians, and everything that is sacred to do so. We can attain our goal if we put all our energy into our efforts. Never again should we tolerate a single blow or insult directed at us or at anyone in our presence.

"We should work conscientiously, for that will speak well of us. But we should refuse to do work which is beyond our strength or to work in unsuitable conditions, and we must do everything we can to help those who are punished for defending themselves in accordance with our instructions. Our people in the kitchen and hospital can give them some material help, and the rest of us should give them our moral and physical support. If a brigade leader strikes one of the prisoners and the whole brigade immediately attacks him, gives him a good beating and stuffs him underneath the bunks, then we'll have won a victory. This, in my opinion, should be the general plan of action for our self-help organization, and once it's been discussed in detail we can proceed with the more detailed, practical aspects of this plan."

The student was not very enthusiastic about my presentation, for he wanted more dramatic action. But after I had convinced him that he was being unrealistic, and allowed him to make some minor suggestions, he became more amenable. Tarashchansky approved, but had doubts about the practical implementation of the plan.

We began cautiously, for we knew how the MVD worked, and knew that if we were discovered, it would try to prove that our modest self-help and self-defence organization was in fact an armed force which was aiming to seize power. Once we had discussed the details of the plan each one of us took on certain responsibilities. I, for example, prepared a handwritten circular summarizing my presentation, and circulated it among the twenty or so prisoners who were already aware of our project. The circular had the desired effect: the prisoners' spirits revived and they gained more self-confidence.

In the autumn we were divided into two groups of "black" hard-labour prisoners and ordinary hard-labour prisoners. The "black" group consisted primarily of nationalists—Ukrainians, Lithuanians, Latvians and Estonians—Vlasovites,[2] and members of the auxiliary police under German occupation who had killed a large number of people. Our camp was renamed the "Black"

Hard-Labour Camp No. 3, and most of the criminals were transferred to the more privileged BOF camp. These changes, however, did not deter us; on the contrary, they even helped us to broaden the scope of our activity, although we remained "underground."

Late in the fall the last shipment of prisoners assigned to the "black" camp arrived from the BOF camp. Among them was my first OUN superior, Fedir (this was his first pseudonym in the OUN), an intelligent man who I felt would have considerable potential. Although he had few organizational skills, Fedir had a journalistic flair which would have been useful to us. We discovered, however, that he had become timid and distrustful, and when he first saw me he appeared shaken and frightened. But eventually he calmed down and began to talk to me quite freely.

One day I explained the situation in the camp to Fedir and told him about the organizational work I had begun. A soon as he heard the word "organization" he gave a start.

"Who gave you the right to do this?" he asked.

"Why, I felt that I was simply doing my duty," I replied.

"I don't want to know anything about this organization of yours."

"That's up to you. But we'll consider you a coward." At this point Fedir got up, left without saying another word, and later I told Tarashchansky and the student about my conversation with him.

"Well, if he doesn't want to get involved we can do without him. We'll carry on the best we can," Tarashchansky declared.

"As soon as I saw him I knew that he was going to be difficult," the student added.

In the meantime we quietly continued our work. New people were brought into our organization only after they had been thoroughly screened, after the person recruiting them into his cell had vouched for them, and after we three had given our unanimous assent. In addition to issuing hand-written circulars, we also wrote pamphlets of a purely educational nature. This literature was passed on from one organizational cell and barrack to another in a prearranged pattern so that we could always keep an eye on it and maintain the conspiratorial nature of our work. The prisoners in our organization, however, were all very conscientious, so there were few problems. All the circulated material was read promptly and always returned on schedule.

The members of our organization were obliged to oppose actively even the most insignificant abuses of the administration's brigade leaders, work assigners and "cultural activists." Not only did they defend other members of the organization, but also promptly and effectively came to the aid of anyone else who had been wronged. The moment a gang-boss or any other lackey of the administration struck a worker, for example, the entire brigade was ordered to beat him up.

Although it was no easy task to rouse prisoners who were physically exhausted, frightened and demoralized, the persistent activity of the inner circle of our organization helped to revive their personal dignity and a desire to defend it.

# Chapter Nineteen

By the end of 1949 approximately fifty of the most capable Ukrainians in the camp were involved in the self-help organization, but there were no great changes in the rhythm of camp life. We needed some dramatic event or "miracle" to occur to convince those who had lost all hope (even if these "miracles" are the work of people who simply have faith in their own abilities). However, the camp administration or, to be more precise, its security office eventually helped us to resolve this problem.

In 1951 I was engaged in fairly light work in the camp's cement factory. Two former students, both of whom had been active in the nationalist movement during the war, also worked in our brigade; one of them, Panchuk, as a stoker, and the other, Utrisko, as a metal worker. I spent a great deal of time talking with them, since they were the most intelligent people in the brigade, but I never revealed myself or the activities or our organization to them. They were simply unsuitable for our work: Panchuk loved to boast, often making a mountain out of a mole-hill, and Utrisko was concealing some dark secret of his past.

Early in the fall of 1951 approximately ten more prisoners joined us after being transferred from a hard-labour camp in Central Asia, one of whom, Khvalynsky, began to visit Panchuk frequently.

"This young fellow who arrived with the latest prisoner transport used to live only four kilometres away from me, and was my orderly in an UPA detachment," Panchuk told me in an enthusiastic but secretive manner. "He informed me that there was an underground Ukrainian nationalist organization in his camp in Central Asia, and when he left the camp it gave him a password so that he could make contact with this organization, and receive instructions about what to do in our camp."

"And you believe him?"

"Of course. He's a good lad; I knew him quite well before I was captured."

"It seems to me that this could be a crude trick intended to trap naive dreamers," I told Panchuk, "for it's ridiculous to talk of setting up a nationalist organization in our camp. But keep in touch with Khvalynsky. Try to tell him as little as possible about our camp, but question him thoroughly about the camp he came from and about the organization he started to describe. Find out more about its actual activities and its aims."

This move, obviously engineered by the camp's security office, showed that the latter knew of our activities, and was trying to infiltrate our organization to encourage the preparation of a major "uprising" which would expose us.

Some time later Panchuk again approached me.

"I spoke to Khvalynsky again," he said, "and he told me that their organization is involved mainly in military preparations, its primary aim being to disarm the division and escape from the camp. Then it would be clear what has to be done next."

"If someone actually did come up with this idea, even with the best of intentions," I noted, "it would serve only the Chekists. In this case, however, I'm sure that we're dealing not with a small group of naive romantics but the organs of the MVD, which are trying to set up a similar organization in our camp so that they can then expose it. Khvalynsky is setting a trap, and anyone touching this trap is already in the hands of the MVD, which will do anything it wants with its victims."

I told Tarashchansky and the student about my conversation with Panchuk, and they agreed with my conclusions. This game, which had been conceived on quite a large scale, both alarmed and amused us. Khvalynsky managed to find himself a job in the cloak-room of the brick factory, and we made sure that he was closely watched both at work and in the barracks. Several prisoners, none of whom knew one another, followed his every move.

One day our informers reported that Khvalynsky had met with the filing clerk of the factory, a free employee[1] who had been awaiting Khvalynsky in his cabin. The next day Panchuk again approached me.

"I've just seen Khvalynsky," he said, "and he told me that his organization has already made contact with him through the filing clerk at the brick factory. One of the bookkeepers in the construction office is acting as a backup liaison person."

"This means that the MVD 'machine' has decided to press ahead with its plans," I thought to myself. The trap had been set rather clumsily, but it was possible that a better plan was in the offing.

Suddenly I was transferred to another brigade in the brick factory, where I was engaged in heavy physical labour. This transfer coincided with the murder of Kucherevsky by Holovko, Borysenko, Kipa and Taras. The latter three persons (who were brigade leaders) and Kucherevsky, their column chief, worked for the MVD, but had a disagreement over some women with whom everyone in the cement factory had been flirting. Kucherevsky had beaten them as a result and had offended their "Cossack pride" (they were from the Kuban area).

The arrival in our camp of the security chief of the Gorlag[2] administration, Major Koloskov, was seemingly connected with this murder. However, an investigation was not necessary because the murderers themselves had brought their blood-stained knives to the main office and informed the officer on duty that they had killed Kucherevsky. The real reason for Koloskov's visit soon became clear. Having realized that his plot to use Khvalynsky had failed, he called for Panchuk.

"What kind of organization were you discussing with Khvalynsky?" he asked him bluntly. "You might as well tell me the truth, because I know everything already and am merely verifying your honesty. Did you know that the punishment for setting up an anti-Soviet organization in the camp is the death sentence? You're still young, Mykola," Koloskov added after a long, calculated pause, "and you have a long life ahead of you. It's your choice: life or death, but you can only avoid a trial and certain death if you co-operate with us. If you agree to my proposal then we'll set a time and a place for our next meeting; if not, then we'll bring charges against you. Understand?"

Panchuk came to me immediately after his meeting with Major Koloskov and repeated, word for word, everything that he had been told.

"And what did you tell him, Mykola?" I asked.

"I agreed to meet with him, for I had no other choice. In my opinion there's nothing wrong with this, for I won't tell them anything. I'm smart enough to give them a runaround."

"All the same, you've fallen into their trap and it's impossible to predict what will happen now. I ask only one thing of you: please inform me of your assignments."

Later I explained to the inner circle of our self-help organization that if I had forbidden Panchuk to meet with representatives of the MVD he would have met with them secretly, and I would have been left in the dark. Therefore I had maintained a neutral attitude, and had simply asked him to inform me about his assignments, for this information was of great value to us.

After Panchuk's third meeting with representatives of the MVD, he told me his instructions:

1.  To discover who in our camp had been sentenced as rank-and-file UPA members but were in fact UPA commanders or high-ranking members of the OUN;

2.  To determine who, although sentenced for their nationalist activities, had actually been serving as spies for foreign intelligence services;

3.  To list his colleagues in the nationalist underground who were still free, and indicate where they were working. To write to them, pretending that he was still in the underground, and pass on any correspondence he might receive to the MVD.

"All right, Mykola, but where is Khvalynsky now?" I asked.

"He's working in the mess hall."

"And has he, as the main organizer, been called out yet by Koloskov?"

"No."

I simply could not understand why the authorities were being so crude in their approach, and thought that perhaps they wanted us to kill Khvalynsky so that we could be accused of murder.

"I have one more request, Mykola. Go and talk with Khvalynsky, as a commander would with his orderly, and insist that he tell you when, where, and in' what circumstances he was recruited as an MVD agent."

"Okay," he replied reluctantly, lowering his head. After this conversation he stopped meeting with me, and soon we issued a circular stating that no self-respecting Ukrainian should associate with Khvalynsky and Panchuk, or even exchange greetings with them. This was a severe punishment, but no one could be penalized for participating in this boycott. Subsequently, Panchuk started to meet with representatives of the MVD on a regular basis. He came to me once more, however, to tell me that he had been instructed to find out who my closest friends and most frequent visitors were. Several other informers confirmed that I was being kept under surveillance.

In 1951 the authorities began to pay us for our work at zek³ rates, which were set at half those of free workers. As a result we set up a special fund for our self-help organization, and by means of our circulars instructed our members to set aside a certain portion of their wages for the organization. Each person gave what he wanted, and thus we could determine how committed an individual was to our cause. Five hundred to 700 rubles came in every month on a purely voluntary basis, and this money was used to help those prisoners who were sick, in penal brigades, or in solitary confinement.

Under the influence of our circulars the workers in the brigades began to demand a just distribution of work and wages. In their opinion everyone had to take turns working in the pits, and this should apply to all the other difficult jobs as well. The brigade leaders, of course, ignored these demands, so the workers, who had always obediently hacked away at the permafrost or solid rock in the depths of the pits, began refusing to go to work. This insubordination on the part of these "slaves" enraged the brigade leaders, and when the plan for pouring concrete and laying bricks was disrupted the administration also became alarmed and started to consult with the brigade leaders, column chiefs, work-assigners and "cultural activists." Soon the brigade leaders began to treat us more harshly. Some of the prisoners who refused to work were imprisoned, others were beaten up, and soon the solitary confinement cells and penal brigades were full. The "troublemakers," however, still refused to work.

One of the most brutal gang-bosses, Baranchyk, started to beat some of the troublemakers in his brigade, a method he had employed with regularity in the past. This time, however, he received a severe beating. The members of the truck repair brigade also began to demand a more equitable distribution of work and wages from their brigade leader, Zarubaev, a tall, strong ruffian who responded by laying into them with his large, meaty fists. This, however, no longer frightened his workers, who knocked him to the ground and, after giving him a beating, stuffed him underneath a bunk.

After these incidents, which set a precedent for other groups of prisoners, the administration and its lackeys became truly alarmed and the security office began to search for ringleaders. I was removed from my job in a laboratory, Fedir Sydorchuk lost his job in the controller's office, Stepan Movchuk was chased out of the KIP section[4] and, finally, Roman lost his job as laboratory brigade leader. We were all assigned to a penal brigade, to load trucks in a quarry, but we refused to work. For more than two months we went out to the quarry every day but did absolutely nothing, and another ten people who refused to work in the penal brigade soon joined us.

The brigade leaders became even more anxious. Eventually one had the idea of preparing a submission to the camp administration alleging that the Ukrainians were preparing to slaughter all the Russians, Poles and other national groups in the camp. The brigade leaders appended a list of names of those who, according to their story, were to carry out this bloody "massacre," and this list of forty Ukrainians included all the prisoners in the penal brigade. Close to thirty brigade leaders, column chiefs, work-assigners and "cultural activists" signed this despicable submission. The camp administration "satisfied" their request, and all those on the list were imprisoned in the isolator.

The last prisoner to join us there was the camp director's orderly. According to the brigade leaders, his role in our "plot" had been to summon all the Russians, Poles and others whom we wanted to eliminate, to see the camp director. Our "executioners" were allegedly waiting for these victims in an annex to the main office, in order to kill them with axes as they went by.

While he was being frisked the orderly had swallowed a piece of paper and the warders had immediately thrown themselves at him, knocking him off his feet and breaking two of his teeth. The paper, however, was already in his stomach, and the administration concluded that it must have contained the list of people to be slaughtered. Soon this orderly, holding the two broken teeth in his hand, was placed in our cell.

"What happened to you?" I asked.

"At one point I lived for a while with a secretary, a free worker who had previously worked in our office, and recently she passed a letter on to me through a friend of hers. The bastards pulled this letter out of one of my pockets, but I snatched it back and swallowed it, for it would have been a shame if the woman had suffered because of me," the orderly said, holding his two teeth and wiping blood from his face.

A few days later the investigators arrived and began to summon us for questioning. None of us took this seriously; we made fun of the investigator and his questions, and in our cell we occupied ourselves by telling jokes and discussing various novels we had read. It was very important for us to keep up our spirits in such situations.

Soon the camp administration began to release us from the isolator, a few at a time. By the end of November 1952, only five of us were still detained. We had spent two full months in the isolator, but our self-help organization had passed food parcels to us every day through sympathetic medical personnel.

Upon my release from the isolator, I was again assigned to the quarry, but I went immediately to see the production chief.

"Either assign me to construction work in Melnyk's night brigade," I told him, "or send me back to the isolator for another two months, before I transfer my belongings to the barracks." At this categorical statement the production chief quickly raised his eyes and stared at me.

"What the hell," he exclaimed finally, "I'll put you wherever you want, as long as we have some peace and quiet." I didn't really work in Melnyk's brigade either, for after getting the approval of the brigades' craftsman I worked at night as a watchman in recently completed buildings and spent my time reading books and newspapers.

In 1952 we hard-labour prisoners had taken the first measures to defend our dignity, and were now more confident of our strength and capabilities. After the failure of the move against us, those who had signed the request to put us away began to adopt a conciliatory attitude toward us. But the administration and its "toadies" also held a number of meetings in a desperate search for some means to crush our movement.

A brigade leader named Sabosiak spoke up at one such meeting.

"We won't be able to take care of the Ukrainian nationalists until they stop treating the isolator as a rest stop. They should fear the isolator, and be forced to work so hard that they sweat blood. Put me in charge of the isolator, give me Papandopolo as an assistant, and I'll put everything in order."

Sabosiak's bold speech greatly pleased the administration, and it immediately gave these two criminals the job of crushing our resistance. Both Sabosiak, a tall, strong Pole from the Ternopil area and Papandopolo, a criminal of Greek background, had been sentenced for murder. It was clear that Sabosiak was the administration's last card, and everyone realized that a final showdown was near.

Sabosiak went about his task in a confident, self-assured manner, and upon being appointed gang-boss of the isolator, he began to abuse brutally all those who dared, even for a minute, to straighten their backs while loading rock from the quarry into wagons. At this point Stepan Shevchuk was placed in the isolator, but continued to refuse to work, since there had been no grounds for removing him from his position as a survey instruments technician. Sabosiak then summoned Shevchuk into the guard hut and, together with Papandopolo and the notorious Baranchyk, proceeded to beat him up. They then summoned all the other recalcitrant prisoners and beat them also. After this incident Captain Tarakhov, the camp director, told the brigade leaders that they should follow Sabosiak's example, and a mood of exhilaration quickly spread among them. They raised their heads and began to threaten the more rebellious members of their brigades, but this situation was short-lived.

One day Stepan Shevchuk and another prisoner, Mykhailo, who had also been beaten up in the hut, armed themselves with a strong steel drill, and just before dinner they entered the workers' mess hall, where the cooks gave them some soup. They placed the drill behind a stove, took off their jackets and sat down to eat. Then Sabosiak ran into the hall and, cursing, started to pummel

Mykhailo. In a flash Shevchuk jumped up from the table, grabbed the drill and brought it down on Sabosiak's head. After a beating, Sabosiak crawled to the forbidden zone and dragged himself to the watch tower.

On the same day, in a different work unit, the gang-boss of a penal brigade struck Roman Zahorulko, who immediately responded by knocking the gang-boss off his feet.

The administration panicked after these two incidents. Sabosiak, Papandopolo and four of their colleagues went to the camp director, asking that they be locked up in the isolator, and afterward all the brigade leaders, work assigners and column chiefs began to gather their belongings and flee to the isolator. In fact, we eventually had to go and persuade these "brave lads" that no harm would come to them if they behaved in a humane fashion.

As a result this entire gang, which for seven years had collaborated with the administration in squeezing the last juices out of us, began to behave much more charitably, assigning us to the work of our choice and treating all the workers with much greater respect. It was clear that the only authority for those who used force was even greater force. Thus we had to do everything possible to build up our strength, while tempering its usage with reason.

A group of Vlasovite prisoners often met to discuss how they could escape from the camp if a war broke out, and had even prepared an operational plan for such an occasion. One of our informers, who was a member of this clandestine group, kept us fully informed of its activities, and recounted one of the conversations he had overheard.

"We have the resources to prepare a good escape plan," one of the Vlasovites had said, "but we lack the fighting strength to carry it out, for 80 per cent of the prisoners are Banderites and we have no contacts with them."

"That's true. They're an ignorant lot, and there's no one we can talk to among them," a second Vlasovite added.

"They may be ignorant, but they've raised their heads and have forced everyone to take them seriously," a third noted. "And they're powerful precisely because, even though someone must be telling them what to do, no one knows who it is."

"So they want us to spill our blood and clear a path for them with our corpses," I thought to myself when I heard about this conversation. Still, it was amusing to hear how they underestimated us.

A second clandestine group in our camp was headed by Bobkov, a former major who spent two years preparing it for an escape attempt before his plan was discovered. We knew about this group, and did all we could to dissuade the prisoners from getting involved in its project.

We were informed about almost all the camp happenings, and were always wary of these groups and their activities. It was impossible for us to treat them and their schemes seriously; they, in turn, simply ignored us. They had treated the Ukrainians, and especially those from Western Ukraine, as cannon fodder to be exploited until we showed our mettle in the latter half of 1952.

In the meantime the administration's confidence in the former auxiliary police and auxiliary police commanders who had served the administration as brigade leaders and in other capacities collapsed, and henceforth the administration itself escalated the campaign of brutality. For example, on several occasions when the division's convoy troops were escorting the prisoners from the camp to the work zone, the division's commander Povstianoi, and his deputy, Nikiforov, ordered the prisoners to drop to the ground, especially when it was muddy. Those prisoners who did not obey immediately were fired upon until they plunged into the mud. The cruelty of the troops increased each day.

# Chapter Twenty

At the beginning of March 1953, Levitan[1] announced on the radio that Stalin had suffered a heart attack, and by the anxious tone of his voice we could tell that he would not recover. Every day the prisoners impatiently awaited more information about Stalin's health, for they all believed that their fate depended on whether he lived or died. The sole topic of conversation at work, in the barracks, and in the mess hall was the latest news about Stalin.

A few days later, I was working on the night shift when suddenly I heard singing outside: it was a group of free workers who were strung across the width of the road, their arms linked together.

"What have you to be so happy about in the middle of the night?" a prisoner called out to them.

"Everyone should be singing—the tyrant is dead!" one of the women in the group replied. The news spread quickly among the prisoners, who threw their hats into the air and shouted with joy. Each prisoner showed his feelings in his own way, but everyone was ecstatic. The Russians, for example, and especially former officers of the armed forces, were pleased that the government would be composed almost entirely of Russians, and their favourites were Zhukov and Voroshilov.[2]

"Danylo!" the office orderly yelled out. "The foreman wants you in his office." When I walked in the foreman, Titerin, was talking happily to someone on the phone.

"The controller just told me that the sale of alcohol has been banned for five days," Titerin told me when he had finished his conversation, "but everyone's drunk anyway. So let's have a drink as well. I put something aside especially for this occasion."

The administration and the convoy troops did not change their behaviour in the wake of Stalin's death, and when spring came the *subbotniki*[3] started. After working a shift we faced two hours of "voluntary" production work as well as additional duties inside the camp before our work day was over, and the extra labour thoroughly exhausted us. This year the division commander arranged for us to do even more "voluntary" work cleaning the division's grounds, although it was both offensive and degrading to take care of the mess made by those who treated us so brutally.

One day, after we had finished a shift in the cement factory, we began "voluntary" work cleaning the grounds around the building, and two hours later Nikiforov, the division's deputy commander, told us to clean the division's grounds. At this point, exhausted by our regular work, lack of sleep, and the extra "voluntary" labour, we could barely stay on our feet and thus refused to pick up our shovels. The division commander then ordered his men to fire over our heads and bullets whistled about our ears, but we all bunched up in one corner of the compound and stood our ground. Dogs were let loose on us and the troops again fired, but we refused to take up our shovels and finally the commander of the convoy troops, fuming with rage, was forced to take us back to the camp.

The brutal behaviour of the convoy troops and the administration helped us greatly in mobilizing the prisoners against them. The tension in the air grew each day as a final confrontation approached, but we had no idea how this situation would be resolved, for this time our opponents were not the brigade leaders, but the administration and the convoy troops themselves.

Events now unfolded quickly and Tarashchansky, the student and myself had to meet every day to discuss the unprecedented flow of information we were receiving. Every provocation and action by the administration and the troops had to be promptly evaluated, and a circular prepared explaining the situation and telling the prisoners what to expect in the future. In our circulars we also appealed to the members of our self-help organizations to ignore the attempts of the convoy troops to provoke them. But although we wanted them to behave in a calm and restrained manner, it was important that they be firm and decisive when dealing with the administration and the soldiers.

"The enemy is trying to provoke us into causing an incident which would give it an excuse to finish us off," we stated in our circulars. "We must prevent this from happening, but we cannot allow ourselves to be defeated and to surrender. We have to maintain and defend our dignity skilfully and courageously, for we are political prisoners who once fought to achieve a better future for our people."

In May 1953 we heard that convoy troops in one of the watch-towers of "Black" Corrective Labour Camp No. 4 had shot and killed two prisoners who had been singing in front of their barracks, and that in protest the prisoners of this camp had declared a strike and refused to work. We were deeply shocked by this incident, since it was clear that a major action of some sort was being planned, and the atmosphere in the camp grew even more explosive.

A few days later we heard from Camp No. 2 (nickname—Medvezhka) that a security officer had shot two prisoners sentenced because of their religious convictions, and that all the prisoners in this camp had also declared a protest strike. Soon afterward the men's and women's zones of Camp No. 5 stopped working, and by the second half of May close to twenty thousand political prisoners were on strike in the Norilsk area. Ours was the only camp where the prisoners were still working, but it seemed that each one of them was close to the breaking point. As a result of the incidents in the other camps, however, the camp administration and especially Bezverkhy, the senior lieutenant and director of the political section, changed their attitude and became conciliatory.

On 1 June 1953, twenty political prisoners (six Ukrainians, the remainder Russians) were transferred to our camp from a prison in Camp No. 4 and were immediately locked up in the isolator. This group was headed by Ivan Vorobev, a former captain in the Soviet army and a native of Leningrad who had gained a legendary reputation because of his many escapes from the camps. On this same day the guards stopped taking us out to work and an uneasy calm fell over the camp.

On 4 June I went to the mess hall for dinner with three friends, but no sooner had we sat down and started to eat when a worker ran in.

"A platoon of security troops just ran past the watch-tower toward the isolator," he announced. We left our dinner, rushed out into the street, and seeing that all the prisoners from the volleyball court were heading toward the isolator, we followed them.

Horrible cries were coming from this building, which had been surrounded by the platoon. Suddenly a tall bearded prisoner burst out of the fire exit:

"The administration is shoving us into Sabosiak's cell so that the trusties can kill us!" he shouted. The prisoners responded by quickly breaking down the wooden fence surrounding the isolator and pelting the soldiers with chunks of brick. The soldiers then broke through the barbed-wire fence and began to flee toward the division's grounds, dragging the unconscious Vorobev along with them.

"Save Vorobev!" shouted one of the prisoners who had escaped into the compound from the isolator. "They're dragging him into the prohibited zone so they can shoot him there as an escapee!" Many of the prisoners then rushed toward the soldiers who were pulling Vorobev up to the barbed-wire fence. They managed to drag him to within two metres of the fence, but were forced to abandon him on camp territory.

Medical orderlies ran up with a stretcher to take Vorobev to the hospital, but at this moment two soldiers on the other side of the fence, with machine guns, shot a few rounds over the heads of the orderlies and demanded that they leave him alone. The orderlies turned back but the prisoners, bricks in hand, remained on the spot to prevent the security troops from dragging Vorobev to the fence and shooting him there, while the soldiers on the other side pointed their guns at Vorobev to prevent him from being taken to the hospital.

Eventually Tarakhov, the camp director, arrived at the scene.

"Give us the key to the isolator," the prisoners demanded, "so we can get at those dogs of yours, whom you've locked up to prevent them from getting their just desserts."

"I refuse—you'd kill them," Tarakhov replied. In the meantime, however, Sabosiak and his group had cut a hole in the ceiling of their cell using a large knife passed on to them by Kalashnikov, a security officer. They escaped to the division's grounds, shaking their fists at the prisoners who had gathered near the isolator. The prisoners again demanded that the administration's lackeys be turned over to them, whereupon the troops' commander, Povstianoi, ordered his men to open fire.

Several volleys rang out as the security troops blindly obeyed the order, and twenty-four prisoners were felled. Six were killed at once, including two young Ukrainians who were standing next to me in the midst of the crowd of prisoners. In fact, all the dead and wounded were young men from Western Ukraine except for the notorious Baranchyk, one of Sabosiak's colleagues, who was hit by a stray bullet. Since the soldiers fired from a point opposite the hospital, their bullets richocheted off the hospital walls, disturbing the TB patients inside.

"General Semenov is on the watch-tower!" someone behind us shouted. I joined the prisoners who immediately ran to the tower, and witnessed an extraordinary sight. The director of the administration of the "black" camps, General Semenov, in all his regalia, was being led by the crowd of prisoners to the spot where the security troops had shot at them, and when he saw the bodies of the dead and wounded he shook his fists at the division.

"What have you done, you scoundrels!" he shouted.

He was taken to Vorobev, whose body, covered with blood, was still lying on the grass near the barbed-wire fence, and after using Semenov as cover by placing him in the path of the division's sub-machine guns, the prisoners took Vorobev to the hospital and then released the general, who quickly made for the division's compound.

"Since even he's run away from us," someone from the crowd shouted, "let the whole camp administration follow him before it's too late."

Another prisoner turned to Captain Tarakhov:

"Take your stinking parasites and get out. Your work here is finished now," he said. Within half an hour the entire administration had left the camp and only the medical personnel remained behind.

The fourth of June 1953 was a memorable day: these extraordinary and violent events had shaken everyone in the camp. All the prisoners had left the barracks and were now in the street, waiting to see what would happen next. No one, however, had any clear idea what to do, although we knew that in such a situation helplessness could be fatal.

The hopes of the uninformed prisoners were centred on the corrective-labour-camp prisoners who had been released from the isolator, whereas the hopes of those who belonged to the self-help organization were focused on the leaders of this group. We were the only organized force in the camp and therefore we had to take maximum advantage of the situation.

Tarashchansky, the student and myself agreed that it would be pointless to take any initiative by ourselves, and that we would have to prompt the prisoners from the isolator to call for an immediate general meeting in our club. Through our own channels we would ensure that everyone knew about this meeting, at which a strike committee would be elected, and that as many Russians as possible, as well as one representative from each of the other nationalities, would be put forward to man the committee. Two or three Ukrainians selected to the committee would suffice to carry our line, for we could mobilize all the other Ukrainian prisoners to give our committee members their full support.

Once the preliminary arrangements had been made we gave the members of our organization their instructions. They were very efficient and one hour later the club was packed. Only one item was on the agenda: the election of a strike committee, and Valentin Vozhdev, who was from the Kuban area, gave the first presentation. He was followed by Morozov, Biliaev, Doronin, Mikhailov and finally Kost Korol, from Bukovyna, who was the smallest and youngest of all the speakers.

"How many representatives should be elected to serve on the strike committee?" Vozhdev asked the audience of prisoners once the speeches were over. After a brief exchange of views and a vote, the prisoners decided on the figure of fifteen.

"I nominate the fearless Vorobev as chairman of the strike committee," one of Vorobev's friends declared, "and since he's in the hospital now I propose that Valentin Vozhdev temporarily replace him." The vote for Vorobev was unanimous and we began to elect the other members of the committee. Nine Russians, three Ukrainians, one Lithuanian and one Latvian were elected. The last member to be elected, Tarkavtsadze, had a German mother and was German in outlook, although his father was from the Caucasus area (the name is Georgian). Tarkavtsadze had been sentenced by the

Nuremberg Tribunal, in accordance with international law, to hard labour for life for his work in the German ministry of propaganda.

During the committee meeting which followed the general meeting each member was assigned certain duties and the committee took on the appearance of a "mini-government." Kost Korol was made responsible for the food supply of the camp, and his duties included receiving bread, sugar and other foodstuffs from the camp administration, transferring these goods to the mess-hall, and taking care of all other matters related to the camp's food supply and distribution. Tarkavtsadze was assigned, in accordance with his earlier profession (but with a higher "rank"), "Minister of Propaganda." He was asked to select a suitable staff for his section which would then mobilize the prisoners, especially before general meetings, to support the course adopted by the committee. The Lithuanian, as a medical aide, was made responsible for all matters related to health, and in particular sanitary arrangements and the hospital.

First, the committee organized a funeral for the prisoners who had been killed. Our carpenters constructed coffins and painted them black, flags of mourning were flown from all the barracks, and three priests officiated at the funeral service. The coffins were carried in a funeral procession throughout the camp before they they were lowered into a common grave near the club. All four thousand prisoners took part in this ceremony. A number of emotional speeches followed, after which each prisoner threw a handful of earth onto the coffins and we dispersed.

The committee decided that it would appoint the former brigade leaders to serve as senior orderlies in the barracks and sections.

"When you worked for the adminstration you squeezed the last drop of sweat and blood from the workers while living at their expense," the brigade leaders were told at one of the general meetings. "Now you'll have a chance, at least partially, to make amends, so take advantage of this opportunity."

The *seksoty*[4]—the administration's informers among us—were given the job of preparing posters bearing appeals to the free citizens of Norilsk, asking them to boycott the camp administration and notify the government about the administration's brutal treatment of the prisoners. They carried out this work conscientiously, and later hung these posters on the sides of several buildings at the edge of the camp.

During the first week of the committee's administration, the prisoners whitewashed the barracks, cleaned up the rubbish in their zone, and put the mess-hall in perfect order (which had never occurred under the camp administration). The committee's political section prepared a number of documents, with testimonies from doctors and many other witnesses, describing the unrestrained brutality and criminal actions of the camp administration, and also prepared a list of the political prisoners' demands. This declared that the administration should be held legally responsible for its criminal activities in the name of the state, and that all political prisoners should be released, even those who had fought against the Soviet state, since the latter was a state of terror and violence, which opposed progress and humanism.

In the meantime the administration had mounted loud-speakers around the camp, which they used to threaten the committee with the most terrible punishments and promise large rewards to those who would speak out against it. This psychological warfare had a very depressing effect on many prisoners. In addition, the camp director instructed Zhdanov, the senior work assigner, to organize secretly an assault group made up of brigade leaders which, at the right moment, was to seize the committee members and lock them in the isolator. Then the administration was to be invited back into the camp.

Zhdanov went about his assignment energetically. He immediately began to draw all the brigade leaders into his assault group, and a week later they were ready. They could have posed a formidable threat to the committee, for they were well-fed and, having served the Germans during the war, were trained to kill. The group planned to arm itself with knives and attack the committee during its forthcoming meeting.

Had it not been for our self-help organization, Zhdanov's group would have easily carried out its plan, for the committee and its administrative network were weak whereas Zhdanov's group had helpers everywhere, even in the committee itself. However, we knew every detail about the formation of Zhdanov's group. We informed the committee about its plot and demanded that a general meeting be called to discuss this issue and to decide what to do with the conspirators. The committee members were terrified when they heard about the strength and plans of Zhdanov's group, but we calmed them down and assured them that everything would be fine. We kept in touch with the committee through Kost Korol, who assured his colleagues that he had the support of all the Ukrainians in the camp.

Zhdanov and all his fellow conspirators were summoned to the general meeting convoked to discuss their plot. From his bed in the barracks to the club, and even after entering the club, each member of Zhdanov's group was accompanied by three to five of our men who had been told what action to take if their "wards" tried to attack anyone. The conspirators immediately noticed that they were being supervised and perceived the merry mood of their "guardians," and many of them lost the desire to proceed with their scheme. But, in accordance with their plan, during the meeting they walked onto the stage, using the back entrance, and stood some two metres behind the members of the committee, who were facing the audience. The "guardians" of the brigade leaders, however, followed them onto the stage.

"Hey lads!" one of our men in the audience shouted. "What are you doing up there on the stage? Why don't you begin your little game—no spirit left?"

The general meeting of the political prisoners of Hard Labour Camp No. 3 was opened by committee chairman Valentin Vozhdev. Korol was the first to speak, and after denouncing the conspirators he demanded that the general meeting resolve to expel them from the camp. "Kick them out!" the audience shouted, although some of the prisoners demanded that Zhdanov's men be tied up and locked in the isolator.

Following Korol, Doronin spoke in defence of Zhdanov, and since he was a gifted orator the audience began to waver. Thus a dangerous situation arose, and I felt obliged to speak out. After my presentation the chairman of the committee called for a vote, and a forest of hands rose to support the expulsion of the conspirators from our zone. There were thirty abstentions, and only Doronin and Holovko voted against expulsion. And so Zhdanov, in the company of seven of his closest associates, left our camp zone, thoroughly humiliated, to report his failure to the camp director. The remainder of his companions, with lowered heads, returned to their barracks and the members of the committee, with a sigh of relief, continued peacefully with their work.

In the meantime the division's security troops had set up eight machine-gun posts around the camp, another eight on the watch-towers, and had brought up two Maxims, all of which were manned day and night. Our strike committee established its own guard posts along the barbed-wire fence opposite these emplacements, and the sentries were changed every four hours. Soon they and the soldiers began to get to know one another.

"See, your relief has arrived and ours is late," the soldiers would note, and our guards freely struck up conversations with them.

"Do you know at whom you're aiming those machine guns? We're workers and peasants just like you; there are no bourgeois and capitalists among us. Why are you preparing to shoot us? We haven't done you any harm."

"We do as we're told," was the reply. "When the orders come to shoot, we'll shoot."

"But that would be a criminal act," our sentries responded.

"We're supposed to carry out our orders, not think about them. Understand?"

Such conversations took place quite often, although in theory the security troops were forbidden to talk to our sentries and were always checking to see if an officer was passing by. We, on the contrary, encouraged our men to enter into such conversations, and they did so openly.

Our self-help organization placed its own personnel on duty in various locations in the camp. They acted independently of the committee's regular network to maintain order in the camp, and their job was to inform us immediately of any incidents involving the political prisoners and the administration. Korol, in the meantime, informed us about events in the committee. He always gave us an advance copy of the committee and general meetings' agenda, after examination of which we gave Korol instructions specifying the position he was to take on each item. Korol was the youngest and smallest member of the committee and always the last to speak. However, he spoke with great assurance at the committee and general meetings, and never allowed his stand to be influenced by anyone else on the committee, including its chairman. If the other committee members disagreed with him he would demand that the matter in dispute be discussed at a general meeting.

The general meetings were held in the club, which could accommodate approximately 700 people. Whenever we had to persuade the committee to follow our lead, our "invisible" self-help organization summoned its supporters to the club where they occupied, according to a prearranged plan, all the available places. As the meeting went through the agenda, and especially when controversial matters were being discussed, our supporters in the audience would speak. There were usually five to seven such speeches, and after each one, all those present would clap and shout their approval.

Under these circumstances, the efforts of Tarkavtsadze's propagandists were totally ineffective.

"There's nothing left for us to do," they told Tarkavtsadze when they returned from their assignments, "for everything's been settled already and they're better informed than we are."

After a few such occasions, the strike committee members realized that whenever they discussed an issue the most decisive opinion was always that of Kost Korol, their youngest colleague. But no one knew anything concrete about the invisible mechanism which supported Korol. Even those in the self-help organization, including Korol himself, did not know how everything was done. They knew only their own specific functions in a given situation. Our "machine" worked very efficiently, with great attention to detail, and our supporters truly put their soul into their work, for they trusted both the nucleus of the self-help organization and their immediate superiors.

Every day representatives of our organization visited the people who had been wounded on 4 June, always bringing them some sugar, butter and white bread. This food was distributed equally among all the patients, including Baranchyk. On the first occasion that we came and handed every single patient sugar and cookies from a parcel received by one of the prisoners, Baranchyk's eyes filled with tears. He was moved that we had not ignored him or sought revenge for his brutal treatment of the prisoners in the past.

Our humane treatment of even our worst enemies greatly displeased the camp administration, which began to devise various provocations. At one point, for example, security officer Vorontsov's wife, who worked as a sanitary inspector in our camp, brought two packets of cigarettes as well as some sugar and butter when she visited Baranchyk, and placed everything on his night table.

"My husband passed this on for you," she told Baranchyk.

"You want my blood, you damn bitch?" Baranchyk shouted, throwing the cigarettes in her face. "So your scoundrel of a husband wants to provoke the other prisoners into killing me, does he? They're putting forward perfectly legal demands, and you're provoking them to commit a crime!" We calmed Baranchyk down and assured him, in the presence of Vorontsov's wife, that no one would succeed in provoking us to commit murder. Then we told Vorontsov's wife to never show her face again in the camp, and on that same day the committee ordered its guards on the watch-tower to bar her from the camp.

# Chapter Twenty-One

Two weeks after the announcement of the strike, a commission from Moscow headed by Colonel Kuznetsov, the Gulag[1] director, finally arrived. Captain Tarakhov, our camp's director, notified us that the commission would be visiting the camp after lunch, and we placed a table covered with a red cloth a hundred metres from the front gates. All the prisoners from our camp assembled some fifty metres from the table, and we anxiously awaited the appearance of this high-level commission from the capital. Eventually a group of military officers left the division's zone, approached the gates to the camp, and the five prisoners elected by a general meeting to negotiate with the commission took their places behind the table. They were headed by Vozhdev, the head of the strike committee, and his deputies Shamaev and Korol.

Finally the gates opened and Colonel Kuznetsov, accompanied by two generals, entered the camp. Radiating contempt and arrogance, they walked up to the table and, ignoring our delegates, greeted the prisoners as a whole. One at a time, according to their rank, the members of the camp administration, including the guards, followed the commission into the camp and stood alongside its members.

"What's happened here, and what do you want?" Kuznetsov addressed the prisoners, again ignoring our delegates.

"First of all," Shamaev told him, "remove your criminals and murderers, headed by Captain Tarakhov, from the camp. Second, we've been authorized by a general meeting of the prisoners to negotiate with the commission. Before entering into any concrete discussions, however, we must ask you to show us your mandates and authorization."

"We'll do nothing of the kind and have no intention of negotiating with you," Kuznetsov said. "We've been authorized by Lavrentii Pavlovich Beria[2] to get to the bottom of this and to hold you responsible."

"If you came to find out what's been going on then you should talk with our representatives who are standing in front of you," one of the prisoners in the crowd shouted. "If you're not interested in doing so and refuse to recognize our representatives, then you shouldn't have bothered to come here."

"He's right!" a number of prisoners yelled out. "If you don't recognize our delegates then we won't recognize you! But before we continue, get those murderers headed by Tarakhov out of our zone!"

Colonel Kuznetsov called Captain Tarakhov over and quietly spoke with him. Then, in a broken voice, Tarakhov ordered his administration to leave the camp and quietly, with lowered heads, they filed through the gates.

"We've been authorized to speak directly to all of the prisoners," Kuznetsov continued, "and not with those who have led you illegally into this mess."

"The criminals are those who just left, headed by your camp director Tarakhov, and Povstianoi, the commander of the division," one of the prisoners said. "Our delegates speak for the prisoners, and are simply opposing legally the arbitrary actions of the administration."

"You'll answer for the consequences of your actions," Kuznetsov said, "and you'll have only yourselves to blame."

"If you came here to threaten us then get out! We have nothing to discuss with you," another prisoner shouted from the crowd, and soon the entire crowd began yelling at Kuznetsov and his escort to leave the camp. When our delegates left the table the crowd also turned their backs on the commission and left the area. Kuznetsov and the two generals stood alone by the table for a few minutes, and then left like outcasts.

Next the executive and members of the strike committee met in the club and decided to write a petition to the government demanding that it send a new commission to our camp with a broad mandate to examine our complaints and expose the flagrant abuse of authority by the administration. The committee was empowered to draw up this petition, and began immediately. Shortly after this meeting, the administration and Beria's commission began to use loudspeakers to threaten us, and the tension between the administration and our camp mounted.

Vorobev left the hospital and took over as head of the strike committee just as a group of former Soviet officers, who had served the Germans during the war, were preparing another plot. The conspirators were led by Borysenko, the brigade leader who had killed Kucherevsky in 1951, together with Kipa and Holovko, and like the earlier group led by Zhdanov, they decided to destroy the strike committee, lock its members in the isolator, and then invite the administration back into the camp.

But Borysenko's group, like Zhdanov's, was unable to carry out its plan, for our invisible but omnipresent self-help organization exposed this conspiracy. The committee assigned three men to escort each one of the conspirators to the committee's headquarters, and they were brought in carrying the knives they had planned to use in their plot. The conspirators soon lost their courage when they entered the headquarters one at a time. Only Borysenko behaved insolently, and he was locked in a cabin and placed under guard. All the others were released. The next general meeting of the political prisoners strongly condemned Borysenko's group, and praised the committee's actions.

Many of the prisoners, and especially the Russians, viewed Vorobev as their Messiah. The adulation heaped upon him assumed legendary proportions, and he breathed spiritual strength and steadfastness into many prisoners who believed him to be an omnipotent and infallible "superman." For a while, his authority counter-balanced the psychological pressure exerted by the administration. But Vorobev and his followers considered this authority to be much greater than it actually was, and they underestimated the other forces in our camp. This, as soon became clear, was at the root of the great blunders made by Vorobev.

Vorobev's first speech at a general meeting of the prisoners was delivered not in the usual fashion, from the stage of the club, but from the film booth, by microphone. This immediately raised the hackles of some prisoners.

"Doesn't he know that he's insulting his audience? Or maybe he doesn't care what they think," some of the hard-labour prisoners in our organization muttered.

A few days later General Semenov called Vorobev out for further talks, to which Vorobev agreed without getting the committee's approval. The negotiations were held on the camp's territory, some ten metres from the watch-tower, with Semenov and Vorobev on opposite sides of the table. No one else was present at these secret talks, which lasted almost an hour, and all the prisoners, standing a hundred metres from the table, anxiously awaited their conclusion.

"The prisoners don't like these secret negotiations with the general," said L., one of the most active members of our self-help organization.

"Agreed," I replied. "This will be the last time he does anything of the kind."

After the negotiations, Vorobev went to the club and, again using the microphone in the film booth, briefly informed the general meeting about his negotiations.

"He spends a whole hour talking with the general, and then talks to us for five minutes, as if he didn't give a damn what we thought," the prisoners said to one another.

"And during his presentation he didn't speak from the platform and look us in the eyes, but used a microphone, so that no one could see him and pose any questions."

"If he ever tries to negotiate by himself again, then we'll have to tell him not to come back, and to join the general outside our zone."

After hearing these comments from the prisoners, I went to see the members of the committee.

"The prisoners don't trust negotiations of this kind," I said. "It would be best if this didn't happen again; otherwise there might be some unpleasant consequences."

"What do you mean—they don't trust me?" Vorobev asked angrily.

"Negotiations with the general concern all of us. We should all decide who is to hold talks with the administration."

"For the time being, as long as I'm head of the committee, I can do without your advice," Vorobev replied arrogantly.

"Your pride and conceit are your greatest enemies. You'll pay dearly for these weaknesses," I said and left the committee's quarters. Later Korol and Shamaev managed to convince Vorobev that he could not behave in this manner, and thenceforth he stopped holding negotiations on his own.

But shortly afterward, I received some more disturbing news.

"A member of Vorobev's group has set up shop in security officer Vorontsov's old office," the student told me. "He's recruiting people into a 'Social-Democratic Progressive Party' of some kind, and is issuing a card with this party's stamp on it to new members."

I was rather amused at this "bureaucrat" working for a new "party," but no matter how comical these "politicians" in Vorobev's group appeared, Tarashchansky, the student and myself had to put a stop to their activities. When we spoke with them, Vorobev vehemently denied knowledge of this activity, and ordered his subordinate to cease recruiting. Then, one memorable night, soon after the "party office" had been closed, I was awakened by Korol.

"Vorobev just held a secret meeting in the building where the 'party office' was located," he informed me. "About thirty prisoners attended, and Vorobev made a speech along the following lines: 'Enough of playing at strikes. It's time to take stock of our situation seriously; in particular, we have to place the camp on a military footing, and to do this we have to set up a number of different military units and a command hierarchy. Our job tonight is to decide which prisoners we'll assign to various command posts. We'll select the regimental commanders from those who are present here tonight, but the battalion and company commanders should be appointed, in absentia, from among the more authoritative Ukrainians, for they make up the main combat force in the camp. Our regiment's aim will be to disarm the division, liberate all the Norilsk camps, capture Dudinka, and make our way to the *Bolshaia zemlia*,[3] where we'll decide what has to be done next.' After this speech the regimental staff was selected and several battalion and company commanders were appointed from those present. Panasiuk, Zahorulko and Kobza were appointed battalion commanders in absentia, and you, Sydorchuk and Bukhalo were appointed company commanders. Today Vorobev will be summoning you one by one to assign you 'officially' to these posts."

"This is a ridiculously foolhardy escapade," I told Korol. "As a result of his egotism and flamboyant imagination Vorobev has completely lost touch with reality! In the morning we'll remove this fool from his position as 'regimental commander' and chairman of the strike committee, and we'll show him his place in the camp! Go back to your quarters and behave as if nothing has happened. We'll soon shake this 'führer' up so badly that he'll never want to repeat these adventures."

A dangerous and complicated situation had arisen, and we had to act quickly and decisively. I sent one of my assistants to fetch immediately Zahorulko, Panasiuk, Kobza, Bukhalo and Sydorchuk. This summons at such an early hour greatly alarmed them.

"I've called you here on a very urgent matter," I told them when they arrived. "Vorobev has just held a secret meeting in the office building, attended by some thirty former Russian officers. They've set up a command structure for a proposed regiment, and have appointed all six of us, in absentia, to be battalion and company commanders. If Vorobev has his way then our strike will turn into a bloody debacle, for he wants to throw the Ukrainian prisoners, with us at their head, at a division which is armed to the teeth while he and a small group escape. He's even prepared a military uniform for himself with a captain's epaulettes, and his closest friends also have military uniforms. Their operational plan is to blow up the boiler room under the division and then use us as cannon fodder, but we'll quash this plan of theirs in the morning. We'll go to the committee's headquarters now, and I'll speak with Vorobev on behalf of our group, but please support me when necessary." This unexpected turn of events alarmed my companions, and we set off immediately for the strike committee's headquarters. When we arrived, Shamaev was there alone, and asked what was wrong.

"We have to see Vorobev."

"I'm Vorobev's next-in-command. What concerns him also concerns me," Shamaev replied, his pride ruffled by my brusque approach. "Tell me what's wrong."

"No, it would be pointless to discuss this matter with you alone. We have to see Vorobev."

"Fedia, go call Vorobev," Shamaev ordered, "and tell him that some people are waiting for him." Presently, Vorobev entered the room.

"Hello! What's the matter?" he asked in an irritated tone of voice, glancing at me in a condescending fashion. Then he turned his head away to emphasize his disdain for me.

"We found out that during the night you called a secret meeting at which you set up a command staff for a non-existent regiment.

You appointed us, without our consent, commanders of non-existent battalions and companies. Who gave you the right to engage in such escapades in our camp? Do you want to sacrifice the Ukrainians so that you can escape? If so, then you're an absolute scoundrel! Call back all those present at your secret meeting now, and tell them, in our presence, that everything you discussed has been cancelled. Understand?" I said, raising my voice.

"Who do you think you are? And what right do you have to tell me what to do?" Vorobev replied. "After all, I'm the chairman of the strike committee."

"From now on we're treating you as a renegade. Do as I say, and quickly! If we have to do it for you, then you'll pay dearly for your actions." Vorobev gave me a look full of hate and, turning to his assistants, told them to summon his associates to the gallery of the club. Thirty minutes later all the regiment's "officers" were there; most of them were Vlasovites, although one (a commander of the "regiment's" field police) had once been a major in the militia. All of them, including Vorobev, were thoroughly dejected.

I decided that it was my duty to break the silence and to start the proceedings on the right foot.

"We're gathered here in connection with the 'secret' meeting held in the former administration's office. Vorobev has something to say about this. Please stand up and clarify this unfortunate situation so that we'll never have to refer to it again."

Vorobev rose reluctantly to his feet, and cast his eyes downward.

"Since everything we discussed last night has become known to certain people who should not have heard about our plans, please consider the matter closed. In view of the circumstances we have to cancel these plans. I'm sorry, lads, that everything has ended in such a fashion," Vorobev concluded and sat down.

"Comrade Shamaev," I said, "please announce that there will be a general meeting of all the prisoners and inform them that, because of ill health, comrade Vorobev requests that he be released from his duties as chairman of the strike committee. Is that correct, comrade Vorobev?" I asked, turning toward him.

"Yes, I'm washing my hands of everything that's going on here," said Vorobev, deeply offended.

"We also no longer consider ourselves members of the committee, and want nothing more to do with you," stated Morozov on behalf of six of Vorobev's companions. A crisis situation now arose in the strike committee, for of the fifteen members, seven, including the chairman, had resigned. We had to select candidates for their posts at once and present them for approval to the general meeting.

Everyone left the gallery in silence. Vorobev and his six faithful companions made for the two-storey barracks where they lived; Shamaev, Korol and the other members of the committee went to the committee headquarters to prepare the agenda for the general meeting; and I went onto the road with my six friends to discuss these new developments. We were all surprised that it had been so easy to dethrone Vorobev and his group of renegades.

Later, I went to see Tarashchansky and the student.

"Well, how did you deal with that 'military leader'?" Tarashchansky asked. I described both the tragic and comic aspects of this affair, and how fortunate it was that we had diverted Vorobev's "regiment" from its fatal course. The camp administration and Beria's commission from Moscow, of course, would have preferred a confrontation.

"Well then, now we have to choose replacements for Vorobev's men on the committee," Tarashchansky said.

"We won't put forward anyone from the self-help organization, because that won't be necessary. We'll simply propose candidates who have shown their mettle during the strike," I said.

"Why shouldn't we put our own people on the committee?" the student asked.

"Why should we do so if we can direct and control the activity of the committee through Korol? The committee won't function any better for it," I replied. After this short discussion we selected six candidates for membership on the committee and chose six members of our organization to nominate them at the general meeting. At the same time we instructed the self-help organization to support actively the candidates chosen and nominated by us at the meeting.

The general meeting went smoothly, and elected all our pre-selected candidates to the committee. Shamaev was elected chairman of this reconstituted committee, which became much stronger and more united after the Vorobev crisis. In addition, Korol's role and stature in the committee were further enhanced.

One day an official who was unknown to us came to our camp together with Tarakhov, the camp director, and approached some of the prisoners.

"I'm Vavilov, the Deputy Procurator General responsible for camps and prisons," he said, taking out his passport. "Here are my papers."

"We're not authorized to check your papers," the prisoners replied. "We'll call the chairman of our committee."

"Fine," the procurator replied, smiling. The guards who had let Vavilov into the camp had already informed Shamaev about his arrival, and having left some instructions with the senior personnel in the barracks, Shamaev went to meet the procurator. As he drew near Vavilov turned his head and gave him a shadow of a smile.

"Greetings, citizen procurator," Shamaev said.

"Greetings, chairman of the strike committee," Vavilov replied. "I flew out here with the specific aim of determining what's been going on in this camp."

"First of all," Shamaev told the procurator, "let's go and take a look at the camp. You can chat with the people here, and then we can get down to serious discussions."

"That's fine with me," the procurator said and took Shamaev by the arm. "Let's go." It was very gratifying to see this tall, sturdy fellow, in uniform and full regalia, link arms as a colleague with our short, emaciated Shamaev, who was dressed in a worn-out camp pea-jacket.

In the meantime, in accordance with prearranged instructions, all the prisoners lined up in columns before their barracks. Shamaev and Vavilov walked up to each column in turn, and after greeting the prisoners Vavilov asked what had happened. We had arranged for three to five people in each column to talk to the procurator, and had briefed them to ensure that each speaker pointed out an example of the camp administration's brutality. But not all the presentations had been rehearsed. For example Liatsky, a former major and former head of a military registration office, came up to Vavilov and showed him a photograph in a newspaper.

"Look at the suit and necktie worn by Thälmann,[4] the leader of the German communists, when he was in a fascist prison," Liatsky said. "And what have I, a Soviet major, been given to wear?"

"You're not Thälmann," Vavilov replied.

"But you're not fascists, yet you treat patriots from your own native land worse than the fascists treated their fellow countrymen."

When Vavilov and Shamaev stopped near the isolator several prisoners described the events of 4 June and showed the former the bullet holes in the hospital. These holes, circled with red paint, testified to the administration's violation of international law, which considered even enemy hospitals to be sacrosanct.

"Is that what really happened?" Vavilov asked Tarakhov.

"I'll talk to you about this later," Tarakhov replied after looking at the surrounding prisoners.

From the isolator the procurator and Shamaev went to the invalids' barracks, where a gruesome sight awaited them. In the barracks yard dozens of legless invalids sat in the first row, those missing both arms sat in the second, and those missing one arm or leg sat in the third. Behind them were blind, deaf or crippled prisoners. All these cripples, approximately 400 in number, had been healthy when brought to Norilsk.

"Yes, this is truly horrible," the procurator said when he looked at this scene. "I'll do everything in my power to do something for these people."

"No one can repair what your curs have already done to us," an invalid in the front row said. "No one can return my legs to me."

"I don't have the authority to resolve all your problems," Vavilov said once the tour was over. "The government will deal with them. All I can do is send two investigators to your camp to look into the incident of 4 June."

"No, a partial accounting of the crimes of the administration and convoy troops won't satisfy us," Shamaev said. "We demand a full, comprehensive examination of all their crimes from 1944 to the present."

"He's right!" the prisoners shouted in approval.

"I understand how you feel," Vavilov replied, "but I haven't been authorized to investigate this whole complex of problems. I'll pass on your demands, but I can't look into them myself."

# Chapter Twenty-Two

For a few days after Vavilov's visit it was quiet in the camp. The administration and the convoy troops no longer provoked us in any way and the loudspeakers were silent. During this lull the prisoners began to organize amateur drama groups and choirs, and in the course of one week five such groups and choirs had been organized by the Ukrainians, Russians, Lithuanians, Latvians and Estonians (only the Belorussians failed to organize a group). Ten days later we were watching one-act plays put on by the drama groups and listening to the various choirs, whose members were dressed in their national costumes. When people have the opportunity to show some initiative they can do wonders! In the meantime Mykolaichuk worked day and night preparing a primitive printing press, and he had an entire arsenal of jars in his workshop containing lead type of various sizes.

The administration soon broke its silence by cutting off our electricity. Work in the kitchen ceased when the ventilators stopped working, and the situation became quite confused. In retaliation Tarkavtsadze blocked the pipe carrying water to the division's grounds and to the buildings in which the camp administration lived with its families, and we waited to see who would last the longer—they without water or we without food.

Soon, however, the wives of the administration personnel protested the lack of water, and negotiations began. As a result our electricity was restored and we let the water flow, but now the administration applied the ninth norm to our camp, in accordance with which we began to receive only 400 grams of bread and two half-litre servings of watery soup every day. These were starvation rations, and had a demoralizing effect on the prisoners. In a few days their eyes lost their sparkle, their smiles disappeared, and they walked around as if in mourning. Only the artist Kharkivsky, as always, kept his sense of humour and entertained the prisoners with his juicy anecdotes.

Only once was there a disturbance, when ten soldiers from the division with sub-machine guns cut through the wire fence and broke into our compound after firing a few volleys into the air. The prisoners guarding this sector fell to the ground, but at that moment Bondarenko appeared on the scene and, giving a shout, ran straight at the soldiers. About a hundred prisoners quickly jumped to their feet and threw themselves at the soldiers, who were so stunned by the courage of these unarmed men that they quickly retreated from the compound and took up positions behind the railway line. Bondarenko's exploit greatly impressed me, for no one could have imagined that this quiet person possessed the strength of spirit which turns even cowards into heroes.

In fact, with their cheerfulness and fighting spirit Bondarenko and Kharkivsky proved to be an inexhaustible source of inspiration even when we were under great psychological pressure and threatened by hunger. Their personal example was much more important than the work of countless propagandists and political instructors. But the starvation rations did their work and the prisoners began to lose their strength. Vorobev's supporters even made plans to break down the doors to our storeroom in order to seize the food inside and sell it, and we were forced to double the storeroom guard.

It was vital to maintain the high morale of the political prisoners even when we were suffering from hunger. Therefore our lads grew very excited when one of the prisoners, a Balt, brought us a magazine which contained designs for paper kites, for we needed kites to carry our appeals to the free citizens of Norilsk. The first kite was built and given a preliminary trial that same day, and successfully passed its first test. Now we had to provide quickly a useful "payload" for the kite.

Mykolaichuk swiftly prepared a number of appeals with the following text: "Free citizens of Norilsk! Boycott the hangmen of the division attached to Hard Labour Camp No. 3. They have murdered innocent workers who built many factories, enterprises and dwellings on the permafrost of the Arctic North." For the first flight we tied a package of fifty appeals to the kite and then attached a long cotton wick to the package. We lit the wick and released the kite, which obediently rose into the air, like a bomber, carrying its cargo of peace high over the city of Norilsk. By the time our hand-winch had released the full one-and-a-half thousand metres of kite-string the burning wick had reached the thread binding the package, and when the wick burned through the thread the appeals began to float down over the city.

Four thousand prisoners, emaciated by hunger, anxiously watched the kite's progress, while on the other side of the barbed-wire fence the entire division and the camp administration took shots at the kite. A group of soldiers ran after the kite to collect our appeals to prevent them from falling into the hands of the citizens of Norilsk. Thus, our first experiment with kites had been a success, and a shout of "Hurrah!" went up from our compound. The administration, however, was furious, since the security police have always feared all forms of publicity.

When we returned the kites to their "base" we found that they had often been shot through several times. After returning from "battle duty" they were handled and examined with loving care, as if they were living creatures. After patching their "wounds," we again attached a suitable cargo to the kites, and directed them along our tested route toward Norilsk. The shooting which followed and our anxiety for the fate of the kites aroused such a fever of excitement among the prisoners that they even forgot their hunger.

For three days we continuously bombarded Norilsk with our appeals and informed the city's inhabitants about the brutality of the camp administration and the convoy troops. Finally General Semenov broke the administration's silence and spoke to us over a loudspeaker.

"Stop playing around with your 'aviation' and you'll receive your full rations today. And call off your strike tomorrow: the prisoners in Camps Nos. 2, 4 and 5 are more sensible than you and have already returned to work. If you want the government to resolve your complaints in your favour then you must stop this anarchy immediately." When the requisite amount of food was handed over to us at the watch-tower, we stopped flying our kites but refused to return to work.

The next day some workers at Plant No. 25 climbed onto the factory roof and, after hanging up a white flag, began to signal to us with their hands. The non-political prisoners in Camp No. 6 also began sending us signals using small flags, and although we could not understand these messages, their persistent efforts indicated clearly that something very important had taken place.

Every second day the base headquarters sent to our camp a horsecart with a sanitary tank to pick up our sewage. When he reached the watch-tower on this particular day the cart driver said in a loud voice, so that the administration personnel could hear:

"Well, boys, all the other camps have ended their strikes; you're the only ones still holding out."

"Go ahead, if you tell them then maybe they'll believe you," the duty officer in the watch-tower told the cart driver, locking him inside our compound while the sewage was being pumped. The prisoners, who were very upset by this news, took the cart driver to the bath-house and began to question him thoroughly.

"It's true that they've stopped striking," he said, "but I mentioned this loudly at the watch-tower so that the administration would trust me. Don't be bitter, because I've got some very good news. Here it is," he said, handing us a copy of *Izvestiia*, "Beria is no more!"

A few of the prisoners grabbed the newspaper and rushed over to the committee's headquarters in the club. A general meeting was called immediately and the short article stating that Beria had been removed from his position and arrested was read out. This news raised the spirits of the prisoners and strengthened their will-power and determination.

We found some technicians among the prisoners who transformed the film projector into a radio receiver, and the committee assigned three well-educated prisoners to take turns listening to the broadcasts and to submit written reports every day on world events. The most important occurrence during our strike was the uprising in East Germany, and especially Berlin, on 17 June 1953.[1] Beria himself had left for Berlin to help crush the uprising, and while he was away Khrushchev and his friends had engineered the downfall of the head of the secret police.

The news of the removal and arrest of Beria depressed the camp administration and the convoy troops no less than it raised the spirits of the political prisoners. For many years these sadists had been given a free rein to mistreat the prisoners and now, after the arrest of their "prince" Beria, they were confused and afraid to continue their criminal activity. In addition, the Moscow commission, which had been acting in Beria's name, lost its mandate, and one of its members, Syrotkin, a lieutenant-general and convoy troop commander, walked alongside the wire fence surrounding our camp and pleaded with us.

"Komsomol comrades, take your ID numbers off your clothing; you're no longer prisoners. All your demands will be met, only stop this dawdling and go back to work."

"Lieutenant-General, what's happened to force you, a general in charge of convoy troops who used to shoot at defenceless prisoners, to address us as 'Komsomol comrades'?" the prisoners asked. "Why, only two days ago you were calling us criminals and fascists and were threatening to shoot us."

Our home-made printing press stepped up its work, and in a single day Mykolaichuk managed to print thousands of appeals to the citizens of Norilsk. Our kites faithfully delivered our statements and appeals to their destination, but the administration began to produce and fly its own kites to intercept ours. Whereas our kites flew at an angle of approximately 35 degrees, their kites carried no "cargo" and, being very light, rose almost vertically. Our competitors then manoeuvred them so that their kite-strings sometimes pulled against ours, and brought our kites down to earth. To counter this tactic, we began to send up five to seven kites at a time, and while the first few were intercepted, the others calmly carried their cargo toward Norilsk. We found this air battle between Beria's offspring and our printed word exposing their crimes to be very entertaining. We were delighted that we had overcome the obstacles in our path and were providing a considerable amount of information to the citizens of Norilsk.

Our statements and appeals proved to be effective, for the citizens of Norilsk did in fact boycott the camp administration. In the schools some children began to abuse and sometimes even to fight with the children of the camp administrators, and the machinists and conductors on the trains that supplied Factory

No. 25 with raw materials clenched their fists when they drove by the camp to demonstrate their solidarity with us.

"Hold tight, lads!" they occasionally dared to call out. "We support you. The hangman Beria is finished now." It seemed that all of Norilsk was on our side, and all the camps for non-political prisoners, especially the neighbouring Camp No. 5, with its 12,000 prisoners, were also sympathetic to our cause and gave us moral support.

The order and tidiness of our camp were exemplary, and all the prisoners, even those who had once fought among themselves, lived in harmony, gaining confidence in their own strength and that of their compatriots. After suffering meagre rations for seventeen days, we had finally won a guaranteed food ration for ourselves, and those prisoners who were ill were even given a special diet.

One day a trader (a civilian) came to the camp store to sell off the remaining goods. The committee obtained from him a list of goods in the store and then prepared its own list, which specified who could buy which goods. Only those chosen by the committee could go to the store, and after everything had been sold the trader approached the committee chairman.

"I've never seen such discipline and politeness," he said. "I never thought that people could change so much in such a short time."

We were very pleased to hear these comments, and everyone realized what disgrace Vorobev's group would have brought upon us had it succeeded in taking over the camp, for in essence his approach was no less disastrous than that of Zhdanov and Borysenko. We had defeated both groups of conspirators through the extremely flexible yet decisive activity of the self-help organization and its nucleus. In its absence Zhdanov's group could have easily tied up the committee members, locked them in the isolator, and invited the administration back into the camp. Likewise, if we had not intervened, Vorobev's men would have succeeded in blowing up the steam boilers underneath the division, and thrown our men against its well-armed soldiers, thereby allowing our well-organized and politically significant strike to end in a massacre. This, in turn, would have provided the administration with a justification for its crimes.

The Ukrainian self-help organization had a decisive influence on the strike committee, especially through the pressure exerted by the general meetings of the political prisoners. Because of this pressure, the committee was obliged to carry out our will, even though it was unaware of our organization's existence. During the strike the Ukrainian self-help organization encompassed approximately 180 political prisoners, each of whom, through personal contacts, had a direct influence on two or three other prisoners. Thus we had the support of approximately 750 of the most active political prisoners, and the club had room for this same number of people. Therefore, whenever we had to pressure the committee to implement our policies, our supporters would occupy all the places in the club.

Every prisoner knew exactly which seat he was to occupy and the role he was to play at a meeting. Those who had to speak out when a controversial issue was raised were scattered throughout the hall and the balcony, and knew the order in which they were to speak. Those in the audience, in turn, knew that their duty was to support our speakers by clapping and shouting their approval. If several prisoners who opposed our policy managed to squeeze into the hall, our people were to interrupt their speeches by stamping their feet and shouting at them. And this was done, when necessary, with such precision and enthusiasm that it was a pleasure to behold.

The Ukrainian self-help organization was a success because its members became involved in the organization through their best and most trusted friends, to whom they were directly subordinated. As for tactics and strategy, we were aided greatly by our personal experience in community affairs and our ability to take maximum advantage of our opponents' weaknesses while concealing our temporary internal crises.

In July, when Shamaev was already chairman, Borysenko's friends, led by Holovko and Doronin, began to persuade individual members of the strike committee that Borysenko should no longer be kept under guard. Through their persistence they managed to persuade almost everyone on the committee that, since Borysenko had been locked up when Vorobev was committee chairman, and Vorobev had now been expelled from the committee, it made sense to release Borysenko.

It was our group, however, that had exposed Borysenko's conspirators, and he had been locked up on our initiative, not only because he had organized a plot against the committee, but also because he had never recognized the strike committee and its regulations. His arrogant, offensive behaviour had insulted and outraged all the political prisoners in our camp, who thus opposed his release.

The committee, however, did everything possible to release Borysenko, and Holovko and Doronin managed to convince Shamaev, the committee chairman, that it was time to let him go. Even Korol had difficulty withstanding the pressure from the other committee members. But, in line with our instructions, he did not state his point of view; rather, he demanded that since the decision to lock up Borysenko had been taken by a general meeting of the political prisoners his release should also be confirmed by the same. Shamaev and the other members of the committee gladly agreed to this, because they enjoyed great respect in the camp at this point and were convinced that no one would speak out against them. Shamaev was a much more skilful and effective speaker and organizer than Vozhdev or Vorobev; he had a keen understanding of a crowd's psychology and how best to manipulate it. Doronin was also a talented speaker, and could almost hypnotize an audience. Thus the two were confident that they could control the prisoners in the club and get them to agree to any stand taken by the committee. They did not know, however, with whom they were dealing. Their audience was not an amorphous crowd without a mind of its own, but a well-informed and disciplined (yet flexible) organization which had already taken a position on every item on the agenda. In fact, they were unaware even that such an organization existed. They depended on Korol to tell them what the Ukrainians were thinking, and since he had said nothing definite about this matter, they believed that the Ukrainians would support them.

As the time of the general meeting approached, Tarkavtsadze, as usual, held a meeting with his propagandists and sent them off to the barracks to make sure the prisoners would unanimously support the committee and approve its plans. The members of the self-help organization, however, had already done their work, and had surrounded the club to ensure that each person would get the seat assigned to him. Ten minutes before the meeting began, Korol secretly gave one of our lads the keys to the two doors of the club, and while the committee was still discussing its plan of action the self-help organization occupied all the places in the hall and gallery.

Ten minutes later the members of the strike committee left their headquarters and took their places behind a long table on the stage. "There's bound to be some opposition today," Shamaev said quietly, as if speaking to himself, after casting an experienced eye over the audience. At this very moment he decided to change the agenda, moving the question of Borysenko's release from the isolator from the beginning to the end. Then he opened the meeting. Five items were on the agenda, and before putting any questions to a vote Shamaev gave an explanation and informed the audience of the committee's point of view. He did this skilfully, and, as was always the case, everyone amicably supported him by voting for the committee's proposals.

Then, at the very end, Shamaev read the proposal concerning Borysenko's release, implying by his tone of voice that this was an unimportant, routine matter that could be resolved quickly. He used the same argument that since Vorobev had imprisoned Borysenko, and had since been removed as chairman of the committee, it was now time to free Borysenko.

The audience, however, had been waiting for precisely this proposal, and after Shamaev finished his presentation a number of prisoners located throughout the auditorium and gallery raised their hands so that they could respond. The first to speak was Shcherba, a young electrician.

"In the camp Borysenko always served as a brigade leader living like a parasite at the expense of the hard-labour prisoners, and furthermore he often beat them up and put them in the isolator. We forgave him his crimes, hoping that he would reconsider his past, repent and act like a normal human being. But—on the contrary—he began to plot against us during our struggle with the camp administration and its lackeys. In addition, he had no respect whatsoever for the rules we established. He went to the back of the kitchen every day, for example, and demanded that the cooks give him what he asked for. Out of 4,000 prisoners he alone turned out to be such a swine. Moreover, it's clear that he was informing the administration about the work of the committee and our activists. We'll consider whether Borysenko should be released only when he appears before one of our general meetings in person, sincerely condemns all his crimes, and promises to become an honest person."

"Scherba's right! Absolutely right!" shouted all the prisoners in the hall, clapping loudly to demonstrate their support. Shcherba's speech was followed by several others in a similar vein, all of which received friendly applause and shouts of approval. After these speeches Borysenko came out from behind a screen, stood quietly for a few minutes with bowed head, and then returned to his original place. This time Shamaev and all his friends understood, more than ever before, that they were simply a tool in the hands of an invisible, well-organized force which supported them only when the interests of the committee coincided with its own.

Having asserted their strength, unity and self-discipline, the prisoners left the meeting with radiant faces. In the meantime Vorobev and the members of his group had been sitting in their barracks, anxiously awaiting the end of the meeting, for they were certain that Borysenko would be released and were afraid of the consequences. When he finally heard about the outcome, Vorobev was surprised.

"I'd very much like to know the identity of the driving force behind this well-oiled machine," he said.

People like Vorobev believed that only someone blessed with supernatural talents can accomplish such things. The strength of our organization, however, lay in our supporters. We simply brought out and refined their better qualities, gave them some direction and, in accordance with a programme which they themselves approved, put them to work. All this, in turn, depended on organizational skills, tactfulness and political sensitivity, most of which I had acquired as a political prisoner in Łomża, and later refined.

# Chapter Twenty-Three

In the second half of July the snow in the valley beyond Camp No. 6 melted.

"You'll be set free when the snow on those hills disappears!" members of the camp administration had always told us in the past, relishing their words since this snow had never melted before and they enjoyed reminding us that we were destined to die amidst the permafrost of the Arctic North.

This period of calm, which lasted approximately three weeks, simply delayed the final resolution of our fate. All major decisions had to be taken in Moscow, which at this point was preoccupied with the Berlin uprising as well as the liquidation of Beria and his closest collaborators. Finally, however, our turn came. On 4 August 1953, at 2am, company after company began to emerge from the division's quarters in strict battle order and surrounded the camp. Eventually sixteen companies, or in other words an entire regiment, of heavily-armed security troops, especially trained to handle large groups of political prisoners, took up their positions. The number of soldiers manning the two Maxims and sixteen machine guns was doubled, with each company having its own field of fire, and officers holding small red flags took their places. This entire operation was conducted in total silence.

In response the hard-labour prisoners left their barracks brigade by brigade, in accordance with our plans, and took up their positions, empty-handed, opposite the companies. This was also done quietly, for each man knew that a final reckoning was at hand, and was ready to face it in a manner befitting a political prisoner.

Finally a menacing voice amplified by loudspeakers broke the ominous silence.

"We're opening the gates now and we're ordering all of you to leave the camp compound. If you don't leave within twenty minutes, then force will be used. Understand?"

This order was repeated three times, but the political prisoners did not move. They stood like a brick wall, and looked bravely into the mouths of the machine guns and Maxims. I headed toward the yeast kitchen and bath-house, near the division's compound, to keep up the morale of the prisoners in this dangerous spot, when suddenly seven trucks full of soldiers, sub-machine guns at the ready, appeared on the road leading to the camp. As the trucks drew near an officer waved his flag, the gates opened, and as the first truck passed through the gates, the soldiers began shooting into the crowd of prisoners at point-blank range. After this truck had crossed the camp and stopped near the barbed-wire fence the others followed, one by one, and the soldiers continued firing at the prisoners. In addition, the bath-house, yeast kitchen and former office building were raked by fire from the supply building and the division's compound. I was standing opposite the division's compound, next to the office building and close to the camp morgue, and was caught in the cross-fire as a soldier from the supply building and a group of soldiers from the compound peppered this corner. I felt it would be senseless to die here, next to the morgue, and I sprinted to the yeast kitchen, which was located next to the barbed-wire fence separating the camp and division compounds. After quickly cutting through this fence, the soldiers surrounded this red-brick building, lobbing in grenades and shooting through its doors and windows. Inside pandemonium reigned, as some prisoners were dying, others, dripping in blood, begged for help, and still others ran from one corner to another. The grenades continued to explode, filling the building with choking gases, and as I huddled in a corner and watched this terrible, senseless scene I was overcome with fear. But I did my best not to show any weakness, and after a few minutes the shooting began to subside. At this point I jumped into the neighbouring room, which was overflowing with old camp clothing, and found six people among the rags who were still alive.

The security troops moved on toward the hospital, main kitchen and two-storey barracks, and the sound of gunfire, exploding grenades and screaming grew louder in the centre of the camp, near the club. There was no point in sitting among the rags, and we decided to leave the building in which we were hiding. But as soon as we did so, warders and soldiers from the convoy troops detained and began to beat us, and we were chased beyond the camp zone and into a two-storey building.

From the yard of this building, which contained many dead and wounded prisoners, we saw Shcherba fall near the club after being shot in the chest. Vasyl Tabotadze, a Georgian and a former UPA member who had been having a feud with Shcherba, was running alongside him when this happened, and ignoring the heavy gunfire Tabotadze ran to his old enemy. He fell to his knees and, filled with grief, asked Shcherba's forgiveness for all his past insults. Shcherba looked silently at Tabotadze and, just before he died, used his remaining strength to exchange the caps they were wearing. I knew Shcherba and Tabotadze well, and could not hold back my tears at this scene. But they were tears of happiness as well as grief, for I was deeply impressed by the nobility of these two men.

In the meantime the warders were running about the camp with axes and crowbars, slaughtering the wounded prisoners. Before my eyes, a warder used a crowbar to finish off the fearless Bondarenko. An ambulance, however, had followed the trucks into the camp compound, and the medical personnel, headed by director Sano, managed to rescue some of the wounded prisoners from these murderers and carried them off to the hospital. Tamara, a medical aide from Armenia, especially distinguished herself by her courageous actions, and literally dragged prisoners out of the hands of their persecutors.

An hour after the attack had begun, the security troops already controlled the sections of the camp next to the division's compound, but it took them another four hours to subdue the entire camp. During this time the troops subjected these defenceless workers, who had built the city of Norilsk while subjected to cold, hunger and extremely brutal treatment, to a steady stream of gunfire and grenades. Norilsk is the site of a very important and strategically vital non-ferrous metallurgical industry, and it is a city of gigantic mines, factories and enterprises. A centre of extraordinary wealth, it has also been the site of unbelievable grief, a hell on earth in the God-forsaken and accursed Arctic North.[1]

The troops finished their work at 6am. Seventy-nine mothers would never see their sons again. The dead were buried in the permafrost, mourned by neither wives nor family. Two-hundred-and-eighty prisoners were registered as wounded and taken to the hospital, while the remainder were taken out into the tundra where, in groups of a hundred, they were led to a table. The camp administration and the same commission from Moscow were sitting at this table. Although Beria had been executed, his system remained intact and the authorities continued to use his methods. The members of Zhdanov's and Borysenko's groups were sitting nearby, and their duty was to tell the administration who should be assigned to which location. They had become accustomed to this dog's work in the employ of the Gestapo.

One by one we were called to the table, where the employees of the security section pulled out our cards, with photographs and comments attached, from a special card file, and the administration's informers suggested what should be done with us. When I approached the table and stated my name, there was a snarl from the informers.

"That's him! It was all his work." At this point a security officer pulled my pea-jacket over my head and began to pummel me about the kidneys.

"Take him to the left," ordered Vorontsov, the senior security officer. I was led away to a group of about a hundred prisoners who were sitting on the ground, and I thought to myself that I had escaped lightly. Just then, however, Vorontsov ran to our column.

"Shumuk!" he yelled, as if he was frightened of something. "Get up! You're in the wrong group."

I stood up, stepped out of the column, and Vorontsov ordered two soldiers from the security troops to take me to the "hole."

"Over there, on the double!" one of the soldiers ordered, pointing the way, and I was led 200 metres to a pit surrounded by small bushes.

"So finally they've given us some work to do!" the soldiers and officers who were standing about the pit shouted with glee as they twisted my arms around my back and handcuffed me tightly. Then I felt a hard blow on the back of my neck and fell straight into the pit, whereupon they stamped all over me and jumped on my back with all their might in order to crack my vertebrae. They kicked me in the sides and hit me about the head until three generals walked up, at which point the soldiers snapped to attention.

"Is that him?" one of the generals asked.

"Oh yes, that's him all right," a second general replied.

"What's your name?" the third asked.

"My hands are numb," I replied.

"Look, his hands are turning black," one of the generals noted. "Who has the keys? Loosen those handcuffs!" It was a full fifteen minutes before the keys could be found, but finally my handcuffs were loosened. Then I stated my name, but the generals were no longer listening and went away.

Ten minutes later Kozlauskas was led up to the pit.

"Look, the committee man has grown his hair back," an officer said and, grabbing Kozlauskas by the hair, kicked him in the stomach. Kozlauskas bent over, fell down, and everyone began to pummel him. Later another Ukrainian was brought to the pit and was given the same treatment.

"Stand up!" an officer then ordered the three of us, "and go in the direction I'm pointing." We obeyed and were escorted by three soldiers, one of whom hit me so hard at one point with the butt of his rifle that I fell down and blacked out for a few seconds. After 500 metres we reached a "Black Maria" whose back doors were open.

"Go in one at a time!" ordered a robust lieutenant standing at one side of the doors. Kozlauskas was first, and as he was about to place his left foot on the back step of the "Black Maria" the lieutenant, with all his strength, kicked him between the legs. Kozlauskas fell and lost consciousness. The soldiers threw him into the van and started to beat him and pull out his hair. The second prisoner received the same treatment. I was next. The lieutenant gritted his teeth and drew his right leg back, but I raised my right rather than left leg onto the step, thereby avoiding the full force of the kick.

"Give it to him good and proper for tricking me!" the lieutenant told the soldiers, who jumped into the van and began to pummel me. However, there were three prisoners inside now, and there was little room for the soldiers to indulge in their favourite "sport."

"Where do we take them?" the soldier who was driving asked the lieutenant.

"Take them to the other 'hole'," he replied. The "Black Maria" set off, and we groaned as we were thrown from one side of the van to another. I had received the worst of it in the first "hole," but I hadn't been beaten up too badly in the van. Fifteen minutes later the "Black Maria" stopped, the doors opened, and three men looked inside.

"Come out one at a time," an officer commanded. I was the first to emerge and a captain, pointing to the wall of a prison which they called the "hole," told us to run to it.

"You were told to run!" one of our guards shouted and kicked me in the side. When I reached the wall a lieutenant with a face like a bulldog told me to lie face downward on the ground.

"Enjoy the smell of the earth while you're still alive, for you'll all be finished off soon," he said. At this moment my two companions in misfortune were chased up to the wall, and were also ordered to lie down in the same position.

"Should we finish them off here, or near the cliff?" the lieutenant asked the captain.

"That would be too good for them. We'll play around with a different one each night; it's more fun then," the captain replied. "But for now we'll pass them one by one to our soldiers for exercise. Shumuk—get up and follow me."

I followed the captain into a dark corridor leading to the prison office. In the corridor four strong soldiers, stripped down to the waist, were already awaiting me.

"Have yourselves a workout with this brave fellow," the captain told them. The soldiers immediately grabbed me by the arms and legs and, raising me above their heads, threw me to the ground six times in a row. Later, after I was taken to the office to be registered, a woman doctor arrived and ordered me to strip naked. My entire body was covered with bruises, and after examining me the doctor turned to the captain.

"I see that he's been doing some boxing," she observed.

"Oh yes, he's quite a boxer," the captain replied and kicked me, with all his strength, in the stomach. I fell and was carried off to a cell. Even the Polish *defensywa* officials had never beaten me so harshly, and for three days I could not eat, drink or even rise from my bunk.

By nightfall so many people had been crammed into our cells that those furthest from the window began to faint from the lack of air. However, we were soon distributed among a number of cells, and five days after the beatings I was feeling better.

A few days after my recovery, several prisoners from Corrective Labour Camp No. 4 were brought to our cell. Among them was a tall, handsome, intense young man.

"Who is he?" I asked one of the prisoners in this group.

"That's Ievhen Hrytsiak,[2] a very brave fellow who led the strike in our camp," he replied.

For nine years we hard-labour prisoners had been isolated from all the political prisoners sentenced to corrective labour, since they had been tried after us. We were anxious to learn how these prisoners had conducted their strikes and what their demands had been, since we had always thought highly of their camps. Stepaniv, Vorotniak and Kolodii had spent many years with some of the corrective-labour-camp leaders such as Herman Petrovych Stepaniuk, Shchura, Horoshko and others, and idealized them. I wanted to meet these legendary figures, but none had ever ended up in our cell.

"Ievhen, you're from Camp No. 4?" I asked.

"Yes," he replied proudly.

"Would you please tell me how your strike started, developed and ended?"

"In the evenings, and especially on our days off, the Ukrainians gathered to sing folk songs. One day a soldier guarding the camp began shouting at them to stop their singing, but they ignored him. Then he started to shoot, killing one prisoner and wounding two others, and this gave rise to our strike."

"And who directed the strike?" I asked.

"I alone, from beginning to end."

"What did you demand from the government, and how did the strike end?"

"I demanded that the murderers be punished. A commission eventually arrived from Moscow and promised to look into all our complaints, so we went back to work."

"Did the prisoners go back to work themselves, or did you order them to do so?"

"I told them to return to work, for their mood was such that they would have returned regardless. That would have been worse for myself and for everyone involved."

"How long were you on strike?"

"Seventeen days."

"We were on strike for exactly two months, and our approach was completely different."

"So what?" Ievhen asked. "You let the Russians get all the glory for the strike, and they ordered you about. There wasn't a single Ukrainian among you who dared to take responsibility for the strike."

"Our intentions were different. We made sure that only Russians were officially in charge of the strike. But we forced this leadership to do our bidding."

"No one sees this; all they know is that it was Russians who gave the orders."

"The Russians always generously praised and rewarded those 'khokhly' who gave their strength, talent and lives to help build the Russian Empire. Now it's time for us to learn how to use the Russians to help destroy this empire. The Russian nation will become truly free only when it ceases to deny freedom to other nations."

Hrytsiak showed no desire to continue the conversation, but it was clear from the expression on his face that he was not convinced by my argument. In general he was an honest, intelligent and observant man, uninterested in personal gain; however, he was also vain, power-hungry and intolerant, and I found it very difficult to talk to him.

"Maybe we also should have led the prisoners out of the compound," Roman Z. said to me later. "By doing so we would have avoided the bloody massacre that took place."

"No, Roman," I replied. "I grow very sad when I think of the political prisoners in hard-labour camps who have died of cold, hunger, harsh work and persecution. But we should be proud of those who died fighting the excesses of this tyranny, for we used only humane means in our struggle. They opened fire on us for our simple refusal to support their lawlessness, and for demanding a public investigation of their crimes."

We spent an entire month in the "hole," and during our incarceration the prison director and the warders created an insidious atmosphere to convince us that we would be executed. The situation was extremely tense, because the prison director was the same security officer who had killed two believers in the Medvezhka camp, and the warders were also murderers. (Even today these men are being protected by the authorities, and some are receiving a sizable pension as a reward for their crimes. Only those who dare to speak and write about these crimes are persecuted.)

Eventually we were transferred from this prison to Dudinka, where we were placed in the hold of a ship which soon set off, along the Enisei River, toward Krasnoiarsk. The prisoners were happy, even though they knew that we were simply being taken to another prison, because finally we had left this terrible peninsula of death: death from cold, hunger and mistreatment, or from bullets, grenades and beatings.

# PART V

# Chapter Twenty-Four

As the boat made its way from Dudinka to Krasnoiarsk we eagerly watched the lighthouses on the banks of the Enisei pass by. Each day the scenery improved. After leaving the depressing tedium of the tundra behind, we entered a taiga zone which initially had sparse vegetation but gradually became more lush. On the ninth day of our trip we arrived in Krasnoiarsk harbour and were transferred to the local prison, which represented "freedom" to us after our stay in the "hole" of Norilsk.

I was placed in a cell with Meletii Semeniuk, Smirnov, a Lithuanian, and Chornobai—a Ukrainian from Vinnytsia oblast. The windows in this prison had iron louvers, and Meletii immediately began a loud exchange with the other prisoners transferred from Norilsk. He knew Herman Petrovych (Stepaniuk), Horoshko, Luka Stepanovych (Pavlyshyn), and many other prominent corrective-labour-camp prisoners. Smirnov also called out to the other prisoners, but these were all strangers to me.

As the evening drew near, Meletii and Smirnov broke a piece of metal off the bed, sharpened it, and used it to begin cutting a hole in the louvers. They did this with remarkable energy and determination, and by 8pm had cut a hole twenty square centimetres in area. Then Meletii took a piece of string, which he had hidden among his personal belongings, attached a note to it, and lowered it through the hole to his friends on the first floor of the prison. They were to tie a packet of tobacco to the string, which was called a "horse" according to prison slang.

We did not use this "horse" for long, because trusties carrying long poles were roaming the prison courtyard. They attached nails to the ends of these poles to "capture" the "horses" weighed down with tobacco or other goods, and our "horse" also met this fate. Such incidents were common in prison and surprised no one. But I was astounded when Meletii and Smirnov knocked on the cell door and told the warder to call his superior immediately. Soon afterward the door opened and the chief warder walked in.

"What happened?" he asked.

"Your lackeys—the dogs with white armbands—have intercepted our 'horse' carrying some tobacco. Please return it to us with its load or call the prison director," Semeniuk told him. The chief warder then stood on a stool and cried out when he saw the hole in the louvers.

"You've broken two important regulations: first, you've cut through the louvers; second, you let down a 'horse.' You violated a third regulation by making a knife to cut through the louvers. And you actually have the nerve to show the prison administration what you've done!"

"To hell with your regulations. Call the director," Smirnov said. The chief warder left the cell and soon the prison director arrived together with two other prison officers.

"What's the matter?" the director asked. Meletii repeated his complaint, after which the director also stood on the stool and looked at the hole in the louvers.

"Quiet, boys, calm down," he said. "We'll look into this, find your 'horse' and tobacco, and return them to you." And the next day the chief warder returned everything just as the director had promised.

A few days after this incident, a prison guard officer took us for a walk and we saw a trusty with a white armband use a long pole to intercept someone's "horse." Semeniuk ran up to the trusty, began to pummel him, and when the officer became involved Smirnov joined in the fight as well. Semeniuk pinned the officer to the wall but realizing how pointless the fight was, I ran up to Semeniuk and pushed him away from the officer. Smirnov then decided to leave the trusty alone, for although stronger than I, both prisoners respected me and would listen to my advice. The prisoners were not punished, and the administration's remarkable and unprecedented patience was a result of Beria's elimination; no one in the administration knew what the next day would bring.

From time to time we were taken to the local offices of the MVD and interrogated about the Norilsk strike. The officials often raised their voices during the interrogations, but never dared to strike us. I refused to give them any information about the strike and eventually they left me alone.

After a month in the Krasnoiarsk prison, we were transferred to the prison in Vladimir for a year. All the prisoners were in a fine, boisterous mood, and the administration treated us quite well in the transit prisons. But the high walls and massive iron gates which seal prisons off from the world always have a depressing effect. Also, prison administrators always share a common mentality. They are criminals, entrusted with power by the authorities, and are never called to account for their crimes; on the contrary, they are paid and awarded medals for their misdeeds. Their faces are so inhuman that at times I would look at them and try to comprehend that they, like everyone else, had wives, children and parents.

At Vladimir prison we were imprisoned in the third block, built during tsarist times, in which several senior officers of the German and Japanese armies were still being held. Our corridors were served by female warders who treated us relatively well. In fact, the behaviour of the prison director and his entire administration was very civilized compared to that of the camp administration.

We were soon transferred, however, to the first block, which had been built after the Bolshevik Revolution. Here the cells were approximately 12–13 square metres in area, with small windows high up on the wall and five bunks attached to the side and back walls of the cell. In the middle, between the bunks, a small table and two small benches were fixed to the cement floor—this was all our "furniture." These cells were depressing and poorly lit, and the administration in this block was much more brutal than in the third or even the fourth blocks; in fact, the first block was like a special punishment prison. Thus foreigners were kept in a "tsarist" prison and treated in accordance with the old tsarist standards, while we were kept in a Soviet prison and treated by Soviet standards.

Every prison is terrible because of its crude violation of human nature; Soviet Russian prisons, however, are the worst of all not only because of the way in which they were built and the extremely harsh treatment of their occupants, but also because of the subtle use of psychological torture. The prison administration places one prisoner who is mentally ill or totally incapable of getting along with his cellmates in every cell so that the political prisoners cannot use their free time to improve themselves. For example, Kovalchuk, who was mentally ill, was placed in our cell. Not only did he attack each one of his cellmates; he would also throw himself at the walls, beat on the door with his fists, and jump onto the window-sill and from there to the table. He made a similar commotion every day, preventing us from reading, writing or even thinking. This made us constantly tense and nervous, exhausting us both physically and spiritually. Kovalchuk was a much greater punishment than the prison itself.

"You can put me in the worst solitary confinement cell, but get me out of here!" I told the prison director.

"I have no right to do that; it's not up to me," he replied. At this point I realized that this system for destroying the political prisoners physically and psychologically had been planned, down to the smallest detail, at the highest level of the penal system.

Fortunately, our stay in the Vladimir prison did not last long. At this time the very foundations of the penal system were being shaken. Early in the spring of 1954 Vavilov, the deputy procurator general who had visited our camp in Norilsk, came to the Vladimir prison and reviewed the decisions on our cases. He arranged for us—the strike leaders from the Norilsk and Vorkuta camps, about 400 persons in all—to be transferred to the Taishet camps. The prison administration prepared us for the trip and took us to the train station, where we were loaded into red freight cars. Soon we were once again on our way to Siberia.

There were few Russians among the strike leaders and the political prisoners as a whole, but they loved to make speeches from the windows of our freight cars when we stopped at train stations along the way to Taishet. At the larger cities we sometimes stopped for more than an hour, and the local people crowded around the train. They had been roused from years of apathy by the atmosphere of anxiety after the death of Stalin and the execution of Beria. Some of the more daring in the crowd even tried to break through the convoy troops surrounding the train to pass food and cigarettes to us.

"Where do you think you're going?" the troops asked, holding them back. "Don't you know who they are? Why they're Beria's men, and you want to help them!" Throughout our trip the convoy troops continued lying in this brazen manner to those sympathetic toward us. As a result, at every railway station we shouted out who we were and why we were suffering in camps and prisons.

There were approximately 140 prisoners in our freight car. All except my friend Fedir and myself had been detained in the Vladimir prison because of the strike in Vorkuta. Initially Fedir had had misgivings about the events which led to the strike in Hard Labour Camp No. 3, but later, at the peak of the strike, he offered to help out with the work of the self-help organization, and we gladly gave him some duties suited to his skills. After our fierce disagreements, only someone like Fedir could have offered me his services and subordinated himself to my command. Such friends are few and far between.

All the other prisoners in the freight car knew one another. Thus Fedir and I decided to find out more about our companions. I made the acquaintance of a Lithuanian colonel who had graduated from a military academy in Holland before the war, and of a Jewish psychiatrist, a former director of a psychiatric hospital in Vilnius. Fedir, in the meantime, spoke with some of the Ukrainians.

Most of the latter belonged to a tightly-knit group of young men with several leaders of whom Ievhen Roniuk, a tall, strapping young man, was the most authoritative. It was clear from their behaviour that they had been much feared in the camps. It was also clear, from their proud accounts, that they had been exploiting the ordinary labourers (whom they contemptuously called "misers") by extorting money from them. They were contemptuous of intellectuals, whom they called "diplomats." If these "diplomats" ever interfered in their racket, they were unceremoniously beaten up; some were even killed. Ordinary criminals, of course, had done the same throughout the camps, but at least they had not pretended to be political prisoners and nationalists, nor had they persecuted intellectuals so openly. But these prisoners, although they considered themselves "Ukrainian nationalists," were brutal in their treatment of genuine Ukrainian patriots.

This group formed a fifth column among the Ukrainian political prisoners. Some of its members were simply carrying out the orders of the secret police, but most of them, although led by the administration's lackeys, were criminals who were interested only in their own personal gain. At this point, however, their criminal activities were unknown to me, and Fedir, as usual, tried to discover something positive in these thugs. We never agreed in our appraisals of people, because he was always impressed by power, even if this power was used negatively. In contrast, I believed that one should oppose the high-handed behaviour of these Ukrainian gangs. I could excuse ordinary criminals in their crimes, but not those who claimed to be fighting for the independence of their people, but were defaming the good name of their nation.

Although there were few negative elements of this kind among the prisoners from the hard-labour camps, and they were powerless, they were quite numerous among the prisoners from the corrective-labour camps. The Ukrainians in the former group were primarily officers or rank-and-file members of UPA detachments, and occasionally OUN members, whereas the Ukrainians in the latter group had various backgrounds. They included, for example, "strybky" who had left OUN self-defence groups in the villages to join NKVD extermination battalions, as well as ordinary criminals who had plundered peaceful families and co-operatives and then left nationalist literature at the scene of the crime to incriminate the OUN. Inexperienced young men were often blackmailed into joining their gangs, and it was much more difficult to fight this fifth column among the Ukrainian political prisoners than to oppose the gangs in Hard Labour Camp No. 3, composed of former German policemen and their commanders, which had co-operated openly with the camp administration.

In short, I was disillusioned by my first encounter with the prisoners from the corrective-labour camps. I was also disappointed by the Lithuanian colonel and the psychiatrist from Vilnius, who may have been competent professionals but were politically rather naive. It was convenient, however, to study these people in the freight car, since no one knew us or paid us any attention.

After five or six days of travel we arrived in Taishet, Irkutsk oblast, and were sent along the Bratsk route to Camp No. 5, which consisted of four long barracks, a dining room, a bath-house and a medical station. One of the barracks housed invalid political prisoners who still wore numbers on the front and back of their clothing. In addition, all the barracks had bars on their doors and windows; in other words, Beria's old methods were still in force here. Once we had settled down we visited the old residents of the camp, i.e., the invalids, and explained to them that political prisoners no longer had to wear numbers, and that locked doors and barred windows were no longer found in other camps. The disabled old-timers, however, listened to us with fear in their eyes.

"Our camp's administration has been briefing us about your arrival for several days now," one old invalid from Volhynia said. " 'Beria's supporters will be arriving here soon,' they told us, 'and they might try to provoke you into disobeying the administration. You must avoid falling for their stories, and inform us about all their tricks'." Other invalids told us similar stories. We were so angry at this slander that we tore the numbers off the invalids' clothes. Then we ripped the grates off the windows and the locks off the doors as the invalids looked on in horror. Next we brought the deputy director of the camp to the invalids and asked them whether he was the one who told them that we were Beria supporters. The invalids remained quiet, but the deputy director was quaking with fear. In those days the camp administration had no idea what the next day would bring and tried to appease us by making a number of small concessions.

The leader of the corrective-labour-camp prisoners established their "staff," which was recognized by the administration, in the dining room. I took great interest in and became acquainted with various prominent people from the corrective-labour camps. Some of their names, associated with various legendary stories, were already familiar to me from my conversations with Meletii Semeniuk, Stepan Romaniv and Andrii Vorotniak. The most famous were Herman Petrovych Stepaniuk, Ievhen Horoshko and Ievhen Shchur.

I did not have to spend time looking for these people, for Stepan Romaniv approached Tarashchansky and myself and said that he would introduce us to Herman Petrovych. Full of curiosity, we followed him to a man with a red beard, of medium height and indeterminate age, who was sitting on one of the lower bunks in a corner of the barracks. He seemed to be an energetic fellow, and his eyes, which were partly hidden behind his glasses, had a perpetually surprised look. After we had shaken hands, Stepaniuk invited us to sit down opposite him, at which point Romaniv left.

"You're from Hard Labour Camp No. 3?" Stepaniuk asked. "I have very little time for you now. Until recently I was in prison, so now everyone wants to talk with me and to ask my advice. I simply don't have time to listen to everyone and give them the proper instructions. So, to get to the point, tomorrow you'll go to Barracks No. 1 and there you'll read Shevchenko's 'Haidamaky'[1] to our lads. Understand?"

"Well, what do you think of this legendary 'leader'?" I asked Tarashchansky after we parted with Stepaniuk.

"Maybe he couldn't see us very well through his glasses and mistook us for youngsters," Tarashchansky replied.

"It would be quite sad if all these great 'leaders' were like Stepaniuk," I added.

During our first few days in Camp No. 5 Stepaniuk indeed met dozens of people. I watched how he behaved during these meetings and it was clear, from the mysterious look he affected and the imperious way in which he shook his ruddy beard, that he spoke to everyone in the same arrogant, authoritarian manner.

On my second day in the camp a handsome young fellow approached me. Speaking rapidly in a clear, boyish tone of voice, he apologized for disturbing me and asked whether I was Danylo.

"I'm pleased to meet you," he said. "I'm Horoshko. We should get to know each other, for we have to work things out so that the prisoners know who's who and whom to obey. The corrective-labour prisoners have been in a number of camps and we all know one another. The prisoners from the hard-labour camps, however, don't know anyone and have been staying quite aloof from us."

"It's good that they're keeping a certain distance," I replied. "Only after knowing a person well, and taking various factors into consideration, is it possible to decide whether that person should be obeyed."

"We decide such matters in the course of a single evening," Horoshko replied.

"Well, in our case it sometimes took years to determine who was who."

"I'll introduce you to an older prisoner, Pavlyshyn, a former member of the krai provid of the OUN. Maybe you'll find it easier to come to an agreement of some kind with him."

"Fine, I'll be glad to make his acquaintance."

"I'll talk to him first, and then introduce you," Horoshko said and left the barracks.

At this point I still respected, at least in an abstract way, the senior-ranking members of the OUN and UPA, and therefore I was interested to meet Luka Stepanovych Pavlyshyn, who had been the krai military director for Galicia. In the evening Horoshko invited me to his barracks, and nearing the stove area where Pavlyshyn was sitting, Horoshko knocked politely on one of the bunks.

"Please come in," Pavlyshyn said as he smiled politely and rose to his feet.

"Luka Stepanovych, this is Danylo Shumuk, from Hard Labour Camp No. 3."

"I'm very glad that we've met; I've heard about you," Pavlyshyn said. Horoshko bowed and left us, and Pavlyshyn suggested that we go out onto the road. We spent about three hours walking around and talking. I described my work in the underground, the circumstances of my capture, and events in the hard-labour camps, but Pavlyshyn listened without much interest. Then he gave me a detailed description of his activities and listed all the posts he had once held in the OUN. He especially enjoyed talking about military affairs, proudly showing off his knowledge of Clausewitz.[2]

"What was the strike like in Camp No. 5?" I asked Pavlyshyn.

"I had left the underground and was working as the director of a secondary evening school in Lviv when I was arrested, so I didn't get involved in the strike. Another fellow here was in the underground until 1950; he's the one who's best informed about these matters, and if you get to know him he'll tell you everything you want to know."

"But I thought that you would have been the one responsible for Camp No. 5?"

"No, the fellow I just mentioned was in charge. Incidentally, I suggest that you introduce one of the lads from the hard-labour camps to Horoshko, for the younger prisoners should be responsible for bringing order to their own ranks."

"The prisoners from the hard-labour camps have lived in strict isolation for many years, so first we have to get our bearings and take stock of these new circumstances. Then we'll decide on our policies." We parted on friendly terms after this conversation.

At first, it was difficult to grasp what was taking place in the camp because only one prisoner from the hard-labour camp was living in the same section as Pavlyshyn, Stepaniuk and Horoshko. This was Ivan Bukhalo from Derman, a tall, polite fellow with a certain natural intelligence. I called him out onto the road one day and, finding a suitable place behind the bath-house, asked him a few questions.

"Ivan, you're an observant fellow—I'd be grateful if you could tell me something about the Ukrainians you're living with now. Whom do you like the most, why, and who has the greatest authority?"

"We've only been here for a few days and it's impossible to learn much in such a short time. I can only give you my first impressions. Look, for example, at the two men who are walking near Barracks No. 4. The one on the left is Mykhailo Marushko, and the one on the right is Ivan Stoliar. I was in the same box-car as Marushko and I got the impression that he was an intelligent person. Everyone in the boxcar treated him with great respect, and he spoke in a calm, intelligent, reasonable fashion. Everyone in our section thinks highly of Marushko; not only Horoshko, but even Luka Pavlyshyn and Herman Stepaniuk. Stoliar is a restrained, introverted fellow who seems to keep his distance from camp activities; he can concentrate on reading a book even when there's a great deal of shouting and other noise in the barracks."

"How does Marushko behave toward the others?"

"He looks down on Horoshko, and although he treats Luka and Herman more seriously he doesn't think much of them either."

"How about Stoliar?"

"He treats Stoliar as an equal."

"And how do the others feel about Stoliar?"

"They all seem to boycott him, but he just ignores them."

"How does Ievhen Shchur behave?"

"Shchur won't have anything to do with Luka, Herman, Horoshko or Marushko, and for some reason he simply hates Stoliar."

"How does Ievhen Hrytsiak fit into this group?"

"Hrytsiak talks mostly with Pavlyshyn, but the others ignore him."

"And how about Ievhen Roniuk and the 'Old Man'?"

"They take Marushko and Horoshko seriously but won't have anything to do with Herman, Luka and Stoliar. It's hard to make any sense out of this mess."

"That's true, but I'd say that Marushko wields the greatest authority in this group."

After talking with Bukhalo I decided to discuss the situation with Tarashchansky and Semeniuk.

"What are your impressions of these new people?" I asked. "How do the prisoners in your sections behave?"

"It's a rather confusing situation because the most 'indigestible' prisoners from various camps have been brought together here," Tarashchansky replied. "I have the impression that various anarchic elements dominated most of the corrective-labour camps. For example, a group of strong young lads led by Roniuk and the 'Old Man' have settled in the section where I'm staying. They behave like ordinary criminals, although the real thieves speak Russian and never emphasize their nationality. But these lads speak Ukrainian and, unfortunately, have the nerve to consider themselves political activists."

"Many other prisoners also live in your section," I noted.

"That's true, but they've been terrorized by the members of this small group, which is the only organized force in the barracks. Almost all the younger men hang around with them."

Later Fedir told me more about the young people in this group.

"About thirty strong fellows armed with sharp knives live in my section. They recognize no authority other than Horoshko and Roniuk, look down on Pavlyshyn and Stepaniuk, and respect only those who can handle a knife as well or better than they can. Do you have any idea what Pavlyshyn and Stepaniuk think of them?"

"It seems that this gang doesn't care what those two think," I said, "because it doesn't take them seriously. In any case, Pavlyshyn and Stepaniuk would more readily side with the gang, as its apologists, than with us."

"A few prisoners from the hard-labour camps have already been drawn into this group," Fedir added. "In our section, for example, Ivan Dovhy sometimes spends all night with them."

"Could you tell Iakymchuk to keep an eye on him and find out where he goes?"

"Fine, Iurko and I will try to find out what's going on."

A few days later Stepan Romaniv came up to me.

"What are you doing?" he asked anxiously. "You don't know whom you're dealing with. They could come up to you at this very moment and beat you senseless or even kill you!"

"What's the matter?" I asked.

"You don't know what's going on? They say that you arranged for Ivan Dovhy to be watched. I just barely managed to dissuade them from going after you, but I wasn't able to stand up for Fedir and Iakymchuk, so they're after those two now."

I found Fedir and told him what Romaniv had said.

"That's bad," he said, "Maybe you should see Pavlyshyn and discuss this with him."

"I'll do that, although he doesn't pull any weight with those thugs."

"But he has some influence on Horoshko, and they take him seriously."

I went to see Pavlyshyn, and just as I began to tell him what I had heard from Romaniv I looked through a window and saw Fedir in the company of four strong lads from Roniuk's gang.

"They've just taken him away," I said.

"Then I can't help you. If Horoshko was here then maybe he could do something," Pavlyshyn noted.

I rose without saying another word and ran after the men who had led Fedir away. Near Barracks No. 3, to which Fedir had been taken, a complete stranger stopped me.

"Don't go in there after them. I beg you!" he said, his voice trembling with fear. "Those animals are capable of murdering you and then boasting that they killed an important stool pigeon. They can do this very skilfully, and can even find witnesses to confirm publicly that you were an informer. They've already killed Kuts Horbenko,[3] a former member of the OUN Provid from Lutsk; Moroz,[4] a former colonel in Petliura's army; and many others. They hold nothing sacred, and have murdered, without hesitation, all those who have dared to interfere in their activities. Ievhen Shchur is the cruelest and most cunning of them all, but Roniuk and the 'Old Man' aren't much better," the stranger told me.

"What do you mean? They simply call people out and kill them?"

"Oh no, they're not so straightforward. If they find it necessary to kill one of your friends then they'll force me, by threatening my own life, to do the job for them. Then they'll force you to go to the security office and take responsibility for the murder, which you supposedly committed because of some personal conflict. And when you've been sentenced they'll try to exploit this as well. They'll gather money from ordinary labourers on the pretext of helping you in prison, they'll praise you for killing an important 'stool pigeon,' and then they'll drink away the money they've collected. That's how that gang operates; I hope that you'll draw the right conclusions. And please don't let anyone know about our conversation," the stranger asked.

"Fine, I'll take this into account. Thanks for the warning and the information."

"I'm Petro," the stranger said and returned to Barracks No. 2.

Roniuk's group released Fedir from its cabin just as Petro finished telling me about these horrors. I wanted to question him at once, but Fedir was totally broken and indicated silently that he wanted to be left alone. I felt sorry for him, but was disappointed that he had given in so easily.

Later it turned out that the members of this gang had been digging a tunnel in Barracks No. 3 and had included Ivan Dovhy in their work. Thus they had accused Fedir and Iurko Iakymchuk of spying on them, whereas we knew nothing about the tunnel and had little interest in it. We did regret, however, that Ivan Dovhy had allowed himself to be recruited into the gang.

Soon almost all of the political prisoners in our camp knew of the ill-feeling between the gang and myself. Occasionally individual prisoners would come to me and describe the crimes the gang had committed. One man approached me near the dining room.

"See that fellow over there, who's walking with a grey scarf round his feet?" he said. "He's a German from Eastern Ukraine and yesterday his boots were taken away."

"Who did this?" I demanded angrily.

"You can go and ask him yourself," the stranger replied.

I immediately called the German aside.

"Who took your boots?" I asked.

The German gave me an inquiring look.

"I didn't tell you that my boots were taken away," he said after a brief pause.

"No, but I heard about it from others."

"To hell with the boots! I've known those people for a long time and would advise you to avoid them at all costs. It would be better for both of us if you just dropped this matter."

"How did they manage to terrorize all of you? Why are you so frightened?"

"If you had spent even a single year with them you'd know the meaning of fear," the German replied. After timidly looking around he walked away and three hard-labour prisoners who had left the dining hall approached me.

"What's going on?" one of them angrily asked. "Yesterday there wasn't enough sugar, and today we didn't get any fried fish. We took this up with the chief cook and he said that if we raised a stink about this we could end up in real trouble."

"Okay, boys, I'll take this up with the person responsible."

I had thought that the prisoners in the corrective-labour camps were of a much higher calibre than the hard-labour prisoners, and that everything had been run more smoothly in their camps. But the opposite was true—in no way were they our equals. Their strike had been a brief, chaotic revolt, and they had been incapable of seizing the opportunity to direct the strike along the right channels. They had been unable to transform this spontaneous outburst of anger into an organized, intelligent and cultured political force. And yet among them were former members of the krai, oblast and okruh provids of the OUN, who had a complete or incomplete higher education and years of organizational experience.

Later I met Horoshko and confronted him with the scandal of the German's boots and the thefts from the canteen. Horoshko did not deny my accusations. He merely argued that the German had stolen from the Ukrainians in some other camps and that it was only these stolen goods which had been taken away from him. Horoshko claimed that he knew nothing about the canteen, and said that he always received the same food as everyone else.

"I categorically oppose the slogan 'steal what has been stolen,' which gives any scum the right to live off the work of honest labourers," I informed him. "If you had returned those boots to their rightful owner then that would have been wonderful. But you took them for your own use, placing yourself on the same level as the German or even below him. You've taken his shame upon yourself and you've cast shame on all the Ukrainian political prisoners. Don't you understand this?"

"I didn't take those boots; I have my own," Horoshko replied.

"I know you didn't take them. The 'Old Man' took the boots and he's wearing them now, but you're the leader of this mob and you're proud of it. That's why I'm talking to you."

"I wouldn't mind if you talked to me alone about this, but you've been discussing these matters with everyone and call us bandits! You're turning the Ukrainians from Eastern Ukraine against us, and if I wasn't around you would have been finished off a long time ago. You don't realize whom you're dealing with," Horoshko said.

Horoshko was the only gang leader with whom I could still talk. In Camp No. 5 he acted to some extent as a brake on the gang and actually prevented it from attacking me, but the tension continued to grow. Roniuk, the "Old Man" and Nykolyshyn simply glared at me, and their gang was just waiting to settle accounts with me. In the meantime Marushko, Stepaniuk and Pavlyshyn looked askance at me and not only turned a blind eye to the crimes of these thugs, but even encouraged and praised some of their actions. Only Stoliar kept to himself and had nothing to do with this gang.

# Chapter Twenty-Five

Three weeks later Ivan Bukhalo was sent to the central hospital, seriously ill with tuberculosis of the spine. The hard-labour prisoners from our camp collected some money and foodstuffs for him, escorted him to the gates, and I took his place in the barracks. Pavlyshyn was two beds away from me, beyond him were Horoshko and Herman Petrovych, and Stoliar, Marushko, Hrytsiak and Shchur lived on the other side. In short, this was the section of the Ukrainian "elite." Druzhynsky and other less well-known members of this "elite" also lived here, and the only hard-labour prisoners in this section were Vasyl Panasiuk, Stepan Shevchuk and myself.

I later discovered that, in other camps, before coming here, the members of this "elite" had feuded bitterly with one another. Their various conflicts, however, were not based on any real differences of opinion, but on personal ambitions and competition for access to the "trough" (the dining hall).

The arrival of the hard-labour prisoners, however, and myself in particular, united almost everyone in this group. When Shchur saw that they were all opposed to me he tried to establish contact with me, but perceiving my hostility, he also turned against me. Only Stoliar remained neutral (at this point Hrytsiak and Druzhynsky were not taken seriously by the others). But who were these people, and what did they stand for?

Pavlyshyn (born in 1907) was an "intellectual" who had readily adopted the superficial emphasis on good manners fashionable in interwar Galicia, and he knew exactly when and to whom he should smile and bow. He was not particularly intelligent but, as mentioned earlier, he loved to talk about military affairs and especially about Clausewitz and his ideas on the theory and practice of partisan warfare. By nature he was a vain and spineless "gentleman" who was especially fond of eating well and having a "good time."

Marushko (born around 1922) was the son of a village head in the Stanyslaviv area, and had studied medicine for four years. He also lacked intelligence, and had worked at the okruh level of the OUN. He had a special "talent" for setting the people around him at each other's throats and then stepping in, as a judge, to settle their disputes. In this way he achieved a central position in the camp, and eagerly kept in touch with all the various warring factions.

Herman Petrovych Stepaniuk was from Eastern Ukraine and had completed a degree in economics. He was an arrogant fellow who posed as an important political activist, often boasting, for example, that he was a member of the UHVR (Supreme Ukrainian Liberation Council). He had few organizational abilities, but was skilled at creating the impression that he was a very able organizer.

Ivan Stoliar (born around 1921) had studied medicine for four years and had apparently worked in the liaison branch of the OUN Provid. Stoliar was remarkably sober-minded, and could shut out all his surroundings when he was reading. He had a sound knowledge of medicine and had more organizational background than anyone else in this group. Stoliar was well versed in the ideology of the OUN, remained loyal to its principles, and was the most honest, determined and intelligent prisoner in this group.

Shchur had completed six grades of elementary school but the rest of his past was a mystery. He was of limited intelligence, treacherous, and always ready to carry out the most despicable acts.

Horoshko was a handsome young fellow who loved attention but lacked experience in organizational matters. In the camp he had gained a reputation as a fearless leader of Ukrainian groups which had fought against former thieves who worked for the administration in the early 1950s. However, this was essentially a struggle for access to the "trough" and for seniority in the camps. Once in control of the camp these new groups established their own order, but the new masters proved to be no better than those they had vanquished.

One day, I met three hard-labour prisoners who were brimming with anger.

"For two months," one said, "we faced the muzzles of the MVD'S machine guns and then braved their grenades and gunfire, and now the likes of Horoshko are pushing us around. They didn't have the guts to stand up against the brutality of the MVD but attack us quite openly, since they know that our principles won't allow us to fight our fellow Ukrainians."

"What actually happened?" I asked.

"We were standing over there, on the road near the canteen, when a cart with groceries drove up. The shopkeeper asked us to unload the cart, and after helping him we each bought a kilogramme of butter and sugar. In the meantime, however, Horoshko set up his own line and had us beaten up because we dared to buy something without his permission."

"We won't start brawling with them over access to the 'trough' or because of the line-up to the canteen," I told them. "That's beneath our dignity. On the contrary; the next time some goods arrive in the canteen not one of the hard-labour prisoners will even go near it. We've shown that we can rise above the interests of our stomachs and we'll continue to do so."

Pavlyshyn and Stepaniuk were sitting in the neighbouring aisle of the barracks, only a metre away, and overheard the entire conversation. When the three prisoners left, Pavlyshyn and Stepaniuk also slipped away. Ten minutes later six tall, young thugs with rolled-up sleeves walked in, with Roniuk, Paliucha and Nykolyshyn at the head, and solemnly trooped through our section. They stopped briefly near the aisle where my bunk was located, and before leaving they stared at me in contempt just as an executioner would look at his victim. The meaning of this demonstration could not have been clearer. Afterward all the apologists for this gang stopped greeting me.

While these events were unfolding another small convict transport arrived from the Vladimir prison. These new prisoners were from the Vorkuta camps, and had been sent to prison because of the strikes which took place there. The most colourful figure in this group was Slavko Pashchak, who had been arrested while completing his studies in French philology at the University of Chernivtsi. He knew French, German, Ukrainian and Polish, in addition to some English, and was well versed in the history of Ukraine and the Catholic Church. A veteran member of the OUN from Lemkivshchyna, he had worked in the municipal and oblast provids of the OUN in Vinnytsia in 1941–2. Marushko and Stoliar immediately included Pashchak in their circle, although Pavlyshyn sometimes took him for long walks.

The Russians in the camp lived in Barracks No. 1. Most prominent among them were the sons of the Russian nobility who had emigrated to Japan, Manchuria and China during the Bolshevik Revolution. The most intelligent, tactful and well behaved of these prisoners was Savelev, a former major in the Japanese secret service. They all had a typical émigré mentality, and were so out of touch with their native country and its people that they were incapable of thinking realistically about the future. They even went to the absurd length of organizing, in a very earnest fashion, elections for the Tsar of all Russia. Three candidates from the camp were put forward for this position (so it was still a relatively "democratic" vote): two colonels and one major, each with his own supporters. Two of the candidates were equally intelligent and influential in the camp, and because of this ambiguous situation they agreed to support the weaker, less influential candidate, and then to form separate parties of their own. In short, the outcome was typical: of the three candidates the most stupid became "tsar."

After the election of a "tsar" and the formation of a "government," the Russians also began to dig a tunnel. To reach freedom the tunnel had to be approximately thirty metres long, and the digging was very difficult. The Russians made a sled shaped like a boat out of small zinc wash-basins, wrote "Ark of Freedom" on it in large letters, and used this "ark" to drag earth from the underground passage. They made a bellows out of old boot-tops to pump air to those working in the tunnel. The Russians had a tendency to be rather pompous, and their activities seemed both comical and ridiculous to us.

Pavlyshyn used to tell the Russians that they were generals without an army, whereas the Ukrainians had both. He of course considered himself to be a general, and Horoshko's cohorts to be an army. This "army," however, never acknowledged Pavlyshyn as its general. Only Horoshko and Roniuk were recognized as its leaders, and then only to the extent that they approved of the high-handed behaviour of their "soldiers."

The MVD discovered the Ukrainians' tunnel when it reached the twenty-six metre mark, and the Russians' tunnel at the twenty-four metre mark. The symbolic "Ark of Freedom" was photographed in all its glory, and some thirty prisoners were taken to the central isolator in Taishet. Among them were Pavlyshyn, Stepaniuk, Horoshko, Hrytsiak, Druzhynsky, Iurko Sakharov (a chess player from Kiev) and Varava (a mathematician).

A few days later Tarashchansky, Fedir and myself (of the hard-labour prisoners) and Marushko, Roniuk and several others (of the corrective-labour prisoners) were also taken to the central isolator. I was placed in the same cell as Marushko and a man named Biletsky.

Since the window of our cell was open, during the exercise period Stepaniuk, Stoliar and Pavlyshyn used to come up to the window to talk with Marushko, and Tarashchansky and Fedir would come to see me. One day Fedir told me that he had heard, via the central hospital, that Horbovy,[1] who had been defence attorney for Bandera and the entire OUN Provid at the Warsaw trial of 1935,[2] was imprisoned somewhere in the Taishet complex of camps. Since I still believed that the founders of the OUN stood head and shoulders above the OUN leaders whom I had met in the camps, I was eager to meet him.

A few days later the security branch of the Ozerlag[3] administration began an investigation into the escape preparations. When questioned, I refused to give testimony concerning the tunnels and escape preparations, because I had not been involved in these activities.

"According to an eternal moral code," I told the investigator, "a slave should never hinder other slaves when they escape; on the contrary, he should help them. I neither helped nor hindered the other prisoners, and therefore I have no desire to discuss this matter any further. The state pays the security organs quite handsomely to guard the prisoners, and yet you want to transfer even this responsibility onto our shoulders, so that the prisoners will guard one another." The investigator summoned two other security officers and, after preparing a document stating that I had refused to give testimony concerning the escape attempt he asked me to sign this scrap of paper. I refused, even though they threatened to imprison me.

Two months later Tarashchansky, Roniuk, myself and a few other prisoners were sent back to Camp No. 5. The others, approximately forty in number, were sent to the Irkutsk prison.

Iaroslav Pashchak greeted me warmly when I arrived in the camp.

"You should see what's going on now that Shchur has gone into action," he told me. "Recently, for example, the storage room in which our invalids kept their clean clothing and the food from their parcels was robbed. At the moment the gang is being led by Shchur and Ipolit Shkursky, who arrived here in the most recent prisoner transport. We have to stick together now."

"Fine, I'm delighted that you're with us," I replied. "But why were you afraid to meet with me earlier?"

"Marushko advised me not to see you. They ensnared me so quickly and so thoroughly that I couldn't take a single step without their approval."

"Why do they dislike me?"

"They never mentioned anything directly to me about this, but one day, in the presence of myself, Pavlyshyn and Stoliar, Marushko said that the hard-labour prisoners had to be brought under control, because they didn't recognize anyone except their Shumuk. In reply Pavlyshyn smiled and said that he had spoken to you about this the first time he met you, but that this conversation had no effect on you. I said that I didn't know you and couldn't say anything about this matter, and Stoliar was silent. Then, after a brief pause, Marushko said that, in his opinion, a few lads should be sent to rough you up, for a person who had been beaten up would no longer have any authority and no one would listen to him. He added that his boys would be glad to do this. Pavlyshyn just smiled when Marushko finished and looked at Stoliar, who remained silent."

"What held them back?" I asked.

"I don't know. They never discussed this again in my presence."

I lived in the same section as Shchur, Tarashchansky lived in the same section as Roniuk and the "Old Man," and Pashchak lived in the same section as Ipolit Shkursky. Between us we ascertained that the gang leaders were supported by a few dozen healthy young lads whose only skill was using a knife, whereas all the other prisoners, and there were hundreds, were opposed to these thugs. But they were passive and had been terrorized by the gang.

The first anniversary of the bloody reprisals against the the strikers of Hard Labour Camp No. 3 was approaching. The hard-labour prisoners decided to honour this day, and set up an initiative group to decide how the bloody tragedy would be commemorated. Every one of the seventy hard-labour prisoners in Camp No. 5 donated some money for this purpose, and preparations were carried out in the strictest secrecy so that Shchur's gang would not hear of them. Only Tarashchansky and myself knew the whole programme for the anniversary, since each participant was aware only of his own specific assignment.

On 4 August 1954 all the political prisoners in Camp No. 5 were notified that when they heard the rail ring they should immediately go to their barracks. People were intrigued by this mysterious announcement and waited impatiently for the signal. At exactly 12 noon one of the hard-labour prisoners went up to the hanging rail and struck it several times. The echo of the ringing rolled across the entire camp, alarming the administration and the guards in the watch-towers, and all the political prisoners immediately ran to their barracks. Probably out of curiosity, Shchur, Roniuk and Shkursky also obeyed the signal.

In each section a prisoner, whom we had appointed beforehand, ordered the prisoners to stand at attention (everyone obeyed the command) and then made a brief statement:

"One year ago today our dearest friends were felled by the bullets of Beria's henchmen and were buried in the permafrost near Shmidt mountain. They courageously laid down their young lives in an unequal battle with a cruel enemy: let us honour their memory with two minutes of silence." At that point everyone fell quiet; even Shchur didn't dare to move, and the first number of our programme was carried out flawlessly.

By 7pm all the tables in the dining hall had been tastefully prepared, at the expense of the political prisoners, to seat and feed 270 people. Each table, for example, had been decorated with two bouquets of flowers, and each guest received an official invitation. All those invited, as well as several uninvited guests from the MVD (no one paid any attention to them) arrived punctually.

The evening opened with a memorial ceremony, followed by supper. We had asked prisoners from all the national groups in the camp to attend, but the Shchur-Shkursky gang had not been invited. Everything was carried out so well that afterward the German, Estonian and Latvian prisoners congratulated us with tears in their eyes. The successful commemoration of the anniversary of the Norilsk massacre boosted the prestige of the Ukrainian political prisoners among the other national groups. Henceforth all the political prisoners began to treat us with much greater respect, and openly showed their disdain for the Shchur-Shkursky gang. In the meantime, however, this gang had become even more violent. One young fellow, for example, had his back broken simply because he called the members of the gang bandits after they had robbed some invalids. When Pelekh broke away from the gang, the atmosphere became even more strained. Plans were afoot to murder Pashchak, Shevchuk and myself; the only question was how best to accomplish this.

One day I went to visit Pashchak, who lived opposite Shkursky. Just before I arrived four gang members came to see Shkursky, and invited Pelekh to sit at the same table with them. When he refused categorically, they began to beat him up, but Pelekh turned out to be a strong, experienced opponent. The five of them were unable to subdue Pelekh themselves so they sent for help. Ten minutes later about thirty thugs with knives at the ready burst into the barracks and threw themselves upon their unarmed opponent. Pashchak and I were only two metres away from Kozii and Semen Bury when they attacked Pelekh, and four gang members, knives in hand, stood near our aisle waiting for us to get involved in the fight. Suddenly Pelekh gave a heavy groan and grabbed his side with both hands, whereupon his attackers immediately melted way. Two orderlies with a stretcher came from the medical station to take Pelekh away, and on the same day he was transferred to the central hospital.

About a hundred people witnessed this bloody incident, and the camp administration also knew what had happened. But in all likelihood the administration had been given instructions not to interfere when these thugs settled accounts with their enemies, because it did not even conduct an investigation into the attack on Pelekh. A few days later, when we were sent to a strict-regime camp (No. 307), and the thugs were sent to a general-regime camp

(No. 26), it became clear that the administration, far from punishing the guilty prisoners, had in fact encouraged their bloody attack on us. However, to prevent us from living peacefully in Camp No. 307 Shchur, Svystun and about seven of their followers were also sent there.

In Camp No. 307 the administration tried to force us to go out to work. The first to obey were Shchur and his gang, and then some of the other prisoners followed. The administration tried to form brigades but the prisoners would not obey its orders and refused to join them. Everyone lived where he wished and worked with the prisoners of his own choice. However, the administration began to look for culprits, and there was no lack of people, such as Shchur, eager to suggest who was behind this insubordination. By this time Shchur was even testifying against his former friends, who were now under investigation in the Irkutsk prison for their escape attempt. In short, he had begun to work openly for the MVD's security section.

Over the past few years the various nationalities in the camp had begun to celebrate their national holidays and invited guests of other nationalities to these festivities. Thus one evening in the fall of 1954, the Latvians invited me and another hard-labour prisoner from Eastern Ukraine to attend their national holiday. They celebrated this event in a lively, joyous fashion, and all went well until a security officer entered the section, took out a notebook, and asked one of the prisoners at the edge of the crowd to give his name. At this moment someone turned off the light, announcing that now we would play a round of "blind man's bluff," and the security officer left so hastily that he dropped his notebook.

Following this incident the administration prepared a list of fourteen prisoners and began to summon them to the watch-tower. But no one responded to the summons, and it was impossible to enforce since the administration did not know our faces. Finally, it brought in the troops and ordered all the prisoners to leave the camp zone. The temperature, however, was more than forty degrees below zero and we had no wish to expose the prisoners to the cold all day on our account. Therefore I informed the camp director that if he was interested only in the prisoners whom he had summoned earlier, and agreed not to bother the others, then we were willing to come out by ourselves. He readily agreed to this, and immediately ordered his troops out of the camp zone. We then took our belongings and left the camp. A "Black Maria" was already waiting for us, and we were driven to the isolator in Camp No. 15. Since the stove in the isolator was broken there was no difference in temperature between the cells and outdoors, but we still had to spend fifteen days in this terrible place. I developed such a bad head cold that the resulting pain continued to plague me for one-and-a-half years, almost driving me insane.

From here, in the winter of 1955, our group, which included five Ukrainians, four Germans, three Latvians and one Russian, was sent to Taishet and then on to the Vladimir prison. The decree on which my prison sentence was based contained all sorts of nonsense, most of which I can no longer remember. Only one point was true—that I had refused to go out to work.

When the decree was to be announced I was summoned together with one of the German prisoners. The charges against us included one identical paragraph: we were both accused of being responsible for the poor work performance of the prisoners in the Norilsk penal camps.

"That's interesting," the German said when he read this paragraph. "How could I have been responsible for this if I've never even been near Norilsk?"

The director of the isolator gave me and my companion a long, hard look, began to leaf through the German's personal file, and finally confirmed that this prisoner had never been in Norilsk.

"Yes, there's been a small mistake," he said, "but that doesn't matter. We'll simply cross this out and think of something else." We never found out what he "invented." The German ended up in the Vladimir prison but was never summoned again concerning this decree.

We were in a cheerful mood on our way to the Vladimir prison. During the entire trip the Germans treated us to excellent food from their German Red Cross parcels, of which they had recently received a very large number. In the prison they were placed in a separate cell and soon afterward, in accordance with an agreement between West Germany and the Soviet Union, they were sent home. In 1955 some twenty Germans from the Vladimir prison returned to West Germany.

On the way to Vladimir, and during my stay in the Vladimir prison, a profound spiritual change came over me. I became alienated from everything associated with the camp, and was overwhelmed with a longing to see my daughter and my native country. In prison I began writing to my children. My daughter wrote more often than my son and sent me, for the first time, her photograph. She was already quite a mature, good-looking girl, full of vitality and a young woman's charm. I looked at this photograph countless times every day, and I sometimes cried secretly when I was writing to her or reading one of her letters.

I spent all 1955 in the Vladimir prison, and read some good books there. The prison administration treated us well, especially in comparison with the camp administration. Thus for me this stay in prison was not a punishment, but a rest from the various intrigues in the camp. However, it was impossible to remain here and I had to leave for a camp in the Bratsk area, the "fiefdom" of the well-known Colonel Evstegneev.

Toward the end of January 1956 we again found ourselves in Taishet, at Transit Camp No. 25. The camp was full of prisoners of all ranks and various nationalities; most were Chinese, Koreans and Japanese, in addition to several Yugoslavs. It was the eve of a mass review of our cases and a large-scale release of prisoners from the camps, and the prisoners hotly debated various aspects of domestic policy and foreign affairs. Some predicted major changes in Soviet internal affairs which would lead to democratization, while others argued that there would be no radical policy changes as long as Suslov, Malenkov, Bulganin and Kaganovich[4] remained in the government.

I spent a whole month listening to these discussions and arguments, for the Taishet transit camp was a veritable debating club at the time. But I no longer sought involvement in these discussions or in any other aspect of life in the camps. I was totally preoccupied, day and night, with thoughts about my son and daughter, and about the forests, marshes, meadows and rivers of my native Polissia. My nerves finally gave out: my arms and legs began to shake, I could not even hold a pen, and sometimes my spoon would fall out of my hand. My heart also began to give me trouble. I was threatened with paralysis, and feared that if I lost the use of my hands I would be unable to write and leave a record of all my experiences.

Next we were taken to Strict-Regime Camp No. 308, where I was greeted by Iurko Sakharov (the chess player from Kiev) and several hard-labour prisoners from Norilsk. I lived with them the whole time that I was in this camp. I decided, however, that it would be senseless to get involved in any of the groups in this camp. I was very weary and felt a great longing to see my native land and my daughter.

I settled in the barracks where both the Ukrainian intelligentsia and the Medvid-Nykolyshyn gang lived. There were twelve intellectuals in the former group, including Sakharov (he was the only one I knew), and the writer Patrus-Karpatsky.[5] There were approximately twenty men in the Medvid-Nykolyshyn gang; Nykolyshyn was the only one of its members whom I knew personally.

There was only one free space in the barracks for me—on the top bunk just above the lads from Medvid's gang. Nykolyshyn was working as a dispatcher at the time, and probably had not yet informed my neighbours who I was and how I felt about such gangs. As a result I had an excellent opportunity, lying in my bunk, to overhear their conversations, which was both an interesting and useful experience. One evening some of this gang's members began to repack their suitcases, boasting about their acquisitions and sprinkling them with napthalene.

"Where did you get such a fine sweater?" the fellow beneath me asked his neighbour.

"Why, from the German major."

"And how did old Pryshliak[6] react to this?" asked another, who had not been in Vorkuta.

"Pryshliak found out about this the next day and resigned himself to what had happened," was the reply.

"And did he keep in touch with you afterward, just as before?" someone else asked.

"What else could he do? And what was so wrong in what we did? They robbed our people blind during the war and shipped our riches to Germany; all that we took from them were twenty suits, sweaters, and pairs of slippers."

"That's true, but after all, wouldn't it be better if the Germans returning home had a good rather than a poor opinion of us? This sort of thing makes us look very bad before foreigners and even before the administration," someone added in a voice which was un-familiar to me.

"So, Stepan, you've become a 'diplomat' now? That's how the rotten intelligentsia talks. We spit on what foreigners think of us. And what do we care about the administration? It lives like a parasite itself at the expense of the prisoners. And the Soviet army, for example, went about looting in Germany no less than the German army in the Soviet Union," someone noted calmly.

"If your goal is to lower yourself to the level of the worst thieves then you're right. But not everyone shares this goal," Stepan replied.

"A lamb won't survive for long among wolves," the same calm voice added.

"If you enjoy being wolves then that's your business. But I can't go along with this," Stepan said quietly.

"Well then, live like a lamb, until you've been broken in," the "wolf" in this dialogue called out as Stepan walked away.

I spent more time with Patrus-Karpatsky than anyone else. He was an unexceptional man, but I was drawn to him by his knowledge, for he knew a great deal about literature and ethnography, had been abroad, and had seen the life of other peoples.

After two months in Camp No. 308 I became seriously ill and was hospitalized. Later I was taken directly from the hospital and transferred on foot, together with many other political prisoners, to Camp No. 307, a special strict-regime camp hidden from public view deep in the taiga.

Here I again met Iaroslav Pashchak and found myself a place, together with Hrytseliak, near his bunk. Pashchak lived in the same section as Volodymyr Vitoshynsky and Vintoniak, two intellectuals who shared a strong love for music and usually kept to themselves. Thus I spent most of my time with Pashchak and Hrytseliak.

# Chapter Twenty-Six

The unforgettable spring of 1956, the spring of the internal political thaw in the Soviet Union, was approaching, and it was widely rumoured that commissions which included people with a mandate from the Presidium of the Supreme Soviet of the USSR were travelling to all the camps for political prisoners to review their court cases and to release approximately 80 per cent of them. All the "politicals" were preoccupied with these rumours.

At one point I discussed the various bands in the camp with Slavko Pashchak.

"Experience has shown," I told him, "that if you have nothing at all to do with these gangs then they themselves split up into separate groups and start cutting one another's throats. It was only in Camp No. 5, where we actively opposed their banditry, that they united against us. They were upset because we, the hard-labour prisoners, refused to recognize their banditry as a heroic political struggle, and not only refused to bow before them and demonstrate our loyalty, but publicly denounced them as bandits."

"I see that this affected you much more than me," Slavko replied.

"Yes, since I had no idea that there were such degenerates among our people."

"Do you think that the members of the OUN Provid were much better?" Slavko added. "I was in Cracow in 1940–1, and the break between the Banderites and Melnykites took place before my eyes. I saw how they fought among themselves, called one another the most disgusting names, and printed all sorts of filth about one another. In the Provid the most brazen people held the most important positions."

"I met Rostyslav Voloshyn of the Provid twice before I was captured, and he seemed to be a fine person and an intelligent politician," I said.

"You can't get to know a person after two official meetings," Slavko noted. "And even if Rostyslav was a good, intelligent person, it would have been impossible for him to change the atmosphere in the Provid for the better."

"I may disagree with the OUN's ideology," I said, "but I don't believe anyone who says that all the members of the Provid were no good, because decent people can be found everywhere. The problem is that envious and power-hungry people are aggressive, whereas good people are modest, thus the former win out over the latter. But the people of other nations also have their problems. Four Germans travelled with us to Volodymyr, where they were imprisoned in a separate cell, and two months later they split into two pairs and started fighting with each other. Both these pairs wrote to me, abusing each other and asking me not to oppose them if they persuaded the prison director to transfer them to our cell."

"It's not so serious if people who have their own state fight among themselves," Slavko noted. "Splits have occurred in all parties; the Russian Social Democratic Workers' Party, for example, split into the Bolsheviks and Mensheviks. But at least they didn't start shooting one another until one of these factions gained power, whereas members of the OUN started shooting one another immediately after the break took place. In 1940 OUN delegates from Galicia, Bukovyna, Transcarpathia and Volhynia secretly crossed various borders and, as friends, went to Cracow to attend the Second Great Congress. But after this Congress, and the split which took place at the time, the Banderites rushed to the border areas before the Melnykites and began sniping at them.[1] So instead of fighting together for independence we began to kill one another. I suppose, after all, that it's best just to avoid getting involved in politics," Slavko concluded.

"If our nation had its own state then I would agree," I noted. "But when I understood, back in elementary school, that Polish children treated Ukrainian children as their inferiors only because we lacked our own state, their contempt provoked me into fighting for independence. This is a political struggle, with a noble aim, but it seems that nothing on earth is so sacred that people cannot defile it in some way. The essence of good and evil lies not in ideologies but in people, and just as no ideology can cleanse a person with dirt on his hands, so such a person can easily sully even the most noble ideology."

Spring came and the long-awaited commission of the USSR Supreme Soviet finally arrived at the Ozerlag camps. The prisoners discussed the commission with great excitement, and began to dream of freedom and meeting their families, friends and acquaintances. But we were in a "special strict-regime" camp, and the Ozerlag administration was in no hurry to have us appear before the commission. Thus the prisoners became more agitated, their hopes alternating with doubts and fears. Some prisoners withdrew into themselves, while others became totally preoccupied by the many rumours in the air. Days, weeks and months went by in this fashion until finally, in the first few days of August, the administration of Camp No. 307 told us to hand in our bedding and remove our personal belongings from the storeroom. This was a clear sign that our turn had finally come.

After dinner we were taken out of the camp and as soon as we passed the gates they fell to the ground, which everyone took to be a good sign. Then, after walking seven kilometres through the taiga, we climbed onto open platforms which were waiting at the railway station and were transferred to Camp No. 11.

Every day twenty-five men were taken from this camp to appear before the commission. Its hearings were held in a local forestry building, and the prisoners had to walk three kilometres to get there. In the evening, after the hearings, the major announced the commission's decisions in his office and an average of twenty men in each group were released. Some prisoners had their sentences reduced by half, and in a few cases the original sentence was left unchanged. But such cases were very rare.

Slavko was called before the commission and released. When some other prisoners and I were summoned, almost all the prisoners who had been released the previous day ran to meet us, their eyes shining with happiness.

"Where's Slavko?" I asked Vitoshynsky.

"He's praying very intensely now, so we didn't dare bother him," he replied. Fifteen minutes later Slavko appeared, asked whether I had been summoned before the commission yet, and when I replied in the negative he told me that he had spent all morning praying for my release.

Just then my name was called. For a few minutes I was anxious and my heart was beating strongly, but by the time I reached the commission's office I had composed myself. Behind a table, in a fairly large office, sat an intelligent, pleasant-looking, middle-aged man who was the head of the commission and a member of the Central Committee of the CPSU (Communist Party of the Soviet Union). A procurator from the Procuracy General, with a dissatisfied, distrustful look on his face sat on the right, and a benevolent-looking elderly general sat on the left.

"Good day!" I said. "My name is Danylo Lavrentiiovych Shumuk. I was sentenced to death by a Military Tribunal in April 1945, but the Supreme Court later changed the sentence to twenty years of hard labour."

"What were you sentenced for?" the head of the commission asked, leafing though the record of my court case.

"For my activities in the Ukrainian nationalist movement."

"And why did you choose this path?"

"I was once a devoted communist and was very active in the communist underground in Volhynia. As a result, in 1935 a Polish court sentenced me to eight years of imprisonment, and I bore all the hardship which followed with my head held high, for I was proud to suffer for my communist ideals. My disillusionment with the Communist Party began after the 'liberation' of Western Ukraine in 1939 by Soviet troops. I could not reconcile myself to the prevailing spirit of formalistic, bureaucratic party-mindedness. I was opposed to repression and enforced collectivization, and I was repelled by the soulless slogans and pompous speeches which I had heard at meetings of party bureaucrats. Although a committed communist, I was ashamed of their rhetoric.

"As a soldier in the Soviet army I was at the front in 1941, in the Zhytomyr and Kiev oblasts, and saw the terrible poverty of the peasants on the collective farms. In the Chernihiv and Poltava oblasts peasants told me about the horrors of the artificial famine of 1933 and the repressions of 1937, and all this served to alienate me from the Communist Party of the Soviet Union.

"I joined the Ukrainian nationalists in March 1943 because of the situation in Volhynia at the time. I had two options: I could either leave for hard labour in Germany or join the Ukrainian nationalist movement, which by then had spread throughout Volhynia. I chose the latter option, in spite of my personal convictions, since the nationalist movement was the only force which, because it opposed the plunder of Volhynia by the German occupiers, united the Ukrainians in this oblast. I didn't occupy any leading posts in this movement, I didn't kill a single soul, and I didn't take part in any fighting."

The members of the commission listened carefully to my account, and after a brief pause the head of the commission turned to his companions and, addressing each of them by his first name and patronymic, asked if they had any questions. I was relieved when they replied in the negative, clearly a good sign. The head of the commission, however, put my court case aside and opened a green folder.

"Your court case is of no real account; I'm surprised that you received the death sentence or even twenty years of hard labour. But you created quite a stir in the camps," the head of the commission said as he pointed to the green folder.

"What did I do that was so terrible?" I asked. "It was not I but the administration that was involved in criminal activities in the camps."

"Listen and I'll tell you what you did," the head of the commission replied and began to read the personal profile prepared by the camp administration. This "profile" was very detailed, approximately fifteen pages long, and was actually a terrible indictment on the basis of which I could have again been sentenced to death. I was accused of ruining the isolator in Hard Labour Camp No. 3 in Norilsk, publishing pamphlets and preparing as well as directing the strike in this camp, editing an underground journal in Camp No. 5 on the Taishet route, inciting the prisoners against the administration, etc.

"What do you have to say about this profile?" the head of the commission asked.

"I'm appalled that your administration dared to submit these fabrications to such a high-ranking commission. You have no facts and no witnesses to support these inventions you've read out to me, and if the drones who prepared this for you are incapable of proving their accusations then it shows that the state is simply wasting its money on them. I fought openly against the high-handed behaviour of these 'feudal princes'—the directors of the administration of the special camps—and their *oprichniki*,[2] because I considered it the sacred duty of every honest citizen, no matter where he or she is, to fight against all manifestations of such behaviour no matter who is responsible."

The head of the commission removed the complaint I had written to the Central Committee of the CPSU six months earlier from the folder. He quickly examined the sections which were underlined in red, showed them to the general and the procurator, and then they consulted quietly with one another.

"We have no more questions," the head of the commission told me when they finished their discussions. "You can go home now."

I bowed and left. Slavko Pashchak, Vlodko Vitoshynsky and Vintoniak were waiting impatiently for me, and I had started describing the details of the hearing to them when a messenger suddenly ran out of the forestry building and called me back to the room where the commission was in session. This puzzled me, for the commission had never called a prisoner up twice before.

"We've decided to free you and annul your conviction," the head of the commission told me, "although you'll be deprived of your rights as a citizen. You should stay here and help us to clarify the confusion about your activities in the camp, but we have no right to detain you. We have only one request: that you write a letter, similar to the one you wrote to the Central Committee of the Party, describing in detail the period of your detention in the camps, and send it to the commission in Moscow."

"Fine, I'll do what I can."

"We hope that you have a good trip and settle down soon," the head of the commission concluded. After I thanked the commission and left the building Slavko Pashchak came up to me with a concerned look on his face.

"What did they want?" he asked.

I explained what had happened and all my other friends warmly shook my hand. In thought and spirit I was already far removed from the camp; I did not have to wait for the major to announce the commission's decisions. On this day the commission released eighteen people: five had their sentences halved and in two cases the prisoners' original sentences were left unchanged.

On the next day we were summoned to the watch-tower and a guard opened the gates. A duty officer called us out according to the standard procedure and a pleasant feeling filled my soul, for this was the first time that we were passing through the gates without a convoy. A truck was waiting for us beyond the gates, and we were transferred from Camp No. 11 to an empty camp on the Vikhorevka. Here we spent two days, while our documents were being prepared, until we received our internal passports.

# PART VI

# Chapter Twenty-Seven

On 20 August 1956 we boarded the "Lena-Moscow" train, and when it began to move a great weight was lifted from our chests. How good it was to leave this land of humiliation and suffering behind!

I fell asleep, and when I awoke and looked through the window it was daybreak, and the train was slowing down. We had reached the Chuma railway station, and women were crowding around the wagons with all kinds of vegetables from their gardens. I left the wagon, bought myself some dry boiled potatoes and a small bunch of green onions for three rubles, and this simple transaction, as well as the chance to meet people who were at liberty, was simply exhilarating! The potatoes were delicious, the fresh morning air a delight, and the whole world seemed to be in a festive mood.

On the way from Vikhorevka to Moscow there was a considerable turnover of passengers in the wagon; they included ordinary workers, bureaucrats, students and young women who were fleeing the virgin lands.[1] The workers cursed Stalin, the students laughed and told anecdotes about Stalinists, and those who were leaving the virgin lands were swearing at everyone. But the bureaucrats, who did not respond to any of the comments which they heard around them, occasionally exchanged brief comments with one another to the effect that this "anarchy" would be short-lived.

It was clear to me that the danger of a new tyranny would continue to exist until every single person who had been involved in the massive crimes of the recent past was thoroughly disgraced.

This included those responsible for the artificial famine of 1933 and those who, in 1937 and later, arrested innocent intellectuals and honest workers, tormented them in camps and prisons, and finally shot their victims. Stalin had released an enormous army of anonymous criminals into the entire system, from top to bottom, and although this army was keeping a low profile, it was simply awaiting an opportunity to lift its head and continue its activities. These criminals could be prevented from returning to their old positions only if they were publicly exposed and denounced.

"Yes," one of the bureaucrats said half-aloud and in a tone of regret to his neighbour in the wagon, "the people have quickly forgotten who transformed backward, semi-feudal Russia into an advanced industrial country, who built Kuzbas, Magnitogorsk, the White Sea and Moscow-Volga canals, and who smashed fascism and expanded the Russian state beyond the Carpathians past Königsberg and into Prussia."

"Yes, they quickly forget the good and just remember all sorts of petty details," his neighbour replied sadly.

"The death of millions of villagers from starvation after their bread was confiscated is not a 'petty detail,' it's a monstrous, inhuman crime!" I said, raising my voice. "Mass repression, torture, executions and hard labour in the Arctic North—these aren't 'trivia' for those who lived through these experiences, or for their hungry and persecuted families. Only bloodthirsty animals could call these terrible crimes 'petty details'!"

The bureaucrat gave me a look that was both frightened and threatening and kept silent. From the neighbouring aisle, however, a man of about fifty who had been listening came up to us and stretched out his powerful arms.

"It wasn't you, Stalin's brood, who built those canals and industrial complexes," he said. "That was the work of those, like me, who were thrown out of our homes throughout Ukraine and whom you deported to these 'projects.' Hungry, barefoot and ragged, we built everything you now boast about before the whole world. And it was not you but our sons who smashed fascism. Stalin and the people around him were responsible for the fascists' takeover of Ukraine and Belorussia and for their advance to Moscow and Leningrad, while the credit for destroying fascist Germany belongs to the people!"

The bureaucrats shrank back from the waving arms of this broad-shouldered fellow and remained silent, while the students in the compartment listened with youthful curiosity.

In the meantime, I was thinking about the October Revolution, which I had once idealized. "He who has nothing shall become everything, and he who was everything shall become nothing." Formally this is what happened, but the transfer of power had not led to any great advance by mankind, for the persecuted became persecutors and vice-versa. Nothing changed for the better; in fact, there was actually an increase in cruelty and intolerance.

Lenin, whose brother had tried to kill the tsar, spent his period of exile in the peaceful village of Shushenskoe, in the Minusinsk valley, which he called the "Siberian Switzerland." Here Lenin studied Marxism, learned English, went hunting and skiing, and skated on the Enisei. But we, ordinary labourers, were beaten, insulted, called "fascists" and "bourgeois nationalists," and were treated in a thoroughly inhuman fashion. And this was not tsarist Russia, but a Russia "free of all oppression and lawlessness."

If the October Revolution had truly resolved all the burning national questions of the Russian Empire, then the Germans could not have seized Ukraine, Belorussia and the Baltic republics and approached Moscow, Leningrad and Stalingrad so easily during the Second World War. And Vlasov could not have created an entire army out of prisoners of war who fought against Russia with much greater zeal than the most select fascist troops. During the First World War the Germans were unable to create an army out of Russian prisoners of war and to throw it against tsarist Russia. And during both world wars the Germans failed to create a single battalion composed of English, American or French prisoners who would fight against the armies of their native countries. Only Soviet prisoners of war took up German arms and deliberately used them against the Soviet army. The presence on the side of the Germans of the Russian Liberation Army (ROA)[2] and of national battalions composed of Balts, Central Asians and peoples from the Caucasus, as well as the Ukrainian SS division,[3] is the clearest proof that not all is well in the Soviet Union, and that the basic problems which once caused the nations of the Russian Empire to rise in revolution are still unresolved.

The number of Russians in the ROA who continued to fight against the Red Army even after the German army capitulated was several times larger than the number of Ukrainians in the SS Division "Galicia" (which also fought against the Red Army), and in the UPA, which fought against both the Red Army and the penal battalions of the MVD. Nonetheless, there were very few Vlasovites in the Arctic camps, and they were sentenced only for individual murders. The Ukrainians vastly outnumbered the Vlasovites, and even Estonians were more numerous, indicating that the penal authorities dealt with the Vlasovites in accordance with the old Russian saying "We'll settle it among friends." The ROA, after all, also stood for a Russia "united and indivisible."

No pamphlets are published and no articles are written about the "atrocities" of the Vlasovites, or about their conflicts with the Red Army. No one even mentions Vlasov and his supporters any more. But large runs of various pamphlets and books about the Banderites and Ukrainian "bourgeois nationalists" are still being published, and these groups are frequently slandered in journals and newspapers.

Who talks or writes in Poland about Polish nationalism, in Romania about Romanian nationalism, in Hungary about Hungarian nationalism, or finally in Russia about Russian nationalism? No one! Why is this so, and why is no one sentenced for nationalism in these countries? This is because there is no national question in those countries. Warsaw talks and writes in its native Polish language, and all institutions and enterprises in Poland operate in Polish. All instruction in elementary, secondary and higher schools is in Polish, and the same applies for Romania or Hungary. These countries are tied to the Soviet Union by political and military treaties, and by economic agreements which restrict their foreign and trade policies. But the Poles, Romanians and Hungarians do, after all, have their own states, national armies and national banks, and there can be no talk of sovereignty in a state without these institutions. But those who live in a bogus "state" such as the Ukrainian SSR and discuss these issues are called Ukrainian bourgeois nationalists, and are sentenced to many years of imprisonment. Such is the sovereignty granted to the Ukrainian "younger brother." And as long as the Russian "elder brother" in ancient Kiev considers the Ukrainians to be "khokhly"[4] and his juniors, then he and his language will continue to rule in the "younger brother's" house.

In short, the most acute problem in the Soviet Union is the national question, and Russia will never follow the example of the Swedes in resolving it.[5] Because of the poverty of their spiritual culture and their expansionist nature, the Russians will never allow Ukraine the possibility of secession. And Ukrainian janissaries will help the "elder brother" to enslave those who would oppose him.

On the fifth day of our trip we reached Moscow. At the Iaroslav station, a rogue offered us his services. He was especially keen to take our suitcases and accompany us to the Kiev station.

"Hey you!" a strong, young man in our group addressed him angrily. "Find yourself some other clients, because you won't get anywhere trying to rip us off. Understand?"

"I understand," the rogue replied and left us. Our group of more than thirty stayed together at the Kiev station. Presently, we were joined by a small group from Norilsk which included three young women who had been freed by the commission. One of them was very good looking.

"How old were you when you were arrested?" I asked her.

"Seventeen."

"What were you tried for?"

"I was a courier for the underground and was caught with some mail."

"Where were you interrogated?"

"In Lviv."

"Were you beaten?"

"And how! There was a brute in the Lviv MVD called Vinogradov who used to twist my braids around his paw and beat my head against the wall so hard that blood would splatter all over the walls," the young woman replied with tears in her eyes.

"They were more brutal with the women than with the men," one of the woman's friends added.

I began to wonder when all this would end. Yes, we had been released, but as long as people like Vinogradov remained in Lviv, Stanyslaviv, Lutsk and Kiev it would be impossible for us to live, work and rest in peace in our native land. For they came to Ukraine with the aim of destroying, with the help of Ukrainian janissaries, anyone who showed even the least sign of national consciousness. Fellows like Vinogradov have no fear of Vlasovites, since in essence they all seek a Russia "united and indivisible." But they are alarmed by seventeen-year-old girls with boundless love for their native country, their people, language and traditions, for the beauty of the Carpathian mountains and the fertile fields of Podillia. They are alarmed by anything which is foreign to them, with its own unique beauty.

Another Moscow rogue came to our resting place in the station and started asking the younger men in our group who they were, where they were from, and where they were heading. This put us on our guard, for it was obvious that it was not mere idle curiosity that brought him here. We kept an eye on him and did not have to wait long. As soon as our neighbours went to the coffee-shop, leaving their suitcases with a few small children and an old woman, he grabbed two of the suitcases and walked quickly away. He wanted the blame for this theft to fall on our shoulders, but two of our lads caught him and beat him so thoroughly that he lost consciousness and medical orderlies had to take him away on a stretcher. The passengers at the station rose to their feet as soon as this commotion started, but no one moved or said a word. Shortly afterward a railway militia captain arrived and came up to me.

"Come along and we'll prepare a statement about this incident," he said.

"I'm not going anywhere, and I refuse to be a witness," I replied. The militia captain smiled, and made the same suggestion to two of our lads, but they also refused. Thus the captain had to look for witnesses among the other travellers.

In the meantime the owners of the suitcases appeared and were informed what had happened. They thanked us for preventing the theft.

Later a young girl of about twelve went quietly from one passenger to another, selling tiny crosses. Along with the other passengers, we gladly bought them, but suddenly the militia began chasing the girl. Fleeing among the passengers, she ran up to us just as the militia caught up with her. Our lads stood up for the girl, and refused to hand her over.

"You should chase the thieves who are stealing suitcases," I said, "not this girl. She's no thief." The men in our group supported me, and the militia left without an argument. They treated us politely, and it was obvious that they had received special instructions about how to handle us.

There was no queue for train tickets to Kiev, and we left Moscow in the evening. On the way I became lost in thoughts about meeting my daughter, about my son who was born and had grown up in my absence, and about my native village and the lovely meadows, fields and marshes among which I had been born and raised. Seventeen years of harsh imprisonment by the Poles, Germans and Russians had exhausted me, and I needed to rest. I dreamt of a quiet haven where I could live in peace and quiet, and above all of seeing my native country and my daughter.

As the train sped onward, my friends eagerly asked one another when they would finally reach Ukraine, and what station marked this spot.

"Ukraine begins at the hamlet of Mykhailiv," I told them. "As soon as we pass through Briansk and the Briansk forests we'll be looking out onto Ukraine."

At the Mykhailiv station we quickly ran out of the wagon and rushed to buy ourselves some tomatoes, green onions and cucumbers. Everyone's eyes shone with happiness, and our lads spent more time looking at the rosy-cheeked salesgirl, who was from the Poltava region, than at the food they were buying. This pleasant woman's warmth, sense of humour, and soft Poltava accent charmed us all, and in their happiness our lads refused to take their change.

In Konotop two young nurses who worked in a hospital in Ternopil entered our wagon and made themselves comfortable in our aisle. They were on their way to Ternopil, and our lads started talking, joking, laughing and singing Ukrainian folk songs with them. It was a pleasant atmosphere and everyone was feeling happy.

"And do you know who we are?" I asked the nurses.

"No," they both replied.

"When you're in Ternopil do you ever hear talk of Banderites?"

"Oh yes. When we were assigned to work there we were given lectures about the Banderites. They're horrible bandits who murdered innocent people," both women replied quickly, interrupting each other.

"Well, all of us here are Banderites," I told them. "We've just been released and we're going home."

"That can't be true. You must be joking—you're not murderers, you couldn't kill anyone."

"We didn't say that we killed anyone," I said. "I was simply sentenced for nationalist activity."

"But is it true that the Banderites are bandits?"

"Bandits are bandits everywhere, whether they're Banderites or Soviet partisans, members of the Polish Home Army or People's Army.[6] The only difference is that they don't always have the same opportunities to engage in banditry."

Our train arrived in Darnytsia before dinner and then continued on its way toward the Dnieper River. Beyond the Dnieper we could see the hills of Kiev, covered by a beautiful leafy forest, with gold-domed churches on the hilltops. As the train crossed the bridge across the Dnieper all my companions, deep in thought, looked at the river, the hills, the churches and the dramatic monuments to Volodymyr the Great.

In Kiev we walked to the Volodymyr Cathedral and from there to the university. We looked at this building, in which the Central Rada, headed by Professor Hrushevsky, held its sessions in 1918, paid our respects to the Shevchenko monument, and returned to the Kiev station. Here our paths parted. Some of the former prisoners headed for Lviv, or Stanyslaviv, or Drohobych, while I and a few others left for the Kovel station in Polissia.

# Chapter Twenty-Eight

My imagination continued to run rampant. Various colourful images carried me back to the world of my childhood and youth, such as my native village and various corners of beautiful Polissia which were dear to my heart: birch groves, marshes overgrown with osiers, choke-cherries and guelder roses, fragrant fields and meadows. It can be a great pleasure to transfer yourself into an imaginary world full of such memories. I had difficulty, however, imagining my daughter as an adult. I always thought of her as a sweet, happy and pretty five-year-old hopping over the flowering potatoes without a care in the world, and playing hide-and-seek with my mother.

It was thirty-eight kilometres from Kovel to the Pidhorodne railway station. This route was familiar and dear to me, for on 26 May 1939, after spending five-and-a-half years in Polish prisons, I had returned home this same way. I was twenty-five years old then, and had returned as a well-trained, committed communist. Now I was forty-two, and had spent eleven-and-a-half years in the Arctic North doing hard labour because of my nationalist activities. The first investigation and trial to which I was subjected and the harsh Polish prisons had not broken me; in fact, this experience only served to harden and discipline me. But Soviet reality, and especially the tragic events of 1933–7, the wounds of which have not healed even to the present day, made me reject communism. By force of circumstance I found myself in the opposite camp, that of nationalism, and now I was again returning to my native village, long after I had lost my faith in communism and had become skeptical about the OUN brand of nationalism. I decided that, insofar as my knowledge and experience allowed, I would thoroughly review and reflect upon my past and the past of my people. My past, ever since I was fifteen, had been closely tied to two antagonistic ideologies, one supported by Moscow and the other by Berlin, which had clashed in Ukraine. It was my fate to have been involved in this clash, and for many years I had suffered a great deal for the sake of both ideologies. Thus it was my duty to reflect on my experiences in a dispassionate fashion, and although this was a difficult task, especially because of the conditions in which I now found myself, I would do everything I possibly could. Such were my thoughts as I returned home a free man.

I did not plan to stay long in my native village. Only our two children linked me to my wife, for spiritually we had nothing in common. My wife did not understand me, and it was impossible for her to do so. Moreover, in 1950 (when I was in the camps) she had given birth to another daughter. I was drawn to my native village only by the passionate desire to see and be with my own children, and planned to settle permanently in another oblast.

On the way from Kovel to Pidhorodne I could not take my eyes off the familiar groves, fields and meadows alongside the railway line. But my impressions when I returned in 1939 had been quite different. Now it was as if I felt a breeze of some undefinable estrangement, coldness and indifference, and I realized painfully that I was no longer destined to live in these parts, that nothing dear to me remained here. The marshes had dried up, the woods had been cut down, tractors had ploughed up the meadows, and the people here had probably changed as well. I wondered, however, whether everything had truly turned into such a grey, gloomy semblance of its former self, or whether it was just that I had grown old and my senses had become dulled.

While I was thinking the train pulled into Pidhorodne. I stepped out of the wagon and looked around. The small red-brick station was gone, as was the orchard in which it had nestled. The alley of enormous old birches through which the railway line had passed was also gone; all that remained was a small, newly built station, finished in stucco, which was in an empty field. Everything was bare and gloomy, and the people also seemed to be vacant, soulless and indifferent to their surroundings. It was only one kilometre from the Pidhorodne station to Boremshchyna. I made my way along a path which had once crossed a stream hidden in a dense thicket of young alders, osiers, guelder-roses, choke-cherries and a delightful birch grove. But now the bubbling stream had been transformed into a sad-looking little brook, with no trees to give it shade, and the never-ending chorus of songbirds was no more. Where once there had been a beautiful wood now there was only a wind-swept field, and when I reached this spot a great feeling of sadness and longing came over me—a longing for the beauty that I had once known. Only the road which approached the village from the south was a comfort to my eyes, for it ran under a canopy of lush willows which I remembered being planted before the war. I walked slowly along this road, examining everything that met my eye. No one, young or old, recognized me; everyone looked at me as if I was a stranger. And, in fact, I was a stranger to them, for they were incapable of understanding my thoughts and preoccupations, and I was indifferent to their everyday concerns. I had lost all psychological contact with my fellow villagers, and it was impossible to re-establish this contact.

My agitation grew with every step. Now I saw the spot where once ducks and geese had swum in a pond, my neighbour's farmstead came into view, and then I saw my own farmstead, although it was not as I remembered it. Once there had been a lush orchard and bee-hives here, but now this area was bare and empty. Two withered pear trees, a walnut tree, and several cherry trees were all that remained. Next to the road was a small house built after the war, during my absence. I quickened my step, and as my heart beat ever faster, I finally entered the house. There was no one in the kitchen so I knocked on one of the bedroom doors.

"Come in," I heard a calm, gentle voice. When I entered I saw a young, delicate woman in a white dress, full of untouched beauty and freshness, standing beside a table. We threw ourselves into each other's arms, and kissed without saying a word. Then we sat down, continued our embrace, and remained silent so as not to interrupt this wonderful moment. Later my wife arrived. She became alarmed when she saw my daughter and me embracing, and then rushed over and started kissing me in a superficial manner. When my son arrived he also kissed me in a distant fashion, as if he had been forced to do so. But poor little Lidochka, who was only six years old and had no real idea what was happening, cuddled up to me as if I was her real father.

Only my daughter and my wife's daughter, born out of wedlock, rejoiced at my homecoming, for my wife and son were not well disposed toward me. When we were alone my wife told me all kinds of nonsense to justify the circumstances which led to Lida's birth, but I never questioned her about this incident, or even mentioned it.

Soon some neighbours, Fedir Mykhalchuk and Nechypir Vlasiuk, arrived, followed by Vasyl Vlasiuk, and they started describing their everyday life and the collective farm, praising one of its managers and cursing another. I considered this visit both ill-timed and inappropriate, because I wanted to be alone in my house with my children.

"It's been a long time now since I lived here," I told them, "so the collective farm doesn't interest me. All I'm concerned about now are my son and my daughter."

During my first few days at home friends, acquaintances and members of the family visited me, but curiosity rather than goodwill seemed to lie behind these visits. Everyone had once known me as a fervent, idealistic and committed communist, and in the past they had all listened intently to my impassioned speeches at various meetings. Therefore they were curious to know what aspect of communism had repelled me and prompted me to turn to another camp. No one dared to put such questions to me directly; everyone waited impatiently for me to explain my behaviour of my own accord. I had to say something; but on the other hand, I could not lie or describe all my experiences in detail. Thus I restricted myself to an abstract explanation along the following lines:

"I have essentially remained loyal to my ideals. I was searching for the truth, thought that I had found it, and shared it with others. But it turned out to be nothing more than a lie masquerading as the truth. This deception greatly angered me and I couldn't forgive myself, since it wasn't just a personal matter—it affected those who had followed me. I wasn't just a mouthpiece for these deceptive ideals; I was also an organizer, and I had a profound belief that these ideals represented the pinnacle of human goodness and happiness. Yet the contrary was the case. So whereas I had once suffered for these ideals, later I suffered because I had been deceived by them, for they were only a pale imitation of the ideals I had been searching for."

Later some of those who had listened to me vulgarized this abstract explanation, edited it to suit their own fancy, and presented it to the KGB[1] in the form of a denunciation. And this was all that the KGB needed to begin preparing another case against me.

I had planned to spend no more than a month with my children, but soon changed my plans. Every day I grew closer to my daughter and could not contemplate parting with her. The days, weeks and months passed by swiftly.

I received three to seven letters a day. Former prison companions from Norilsk wrote to me from all corners of the Soviet Union and Stepan Semeniuk, who wrote to me from Poland, sent me Polish magazines and newspapers. Gomułka and Spychalski[4] had recently been released from prison in Poland, and the Sixth Plenum of the Polish United Workers' Party opened with Gomułka participating in its proceedings. A fresh breeze of humanism and democracy was blowing from Poland, and Moscow grew alarmed when the plenum condemned the party's internal policies. Khrushchev and Bulganin arrived in Warsaw without an invitation, and troops were sent to the Polish border day and night. Tension mounted, and Khrushchev and Bulganin demanded a meeting with Ochab and Cyrankiewicz.[5] But the plenum decided that Gomułka should accompany these two officials to the negotiations, which took place in very strained circumstances.

Gomułka was subsequently elected first secretary of the PUWP and at his lead the plenum attacked Politburo member Zenon Walko for instructing the press to describe the Poznań strikes as a bloody putsch organized from abroad by foreign intelligence agencies. Gomułka strongly attacked the Politburo's position on the events in Poznań, stating that the working class does not take up arms without reason, and thus rehabilitated those who had actively opposed the government's policies. Gomułka then dissolved the unprofitable collective farms and the harassment of individual landowners ceased. The new leader's authority literally grew by the hour as he became the favourite of the entire nation, of communists and non-communists alike.

I was pleased by these developments, and was proud of Gomułka. If he had been in power for only four or five years, as is the case in democratic countries, then this period might have left its mark on Poland's history. But Gomułka ruled for fourteen years, and power of this kind can corrupt even the best and most noble people. Such authority eventually destroyed Gomułka, a truly simple, humble and humane person who had once been accessible to everyone.

Shortly after the crisis in Poland, a tense political situation arose when England and France became involved in the Suez crisis. Collective-farm workers in Western Ukraine stopped work and everyone rushed to the shops, which were emptied within two days. The Central Committee of the party then ordered party officials to lecture the citizens on the international situation, assuring them that the Suez conflict would not develop into a war and that everyone should continue working. The first secretary of the party's raion committee came to our village to give this lecture, which my daughter and I attended. He spoke in a crude mixture of Russian and Ukrainian (*surzhyk*) and he confused the sequence of events so badly that if anyone had recorded his lecture and sent the tape to the Central Committee of the party the speaker would have immediately lost his job.

Later in 1956 a revolt also took place against Rákosi's dictatorial regime in Hungary,[4] and Imre Nagy[5] came to power. The echoes of this uprising were soon heard in Ukraine, and work on the collective farms again ground to a halt. Some women even began to threaten the hated brigade leaders and collective-farm chairmen. It was a complicated situation, and there was tension in the air. When the fighting in Budapest and throughout Hungary began to favour the rebels, there was a possibility that Hungary might leave the Warsaw Pact, an action which, in the eyes of the Soviet leaders, would have set an extremely dangerous precedent. Therefore Khrushchev's government ordered Soviet troops stationed in Hungary to crush the uprising.

After these bloody events in Hungary the political prisoners who had been set free after Stalin's death began to face various new pressures. Every attempt was made, for example, to chase us out of the western oblasts of Ukraine, and the local authorities began to treat not just me, but even my children with open hostility. My house was placed under surveillance to discover whether or not any strangers visited me, and the collective-farm chairman began pressuring me to start working. I had to leave this area, but had no idea where to go.

One of my old friends from the communist underground lived in Dnipropetrovsk, so I decided to visit him. He immediately recognized me although we hadn't seen each other for seventeen years, and even though he was a member of the party, he received me warmly. It took me seven days to find a room and then the passport office refused categorically to register me[6] in Dnipropetrovsk and treated me in a rude, hostile fashion. My situation seemed hopeless.

After nine days, I left Dnipropetrovsk for Kiev, where I stayed with my niece Dusia. I wanted to have a good look at Kiev, and for the first time I saw the Pecherska Lavra, the Cathedral of St. Sophia, the Golden Gates[7] and the grave of Askold. These famous monuments testified to the great cultural achievements of the Ukrainians, and revived my faith in this nation. At one time Ukraine had been an iron shield defending European culture before the barbaric East, and the mightiest kings in Europe used to consort with the Kievan princes. But little remains of the glorious past; now these monuments alone remind the Ukrainians of the advanced culture and spiritual greatness of their ancestors.

When I returned to Boremshchyna I found that my daughter was depressed by the atmosphere in the village and offended by the behaviour of the authorities.

"Father, it's impossible for us to continue living here," she said. "People are being recruited now to resettle in the Crimea and in the Dnipropetrovsk and Kherson oblasts. We should sign up and move away from here."

I had not considered moving my whole family because I knew that my wife and I could never live in peace with each other. Only our children kept us together, and when they married we would have nothing left in common. But I could not refuse my daughter's request.

I no longer had any rapport with the villagers of Boremshchyna. Their concerns did not interest me, and they were incapable of understanding me. In addition, the village had changed a great deal since the war. The number and quality of the buildings in the village had increased, and the number of educated people had grown considerably, but the spiritual culture of the village had declined. The old folk songs, for example—the moving vesnianky, the Kupalo and Petrivka songs[8]—were no longer heard. Instead of their happy sound, in the evening one heard the wild shouting of drunks, since the villagers now drank more spirits in a day than they would have drunk in a month before the war, and in the evening the villagers locked their doors to prevent drunks from barging in and causing a scene.

One evening there was a knock on our door. When we opened it two strangers entered the house.

"Does Dubii live here?" the older of the two asked.

"No, he lives two farmsteads down the road," my son answered and pointed in the direction of Dubii's house. But these "guests," who had no intention of going to Dubii's, sat down, uninvited, and started asking me who I was, where I was from, and when I had arrived in the village.

"Who are you?" I asked. "You were supposedly looking for Dubii and all of a sudden you've begun to interrogate me."

With an arrogant flourish the older man took out a small red booklet, handed it to me, and I discovered that I was dealing with Captain Kramsky of the KGB.

"I'm originally from the Ivanov oblast, in Russia, but I came here voluntarily, out of sympathy for the Ukrainian people, to help them rid themselves of nationalist bandits. In Volhynia we smashed the Dubovy and Rudy bands; do you know them?" Kramsky suddenly asked.

"No I don't, just as I don't know you," I replied in a hostile tone of voice.

"Which of the leaders of the nationalist bands did you know?" Kramsky persisted.

"I didn't know any 'bandits.' And don't ask me any more questions of this kind," I replied angrily.

"Well, I'm sure that we'll meet again, despite your negative attitude," Captain Kramsky said with a smirk on his face as he and his companion rose and left the house.

This "visit" greatly upset me, and I thought to myself that my problems were starting all over again.

Two weeks passed. Then, late one evening, someone knocked, police-style, on the door. I was enraged by this insolent intrusion and told my son not to open the door, although the knocking and shouting grew louder.

"Who are you, and what do you want?" I demanded.

"Open up! We're from the KGB," someone shouted.

I opened the door and two men who were strangers to me burst into the house. My son, however, recognized them—one was an assistant veterinarian and the other was the veterinarian's orderly—and both were thoroughly drunk. I was very curt with them, and they excused themselves by saying that they had actually come to buy the house from me.

We registered for resettlement in Dnipropetrovsk oblast, and the date of our departure was set for 17 March 1957. We were assigned to the Shchors collective farm in the village of Slovianka, Mezhiv raion, and early on the morning of our departure we loaded our belongings onto a truck, boarded up the doors and windows of our house, parted with our farmstead and then drove out of our beloved yard. The villagers watched us coldly and silently as we left, but the driver stepped on the accelerator and five minutes later we left the village behind.

The people who were to be resettled from three local raions all congregated at the station in Liuboml, where several railway wagons were set aside for us. We were the only settlers heading for Dnipropetrovsk oblast—everyone else was heading for the Crimea—so the director of the recruitment and resettlement programme told us to load our belongings into a wagon going to the Crimea.

"But we've been assigned to Dnipropetrovsk oblast," I protested.

"No one else is going to Dnipropetrovsk oblast from here and I can't give you a separate wagon," the director said. "Go along with the settlers heading for the Crimea as far as Kovel, and there you can transfer your belongings onto the train going to Dnipropetrovsk oblast."

There was no alternative, and we were forced to accompany the settlers going to the Crimea.

In Kovel there were three trains for the settlers; one going to the Crimea, another to Kherson and a third to Dnipropetrovsk oblast. However, the railway management in both Kovel and later Kivertsi refused to transfer us to the train for Dnipropetrovsk, and thus we travelled to the Crimea.

From Dzhankoi station our railway wagon was sent in the direction of Kerch, to Petrov station, Semykolodiaziv raion. Everyone else unloaded their belongings but the Crimean oblast authorities refused to accept us and did not want to send us to our original destination at their own expense. The railway administration charged for a railway wagon which was kept idle, and thus we were "orphans" for two days. On the morning of the third day I sent a telegram to Mohyla, the director of the Council of Ministers' recruitment and resettlement bureau in Kiev, and on that same day the authorities in Kiev ordered that our wagon be sent immediately to Mezhiv station in Dnipropetrovsk oblast in accordance with our original assignment. By 25 March we were in the village of Slovianka.

Initially, we were quartered with a widow in a small room approximately nine metres square, and after a few days, I went to work on the collective farm. I was first assigned to be a tractor hand, but I caught a cold doing this work and became quite sick. Later I joined a construction brigade.

Three weeks after we arrived in Slovianka my daughter started to work as a nurse at the raion hospital, and my son also began to work on the collective farm. The collective-farm administration gave us the plans for a house and we quickly dug the foundations for our new home.

Toward the end of April the raion authorities appeared in the village and called a general meeting to discuss the transformation of the Shchors collective farm into a state farm. The head of the raion executive committee and the director of the collective farm approved this step, but the meeting was attended mainly by women who worked on the collective farm and were quite attached to it, since they had organized it themselves. Therefore they were strongly opposed to the establishment of a state farm.

The authorities, however, insisted on having their way. Individual discussions were held with the most stubborn opponents of this plan, and threats were made that the "culprit" behind this opposition would have to be found. And so the audience finally voted in favour of the state farm.

Personally, I preferred a state to a collective farm, for the working day on a state farm was only eight hours, and it was much easier to get permission to leave a state farm. This was important to me, for I was anxious to leave the village eventually. First, however, I wanted to build a house here and then wait until my daughter entered an institute to continue her education.

The state farm, however, was in no hurry to let me go ahead with building a house. The director of the state farm said that the administration did not have permission to build houses for new settlers. But it was impossible to continue living in our cramped quarters. We finally moved to the plot of land allotted to us and lived out in the open, under the sun and rain. We endured these difficulties patiently, but our situation became increasingly intolerable. Neither the director of the state farm, who had already built himself a luxurious house, nor the head of the raion executive committee cared that we were living under the open sky. The latter's only concern was to fulfill the plan for delivering grain to the state. Neither of these officials would even discuss our problem.

I wrote to Levkovtsev, director of the Dnipropetrovsk oblast executive committee's recruitment and resettlement bureau. Levkovtsev then wrote to the chairman of the raion executive committee and to the director of the state farm, but they ignored his intervention. Finally I again wrote to Mohyla in Kiev, and it was only thanks to his pressure that the raion executive committee provided me with the wood I needed and the state-farm director provided a truck to transport the building materials for the house. I built the house that summer and thatched it temporarily with reeds. Since I planned eventually to cover the roof with slates, I put in a request for slates to the management of the state farm.

I worked like an ox from dawn to nightfall for eight months. I did very little reading or writing and reduced my correspondence with my friends to a minimum. One day, however, Slavko Pashchak visited me unexpectedly. We greeted each other warmly, had something to eat, and then began to discuss our personal affairs. Slavko's situation was no better than mine. He was on his way to Donetsk oblast in search of work, because he had not been allowed to stay in Odessa. Our brothers—former political prisoners—were being harassed no matter where they were.

For a while it seemed that I was going to be left in peace. But a suspicious-looking fellow, who often visited the office of the state-farm administration, began observing me with a great deal of curiosity. After years of harassment by police of all kinds I had developed a certain sixth sense which allowed me to identify immediately a security official. I could not imagine what I might have done to warrant this attention, but I was constantly aware of his persistent gaze, which followed me like a shadow. It was clear that a web of some kind was also being spun around my wife and daughter, and every day I became increasingly aware of the operation of this police machine. The circle was closing.

# Chapter Twenty-Nine

On 18 November 1957, late in the afternoon, the director of the state farm, accompanied by a veterinarian, drove into our yard. The director jumped out of the car, greeted me with a smile, and told me that he had just received a phone call from Levkovtsev in Dnipropetrovsk.

"He has the slates for your roof," the director said. "Tomorrow at dawn our truck will be going to Dnipropetrovsk to pick up some farm equipment, and it can stop for you on the way. You can bring the slates back with you in the truck."

"Fine, I'll be waiting for your truck tomorrow morning," I replied.

"I can see that you've almost finished the house."

"Yes, we're already living in it, although the ceiling hasn't been plastered and the floor hasn't been laid yet."

"If you've already lathed the ceiling them I'm sure that you'll get around to plastering it. As for the floor, take some measurements to find out how many boards you'll need and somehow we'll take care of this as well."

The director was being exceptionally polite and generous to me, and I was surprised by his positive attitude.

Just before dawn the next day, a truck stopped in front of our house. I opened the door and invited everyone to come in. There were six passengers: four men and two women. Then I noticed that two of the young men, who were quite well dressed, were following all my movements carefully. I became suspicious and for a moment thought that maybe the KGB was behind this story about the slates.

But I dismissed this suspicion. I could not imagine what the KGB might want from me, since I had spent all my time building the house and working on the state farm or my private plot. Ever since I had left the camps I had neither been involved in any political activity nor planned to do so, for the ideologies which had been popular among my fellow Ukrainians were now foreign to me. I hated totalitarianism in all its forms, both internationalist and nationalist, and therefore I had decided to avoid involvement in social and political activities altogether. Nonetheless, since I considered it my duty to rethink and analyze all my previous activities, I had looked everywhere for relevant materials.

The chief mechanic of the state farm rode in the truck's cabin along with the driver while the others and myself rode in the back. We stopped in front of the state-farm administration building in Dnipropetrovsk and the mechanic went inside while we remained seated. I waited impatiently for the mechanic to return so that we could agree on where I could find him once I had settled my affairs, but the mechanic took his time. I kept my eyes on the building and noticed that everyone went in and out in a businesslike fashion except for one man, approximately my own age, who was wearing a long, leather coat. It was the same man who had looked me over in the courtyard of our state-farm headquarters, and he was leaving the administration building in anything but a businesslike fashion. He shifted slowly from one foot to the other, as if unsure whether to go on or turn back, but then he continued on his way and looked at us with seeming indifference. When he reached the road he turned to the left, and after walking some fifty metres he stood behind a ZIM car and continued to look at our truck. This fellow and his strange behaviour again began to trouble me, but since I had not been involved in any "anti-Soviet" activities, I decided not to worry.

When our mechanic finally returned we drove to the state bank. The mechanic entered the bank while I went to the oblast executive committee building to see Levkovtsev. As I was about to open the door to this building, the same man in the leather coat appeared from nowhere and asked whom I wanted to see.

"Levkovtsev, the oblast recruitment and resettlement director," I said.

"Finally! I'm Levkovtsev and I've been driving around the whole city looking for you. Please get in the car," he said and pointed to the open door of a black ZIM. As I approached the car two young men jumped in, I followed, and "Levkovtsev" sat down next to me. The car accelerated and we sat in silence. I knew immediately into whose hands I had fallen, but I remained calm, for I could not imagine what charges could be brought against me.

"Will you be staying in Dnipropetrovsk overnight?" "Levkovtsev" asked.

"I don't know how quickly the mechanic will settle all his affairs and load the agricultural equipment onto the truck. If he manages then we'll leave today."

"Do you have a place in Dnipropetrovsk where you can spend the night?"

"Yes."

"Where and with whom?" "Levkovtsev" asked quickly.

"At Makar Maslianka's, on Dimitrov Street."

"And where does he work?"

"At the Petrovsky metallurgical factory."

These questions were followed by another tense silence as the car sped along until iron gates and a guard appeared before us. When the guard saw the ZIM and its familiar licence number he opened the gates and we drove into the back-yard of a massive building shaped like a horseshoe. We were driven up to the doors of this building and "Levkovtsev" hastened to deliver me to my destination. We entered a wide foyer and immediately turned onto the stairs. One of my "companions" went ahead of me while two others walked behind me—clear evidence that I had been arrested.

When we reached the fourth storey, "Levkovtsev" opened his office and gestured to me to enter. It was a huge office; on the left, next to the wall, there was a massive safe, and on the right a sofa.

"Take your coat off and sit down," "Levkovtsev" said. He took off his coat, hung it up and then left, leaving me with a young man who sat down opposite me. He began to ask me casually how I liked Dnipropetrovsk and what other cities I knew, and then asked me if I had been to Lviv and Uzhhorod. These questions suggested to me that I was suspected of being involved with border crossings into Hungary to participate in the Hungarian events. In the meantime "Levkovtsev" re-entered the room, gave the young man a signal of some kind, and again disappeared. This prompted the young man to ask me to show him my personal documents, and I took out my wallet and was about to give him my passport when he eagerly grabbed the wallet and started to leaf through my papers. But when he found nothing "subversive" he returned everything to me. Soon afterward "Levkovtsev" came back, asked me to follow him, and we entered another, much smaller room.

"Levkovtsev" told me to sit on the left, next to the wall, and I sat there while he walked back and forth, looking at me inquisitively. Suddenly a blond, middle-aged man entered. He had a commanding tread which seemed to underline his authority in this ominous building.

"Good day, Mr. Shumuk," the blond said, looking at me in a friendly manner.

"Good day," I replied. "And when did you people begin to use such a polite form of address?"

"All your friends honour you in this fashion in their letters," he replied.

"First of all I'd like to know who I'm dealing with, and what law authorizes you to read my letters?" I asked.

"Right now, Mr. Shumuk, you're dealing with counter-intelligence officials," the blond replied, "and we're the ones who ask questions. Understand?"

The man who had introduced himself to me as Levkovtsev was in fact Major Hura, who at that time was deputy head of the security branch of the Dnipropetrovsk oblast KGB. The blond, Sverdlov, was also a major and a deputy head of the security section, but in addition he also occupied a post in the republican KGB.

"I don't understand what grounds you have to bring me here, and what you want from me," I said.

"Don't rush; you'll soon find out everything you need to know," Sverdlov told me. "Just remember where you are, because only those who use their heads and co-operate with us leave this building without any problems."

"You have no grounds to arrest me and I refuse to make any deals with you."

"If you turn out to be unco-operative then it will only be the worse for you, for we'll have to bring charges against you. Think, Mr. Shumuk, think carefully, for your senseless obstinacy could get you into a great deal of trouble. And I know very well what I'm talking about."

"Please don't insult me," I replied. "Only scum who have no self-respect and who hold nothing sacred would make a deal with you. Just as I have no respect for those who collaborated with the Polish *defensywa* or the German Gestapo, I despise anyone who would collaborate with you. Such wretches are always of the same ilk; in fact, the same people have often served all these masters."

"All right, so now we'll talk about your case," Sverdlov said and opened a red folder. Inside were photocopies of my letters to Iaroslav Pashchak, Luka Pavlyshyn and Stepan Semeniuk in Poland, and the folder also contained photocopies of their letters to me. In our correspondence we had never even mentioned or discussed our views of the Soviet system and communism. On the contrary, in my letters I had written only about my attitude to the non-communist political parties in prewar Western Ukraine, and my feelings about events in the camps in the last few years. I had been very objective about my experiences, but unfortunately neither the communists nor the nationalists tolerate an impartial stance. They love to point their fingers at each other but are reluctant to hear the truth about themselves. I am equally familiar with both sides, and I have met fine people in both camps, but unfortunately they never had any decisive influence. Careerists who were greedy for power and were extremely intolerant when it came to even the slightest criticism always managed to gain the most important positions, while decent, humble people were always pushed into the background.

Sverdlov picked out several photocopies, questioned me about the meaning of various words, sentences and paragraphs in my letters, and on the basis of these letters, tried to extract the information needed to charge me under a certain article in the criminal code. He did all he could to concoct a "group" case, but I fought to prevent this. I had considerable experience in such matters, but unfortunately made a mistake during the interrogation. In trying to ensure that no one else would be implicated in my case, I ended up entangling myself quite badly. Instead of attempting to explain or justify my letters, I should simply have refused to answer the questions. Every question is prepared by a special group headed by the director of the investigating section. No matter how the person being questioned replies, his answers still place him in the position of a guilty party and sooner or later he is thoroughly confused by this tactic.

For example, the investigating authorities always enjoy preparing questions which are worded in the following fashion: "When and in what circumstances did you begin to oppose the Soviet regime?" This immediately assumes the guilt of the person being questioned, and one should either refuse to answer the question, or give the following reply: "You arrested me, so it's your duty to prove my guilt. I'll defend myself at an open trial." And one should stick to this position to the very end. But at the time I was unable to do this. My basic error was that I answered their questions, thus recognizing that they could play a role in determining my guilt or innocence. Fortunately, no one else suffered as a result.

The director of the oblast KGB and all his deputies attended the first phase of the interrogation. First I was cross-examined by several people who subjected me to a barrage of questions. Many of the questions were nonsensical, but a few serious questions were always included. In such situations, someone who knows human psychology can easily perceive the difference in the way the person being questioned responds to fictitious accusations and those based on fact. It is difficult to avoid this trap, and therefore one should ignore these devices and simply refuse to answer any questions.

Sverdlov conducted the interrogation for the first two days, while Hura wrote down the minutes. There was almost no pause in the questioning, and I was not allowed to leave the office. The first day was essentially devoted to my correspondence. In those cases where the KGB officials could not understand certain passages in this correspondence, they tried to extract explanations which would incriminate me under sections nine or eleven of Article 54–1 of the Criminal Code.[1]

They also read out and demanded an explanation of certain passages from Pashchak's and Semeniuk's letters. In one of his letters Semeniuk had written along the following lines: "I've just taken a holiday in the Tatra mountains and on my way home I visited Cracow and Auschwitz, where I examined the death camp built by the Germans. Everything there was built with typical German quality and efficiency, and to judge from their work one would think that the Germans were planning to settle there permanently. When

I examined the ovens in which the Germans cremated their victims it was difficult for me to believe that a nation which gave rise to Beethoven, Strauss, Bach, Hegel, Goethe and Schiller could also give birth to terrible executioners such as Hitler, Himmler and their bloody Gestapo. Next to these ovens stood a gallows, painted black, on which the first director of this camp was hanged. It would be very good if the directors of the camps and prisons in Lutsk, Lviv, Dubno, Rivne, Vinnytsia, Norilsk, Kolyma, Vorkuta and Karaganda were to come here and take a look at this exhibit.... " Later he added: "There will be no peace on earth as long as there is injustice."

"It's easy to understand why he's so upset about the Germans," Sverdlov said when he finished reading out this letter, "but tell me why he includes our prison and camp directors in all this, and why he thinks they should go to see these gallows?"

"Ask the author. I had nothing to do with this."

"So it seems that you're a coward who's afraid even to tell me what this letter is all about. Semeniuk clearly has in mind the executions which took place in our prisons during the war and in the camps during your revolts. Yes, we shot people and we'll continue to do so. And in the event of a war no one, not a single one of you will escape our eye and sword."

"I don't doubt that," I said, "but only sadists relish killing other people. And if a war breaks out your safety also isn't guaranteed in any way."

"It's a shame that I didn't get my hands on you ten years ago. If I had you between my pincers you'd be singing a different tune," declared Sverdlov, who was clearly nostalgic about the "good old days."

After this wrangle with Sverdlov, Major Hura came over to me.

"We're trying to save you," he said, "to get you out of this mess. But you're as stubborn as an ox and you're putting your own head in a noose. What happened in the past, happened. But now that you've ended up here you have to bring everything out into the open, understand?"

"I didn't know that you arrest people in order to save them. And they're so perverse that they actually reject your good deeds!"

"You haven't been formally arrested yet," Sverdlov reminded me gently. "You still have time to think things over and to prevent yourself from getting arrested, for everything is in your hands now."

"Tomorrow you could return home with the slates," Hura added, "and no one would ever know that you were here. And in a few months you could have a job managing your section of the state farm."

"Are you again suggesting that I become an informer?"

"We're simply suggesting how you can be of the greatest benefit to your people," Sverdlov replied.

"Those who used to beat up their victims have no right to talk about the good of the people. That's sheer hypocrisy."

"We did this only with bandits, not with ordinary people!" Sverdlov shouted.

"Your distinction between those who are 'bandits' and those who aren't has no meaning for me."

"Fine. It's 4am now. We'll meet again at 8am and I hope that by then you'll have come to your senses," Sverdlov said.

Two young men were playing chess in Major Hura's office, but when he entered they jumped to attention. Hura gave them a signal and they sat down and looked me over.

"You can rest here on the sofa, Lavrentiiovych. I trust these young lads won't bother you," Hura said and left the room. The "lads" continued their chess game and I dozed off.

At 8am Major Hura reappeared.

"What would you like for breakfast, Lavrentiiovych?" he asked politely.

"I only want something to drink," I replied. "Bring me some tea." I was served two cups of tea and some bread and butter with a piece of sausage. Afterward I was called into the office next door, where Sverdlov awaited me.

"How did you sleep, Danylo Lavrentiiovych?" Sverdlov asked. "Have you had some breakfast?"

"Yes, I've had breakfast."

"I hope that you're going to be more sensible, Lavrentiiovych."

"You're not starting off in a very serious fashion," I told Sverdlov. "The categories we use in our thinking are completely different, and what you call good and intelligent is base and stupid to me." And once again the senseless wrangling, shouts and insults began.

Sverdlov wanted the two of us, there and then, to fabricate an "underground nationalist organization." But when I refused categorically, he raised the question of the Norilsk strike. Sverdlov wanted to prove that the strike in Hard Labour Camp No. 3 had been organized by Ukrainian nationalists, that I had organized an OUN network with all kinds of directorates among the prisoners, and that the propaganda, financial and SB (internal security) directorates were especially active in the camp. To prove his "knowledge" of this fictitious OUN network in Norilsk, he told me exactly when I had entered and left the Vladimir prison, the number of my cell, and quoted a phrase I had allegedly uttered at one point: "The Organization of Ukrainian Nationalists is active wherever Ukrainians are found."

I recognized this phrase as one Mykola Panchuk had used in a conversation with Stepan Shevchuk at the Norilsk cement factory in 1952. It had been intended as bait for Shevchuk, but the security section had been informed that these were my words. Sverdlov's use of the phrase showed that he had carefully studied all the false information supplied by the camp agents in Norilsk.

But all the primitive discussions which Sverdlov (who had an enormous ego) tried to conduct with me were fruitless. No one could prove that the OUN had been active in Hard Labour Camp No. 3 in Norilsk, for the simple reason that the OUN, and in particular the SB, did not exist in this camp. What *had* been active in this camp was a modest, humane "self-help" organization which had committed no crimes and had acted in an exemplary manner at all times. I considered my activity in this organization to have been the high point of my public activity, and I am very proud of every member and of all the prisoners in Hard Labour Camp No. 3. They fought bravely for their lives and dignity, and adhered strictly to humane and noble norms of behaviour.

On 20 November 1957, my quarters were searched and all my manuscripts confiscated. The next day I was presented with a warrant for my arrest, issued by the Volhynia oblast KGB and signed by the Volhynia Procurator as early as June 1957. Thus five months had been spent planning my arrest before the KGB dared to take this senseless, criminal step.

On 21 November my case was passed on to Captain Moroz, the Dnipropetrovsk oblast KGB investigator. He was a tall, broad-shouldered fellow with coarse features. Later it became clear that his appearance was his only real qualification for the job, since he was stupid and primitive.

Early in the evening I was taken to the KGB's internal prison in the basement where the necessary forms were completed, my fingerprints were taken and I was placed in a cell. And once again there were iron grates on the window, locks on the doors, cold, soulless looks from the warders, the usual prison gruel and prison routine. When I was a political activist and was involved in the underground I had been prepared for the worst possible situations and I faced everything which happened to me calmly. But this time it was different. I had not been involved in any conspiratorial activity, and I had been all set to lead the quiet, peaceful life of a manual labourer. And then, without warning, I was rearrested and found myself in prison. This was a heavy blow, and I found my surroundings much more depressing than anything I had ever experienced before. I was very bitter, for at times this whole affair seemed to be a crude joke. I just could not believe that I could be arrested and tried for no reason at all.

For a long time, stupefied, I walked back and forth between the cell door and the window. Then I fell asleep with horrible thoughts, and nightmares kept persecuting me. When I awoke in the morning I imagined I was at liberty, but then I glanced at the window and door and it was as though a sharp knife had been plunged into me.

After the inspection and breakfast I was summoned for questioning. The investigator, Moroz, sat behind a writing table in a tiny office in which he looked like a giant. There was a small safe in one corner behind Moroz, and a portrait of Khrushchev was hanging on the wall. To the right of the door there was a cupboard, and a large portrait of Stalin was standing on it. Captain Moroz told me to sit on a chair in the corner to the left of the door, opposite the table. From this position I could see Stalin coldly and ruthlessly looking at me, Captain Moroz, and the portrait of Khrushchev, which was occupying Stalin's old position of honour.

"Well, let's begin," Moroz bellowed, casting a significant glance at the portrait of Stalin.

"So in practice you continue to follow his line," I said and smiled. "But if he was to rise from the dead he wouldn't forgive you for removing him from his place of honour. He only liked those cowards who were afraid of him alone, and would even die for him. Yet none of you have lifted a finger or said a single word in his defence."

"Shut up!" Moroz yelled and jumped up from behind the table. I was silent while Moroz shook his enormous fists above my head. Then he returned to his place.

"You've spoiled my mood," he said. "Do you realize that?"

"Please don't address me in the first person," I replied. After this altercation Moroz addressed me in the second person and started asking me questions concerning my case, referring to a list in front of him. After every such quarrel I swore to myself that I would never tangle with him again. I knew that it was best to say as little as possible, but I could not adhere to this policy and only made the situation worse for myself.

Soon Moroz began to question me about the Norilsk strike; he also was trying to establish that the OUN had been operating in the hard-labour camp. A thick dossier dealing with my imprisonment in the camps was lying on Moroz's table, and it contained all the denunciations of my activity which had been prepared by various agents in the camp. On the basis of these denunciations the investigating group was trying to put together a court case which would demonstrate that I was responsible for organizing an OUN group in the hard-labour camp and was behind the strike. Over a hundred questionnaires had been prepared for the former hard-labour prisoners who, according to information provided by secret police informers, had known me in the camp. These questionnaires were then sent to the places where the former prisoners now lived so that they could be questioned about my case. But this proved futile. None of these prisoners gave any incriminating evidence against me, and their statements were not even included in my dossier.

A month later I was transferred to a cell which contained two other prisoners. One had been brought in from the Mordovian camps for an investigation of some kind. The other was from a camp for non-political prisoners in Dnipropetrovsk, and had been paired with me deliberately. He said that he had been accused of scattering nationalist leaflets at the Piatykhatka station, and told me various other tales about his "collaboration" with the nationalists. He was actually quite good at putting together these stories.

It soon became clear that my correspondence was of no real significance. The KGB failed in its attempt to manufacture an OUN cell in the Norilsk hard-labour camp, and with every passing day Captain Moroz grew angrier and more frantic. Finally a "subversive" passage was found in one of my letters to Slavko Pashchak: "So, Slavko, after your departure my son asked, to my great surprise, 'Father, why is Albania so small yet independent, and Ukraine so large but dependent on Russia?' This is a sign that my son is beginning to think for himself." This passage in a letter photocopied by the KGB drove Moroz into a frenzy. My son was summoned and questioned by the KGB on two different occasions, for it appears that even a child's awareness of the inferior status of his nation, and dissatisfaction with this state of affairs, is more dangerous than dissatisfaction with the social or even the political order, and is of great concern to the authorities. The greatest fear of the regime is that people in general will become aware of the subordinate role of their nation, and this is why those who bring this situation to the attention of the people are pursued with such ferocity. This is also why Captain Moroz began to threaten that both my daughter and my son would find themselves in court together with me.

In the second half of January 1958, a gloating Moroz told me that two days previously my daughter had been summoned to the prison.

"She finally came round," he said. "She recently married a fellow whom you didn't even want to see around your house and we asked her how she thought you would react to the news of this marriage. 'I was born and grew up in the absence of my father,' she said, 'so it's none of his business whom I marry. I'm sick and tired of all the trouble we've had because of him.'"

This news was a greater blow to me than any sentence I could have received, even the death sentence.

"From this day on I refuse to enter your office," I told Moroz, "and you won't get a single word out of me until you allow me to see my daughter."

"You forget where you are—no one gives us ultimatums," Moroz said and went to see the director of the investigating section.

I was taken back to my cell, but could not sleep and had completely lost my appetite. For three whole days I neither ate nor closed my eyes. On the fifth day I was summoned by the director of the investigating section.

"What's wrong? Why do you refuse to talk with the person investigating your case?" he asked.

"I refuse to talk with anyone until you allow me to meet with my daughter."

"But are you sure that your daughter wants to see you? Perhaps not," my tormentor noted.

"Please take me to my cell," I asked. "I refuse to continue this conversation."

# Chapter Thirty

Two days later I was sent from Dnipropetrovsk to Kiev and then on to Lutsk, where I was the only prisoner in my cell in the internal prison of the Lutsk KGB. For three weeks I was left alone in this cell, but instead of alarming me this waiting game on the part of the KGB began to anger me. Thus, during one of the inspections I told the prison director that unless the investigation into my case was completed by the end of the month I would be forced to declare a hunger strike.

"I have no jurisdiction over the investigating authorities and I can't force them to finish your case," the prison director replied.

"Actually I'm not concerned about the investigation; I'd like to see my daughter. Give me permission to meet her before the investigation is completed and I won't complain about the delay with my case."

"I'll inform the KGB chief of this; it's his business."

The next day I was summoned to the prison office, where a KGB lieutenant and captain were waiting for me. Both these men, who were in their thirties, appeared to be fairly intelligent.

"My name is Matviienko," the captain said after looking me over with a policeman's trained eye, "and I'm going to be in charge of the investigation into your case. This is junior lieutenant Kolchyk, who'll act as a secretary. Do you have any reservations about us?"

"How can I have any reservations?" I asked. "I don't even know you."

"And how do you plan to conduct yourself? Are you going to be honest with us, or not?"

"First of all, I'm not a criminal. Second, I don't think that this office has seen much in the way of 'honesty'."

"There's no reason for us to start quarrelling already. Once your dossier arrives from Dnipropetrovsk I'll study it and then we'll have a talk. I'll write down only what you tell me, or, if you prefer, you can type your answers up on my typewriter," Matviienko said. Kolchyk, in the meantime, remained seated, examining my profile.

Ten days later I was summoned again, and this time all the handwritten materials that had been confiscated during the search of my quarters were laid out in front of Matviienko.

"Judging by these materials, you're not at all the person you pretend to be," Matviienko said. "You claim to be innocent of all wrongdoing but your letters show that you're an out-and-out nationalist."

"Show me or read out those passages in which I've praised nationalism and cursed the Soviet regime, or where I called upon anyone to oppose the Soviet authorities," I replied.

"Oh no! You're not so stupid that you write about this openly. You've done this in a more veiled, sophisticated fashion. For example, why did you copy out Sosiura's poem 'Love Ukraine'[1] five times? And why did you underline the title of the poem 'The Desecrated Grave'[2] in Shevchenko's *Kobzar*, and underline every word of the passages in which Shevchenko curses Khmelnytsky?"

"So now you've turned Shevchenko and Sosiura over to the nationalists? If so, you've done the nationalists a great service."

"We have in mind not all of Shevchenko's or Sosiura's works," Matviienko noted, "but only some of their poems. You copied out 'Love Ukraine,' but you didn't even mention the critique of this poem."

"This critique states that even Bandera could have been responsible for such a poem. This evaluation puts Bandera in a very favourable light—no Banderite could have praised him more highly."

After this discussion Matviienko moved on to his official questions, all of which dealt with the confiscated materials. He would ask me, for example, why I had written a certain word, sentence or paragraph, and what I had in mind at the time. I was interrogated in this way for a month, and the most "subversive" item found among my materials was the poem "The Woman." I had not written this poem, but simply copied it out, and the initials "P.K." were found at the end of the poem. The interrogators claimed, on the basis of these intials, that the poem had been written by Patrus-Karpatsky, and pressed me for a long time to confirm their suspicions. Finally they told me that if I didn't want to name the real author of the poem, then I would be held responsible for it.

Toward the end of this investigation I was shown the testimonies on which my arrest had been based, and was stunned by the brazen slander which they contained. The main witness against me was Iakiv Shyts, a former neighbour of mine whom, to my later regret, I had recruited into an underground Komsomol organization in my youth. He stated that when I returned home in 1956 I spurred him to speak out against the Soviet regime, the party, the Komsomol and the collective-farm administration in the village. He also stated that I had cursed Khrushchev and Kyrychenko[3] in his presence, calling them drunkards and idiots.

The second important witness against me was Fedir Mykhalchuk, who had been my nearest neighbour. After the war Mykhalchuk had belonged to an extermination battalion, setting up ambushes for Banderites, and in 1956 he was working as a brigade leader on the collective farm. The third witness was Shyts' mother, Ievdokha, the fourth was Petro Minchuk, and the fifth was Nechypir Vlasiuk.

Fedir Mykhalchuk also claimed that I encouraged him to speak out against the collective farm and the Komsomol, and that I recommended the dissolution of these organizations. The interrogator's insistence that I confirm all these statements struck me as senseless, since I could not believe that any sober-minded person could demand such a thing. If I had intended to engage in anti-Soviet activity of some kind then I would never have approached people such as Shyts or Mykhalchuk. This would have made as much sense as trying to organize the KGB to oppose the Soviet regime. No organization needs people of this kind. As for the other witnesses, Shyts' mother and sister were regular witnesses for the KGB and had already testified against a large number of people. For many years Petro Minchuk, who was a drunkard, had been a store-keeper on the collective farm, and he was perfectly willing to testify against anyone to stay in the good graces of the authorities, who could always find an excuse of some kind to harass him.

Nechypir Vlasiuk started to slander me in his statement, but then thoughtlessly mentioned that both Vasyl Vlasiuk and Fedir Mykhalchuk were present during my "anti-Soviet speech," and therefore they were required to confirm the details. But it turned out that Vasyl Vlasiuk was a decent person and Mykhalchuk could not get his story right, so both failed to uphold Nechypir's statement. And when I was brought face-to-face with Nechypir even he withdrew his earlier statements. However, it was impossible to neutralize Shyts and Mykhalchuk, for they kept to their story that I had spoken to them individually, and that no one else was present at the time. When I confronted Shyts in person he was at first unable to say a word, as if a bone had stuck in his throat. But with the encouragement of the procurator and investigators, he regained his composure and confirmed his story. Actually, at this "face-to-face" meeting he was hidden behind a wardrobe. I briefly saw his nose on two occasions but never looked him in the eyes. Fedir Mykhalchuk was also unable to say a word when we met; he was simply struck speechless, but his silence was interpreted as confirmation of his earlier testimony.

Before I was summoned, all these witnesses were taken to the investigator's office, and I was called in only after they had been suitably prepared and encouraged. When I arrived I was harangued to give the witnesses more courage. Kolchyk was an active participant in this psychological offensive. At the time he was just learning the ropes as an interrogator, although now he is quite well known.[4]

I was alone in my cell the first month in Lutsk, but later I was joined by an elderly man from Romen who had also been accused of nationalism. He kept talking about the inevitability of a third world war and was waiting for the United States to explode atomic bombs over the Soviet Union. But when I said that there would be no such war between the two countries, that I was essentially opposed to war and the detonation of American atomic weapons, and explained why I felt this way, he lost interest in me and soon afterward was removed from my cell.

A few days later a young fellow from Polissia replaced him. He had been sentenced to five years' imprisonment because several people who had been killed by the Banderites were buried in his barn. He was charged according to the article of the criminal code which the prisoners mockingly called "he knew but didn't tell." The event which led to his arrest happened when he was a small boy, but he was only sentenced after he had finished his army service, married and had children.

I was then transferred to the cell of a sick man who had been accused of murdering many people in his village. A few days later I was summoned by the director of the investigating section, Colonel Cherviakov.

"Have your most recent cellmates told you what they've been accused of?" he asked.

"No, they haven't."

"Is that so?" Cherviakov asked with a drawl which emphasized his disbelief. "Then I'll tell you. The young fellow from Polissia was a witness to a number of murders which were committed by the Banderites in his barn. And the second, older fellow killed about twenty people in his village."

"Why are you telling me this? It doesn't have anything to do with me."

"You're mistaken. You have a great moral responsibility for these terrible crimes, for you were one of those who inspired them."

"According to this logic, I also inspired your colleagues who shot thousands of people without an investigation or trial in Lutsk, Dubno, Rivne and Lviv in 1941, for I was once a tribune for communist ideas," I replied, raising my voice. "But you and your terrible crimes caused me to abandon my communist convictions and inspired these people to commit the crimes for which you are now trying them. You and your colleagues are behind all these terrible murders."

"If you don't reconsider your values it will be very difficult for you," the director of the investigating section stated menacingly and ordered that I be taken away.

The date of my trial was set for 5 May 1958. Four armed guards escorted me to the oblast court building. The courtroom was empty until the procurator arrived with a young woman. They were chatting cheerfully and laughing. The procurator went to the left, taking his place as state prosecutor. The woman went to the right and sat in front of me, at which point it became clear to me that she was to play the role of lawyer for the defence in this farce. I was curious to see how she would perform her role; how she would address me, what questions she would ask, and what advice she would give me. But she did not even glance at me, and continued to smile coquettishly at the procurator.

Soon the order came for everyone to rise, and the judge, my court dossier under his arm, walked in from a side room accompanied by two assessors. After the judge, Belov, had taken his place behind the table, he began to read out the charges against me, which were essentially based on the witnesses' testimonies. Then he began to question the witnesses, beginning with Shyts, who confirmed the earlier testimony he had given to Captain Kramsky of the KGB. Then Mykhalchuk was questioned, and, as had happened when I last met him face-to-face, he couldn't utter a single word. Finally the judge asked him one last question:

"Do you, Mykhalchuk, confirm the testimony which you gave during the investigation?"

"Yes, I do," Mykhalchuk replied, and his answer fully satisfied the court.

After all the witnesses had been questioned, I was given an opportunity to speak. In my statement I stressed that none of the materials confiscated from my quarters, and none of the letters intercepted by the security apparatus, contained even a hint of any appeal to oppose the Soviet regime. As for the witnesses, I stated that their testimonies were a complete fabrication that had been crudely concocted by Kramsky and then simply signed by the so-called witnesses. I mentioned, for example, the way in which Nechypir Vlasiuk's testimony had been shown to be completely unreliable.

During my speech the judge chatted with the assessors and did not pay me the slightest attention. In fact, it was clear that the entire trial was a formality, and that everything had already been decided by the KGB. When I had finished the procurator made a rather vague, general presentation in which he mentioned that I had been sentenced previously for nationalist activity, and therefore demanded that the court sentence me to ten years of imprisonment. Then the court gave the floor to the defence lawyer, who requested that the court not take into account that I had not worked for six months after being released from my previous imprisonment. This was the full extent of her "defence," after which the court adjourned for deliberations.

The verdict, which was written in an abominable mixture of Ukrainian and Russian, was then read out to the court. Nothing in the verdict was clear to me except that I had been sentenced to ten years of imprisonment; everything else was an irrelevant nightmare. All these court proceedings, of course, were held behind closed doors.

In the Soviet Union, the KGB, the procuracy and the courts were supposedly created to defend the Soviet people and state order. But instead of fulfilling their mission in public, before the people, for some reason these institutions carefully hide themselves and their work from those whom they are supposedly protecting. I was first tried in 1935, in Poland, for my work in the communist underground, and this was now the second time I had been tried in the Soviet Union for anti-communist activities. So, logically, I and not the KGB, the procuracy and the court should have feared a public examination of my case. But in the Soviet Union logic is inverted in such a fashion that these so-called "defenders of the interests of the people" hide this "defence" from those they are allegedly "protecting" as if it was the greatest of secrets.

But I do not fear the people, or feel ashamed before them. On the contrary, despite the threats of the authorities I would gladly do everything within my power to publicize my activities and the motives behind my behaviour. I have already been imprisoned for twenty-seven years in Poland, in a German prisoner-of-war camp and in the USSR.[5] And when I publicize my story, in all likelihood I will end my days in harsh captivity. But I am fully aware of what I am doing, and I have an obligation to inform my people what induces me to take this path, this search and struggle for the truth.

I know that what I have to say will not be to the liking of either the communists or the apologists for the OUN, and will not please the Poles, Russians or Germans, but I cannot (and have no right) to tell my story in any other fashion. They can all cast stones at me, but I will not change my behaviour to conform to prevailing political trends.

I have taken many wrong turns, and have made many mistakes, but I always followed the voice of my conscience and ignored all threats, obstacles and suffering. Apologists for the communists and nationalists have accused me of revisionism, but I never fully committed myself to either of their ideologies, for I was committed only to searching for the truth.

Soon after the trial I was transferred from the internal prison of the KGB to the ancient Liubart castle in Lutsk, which had once been a forbidding fortress looming over the beautiful Styr River and had now been transformed into a prison.

It was the end of May. The chestnut trees were in blossom, and beyond the Styr an unbroken expanse of meadows turned green and burst into bloom before my eyes. Girls walked along the banks of the Styr in the evening and, looking at their reflections in the water, they sang ancient folk songs, as had always been the custom. As I looked upon the beauty of my native countryside, which was so dear to my heart, I thought how wonderful it would be if these Sverdlovs, Kramskys and Belovs had not come to our Ukraine. These occupiers provoked discord and fratricide among our people, and now play the role of bearers of justice. In their absence my neighbours would not have given false testimony against me, for they are also the unfortunate victims of these intruders.

With their vile actions these Sverdlovs, Kramskys and Belovs cause great harm not only to the Ukrainian people but also to the Russian people, who gave the world great figures such as Lev Tolstoy, Chekhov, Dostoevsky, Dobroliubov and Herzen. It is the Russian interlopers on our territory who are feeding the fires of antagonism among people in general and among nations in particular. If it were not for the excesses of Polish and Russian chauvinism in Ukraine, there would have been no OUN, no Banderite movement and no fratricidal butchery. It was Great Russian chauvinism which gave birth to the term "Ukrainian bourgeois nationalists" and to the nationalist movement. Why is the percentage of Russians, Romanians and Poles sentenced for political reasons in their own countries much lower than that for Ukrainians, Lithuanians, Latvians and Estonians? And when the former are sentenced, it is not for nationalism, since nationalism is born of the direct subjugation of one nation's population by another, no matter what form this subjugation assumes—direct and open occupation, or supervision by an "elder brother," "guardian," or "defender."

Nationalism will continue to be a problem as long as Ukraine does not have its own separate economic life, its own central state bank, its own army, and its own higher and special secondary institutions which function in Ukrainian. It is not a bourgeois order

I am seeking for Ukraine, but democracy and independence. For me the Russians are a fraternal Slavic nation and I would like to live in harmony with them, but I cannot regard myself as their "younger brother." This offends my sense of personal and national dignity.

If the Russians attain a level of spiritual awareness such that they are ashamed to play the role of an "elder brother" to other nations in such a hypocritical fashion, then they will gain great respect among the other nations of the world. And only then will they have the moral right to talk of justice and humanism. The Russians will never be free unless they overcome their chauvinist and expansionist spirit, for a nation which enslaves other nations, even if it is playing the role of an "elder brother" and "guardian," cannot allow its own people to enjoy true democratic freedoms and a tradition of humanism. But this can only occur when Ukraine stops seeing itself as an inferior "younger brother." I bear no hatred toward any nation. I do not belong to any political party and I do not intend to oppose the existing state order. But I will not assist in or approve of the present regime's Russification of the political, economic and cultural life of Ukraine. The physical or spiritual destruction of a nation is an enormous crime against all humanity, since it involves the destruction of a unique aspect of the human spirit.

I firmly believe, however, that the Ukrainian nation will survive. It was the first nation, in a Europe of mighty sovereigns, to establish a free society of Cossacks in spite of the powers that be, and it gave birth to Shevchenko, Franko and Lesia Ukrainka,[6] three titans of the Ukrainian spirit and culture who are an eloquent testimony that we are not a dying nation. But I have digressed from my story.

In the Lutsk prison I was housed alongside common criminals, most of whom were embezzlers. They included book-keepers, store and warehouse managers, an agronomist and a sugar industry engineer. All were loyal to the Soviet regime, approved of the government's policies, and possessed no views of their own. Their only regret was that they had received insufficient access to the "trough," and that they were sentenced after trying to enrich themselves at the expense of their country.

I slept next to the book-keeper of a butter factory, an older, congenial fellow with a good sense of humour. Once, during an exercise period, he told me that his wife had been killed by Banderites.

"I have a second wife now," he told me, "and I don't feel especially bitter toward the Banderites. They, after all, are the brothers, friends and neighbours of those who were shot by the NKVD during the first few days of the war in 1941. They were buried in a large pit right underneath this exercise yard." When he finished his story I couldn't help looking at the ground beneath my feet and imagining this terrible tragedy.

# PART VII

# Chapter Thirty-One

At the beginning of June 1958 I was summoned to join a prisoner transport which was heading for Kiev. I arrived there the next day, and soon afterward I was taken to Moscow, where I stayed in the Krasnaia Presnia All-Union transit prison. After a week in this prison I was sent to Vorkuta, and spent almost three days travelling to this area in the far north, beyond the Arctic circle. It was not an easy journey, for I was leaving behind my native Ukraine, and I sank slowly into a depression as the landscape became increasingly more desolate and the trees gradually thinned out. On the third day of this trip we finally reached the Vorkuta area, the realm of snow and tundra. It was the first half of June and snow still covered this land of human tears and sorrow, of man's cruelty to his fellow man.

On the evening of the third day I was in the Vorkuta transit camp, where I met some prisoners who were leaving the camps for new investigations into their cases, and others who were heading for the camps. This was a clear sign that the political prisoners were coming under great pressure, that reactionary forces were once again raising their heads and Beria's henchmen were beginning to reassert themselves. Since I knew that I was being taken to the strict-regime camp, I asked the prisoners who were leaving the camps about conditions there. One young man had just left the strict-regime camp, which at that time was located near a cement works, and told me that it consisted of only two barracks.

"And who are the best-known prisoners in this camp?" I asked.

"Among the Ukrainians, Hryts Pryshliak and Herman Petrovych Stepaniuk, among the Lithuanians Father Racunas, a doctor of theology, and among the Russians, Revolt Pimenov,[1] a professor from the University of Leningrad and Feliks Krutikov, a former member of the Soviet diplomatic corps."

Of all these people I knew only Stepaniuk personally, although I had heard about Pryshliak. By this time I was no longer interested in most of my fellow prisoners. Only those who stood out from the crowd still intrigued me.

At the strict-regime camp I was assigned to a barracks which housed primarily Lithuanians, Latvians and Russians. Three Lithuanians took me under their wing and invited me into their circle, where they shared the food which they received from home or bought at the camp's canteen. I was touched by their friendliness and hospitality. It showed that, no matter what the circumstances, one can always come across fine people.

A lively young Russian, who had a former thief (a crippled hunchback) serving him as an "orderly" of sorts, lived opposite me in the barracks. This quick-witted prisoner had a higher education and such a good memory that he could read a page from a book, put the book aside, and then recite the contents of the page by heart. It turned out that this was Krutikov, of whom I had heard earlier. He was from a well-known Russian noble family, in which French as well as Russian had been used in everyday life, and his grandmother had taught him to speak French when he was only four years old. His French was equally as good as his Russian; in fact, he had a flair for languages, and mastered Lithuanian in little more than two months.

Before his arrest Krutikov had worked for the Soviet Embassy in Paris, where one day he fell into a trap set by French counter-intelligence and was forced to agree to work for the French. When Krutikov returned to the embassy he told his superiors what had happened, but despite his confession he was still sentenced to twenty-five years in corrective-labour camps. Although Krutikov's memory was phenomenal, he had no particular creative talents and was not a very moral person. He did not scruple, for example, to apply his skills as a former intelligence officer to all kinds of petty camp affairs, although this sort of thing no longer really surprised me. If Kamenev, for example, had been a prison informer in Bukharin's group,[2] then why should not Krutikov, with his aristocratic background, perfect his skills among people with whom he actually had little in common?

Krutikov spent his time trying to devise a way to earn himself the right to be freed before the end of his sentence.

"Professors Ramzin and Ochkin, who were sentenced in the 'Industrial Party' case,[3] built a new kind of steam boiler in the camps and were released as a. result of their invention. What could I do to get myself released?" Krutikov once asked one of his friends.

As for Stepaniuk, he had changed completely, and had lost his egotism and his aspirations to become a "leader." He had come down to earth from his earlier flights of fancy, began to work conscientiously in the camp, and even began to play up to the camp administration.

Pimenov, whom I knew only casually, had a long, full beard which gave him a very solid, respectable air. He worked energetically on various construction projects along with Stepaniuk, but on the whole behaved in a restrained, moderate fashion, and neither pandered to the camp administration nor antagonized it in any way. I saw Pimenov one day when he was playing volleyball, and he cut a rather childish figure. I had difficulty believing that he was a former professor of mathematics, but later, when I overheard him talking to Krutikov, I realized that he had a lively, sharp mind and that, given the right conditions, he would have been an outstanding scholar. Somewhat later I met Racunas. He was a highly educated and cultured person, and at the time was writing a book entitled "The Child, the Individual and Society." When we were transferred to Irkutsk oblast, on the Taishet route, we became close friends.

Eventually I again arrived at Vikhorevka, in the camp (No. 11) from which I had been freed in 1956. It appeared that captivity was a permanent state of affairs for me, and that freedom was to be only a brief interlude in my life. At Camp No. 11, I met Druzhynsky, whose second sentence had been imposed earlier than mine.

"I'll introduce you to Duzhy,[4] a member of the Provid of the OUN," he told me.

"Fine," I replied.

"There he is!" Druzhynsky exclaimed, grabbing me by the arm and pulling me along.

"Petro Afanasiiovych!" Druzhynsky shouted.

Duzhy stopped, and after introducing us Druzhynsky left us alone.

"Where are you from, Mr. Shumuk?" Duzhy inquired. "And what kind of an education do you have?" he asked before I finished answering his first question.

"Secondary," I replied.

"I have a higher education," Duzhy noted arrogantly. He asked me no more questions, but started talking about himself, his great knowledge and his exploits.

Duzhy was then living with Fedir Orobets, Ivan Kochkodan and Mykhailo Kolesnyk. Orobets was the real name of the UPA military okruh commander who had been known in Rivne oblast by the pseudonym Vereshchaka. He was a tall but slightly stooped man who had once been the scourage of Polissia. Battalion commanders had jumped to attention before him and both friends and foes had trembled in his presence, but now, in the camp, he was harassed and persecuted by both the prisoners and the administration.

The prisoners persecuted him because he had broken down under interrogation and told the investigators everything he knew—and he knew a great deal. The administration harassed him because of the horrendous charges brought against him. Vereshchaka recognized me, but for personal reasons I pretended not to know him and he did not inist on renewing our acquaintance. Vereshchaka had liver problems of some kind and died shortly after I arrived.

Kochkodan, a philologist, was an unfortunate man whose continued imprisonment was a pure accident. He was not released by the commission in 1956 because, before its hearings, he had been sentenced in the camp for a murder which he could not possibly have committed. Not only had one of his arms been partly crippled because of an old accident in a bicycle race, but in addition he was simply incapable of committing such a crime. However, since a murder had been committed in the camp, the administration had to find someone to put on trial in order to close the case. The real culprits were shrewd criminals who cast the blame on Kochkodan. This method of covering one's tracks had been used quite frequently in the camp, and the administration knew that Kochkodan was not responsible for the murder. But the easiest way to close the case was to accuse and sentence this innocent man.

Soon I found myself in Kozachok's brigade, which consisted almost entirely of Ukrainians. Some considered themselves to be "merited activists" and therefore above camp work, although they were even more preoccupied with money than the other prisoners. This set the stage for frequent conflicts between Kozachok and the group of "merited activists," which was headed by Adamiv and Fits.

Fits had one redeeming quality: he was quite serious about furthering his education and studied conscientiously during his free time. Unfortunately, he also had a strong lust for power. This "sickness" was a contagion in the camps, although in other prisoners, most of whom had no desire at all to improve themselves, it assumed an even worse form.

Druzhynsky tried to associate with Adamiv and Fits, but they did not take him seriously. In fact, they would not even acknowledge the authority of Duzhy, and considered themselves the real leaders of the whole camp. Since they did not know who I was, I had an excellent opportunity to see them as they really were.

Adamiv and Fits were better men than Shchur, Shkursky and their associates, but in essence they were all of the same ilk. They were quick and eager to use force against their fellow Ukrainians, but cowards when it came to standing up for their rights and opposing the brutality of the administration. For them the most important thing in life was to eat well, dress well, and have something to drink. And since it was difficult to achieve this by the sweat of one's brow, they made themselves out to be great "fighters" for the national cause, and forced the other prisoners, in the name of this cause, to surrender a part of their earnings to them. The exploitation of one group of prisoners by another was quite useful to the administration, and thus it did nothing to hinder this activity. First, the "activists" simply did away with those prisoners who stood up to them. Since those who opposed this exploitation also opposed the tyrannical behaviour of the administration, this could not but please the administration. Second, this parasitic activity helped to undermine the foundation of national solidarity in the camp. Therefore, in essence these "activists" and the camp administration were helping one another.

Kozachok was born in the Sokal raion of Lviv oblast. He was a practical, quick-witted fellow, and basically not a bad person. I was surprised, however, that he had accepted the post of a brigade leader in the camp, for once they became brigade leaders even the most noble prisoners became scoundrels within a year. Brigade leaders were appointed by the camp administration to squeeze as much work as possible out of the prisoners, and to inform the administration about those who resisted this pressure. The administration worked hard to ensure that the prisoners exploited one another, both during and after the normal workday. Those selected to supervise their fellow prisoners became the ears, eyes and feelers of the administration in the camp, which rewarded them by payment and unlimited access to the camp "trough"—the dining hall.

As a rule these positions were filled by people who had fulfilled similar functions in the German Gestapo or in Vlasov's army. Among the Vlasovites there were some decent people, but almost all the prisoners who had once collaborated with the Gestapo now collaborated with the KGB; that is, they simply continued working according to their "profession."

This whole system of exploitation, which tried to destroy the moral standards and national consciousness of prisoners, operated very effectively until 1952–3, and between 1944 and 1952 millions of honest labourers died from hunger, cold, hard work and the unbelievably brutal conditions in the Arctic North, the Soviet Far East, Irkutsk oblast, Kemerovo, Karaganda and Balkhash.

In 1952 this system for destroying prisoners was undermined by the growing protest movement among the political prisoners, which had as its first target the well-fed lackeys of the administration. In 1953, massive strikes of political prisoners in Norilsk and Vorkuta shook the very foundations of the camp system. The bones of countless prisoners from Ukraine and the Baltic states lie under Norilsk and Vorkuta, with their dozens of mines and great metallurgical factories, and under Karaganda and Magadan. But in 1953 these persecuted, starving slaves finally rose up against the all-powerful tyranny of Beria's henchmen, and the moving force behind these uprisings, unparalleled in the history of the camps, were the Ukrainians and the Balts.

It was far easier, however, to mobilize the prisoners to fight against a blatant evil than against those who passed themselves off as "martyrs for the national cause." The prisoners who had bravely faced the machine guns of Beria's thugs could not bring themselves to lift a hand against their fellow Ukrainians. Shchur, Shkursky and their ilk, who were aware of this, calmly, and without fear of punishment, persecuted and murdered those who dared to condemn their shameful behaviour. These "activists" were often renegades from OUN village self-defence groups who had joined NKVD extermination units toward the end of the Second World War and later. On the instructions of the NKVD, they had masqueraded as members of the OUN, and robbed and killed the finest people in our villages. They continued their criminal activity in the camps, and often succeeded in trapping completely innocent young men in their criminal network. The old OUN leaders in the camp opposed neither these parasites nor the tyranny of the camp administration, for they usually played a passive role in the camp, and in some cases they even played along with the disreputable elements among the prisoners. By 1958, however, relatively few of these "activists" remained in the camps.

Soon Duzhy and Kolesnyk were transferred to Strict-Regime Camp No. 26, and a few days later Fits, Druzhynsky and myself, and eventually Kochkodan, joined them. We all settled in the same section of this camp and most of the prisoners grouped themselves around either Fits or Duzhy, although I kept my distance from them. Later Ivan Goi and Racunas arrived and settled in our section. Goi was a modest, sincere person and we immediately became good friends.

One day Duzhy made a remark before all the residents of our section which was clearly meant for me.

"Volhynia is full of communists," he stated.

"Perhaps," I replied, "but we 'Volhynian communists' formed UPA units as early as 1942, and in 1943 we didn't allow the Germans to take a single cow out of Volhynia. Our 'pro-communist' youth joined UPA detachments, while you in Galicia were feeding the Germans to the very last day and sent your youth off to Germany as labourers or to join the SS division 'Galicia'."

After this discussion we virtually stopped talking to each other and I spent most of my time with Ivan Goi. He was an ordinary rank-and-file member of the UPA, and had only seven years of formal education, but he caught my attention initially because of his eagerness to help other prisoners who had suffered a misfortune of some kind. One day, however, Hlyva, prompted by Fits, struck

Goi in the face for the sole reason that Goi had been ignoring the Fits group. Everyone else in this group immediately pulled out their knives in what was clearly an attempt to provoke us into a fight. However, we did not react to this provocation, which would have benefited only the administration.

The administration never harassed the Fits group in such conflicts, whereas those who opposed it were immediately sent to jail. Thus the administration knew who posed the greatest danger to its security. Ivan Goi, for example, was a great threat as one of a group of prisoners in Kolyma who had once disarmed a division of internal security troops and then, arms in hand, tried to reach Alaska. All the divisions in Kolyma were thrown against them and only two prisoners survived the unequal battle which followed, of whom the wounded Goi was one. The administration feared Goi more than all the other prisoners put together, and examined his bed as often as three times each night to check whether he was asleep. And yet Goi who, empty-handed, had been the first in Kolyma to attack one of the division's officers and disarm him, had to suffer a slap in the face from a whelp in the Fits gang to prevent the Ukrainians in the camp from killing one another. Only a small proportion of the Ukrainian prisoners in the camp belonged to the Fits gang, but these scoundrels took advantage of our reluctance to fight with them and did the administration a great service. Thus three antagonistic parties were formed in our section, in which no more than thirty Ukrainians were living. In comparison with Hard Labour Camp No. 3 in Norilsk this was a terrible nightmare and I felt ashamed to look non-Ukrainians in the eye.

One day, early in 1959, I came across a copy of *Literaturna Ukraina*,[5] and scanning the newspaper's headings, I came across a piece of literary criticism devoted to the poems of Patrus-Karpatsky, whom I had met in the camps in 1956. It was a profound article, but the name of the author—Ivan Dziuba[6]—was unfamiliar to me. At the time I could not imagine that a bold, cultured and talented new generation of Ukrainian writers and activists would arise during my lifetime. But by 1959 such a generation was beginning to raise its head and Ivan Dziuba was to become one of its best-known spokesmen and representatives. This generation gained a higher education, became active in cultural and public life in Ukraine and, with its passionate and powerful words of truth, began to chip away at the glacier of fear in which the Ukrainian people had been entombed.

From Camp No. 26 we were first transferred to Camp No. 16 and then to Camp No. 10. Here Ivan Goi, myself and several other prisoners kept our distance from the other residents of the camp and we went to live in a separate barracks. However, I did get to know one of the prisoners, Vasyl Karkhut,[7] who had been living in Camp No. 10 before our arrival there. A medical doctor from the older generation of Galician intellectuals, Karkhut had an extraordinary memory and was very knowledgeable not only about medicine, but also about literature, having been a writer in his youth.

Because of the specific circumstances in Camp No. 10 Duzhy's attitude toward me changed for the better, and out of curiosity I sometimes listened to him when he talked about his colleagues in the Provid of the OUN. His accounts were of great interest to me, because they helped me to draw my own conclusions about the members of this Provid and the UHVR. On the whole, these conclusions were rather negative.

The strength of the OUN lay not in its Provid, but in the middle levels of the organization, in its fanatically loyal lower ranks, and in the units of the UPA. However, there were actually relatively few OUN members in the UPA command staff. Thus even the UPA-North chief of staff, Colonel Stupnytsky, was not a member of the OUN.

In Camp No. 10 Goi and I cut ourselves off from the other prisoners, and lived a separate life. We did not go out to work, so we had ample free time. I occupied myself by growing onions, radishes, cucumbers and potatoes in a small garden. This gardening and reading brought me a great deal of peace and satisfaction, and enabled me to forget temporarily the quarrels among the other prisoners.

# Chapter Thirty-Two

In the fall of 1959 I was transferred from the strict-regime category and was sent to Camp No. 601 in the Taishet area. Here all the prisoners worked in a furniture factory, and I was assigned to Vorotintsev's brigade, to work on a frame saw. Vorotintsev, who had been a major in Vlasov's army during the war, was a member of the "council of activists" set up by the camp administration to help strengthen its control over the prisoners, and he went out of his way to serve his masters faithfully. His brigade also included a Pole, Mikołaj Tichanowicz, who had been a major in the Polish *defensywa* before the war. Once he had persecuted and arrested people like myself, but here, in far-off Siberia, we became almost close friends. He was an intelligent, friendly and sensitive person; moreover, he was well-informed about a number of subjects which interested me.

Tichanowicz and I had many mutual acquaintances from Norilsk, since he had been imprisoned in the Medvezhka camp, and participated in the strike that took place there. He told me, for example, that Mykola Panchuk from Hard-Labour Camp No. 3 was in our camp, that he was working as a brigade leader, and that he was a member of the "council of activists." This did not really surprise me, for after becoming an informer for the MVD's security section in the Norilsk camp, it was easy for him to stoop to all kinds of villainy. Later Tichanowicz told me that Panchuk had befriended the KGB security officer in the camp, although the former justified this before the other prisoners by claiming that they had once studied together in high school.

Later, when I had more time, I asked Tichanowicz about the operations of the Polish *defensywa* before the war. He told me that after his training, he was assigned to infiltrate the communist underground, and eventually attained the post of secretary of a raion committee of the Communist Party in Upper Silesia, while one of his colleagues from the intelligence school became a member of the okruh committee. However, local party officials eventually realized that someone was subverting their organization, and suspicion finally fell on Tichanowicz. At this point Tichanowicz's colleague in the okruh committee ordered him to flee. Immediately afterward, however, this colleague submitted documents to the okruh committee exposing Tichanowicz as a Polish *defensywa* agent, thereby gaining its trust.

Tichanowicz claimed that for every fifteen communists in the party there had been one *defensywa* agent, and that all the literature used by the communists, as well as all Comintern directives, reached the Central Committee of the Communist Party of Poland (CPP) only after they had been delivered to the Polish ministry of internal affairs and suitably "processed." Polish *defensywa* agents, for example, ensured that the tribunal of the Central Committee of the CPP arranged for the execution of some of the staunchest communists, who had resisted all attempts by the government to recruit them as agents. Tichanowicz told me a great deal about the methods employed by the Polish *defensywa*, and his accounts made me realize the terrible and repugnant nature of all underground activity.

Tichanowicz sometimes visited Milhul, another Pole whom I also knew from Hard Labour Camp No. 3 in Norilsk. Milhul was a physician (all the political prisoners who were physicians carried out their profession in the camps), and approximately three weeks after I arrived in Camp No. 601 he informed me that he had just transferred Dr. Volodymyr Horbovy from the central isolator to the camp hospital. I was delighted that finally I would have an opportunity to meet Dr. Horbovy and to question him about the 1935 trial of the OUN Provid, and about the OUN Provid in general (especially Bandera). These issues had not ceased to interest me, for, after all, Bandera's name had become widely known, and the nationalist movement, which had encompassed all Western Ukraine in 1943 and even spread into Eastern Ukraine, had been named after him.

History will be the final judge of the Ukrainian nationalist movement, but in Western Ukraine it was truly a mass movement, a movement of the people. In fact, both the nationalist and communist movements were indigenous to Western Ukraine, but they were plagued by forces which cast a dark shadow over these movements and the nation which produced them. Now that the communists are fully entrenched in power, and have total control over everything printed or broadcast in the Soviet Union, they are doing everything within their power to defame the nationalists and especially the Banderites. But in reality the crimes of the Banderite SB were a response to the crimes of the NKVD. The bloody reprisals of the nationalists would not have taken place had it not been for the enforced collectivization of Western Ukraine in 1940, the arrests and deportations to Siberia which accompanied this action, and the mass executions in the prisons of Western Ukraine immediately after the outbreak of war in 1941. I have no intention of justifying the criminal activities of the SB, but this does not mean that I will play down the bloody crimes of the NKVD.

One autumn evening I went to the camp hospital to visit Dr. Horbovy, who was very sick and weak at the time. He had once been a strong, sturdy man, but systematic undernourishment had taken its toll, and the basic cause of his illness was simple exhaustion. Horbovy was restrained when I first met him, but became more open when I told him that I had been in the same camp as Milhul. He knew many of the Ukrainian prisoners whom I had met in the camps, and was interested to hear my impressions of them. He was disappointed that I had such a low opinion of Hlyva and Fits, and tried to excuse their behaviour, but I told him that I wanted nothing to do with such people, who were a disgrace to the good name of the other political prisoners.

"Well, what can we do?" Horbovy asked. "After all, they're fellow Ukrainians."

"That's our misfortune, that they're fellow Ukrainians," I replied. "How on earth did people like that ever get involved in a political movement?" Thus my very first meeting with Horbovy started off on the wrong foot. All the Ukrainians in the camp had a great deal of respect for Horbovy; none had ever been so straightforward with him, and this offended his pride.

Soon afterward Horbovy moved back to the central isolator, but a few days later he was brought back to Camp No. 601 and was assigned not to the invalids, but to the brigade in which I was working. The security section in the camp did this deliberately, hoping that we would argue with each other, for in the course of such arguments the security officers, with the help of their agents, acquired all kinds of valuable information. However, Horbovy and I both realized this, and tried to avoid contentious issues.

In the spring of 1962 Horbovy was taken to Lviv and I was transferred to Camp No. 7 in Mordovia. Here I met a number of old acquaintances, including Roniuk, Marushko and Hrytsiak. I was assigned to the barracks in which Marushko and Tichanowicz were quartered. Ten days after my arrival the camp director appointed Marushko leader of our brigade. By this time he was openly serving the camp administration, and he was appointed brigade leader because he had been one of the first prisoners to join the "council of activists" in the camp. Marushko watched me carefully to see what stance I would take toward the administration and the "council of activists."

I immediately told all my acquaintances that I would not participate in the activities of any camp organization, since I considered the whole system to be criminal and inhuman, and refused to help it cover up its crimes. Many attempts were made to recruit me into the ranks of the "voluntary guards" or "cultural activists" in the camp, and I had come under considerable pressure to join the editorial board of the camp newspaper. But I refused categorically to co-operate with the administration, which I felt that no self-respecting political prisoner could do, even in return for an immediate release.

My position upset many of the prisoners I knew, including Marushko. But in time even Marushko stopped boasting about his co-operation with the administration, and eventually became ashamed of his behaviour. He told me that Stepaniuk and Pavlyshyn were in Camp No. 7, and that they were also loyal to the administration. Pavlyshyn had even been taken to Moscow to declare and demonstrate his loyalty to the KGB.

"And what was he assigned to do when he returned to the camp?" I asked Marushko.

"He was told to persuade all the other Ukrainians to follow his example."

"Did he carry out his assignment?"

"Of course. He was quite proud of the fact that Moscow had given him such an important mission."

"Did Pavlyshyn say whom he talked with in Moscow, and the topic of their conversation?"

"Basically he described how well he was received, and how he was even given the title of 'general.' But he didn't want to say anything about the contents of his discussions with the KGB."

"The KGB must have some good psychologists, for they obviously knew a great deal about his weaknesses. The very fact that someone addressed him as a 'general' must have given him delusions of grandeur and completely disarmed him, for he loves good living, pomp and ceremony more than anything else in the world."

"Times have changed," Marushko noted. "Now everyone is preoccupied with the thought of gaining freedom at any cost, whether by overfulfilling their quotas and getting time off, by petitioning the authorities for an early release, or even by getting a pardon. No one has suffered because I became a brigade leader and a member of the 'council of activists.' On the contrary, I'm trying to make things better for everyone. You can see what's going on now: even members of the Provid are recanting and writing petitions pleading for a pardon. Vasyl Kuk[1] recanted and wrote a whole brochure condemning the nationalists. Stepaniuk and Duzhy petitioned for pardons and have also written disgraceful articles for the Soviet press. I haven't stooped to that kind of activity, and I'm not a member of the Provid. But I do want to be released after serving two-thirds of my sentence, and that's why I joined the 'council of activists'."

"Do as you wish—that's your business. I don't know Kuk personally, but I know Duzhy and Pavlyshyn well, and I don't give a damn about these members of the Provid and their ideology. If I refuse to collaborate with the camp administration and to petition for a pardon, it's not for the sake of the honour of the OUN, but because my own conscience and my sense of personal dignity won't allow me to do so. For me, both those who are recanting and those to whom they are recanting are equally contemptible. Duzhy, Pavlyshyn and Kuk have no right to slander the OUN, for they themselves and their criminal acts represent everything that was worst in the OUN."

I operated a power saw in Marushko's brigade, cutting up wood for furniture, and I used to work the entire day, without leaving the bench. I never asked Marushko for any favours, but should say in fairness that, as a brigade leader, he was always good to me. In 1961 he went to work in a hospital as a medical intern.

In the fall of 1961 Hryts Pryshliak was assigned to work in the furniture factory, but by now Horbovy and Karkhut were invalids and therefore did not have to work, although Karkhut eventually managed to find himself work as a physician. He did not share the views of the Banderites in the camp; in fact, he even felt a certain aversion for them. However, he maintained good relations with Horbovy and the other prominent Banderites.

My critical attitude toward the OUN, and especially my categorical condemnation of the crimes of the SB, was not to the liking of a number of prisoners, especially Horbovy and Pryshliak. They not only approved of those who had committed these crimes; they even tolerated those who had publicly vilified themselves and the OUN. But they could not tolerate me, even though I had not broken down under interrogation and, unlike so many others, had refused to write any articles for the official press condemning the OUN.

In essence, all parties of a totalitarian nature are similar. Thus, even today, the Communist Party and the Soviet government are paying substantial pensions both to those who organized the famine in 1933, and those who, in 1937 and later, deprived millions of innocent people of their freedom, and tens of thousand of their lives. The party and government ensure that these terrible, shameful crimes are never mentioned. On the contrary, they continue to persecute and punish those who dare to speak out against these crimes and their perpetrators.

The ghosts of those who died during the famine or were later executed will continue to haunt Ukraine until the people publicly condemn all those responsible. Not only are they still alive in every raion centre, collecting pensions, they are striving actively to renew the old order. And, to this day, some of them remain at the summit of power and continue their criminal deeds in the name of the government.

Only democracy can save humanity from the dangers of tyranny, both of the right and of the left. And only the unlimited right, guaranteed by law, of all citizens to express, disseminate and defend their ideas makes it possible for the people to control and direct the policies of the government. Without this right, and in the absence of a legal opposition, there can be no talk of democracy and democratic elections to a parliament.

# Chapter Thirty-Three

In 1962 I had an operation for varicose veins in the central hospital of Camp No. 3. It was a tricky operation, and the post-operative period was particularly difficult. Later, in 1964, I had an operation for a ventral hernia in the same hospital, and this is when I first got the urge to start writing my memoirs. In fact, I began immediately after I entered the hospital. At this point Horbovy also entered the hospital, and I was glad to have an opportunity to question him about the activities of the OUN Provid. Horbovy greeted me politely and was pleased that we had met again. When we were in the hospital we spent almost all our time together, and he told me a great deal about the internal politics of the OUN.

After the war Horbovy had worked as a consulting lawyer in the Czechoslovak ministry of agriculture, but the Czechoslovak government soon extradited him to Poland. In 1947, when he was being interrogated in Warsaw, he was beaten very severely and jumped out of a window in the second-floor office of the director of the interrogation section, breaking a leg. Afterward he was sent to the Soviet Union, and spent three years under investigation by the KGB at 33 Korolenko Street in Kiev. He was beaten badly there too, but the authorities did not break his spirit, and in the camps he refused to pander to the administration. The only thing I disliked about him was his tolerance of all kinds of political rogues and degenerates, but he was a poor judge of character and too trusting. In addition, he had a great weakness for people who flattered him and used the title "Doctor" when addressing him.

After the strikes in 1953, and until the fall of 1956, the government made a number of concessions to the political prisoners which were unprecedented in the history of the Soviet Union. But beginning in the fall of 1956 the government again reverted to a policy of repression. Thus, in 1963 we were restricted to receiving two parcels, each weighing five kilogrammes, per year. In 1964 it was forbidden to sell sugar, bread and any kind of fat or oil in the prison canteen, and only those who collaborated with the administration were allowed to receive the two parcels to which each prisoner was theoretically entitled. The conditions in the camp, as well as the quality of the food we received, continued to deteriorate. But each Wednesday, during the political education sessions, detachment commanders brazenly and shamelessly lectured us about the "humanism" of Soviet rule.

When we were forced to listen to these ignorant, cynical lectures about "humanism" I felt as if I had been bound hand and foot, that my persecutors were spitting in my face and taunting me, and that I was totally incapable of defending myself. It is the height of mockery when a parasite who is living off your sweat and blood forces you to respect him and to listen to his "lectures." No one will ever devise a more terrible way of debasing human dignity.

Sometimes prisoners simply could not tolerate this treatment, and committed suicide by climbing the fence surrounding the camp in broad daylight. I saw one such incident in Camp No. 7, when a prisoner with a ladder on his shoulders climbed over the barbed wire marking off the "forbidden zone," placed the ladder against the wooden fence surrounding the camp, and calmly started climbing the ladder. The camp guards could have easily captured the prisoner, but they shot him in cold blood, just as he was about to climb over the barbed wire at the top of the fence. And so, poor soul, he remained hanging on this wire until Shved, a notorious brute of an officer in the camp, removed him. Three prisoners in Special Strict-Regime Camp No. 10 also committed suicide in this fashion.

In 1964 I only had three more years to serve before the end of my sentence, and I decided to work in the polishing workshop. This was the least healthy workshop in the furniture factory, and any prisoner who was willing to work there was welcome to do so. By spending some time here I could save some money so that I could clothe myself properly upon my release. My instructor in this workshop was Pavlo Kulyk, whom I knew from my stay in the Taishet camps. Born in 1928, in Tarashchanskyi raion, Kiev oblast, he was a slim, handsome fellow who was warm-hearted and sensitive to the misfortunes of other prisoners.

I was a poor apprentice, and had great difficulty handling the cases I was supposed to polish. Although not the best of instructors, Pavlo was extremely patient, for I spent a whole month spoiling cases, and he had to fix them afterward. But with great difficulty I finally mastered this job, and eventually became one of the best polishers in the workshop. It was not easy spending the whole day working with acetone, but I came to enjoy this job, because it allowed me to work on my own.

While I was still in Camp No. 601, in the Taishet area, I heard that Kulyk was now serving his second sentence. I was curious to know what had driven this young man to show such dissatisfaction with the Soviet regime, and one day I asked him why he had been sentenced.

"I was first sentenced when I was serving in the armed forces," Kulyk replied. "I was with the navy at the time, and a court case was brought against me because I sometimes made fun of the political instructors during the political sessions we had to attend. They couldn't do anything about my making fun of their lectures, but when a group of sailors escaped to Turkey from our battleship I was arrested because I had also requested shore-leave for that day, although I had remained on the ship because I didn't receive a pass. I was arrested the second time for preparing leaflets critical of the regime. I bought myself a typewriter, typed up these leaflets and distributed them all on my own."

"Why did you do this?" I asked.

"I can't forgive the authorities for the famine which they created in 1933," Pavlo replied.

"Do your remember this famine?"

"I remember everything, because this isn't the sort of thing that can easily be forgotten."

"Can you tell me what you remember?"

"It's difficult to describe everything. Our little hamlet was called Komyshky and it consisted of twelve households, of which only two, those who owned cows, didn't suffer any deaths because of the famine. Four families were completely wiped out, and deaths occurred in six other families. My family survived only because we had a milch cow."

"How did this happen? Weren't you given any grain by the state?"

"No, everyone was initially issued grain for their work-day units[1] in the fall of 1932, but in December an order was issued stating that by a certain date all collective-farm workers had to hand over all the grain they had received from the state. After this date members of the Committee of Poor Peasants,[2] together with representatives of the raion executive committee, went from house to house and confiscated every single morsel of grain they could find. My father hid two sacks of wheat in the garden, but because of the constant searches we were unable to make use of this grain. My father was afraid that he would go to jail if the wheat was found, so he finally dumped one sack down a well and scattered the other in the fields. However, one search party found a pail of beans in our attic, and even this was enough to have us threatened with imprisonment."

"In 1933 I was very active in the communist underground in my district in Volhynia and I did everything I could to dispel the rumours concerning a famine in Soviet Ukraine. I'm no longer a communist; in fact, I've been sentenced twice now as a nationalist, but I still find it difficult to believe what you're telling me."

"You were all idiots," Pavlo retorted angrily, "and the Poles were fools to imprison you for your communist activity. They should have just chased the lot of you across the border into the Soviet Union. There you would have all died of hunger in the 'paradise' you were fighting for in Poland, and you would have stopped bamboozling your fellow citizens."

"Who confiscated your grain? Were they people just like you, your neighbours?"

"Not just neighbours, even relatives were involved. For example, one of our neighbours, a distant relative called Ievtukh Komashko, was the first organizer of the Committee of Poor Peasants in our area, the members of which later became the 'activists' of the collective farm. In 1933 they confiscated grain from the employees of their own collective farm, but then they themselves ended up dying of hunger. I'll never forget the terrible moment when my father and I went to see Komashko. Through an open window I could see his daughter Katria lying on a bench. Her hair was hanging down from the bench, and from the way it was moving it seemed that she was alive. But it was only the wind blowing her hair, for she was dead and her body was already decomposing.

"Katria's mother, Ielysaveta, was lying on the stove alongside her second daughter Motria; her son Petro was lying under the stove; and we found Ievtukh's body in the garden. My father placed their bodies in his cart and drove them to a large pit in the graveyard—such was the fate of the organizer of the Committee of Poor Peasants in the village of Velyka Bereznianka. Many others like him died in the same fashion, but some are still alive and occupy various high positions. Those who were involved in grain confiscations and caused others to starve were never punished, but I was imprisoned for simply daring to write about their crimes.

"All that I can remember from my earliest childhood are scenes of horror. Even before the famine Komsomol members used to ride horseback on our village priest, derisively pulling his beard, and Hapka Radchenko once demonstratively danced on top of the church icons in front of the entire village. My mother was approached a number of times, even after the famine, to become an atheist.

"From April to June 1933 more than 700 people in our village died of starvation, and some even resorted to cannibalism. Seven children's heads were found in the ash-pit of one house, and one child's head was raked out of the ash-pit of our neighbour's house. My mother used to tie me to a table-leg so that I wouldn't run out of the house and disappear. Now the people of Velyka Bereznianka live quite well and have already forgotten this great tragedy, but I can't get it out of my mind. That's why I'm being punished now."

This artificial famine is now long past. But as long as this crime and the criminals who were behind it remain unpunished, and those who condemn this evil continue to be persecuted, the possibility that a similar horror may take place some day cannot be excluded. And before they can gain the moral right to demand punishment for fascist criminals, the Soviet authorities must at least have the courage to condemn publicly all those who were behind the artificial famine of 1933 and the massive arrests and executions which followed, especially in 1937. How can they proclaim their state to be the "most humane" in the entire world if they continue to conceal and pay pensions to the very worst kind of criminals? Such a cover-up can only be the work of people who fear that exposing these horrors would expose their own role as accomplices.

Khrushchev once promised to start unravelling this terrible mess, which began with Kirov's murder.[3] But someone must have suggested to him that the thread of guilt could lead back to him, since he was a member of the CPSU Central Committee from 1934 and the Politburo from 1939. And as for the events of 1933, even Khrushchev never mentioned a word about them.

One day in 1964 Captain Krut of the KGB called me to his office and returned the handwritten materials his predecessor Lytvyn had confiscated from me.

"You should request a pardon," he told me. "You've completed two-thirds of your sentence now and it's time you were released."

"If I requested a pardon I'd have to name and condemn the crime I committed," I replied. "How can I do this if I'm not a criminal?" Thus I failed to reach an agreement of any kind with Captain Krut, although he did return the first part of my memoirs to me.

I worked quite conscientiously in the camp during the last few years of my second sentence, and devoted most of my free time to reading and writing. I rarely conversed with my neighbours at work or in the barracks, but this in itself did not suffice to please the administration. It wanted me to condemn my past, to use every opportunity to praise the "educational work" of the camp authorities and thank them for their good work in "reforming" the political prisoners. Of course, the administration did not consider us to be *political* prisoners; they never used this term when referring to us.

"Only Bolshevik-Leninists who were imprisoned in tsarist jails before the revolution can be considered political prisoners," one of the camp supervisors told me one day. "As for you—you're state criminals." It would have been a waste of time to argue with him, or to point out the precise meaning of these words, and thus no one reacted to such nonsense.

# Epilogue

*In the fall of 1967 Danylo Shumuk was released after completing the ten-year sentence he had received in 1957. In the meantime Shumuk's marriage had completely fallen apart and he settled down in the town of Bohuslav, Kiev oblast, where he was employed as a watchman at a "Young Pioneer" camp.[1] He lived there alone for almost two years and in his free time he worked on his memoirs, which he had begun writing during his imprisonment in the Mordovian corrective-labour camps.*

*In 1968–9 Shumuk made several trips to Kiev, where he became acquainted with members of the young Ukrainian creative intelligentisa sometimes known as the* **shestydesiatnyky** *(literally, "people of the sixties"), whose spokesmen at that time were Ivan Dziuba and Ivan Svitlychny,[2] and in 1969 Shumuk received permission to live in Kiev. In a* **samvydav** *document written in 1979, on the occasion of Shumuk's sixty-fifth birthday, members of the Ukrainian intelligentsia in Kiev wrote:*

*We...met and befriended Danylo Shumuk shortly after his release in 1967 from the Mordovian camps. These were the memorable sixties, a period of national renaissance in Ukraine.... It was always interesting to talk with him, and he struck us as a dedicated, honest and sincere person who follows only the voice of his conscience. He values truth and compassion above all, and despises all forms of hypocrisy and conformity to the powers that be....*

*The ideal and aim of Shumuk's life—a free and democratic Ukraine—were and remain our ideal and aim as well. True, we did not always agree with him, and we engaged in lengthy arguments and discussions, but in essence we were of the same mind....*

*In effect Shumuk's ideals and his understanding of the truth have not changed since his youth. They are—freedom, justice and happiness for his people.[3]*

**Between the fall of 1967 and late 1971 Shumuk completed his memoirs, which were circulated among the members of dissident circles in Kiev. However, the only segment of Shumuk's memoirs covering the period 1967–71 to reach the West describes a trip he made to Odessa in 1970 and his conversations with an old friend from the hard-labour camps.**

*[Editor]*

At the beginning of April 1970 I arrived in Odessa for treatment at the Lermontov sanatorium. Odessa thoroughly depressed me, for in Kiev one could occasionally hear Ukrainian here and there, but in Odessa—never, and in the streetcars, buses, canteens and shops I was mocked every time I opened my mouth. One day I was in a streetcar when a woman looked at me intently and then spoke to me in Russian.

"Young man, you're dressed quite well and you have a fairly intelligent face, yet you can't speak properly. Don't you know Russian?"

"Why, the *khokhly* have become so impudent, even here, in Odessa," another woman added, "that I was even asked to fill in a form in Ukrainian. 'I didn't just come off the farm,' I told them, 'I'm from Odessa.' So I simply ignored them and filled in the form in Russian."

"When I go to Moscow or Leningrad I'll speak Russian there," I replied. "But in Ukraine I'll speak only Ukrainian, no matter where I am."

"So we have a Banderite here—he considers even Odessa to be part of Ukraine," a man at the other end of the compartment sneered. I saw that there was no point in arguing with these people and kept silent, although my fellow passengers continued to stare at me as if I was a criminal of some kind.

A few days after this incident a man ran up to me.

"Hello, Danylo!" he exclaimed. "It's been years since I last saw you!"

I responded to this greeting and stood rooted to the spot, straining my memory to remember who this stranger might be.

"What! You don't remember me?" the stranger said and took off his hat.

"Oh, Slavko Pashchak!" I exclaimed.

"Yes, it's me. What brings you to Odessa?"

"I came here for medical treatment; I'm just returning now from the Lermontov sanatorium."

"And where are you heading?"

"I'm taking streetcar 13. I have a room on Chornomorska Road."

"We'll go together. I'm heading that way to see my brother."

When we reached Chornomorska Road we went to a cafeteria and then spent about an hour walking the streets and talking about our experiences in the camps.

"Danylo, you've always been an honest person," Slavko said toward the end of our conversation. "Tell me, don't you regret that you broke with communism and wasted your entire life supporting nationalism so that now you have nowhere to turn?"

"You have a very distorted view of my switch from communism to nationalism," I replied. "If nationalism is a yearning for freedom and independence then I have always been a nationalist, even when I belonged to the CPWU, and will remain a nationalist to my dying day. But if nationalism is characterized by the ideology of the OUN then I never was and never will be a nationalist. The Communist Party proved to be incapable of solving the problems it was established to resolve, and that's why I abandoned it. And I joined the OUN because in 1943 it was the only force fighting the German occupiers in Volhynia, which at that time was the most important consideration for me.

"In France the resistance movement was organized and directed by democratic forces, since only they could lead such a movement in a nation-state which had just lost its independence and democratic order. But in the case of our nation, which lost its independence a long time ago, there were no such forces. Our so-called democrats were opportunists, from our old hereditary intelligentsia, who had learned from their fathers and grandfathers how to adapt to various waves of conquerors and how to serve them. Because of the circumstances in which we found ourselves, the spirit of revolt and struggle arose from the depths of the masses, which were mobilized and led by the totalitarian forces of the CPWU and OUN.

"As for regretting the path which I have chosen, I have never done so and never will, for I consider it contemptible to be a hypocrite for the sake of utilitarian comforts or the opportunity to taste power. We have only one life to live, and everyone has to make his or her own choice: to live for bodily comforts and passions, or for freedom of thought and convictions. When faced with such a choice we have to make certain sacrifices, and everyone sacrifices that which he or she values least."

Slavko had no desire to reflect on these issues, and after giving me his address he invited me to spend Easter with him and his family. I accepted the invitation gladly, and the next day I duly arrived at Illichivka Street. Slavko's wife greeted me, and he came home soon afterward. After we had drunk some champagne and eaten our fill Slavko asked me why I had never married.

"In my situation," I replied, "at my age, with my health, without lodgings, without a diploma or profession and without prospects for a pension of any kind, constantly harassed and persecuted, and after my psychological upheavals, it would be impossible to get married. Establishing a family requires a certain talent and total dedication to that family. I lack these qualities, and have dedicated myself to other endeavours. It would be better if I kept clear of a family and emotional involvements."

"That's true. I'm not quite myself either. I yell and swear at my wife, swear at my daughter, swear until I'm exhausted, and I'm not even sure why. We're like fish out of water. Incidentally, how much do you make at your present job?"

"Eighty roubles a month."

"That's peanuts, Danylo. Move to Odessa and I'll pay you one hundred-and-twenty roubles a month."

"What's this, Slavko? You're talking like a businessman now!"

"I work as a brigade leader of brick-layers at construction sites and could get you a job there."

"But can you get me registered in Odessa?"

"Oh no, that's not up to me."

"So you see, Slavko, 'white niggers' like me have more difficulty getting permission to live in Kiev or Odessa than the real, African negroes."

"That's true, Danylo, but I'm concerned that you might get involved with the new generation of politicos in Kiev."

"Whom do you have in mind?"

"Whom? Why Dziuba, Svitlychny, you know."

"Where did you hear about these people? What do you know about them?"

"Why are you questioning me like this, as if I was a child? Every member of the intelligentsia in Odessa knows them."

"That's not true, Slavko. Even in Kiev not all the intelligentsia know them."

"I'm not saying that everyone knows them personally, but every teacher and doctor in Odessa has heard about them."

"All right. So what does this intelligentsia know about their 'subversive' activity?"

"They know everything, but are doing absolutely nothing themselves. The Soviet 'machine' crushed the Central Rada in the twenties, it crushed the entire nationalist movement during the Second World War, and it will crush these new politicos as well. As for the masses, their main concern is to eat well, dress well, drink, watch soccer on television and have a good time. This is all they think about, and to a large extent they've achieved their goals. They don't give a damn about independence and their native language, culture or customs. What can a small group of members of the intelligentsia do when the entire working class chatters away in Russian and doesn't even want to hear talk of independence? You don't know what's going on these days. But I do. I've been working in Odessa as a brick-layer for fourteen years now, and I know what makes the workers tick. And nothing can be accomplished without them. We're not a true nation, Danylo, we're just a 'Little Russian folk' which prides itself on its borshch and dumplings and nothing else."

"But Slavko, I know Svitlychny and Dziuba personally and can state categorically that the intelligentsia in Odessa have been misinformed about these people in order to create the kind of public opinion the authorities desire. They are not and have never tried to act as 'politicos.' They're very intelligent, talented, humane and modest writers who, motivated by a sense of public duty, have stood up in defence of their native language and culture and the elementary human right to express one's opinion. In my opinion they're exemplary persons, and I, with my shattered nerves, can't even hope to match them. I'd probably disagree with them in many respects as far as their world-view and politics are concerned, but there's no real need for us to define and clarify these differences, for they're not members of an organization of some kind. They're people who are totally independent of one another in their thoughts and actions.

"The use of the label 'Ukrainian bourgeois nationalism' is an old, tried method used by Russian chauvinists to frighten those who dare to oppose their offensive. But they don't stop at frightening people, for they also use slander, dismissal from work, locks, barbed wire, hunger and all manner of physical and moral persecution to achieve their ends. We're living in an era of powerful national liberation movements, in an era of national self-awareness on the part of even the most backward peoples. Russian chauvinist reaction is supporting these movements, throughout the entire world, for its own political purposes, but uses the most brutal methods to crush similar movements in its own back-yard."

"Danylo! They'll put you away again, and at your age, with your health, you won't survive another sentence. And it won't be Russian chauvinists who'll imprison you—it will be your fellow Ukrainians."

"I've already spent most of my life in captivity, and if necessary I'll die there. This would be just one more crime on the conscience of our present-day janissaries. But every nation in the world has had its renegades. Joan of Arc, after all, wasn't tried by an Englishman, but by a Frenchman, Cauchon."

"Danylo, no one needs your struggle and your suffering. You'll die and no one will even have a good word to say about you. You'll be condemned, and the condemnations will come not only from enemies and strangers, but from your relatives and former friends as well. And some people will simply call you a failure who never learned how to live a normal life."

"I know, Slavko. But I can't change, and even if I could I wouldn't want to do so."

*Danylo Shumuk was rearrested on 14 January 1972 during a concerted KGB offensive against Ukrainian dissenters.[4] This offensive was part of a broader, "all-Union" campaign against dissent, but the scale and severity of the crackdown in Ukraine was exceptional, for "the evidence suggests that the aim of this campaign was to terminate and, if possible, reverse those social processes which had brought about the revival of cultural and public life in Ukraine during the 1960s."[5]*

*Shumuk's trial took place in Lviv on 5–7 July 1972. He was charged, under Article 62–2 of the Criminal Code of the Ukrainian SSR ("anti-Soviet agitation and propaganda"), with preparing and circulating his memoirs, circulating articles by Milovan Djilas[6] and Ivan Dziuba, making anti-Soviet statements, and writing a letter to Ivan Svitlychny which had been confiscated from the addressee and was judged to be a "programmatic document." Shumuk, as one previously convicted of "especially dangerous crimes against the state," received the maximum penalty prescribed by Article 62–2: ten years in a special-regime corrective-labour camp to be followed by five years of internal exile.[7] At the beginning of October 1972 Shumuk arrived at the camp where he was to spend most of his sentence: Mordovian Strict-Regime Corrective Labour Camp No. 1–6.[8]*

*According to Amnesty International, the Mordovian ASSR and the Perm region contain the largest concentrations of known prisoners of conscience in the USSR, and Mordovian Camp No. 1–6 holds all the prisoners of conscience known to Amnesty International who are serving special-regime sentences.*

> *No report on imprisonment in the USSR could avoid singling out the special-regime colony in Mordovia. This camp has the worst features of both prisons and camps...the cramped and unhygienic conditions of the prisoners' cells, the unhealthy and exhausting nature of the compulsory labour, the meagre and miserable food rations and the lack of possibility for exercise combine with other deprivations to make it probably the most punitive known corrective-labour institution [in the Soviet Union]. What makes it particularly dangerous for its inmates is that all are serving lengthy sentences of imprisonment—more than 10 years in virtually all cases. Furthermore, the prisoners of conscience there are all "recidivists," and must endure these appalling conditions after having served long terms of imprisonment previously.[9]*

*In 1972 Amnesty International began an investigation into the case of Danylo Shumuk and in December of that year the International Secretariat of Amnesty International adopted him as a prisoner of conscience. Through its research and investigation, Amnesty International concluded that Shumuk had been incarcerated and deprived of his liberty, especially since 1957, solely for having exercised his rights, guaranteed under Soviet law and proclaimed in international covenants, to freedom of expression.*

*During the seventies a large number of statements, appeals and open letters prepared by prisoners of conscience in Soviet prisons and corrective-labour camps reached the West, and these documents show that Danylo Shumuk was an active participant in the human-rights activities of the inmates of Mordovian Camp No. 1–6, most of whom were also prisoners of conscience. One of Shumuk's first acts (on 10 December 1972) was to apply to the Presidium of the Supreme Soviet of the USSR to have his Soviet citizenship withdrawn,[10] and on 1 August 1974 he appealed to the United Nations Human Rights Commission about this matter:*

> *As I have already appealed twice to the Presidium of the USSR Supreme Soviet to relieve me of the "honourable title" of citizen of the Soviet Union ... but on both occasions without result, I am forced to appeal in this matter to the Human Rights Commission of the UN, and to the free world in general—to help me to rid myself of this "honourable title." ... I still have to serve seven years of oppressive imprisonment in a special-regime camp, in a crowded cell—two square metres to a man—which is kept locked all day, on an extremely inadequate diet, with five more years of exile to follow. Considering my age and the serious state of my health this is a life sentence—it is murder. I do not wish to die in harsh captivity, in an alien, hostile environment, as a citizen of this state, and thus bear responsibility for all the evil deeds committed by the USSR's punitive agencies—this is why I renounce my Soviet citizenship. ...* [11]

*Danylo Shumuk soon became involved in the prisoners' struggle to be recognized as **political** prisoners rather than common criminals. He was one of five Ukrainian prisoners, for example, who sent an appeal to the Commission of Human Rights in the USSR in November 1974 calling for action to alert world public* *opinion to the fallacy of the claim that "in the USSR there are no political prisoners, only criminal offenders." This appeal also mentions that KGB officials had offered to release certain political prisoners in exchange for their "condemnation of their past."[12]*

*Other statements signed by Shumuk described the brutal treatment of political prisoners by the penal authorities. In a "Memorandum to the Presidium of the USSR Supreme Soviet" prepared in December 1977, Shumuk and eight other signatories stated that at the end of 1976 the camp administration instigated a number of hostile actions by common criminals against the political prisoners. According to the memorandum this represented a continuation of the traditional policy of using the worst criminal elements to terrorize the other prisoners.[13] Shumuk also participated in numerous hunger strikes, including the traditional hunger strikes which marked Political Prisoners' Day (30 October) and the anniversary (12 January) of the beginning of the 1972 campaign of repression in Ukraine.[14]*

*Shumuk signed a number of appeals on behalf of his fellow prisoners of conscience. They included an appeal to the Holy See, the World Council of Churches and other religious bodies on behalf of Father Vasyl Romaniuk, a Ukrainian clergyman who received a ten-year sentence "for being an especially dangerous recidivist,"[15] and an open letter "To the people of Israel, to all honourable Ukrainians and Jews of the world and to academician Sakharov" on behalf of Edward Kuznetsov, who had begun a lengthy and dangerous hunger strike on 17 December 1977.[16] In addition, Shumuk, who was aware that any signs of intolerance or chauvinism among the political prisoners would be exploited by the authorities, was a founding member of a special committee in Mordovian Camp No. 1–6, which included among its tasks "the promotion of a friendly climate among political prisoners, unity among different nationalities, mutual respect and recognition of the humanitarian rights of individual prisoners of all ideological persuasions who have been convicted because of their political beliefs, and also the condemnation of anti-Semitism."[17]*

*Shumuk co-authored and/or signed a large number of other documents in the camps, of which only a few are available in the West. They include: a greeting to the American people on the occasion of their Independence Day from political prisoners in the*

*USSR; an open letter to Leonid Brezhnev concerning the draft USSR Constitution; an appeal to Soviet public opinion concerning a campaign by the Soviet press to discredit political prisoners; an appeal to athletes participating in the Olympic Games in Moscow in 1980; and an appeal to "Christians of the World" asking them to defend the right of prisoners of conscience to observe religious practices in Soviet prisons and corrective-labour camps.[18]*

*Shumuk's active role in various human rights activities in Mordovian Camp No. 1–6 is all the more surprising when one takes into consideration his steadily deteriorating health. During his imprisonment Shumuk suffered from a number of ailments, including aggravated stomach ulcers, chronic ear inflammations, a nerve problem which frequently disabled his right arm, neuralgia of the trigeminal nerve, a severe case of varicose veins, and heart pains. The medical care available in the corrective-labour camps was so inadequate that Shumuk's condition became critical and he was hospitalized on several occasions; he spent almost three months in a hospital early in 1977, for example, because of severe ulcer problems.[19]*

*Shumuk's case, however, quickly gained considerable publicity in the West. Danylo's nephew, Ivan Shumuk, who grew up with Danylo and now lives in British Columbia, began writing to his uncle soon after news of his arrest and trial reached the West, and since that time Danylo's relatives and Amnesty International have launched several appeals for his release. In his letters Danylo Shumuk has expressed a desire to emigrate to Canada and join his relatives there, and in 1977 his case was mentioned three times in the Canadian House of Commons. As a result, during unofficial talks with Soviet officials at the Conference on Security and Co-operation in Europe in Belgrade in late 1977 and early 1978, the Canadian government raised the question of Shumuk's possible release from imprisonment and emigration.[20]*

*Shumuk's health continued to deteriorate throughout 1978. In September 1978 several of his fellow inmates prepared an appeal addressed "To the Parliament and Government of Canada."*

> *We, political prisoners of the "Sosnovka" concentration camp, have learned that the Canadian Parliament is taking specific measures for the release of Shumuk.... We appeal to you to multiply your efforts, for Shumuk's state of health is disastrous....*

*By Soviet standards the remainder of Shumuk's sentence is a mere trifle; however, burdened as he is with many illnesses, he is not likely to live until 1987 and thus get the chance to insist on his right to emigrate to his relatives in Canada and live out the rest of his days there without fear of another arrest.*

*We, Soviet political prisoners, not only receive practically no medical assistance from the so-called doctors assigned to the concentration camps, but are also deprived of the right to receive medicine from outside the camps, even though for years the camp pharmacy has had nothing but aspirin.*

*Shumuk is wasting away under our very eyes. Our efforts to compel our gaolers to provide Shumuk with qualified medical assistance have come up against cynical malice: Shumuk's steadfast principles and inflexible will, his whole life, are hateful and terrifying to them, as a living indictment and witness and a call for retribution.*

*We appeal to you with gratitude for your concern for our fellow prisoner and urge you to do everything you can so that he may be released as soon as possible.[21]*

*At one point there were fears that Danylo Shumuk had stomach cancer, and in late September 1978 the eminent Russian physicist Andrei Sakharov stated at a press conference with Western correspondents that Shumuk was close to death.[22] This news touched off widespread appeals for his immediate release from his family, from Amnesty International groups, and from political figures in the United States and Canada, but to no avail.*

*On 3 November 1978 the Canadian House of Commons unanimously passed a motion proposed on that date by Member of Parliament Mark MacGuigan: "That this House strongly urge the Soviet government, taking into account Danylo Shumuk's ill health, to release him from imprisonment."[23] In response, the Soviet Embassy in Ottawa issued a number of press releases in which Shumuk was depicted as a "Nazi collaborator" and a "war criminal."[24]*

*On 1 March 1980 a number of prisoners from Mordovian Camp No. 1, including Danylo Shumuk, were transferred to Perm Camp No. 36, to a new special-regime zone half a kilometre from the strict-regime zone.[25]*

*On 1 May 1980 Shumuk was taken to the hospital (he was suffering from retching, dizziness and fainting), and in letters to his relatives Shumuk expressed concern that, because of his age and poor state of health, he might not survive the difficult trip into exile which he was to face at the end of 1981.[26]*

*Transportation from places of imprisonment to places of exile is one of the most trying aspects of the entire process of imprisonment in the USSR. During the frequently lengthy journeys prisoners are locked in overcrowded railway carriages and are at the mercy of arbitrary treatment by guards. Prisoners in transit receive inadequate food, water and medical attention and suffer further hardships during stopovers in transit prisons, since the common criminals with whom prisoners of conscience are detained in these prisons often use this opportunity to rob and beat up their cellmates.[27]*

*Unfortunately, Shumuk's fears were fully justified:*

> *My trip into exile [December 1981–January 1982] caused me more suffering than all the ten years which I spent in the special-regime camp. I was taken south, then back north, then back south once more.... I spent a total of fifty-one days in transit. This experience totally exhausted me.... In addition to the suffering and the indignities to which I was subjected, three hundred pages of handwritten manuscript were confiscated from me.[28]*

*Prisoners of conscience serving sentences of internal exile are faced with many hardships. They are almost invariably sent to remote parts of Siberia, Kazakhstan (the Kazakh SSR) or the Soviet Far East, and all prisoners in internal exile are subjected to stringent restrictions on their freedom of movement, even within the limits of their district of enforced residence. They are required to report regularly to the police, and many are subjected to harassment and have great difficulty in finding accommodation and even menial jobs.[29]*

*Danylo Shumuk was exiled to Karatobe, a village in Uralskaia oblast, western Kazakhstan. This area is very thinly populated (mostly by Kazakhs), and the nearest town (Uralsk) with a proper hospital and decent medical services is 250 kilometres from Karatobe. Since Shumuk did not receive a pension of any kind he had to provide for himself, and despite his age and ill health he could find work only as a physical labourer. In the first few months of exile Shumuk worked as a furnace stoker:*

*This work is hardly appropriate for someone of my age and health, but what can I do when I have to pay for the hostel where I'm staying and have to buy something to eat. If I don't fall ill then I'll be working here until April 15, and after this date I have no idea what will happen and what kind of work I'll be offered. In short, it's no great relief to me that I'm no longer behind bars and surrounded by fences and barbed wire.*[30]

At the end of April 1982 Shumuk was given a job planting trees and tending a small park in Karatobe, for which he was paid seventy rubles a month. Soon afterward he left the hostel in which he had been living and began renting a small, primitive, clay dugout.[31]

Danylo Shumuk's health has continued to deteriorate, and on several occasions his condition has required hospitalization in Uralsk. His health problems, and especially his ulcers, have been aggravated through an inadequate diet; milk, other dairy products and meat are rarely found in Karatobe, and when they are found prices are very high. Thus, since it is increasingly difficult for him to work as a manual labourer and earn his keep, Shumuk has become heavily dependent on food packages which he receives from family, friends and Amnesty International groups in the West. Equally important, however, are letters and postcards from the West which provide him with valuable moral support. But the Soviet authorities often deprive him of even this last source of comfort. Many of the packages and letters sent to Shumuk never reach their destination, and his numerous complaints to the Soviet postal authorities have fallen on deaf ears.

Since his last arrest in 1972 Danylo Shumuk has received several offers from the penal authorities of release from imprisonment in return for a "condemnation of his past," but he has refused steadfastly to "repent," and the Soviet government now seems determined not only to ensure that he serves his term of exile in full, but also to isolate him totally from the outside world. From his letters it is clear that Shumuk has never placed any real hope in the "benevolence" of the Soviet regime and the possibility that he might be allowed to leave the Soviet Union for Canada. He has now fully reconciled himself to the fact that, in all likelihood, he will die in exile.

# Notes

## Chapter One

1. One desiatyna equals 2.70 acres.
2. The "reading room" tradition was still strong in Western Ukraine during the interwar period. The Ridna Khata (Native Home) society, which co-ordinated the cultural-educational work of reading rooms in Volhynia, performed the same function as the Prosvita (Enlightenment) society in Eastern Galicia, but in the late twenties it was under the complete control of Selrob and was dissolved by the Polish authorities in 1930.
3. Selrob (Ukrainske Seliansko-Robitnyche Sotsiialistychne Obiednannia or Ukrainian Peasants'-Workers' Socialist Union), a mass, legal pro-communist movement, was established in October 1926 by the merger of the Volia Naroda (People's Will) Party and Selsoiuz (Ukrainian Socialist Peasants' Union). The CPWU played the role of a mediator in the negotiations between the two groups. In September 1927 Selrob split into Selrob and Selrob-Left, and in May 1928 elements from Selrob joined Selrob-Left to form Selrob-Unity. The latter functioned until dissolved by the Polish authorities in September 1932, whereas Selrob declared its self-dissolution in December 1929.
4. Mykola Khymchyn headed the nine-man Central Committee elected by the First Congress of Selrob-Left in 1927.
5. *Vikna* (Windows) was a monthly journal devoted to literature and the arts published by Sovietophile writers in Lviv from 1928 to 1932.
6. The term Komsomol (Leninist Young Communist League), which usually refers to the youth wing of the Communist Party of the Soviet Union, was also used to refer to the youth wings of a number

of other communist parties. The youth wing of the CPWU, the Union of Communist Youth of Western Ukraine, had approximately 2,000 members in the early thirties and, like the CPWU, was disbanded in 1938.

## Chapter Two

1. The artificially induced famine of 1932–3, which affected Ukraine, the Kuban (northern Caucasus) and the area inhabited by the Volga Germans, was a product of Stalin's rapid and brutal drive to collectivize Soviet agriculture. Ukraine suffered the greatest losses in life; a total of at least 4.5 million persons.
2. Pochaiv is the site of a well-known Orthodox monastery which was founded in the sixteenth century.
3. *Defensywa* was the popular name given to the Polish counter-intelligence organs of the interwar period.
4. Beating prisoners on the soles of the feet (*falanga* or *bastinade*) is a very painful form of torture which is still commonly used throughout the world.

## Chapter Three

1. Andrii Marchenko (1908–43): prominent organizer of the Ukrainian nationalist underground in Volhynia. In 1942 Marchenko was imprisoned by the Germans in Lviv and was executed by them the following year.
2. Volodymyr Starosolsky (1878–1942): lawyer, sociologist and politician. Starosolsky was active in the Ukrainian social-democratic movement and served as a defence attorney at a number of important trials of Ukrainian political prisoners during the interwar period in Poland. After the Soviet occupation of Lviv, Starosolsky taught briefly at Lviv State University but was soon arrested, sentenced to ten years of imprisonment, and died in a prison in Western Siberia.
3. The "Internationale" is a hymn (text composed by Eugène Pottier in 1871 and music written by P. Degeyter in 1888) which became recognized as the "hymn of the international proletariat" after the First Congress of the Second Communist International (1889).

Chapter Four

1. Stepan Bandera (1909–59): political activist and leader. In 1933 Bandera became head of the OUN krai provid. He helped organize several terrorist actions in Galicia in the early thirties and was arrested by the Polish authorities in June 1934. After trials in Warsaw and Lviv, Bandera was sentenced to death, but this sentence was later commuted to life imprisonment. He was released from prison during the partition of Poland in 1939 and soon became leader of the "revolutionary" OUN faction which arose during 1940–1. He was detained (and later imprisoned) by the Gestapo in July 1941 after refusing to withdraw the "Act of Proclamation of the Ukrainian State" announced by a group of his followers in Lviv on 30 June 1941, shortly after Germany's invasion of the USSR. Bandera was released from imprisonment in September 1944, and from February 1946 until his assassination by a Soviet agent in 1959, he headed the Foreign Branch of the OUN. His followers were popularly known as Banderivtsi (Banderites), although the term Banderites was often used in the Soviet Union after the Second World War to refer to all Ukrainians suspected of nationalism.

   Bronis aw Pieracki (1895–1934): Polish minister without portfolio from 1930 to 1931 and minister of internal affairs from 1931 to 1934. The OUN considered Pieracki to be responsible for the brutal "pacification" of the Ukrainian population of Galicia in September-November 1930, and for various repressive measures against the Ukrainian nationalist movement. He was assassinated in Warsaw on 15 June 1934 by Hryhorii Matseiko, an OUN member who later fled the country, and the assassination was followed by the arrest of a number of prominent OUN members, including Bandera.

2. The Comintern is an abbreviation used to designate the Third (Communist) International, which was established in March 1918 and disbanded in May 1943. Parties wishing to join the Comintern had to adopt what was essentially a Bolshevik Party model, and the organization was dominated by the representatives of illegal communist parties who lived in Moscow as well as by the spokesmen of the CPSU. The Institute of Red Professors was a training institute, established in 1921, for cadres, party activists and teachers of the social sciences in higher educational establishments in the USSR. The institute was reorganized in 1931 and replaced by a number of specialized institutes, which were all disbanded in 1938. The Institute of Red Professors was not formally affiliated with the Comintern.

3. The International Organization for Aid to Revolutionaries (also known as the International Red Aid) operated under the guidance of the Communist International between 1922 and 1939 and provided aid to communists, non-communists who followed the lead of the Comintern, and those whose arrest and trial exposed "class justice." The Soviet section of this organization had the largest number of members and provided most of its financial support.

4. Zenon Nowak (born 1905): an activist of the Communist Polish Youth Union during the twenties and a member of the Central Committee of the CPP from 1932 to 1938. Nowak was a member of the Politburo of the Polish United Workers' Party from 1948 to 1956, and was a spokesman for the Stalinist faction of the party in 1956, becoming notorious for his anti-Semitism. Nowak has occupied various party and state positions in Poland, and was Polish ambassador to the USSR from 1971 to 1981.

5. The Communist Party of Western Belorussia (CPWB) was, like the CPWU, a territorially autonomous organization of the CPP. It was established in 1923 and had approximately 4,000 members in 1933. It enjoyed considerable public support in the late 1920s, and Belorussian pro-communist lists received 140,000 votes in the 1928 elections to the Polish Sejm.

6. A series of purges, beginning in 1933, eventually resulted in the physical liquidation of many leading members of the CPWU. Ivanenko (*pseud.* Baraba) headed the CPWU from 1929 until 1933; he and Myron Zaiachkivsky (*pseud.* Kosar) were both removed from the Central Committee of the CPWU at the Second Plenum of the Central Committee of the CPP (24 November 1933), and during the Fourth Congress of the CPWU both were accused of belonging to the Ukrainian Military Organization, working for the Polish security police, etc. Soon afterward they were liquidated.

7. Julian Leński—real name Leszczyński (1889–1939): an activist in the social-democratic movement before the First World War, occupied various important positions in both the international and Polish communist movements (where he represented an ultra-left-wing position) during the interwar period. From 1929 Leński was a member of the Presidium of the executive committee of the Comintern and was also the General Secretary of the CPP.

Gustaw Henrykowski—real name Saul Amsterdam (1898–1937): a member of the Central Committee of the CPP from 1923. Henrykowski worked for both the Comintern and, in various capacities, for the CPP.

Gustaw Rwal—real name Reicher (1900–38): an activist in both the Polish and international communist movements during the interwar period. In 1928–9 Rwal was a member of the executive committee of the Comintern and worked with the Foreign Bureaus of the CPWB and CPWU. In 1937 he was a CPP delegate to the Central Committee of the Spanish Communist Party. Leński, Henrykowski and Rwal were all arrested in 1937 by the Soviet authorities and were liquidated soon afterward. All three were posthumously rehabilitated in 1955–6.

8. On 30 September 1938 Colonel Józef Beck, then the Polish foreign minister, issued an ultimatum to the Czechs demanding that they cede the Zaolzie (Trans-Olza) area of Czechoslovakia, which had a large Polish population, to Poland. This ultimatum followed a long campaign of pressure on Prague on behalf of the Polish minority in Czechoslovakia, which exploited the widely held anti-Czech feelings of the Poles. The Czechs accepted this ultimatum on 1 October 1938.

## Chapter Five

1. The Russian abbreviation of the People's Commissariat for Internal Affairs, which operated from 1917 to 1924 and from 1934 to 1946. It also functioned as the organ of state security from 1922 to 1924 and from 1934 to 1943.

2. No precise count of the number of Polish citizens deported to the USSR is available, but the Polish Government-in-Exile estimated that 1.2 million persons were resettled in the Soviet Union from Poland during the first two years of the war. About half the deportees ended up in labour camps and prisons, and the other half were sent to settlements all over the Soviet Union. Approximately one-quarter of the deportees were children fourteen years of age or younger.

3. Some 665,000 Soviet military personnel were encircled and captured by the Germans in the Kiev area in mid-September 1941, and it is estimated that a total of more than 5.7 million Soviet military personnel were captured by the Germans during the entire campaign on the eastern front. Approximately 3.3 million Soviet prisoners of war were shot or died in captivity, and the majority of these deaths occurred between June 1941 and February 1942.

4. The Khorol death camp was located on the site of a brick factory, and the pit described by Shumuk had been used before the war to provide the factory with clay. According to Soviet sources over 55,000 prisoners-of-war died in the Khorol camp.

Chapter Six

1. The Ukrainian Military Organization (UVO) was a paramilitary organization established in 1920 to co-ordinate the activities of veterans of the struggle for Ukrainian independence during and immediately after the First World War. The Union of Ukrainian Nationalist Youth (SUNM) was established in Galicia as a central co-ordinating body for Ukrainian nationalist youth. The SUNM, two similar organizations in Czechoslovakia, and the UVO were instrumental in founding the OUN in 1929. Plast is an organization devoted to the patriotic upbringing of Ukrainian youth which was founded in 1911 as a Ukrainian counterpart to Baden-Powell's Scouts. Many of its members were active in the nationalist movement.

2. The "decalogue" of the OUN was a statement of principles that every member was expected to memorize. It was written by a leading member of the OUN, Stepan Lenkavsky (1904–77), and first published as an insert in the underground OUN newspaper *Surma* in the summer of 1929. For the official text, which differs in minor respects from the version cited by Shumuk, see P. Mirchuk, *Narys istorii Orhanizatsii Ukrainskykh Natsionalistiv* (Munich 1968), 1:126.

3. The "44 Rules of a Ukrainian Nationalist" were written in the early 1930s by Zenon Kossak (1907–39), a member of the OUN krai provid. Intended to inspire the youthful membership, the rules stressed discipline, dedication and struggle. For the text, see Mirchuk, 128–9.

4. The symbol of the trident became the hereditary pre-heraldic badge of the descendants of Volodymyr the Great (980–1015), a medieval ruler of Kievan Rus'. The trident was adopted as the national device of the Ukrainian People's Republic in 1918, and since then it has served as a symbol of Ukrainian nationalism.

5. Ulas Samchuk (born 1905): Ukrainian writer and journalist from Volhynia. Samchuk was editor of the newspaper *Volyn* (published in

Rivne) from 1941 to 1943. Since 1948 Samchuk has lived in Canada, and is a prominent Ukrainian émigré author. His major works are the trilogies *Volyn* and *Ost*.

6. According to Shankowsky's lengthy critique of the Shumuk memoirs (published in issues 1–4 of *Vyzvolnyi shliakh*, 1975), Lisovyk's real name was Lutsiv, not Lutsyk, he did not work for the SB, and he was not a member of the personal guard of Bulba-Borovets (as Shumuk later claims). The SB, which had a reputation for ruthlessness, acted as a security service for the OUN, to which it was directly subordinated.

7. *Literaturno-naukovyi vistnyk* (Literary-Scientific Herald) was a monthly journal published in Lviv from 1898 to 1906, in Kiev from 1907 to 1914, and again in Lviv from 1922 to 1932. *Literaturno-naukovyi vistnyk*, founded by the Ukrainian historian Mykhailo Hrushevsky, was the most prominent Ukrainian literary and socio-political journal of its time.

8. Mykola Khvylovy—real name Fitilov (1893–1933): Soviet Ukrainian writer and leading figure in what is known as the "Literary Discussion" in Soviet Ukraine (1925–8), in which Ukrainian writers engaged in a debate on the nature of art and literature and on their place in the Soviet state. Khvylovy's orientation toward Europe and its corollary—"away from Moscow"—drew the displeasure of hard-liners in Kiev and Moscow (Khvylovy and his followers were promptly branded "bourgeois nationalists"), and Khvylovy eventually committed suicide (on 13 May 1933), during a widespread purge of the Ukrainian literary and intellectual elite. The fifth issue of the journal *Vaplite*, which Khvylovy helped to edit and which frequently attacked various "sacred cows" of the Soviet literary scene, contained the first instalment of Khvylovy's novel *Valdshnepy* (The Woodsnipes), which was bitterly attacked by the authorities as a "nationalist" work. The second section was published in *Vaplite*, no. 6 (1927), but all copies of the journal were confiscated by the censors and destroyed.

9. Aglaia is a strong-willed Ukrainian amazon in *The Woodsnipes* who has a strong influence on a frustrated communist.

10. MTS: abbreviation for Machine-Tractor Stations, state centres for agricultural machinery located in rural areas in the USSR, from about 1928 to 1958.

Chapter Seven

1. The term "Easterners" is used to denote Ukrainians from Eastern (prewar Soviet) Ukraine. "Western Ukraine" was a term used in a broad sense after the First World War to designate Ukrainian territories in Poland, Romania and Czechoslovakia, although in a narrower sense this term was used to designate those Ukrainian territories held by Poland.

2. Bohdan Khmelnytsky (circa 1595–1657): Hetman of Ukraine, 1648–1657. After holding various responsible posts in the registered Cossack army, in 1647 Khmelnytsky, the son of a petty Ukrainian nobleman, fled to the lower Dnieper region where, with the help of free, non-registered Cossacks, he took over the Zaporozhian Sich and was elected leader (hetman) of the Sich Cossacks. In 1648 Khmelnytsky led a successful Cossack uprising against Poland which coalesced with a mass peasant revolt and with a religious war of the Orthodox against the Catholics. Searching for allies to strengthen his position, Khmelnytsky entered into the Pereiaslav agreement (1654) with Russia which eventually led to a drastic weakening of the Ukrainian Cossack state.

3. The Zaporozhian Sich was the military and political centre (just below the Dnieper rapids) of the territory controlled by Ukrainian Cossacks (with interruptions) between the sixteenth and eighteenth centuries. Khortytsia is an island in the Dnieper which was an important stronghold of the Sich. During the Second World War the term Sich was used by Ukrainian nationalists to refer to local Ukrainian strongholds in Volhynia and Polissia.

4. Shumuk is probably referring to schools that trained Ukrainians for service in auxiliary police units, since the German civilian administration (which replaced the military authorities in Volhynia soon after the German invasion of the USSR) did not permit the operation of military schools that trained Ukrainian personnel for service in autonomous Ukrainian military units.

5. Dmytro Kliachkivsky—*pseud.* Klym Savur (died 1945): a member of the OUN Provid, Kliachkivsky was imprisoned by the Soviet authorities in 1940–1. In the latter half of 1943, Kliachkivsky became the commander of UPA forces in Volhynia (later UPA-North) and was killed in battle with Soviet forces in 1945.
Leonid Stupnytsky—*pseud.* Honcharenko (died 1944): a colonel in the army of the Ukrainian People's Republic, Stupnytsky became Chief of Staff of UPA forces in Volhynia in 1943 and was killed in battle with Soviet forces in 1944.

Symon Petliura (1879–1926): a Ukrainian political activist and prolific essayist in the prerevolutionary period who became the first General Secretary for Military Affairs of the Ukrainian Central Rada government in Kiev in June 1917. In November 1918 Petliura became the Chief Otaman (leader) of the army of the Ukrainian People's Republic, and in February 1919 he became head of the Directory of the Ukrainian People's Republic. After the failure of a joint Ukrainian-Polish campaign against the Bolsheviks in 1920, Petliura continued his political activities abroad. In 1926 he was assassinated in Paris by Schwartzbard, who claimed that he was avenging the pogroms against Jews in Ukraine in 1919.

6. Taras Borovets—*pseud.* Bulba (1908–1981): Ukrainian political and community activist in Polissia who started organizing a Ukrainian underground in 1940 and established paramilitary units after the German invasion in an area which he called the "Polissian Sich." The units of this Sich were formally included in the German auxiliary police system. But the Germans had difficulty controlling Polissia, a centre of Soviet partisan activity, and relied on Borovets to keep the situation under control. Borovets decided to liquidate the "Polissian Sich" (which had its headquarters in Olevsk and not, as Shumuk states, in Sarny) in November 1941, after the Germans refused to recognize the autonomy of his forces as a Ukrainian military formation, and his units began to take part in skirmishes with German forces in April 1942.

7. Dmitrii Medvedev (1898–1954): employee of the Cheka, the Unified State Political Administration and the People's Commissariat of Internal Affairs of Ukraine from 1920 to 1935. From June 1942 until March 1944, Medvedev commanded the *Pobediteli* (Conquerors) Soviet Partisan Detachment, which operated in the Rivne and Lviv oblasts of Ukraine. Medvedev wrote several books after the war which were based on his experiences.

8. The *Volksdeutsche* were persons living in territories newly occupied by the Germans during the Second World War, who were (or claimed to be) of German origin and were accepted as such by the occupying forces.

9. Several thousand Czechs settled in Volhynia in the last decades of the nineteenth century. Most of these Volhynian Czechs were repatriated after the Second World War.

10. The incident in Malyn described by Shumuk occurred on 14 July 1943. According to Shankowsky this incident was not provoked by one of Medvedev's raids; rather, it was part of a broader campaign of

reprisals against the local population conducted by the German anti-partisan expert Erich von dem Bach-Zelewski.

## Chapter Eight

1. This is probably a reference to an UPA ambush in May 1943, on the highway between Kovel and Rivne, which resulted in the death of Viktor Lutze (born 1890), Röhm's successor as Chief of Staff of the SA (Sturm-Abteilung).
2. Boremsky was the pseudonym used by Danylo Shumuk in the UPA, and was derived from the name of Shumuk's native village, Boremshchyna.
3. Gottfried Leibnitz (1646–1716): German scientist and philosopher, influential writer on logic, mathematics, science, law, history, linguistics and theology.
4. The Zahoriv monastery battle took place on 14 September 1943. According to Shankowsky the platoon commander did not commit suicide during the battle (as Shumuk claims).
5. The term in the Ukrainian original is "Liakhy," an old Ukrainian name for the Poles which in modern times acquired a negative, contemptuous flavour.

## Chapter Nine

1. The OUN and the UPA were interested in forming a common front with the non-Russian peoples of the Soviet Union and a "Conference of Captive Nations," which was attended by representatives of thirteen different national groups, was held on 21–22 November 1943. Most of the non-Ukrainian representatives were delegates from separate ethnic combat units attached to the UPA.
2. Halyna—real name Iakiv Busel (died 1945): leading member of the OUN in Volhynia and a member of the OUN Provid. Busel headed the OUN socio-political directorate in Volhynia, in which Shumuk served as an instructor.
3. Rostyslav Voloshyn—*pseud.* Horbenko, Pavlenko (1911–44): head of the Union of Ukrainian Student Organizations in Poland (1933–4), imprisoned by the Poles (1934–5) and later by both the Russians and

Germans as an OUN activist. Voloshyn helped organize the UPA in Volhynia and from August 1943 he was a member of the Bureau of the OUN Provid. Voloshyn was the chairman of the First Assembly (July 1944) of the UHVR (Supreme Ukrainian Liberation Council), which was created as a political superstructure for the UPA and to act as a political body representing all Ukrainian groups committed to the independence of their country.

4. Mykola Lebed—*pseud.* Maksym Ruban (born 1910): an OUN activist who was sentenced to death in 1935 for participating in the plot to assassinate Pieracki. This sentence was commuted to life imprisonment, and Lebed was freed from prison after the German invasion of Poland. After Bandera's arrest in 1941, Lebed headed the OUN until May 1943, and was a founding member of the UHVR as well as its General Secretary for Foreign Affairs. The conflict between Okhrym (Kliachkivsky) and Lebed, to which Shumuk refers, may have been a result of a dispute within the OUN concerning the creation of armed units in Volhynia to combat the Germans. Although Shankowsky claims that this dispute was settled in February 1943, a regional dispute between native Volhynian nationalists and underground activists from Galicia continued for some time after this date.

5. According to Shankowsky, Volodymyr (real name Anatolii Kozar, from Piddubets) was not the first deputy of the district SB director, but the intelligence chief for the staff of the Tury UPA group.

6. The term "Cheka" comes from the initial letters of the first two words in Russian for the "Extraordinary Commission for Struggle with Counter-revolution and Sabotage," the original Soviet secret police organization. The term "Chekist" is used to refer to a member of the Cheka or of any of its successor organizations.

7. During the period immediately following the German invasion of the Soviet Union, most of the political prisoners in the western areas of the USSR (including the newly acquired areas such as the Baltic states and Western Ukraine) who could not be deported eastward were shot. It is estimated that about 4,000 Ukrainian political prisoners were executed in NKVD prisons in Lviv, and that some 3,000 political prisoners were murdered in Lutsk. Many of those deported were killed before they reached their destination.

Chapter Ten

1. The ideology of the Bandera faction of the OUN began to undergo a change in 1942, after members of the "expeditionary groups" which it sent into Eastern Ukraine were exposed to the conditions in this area and the attitudes of the local population. These new ideological influences were clearly evident by the time the Third Extraordinary Congress of the OUN was held on August 1943. Thus the congress' programmatic resolutions devoted considerable attention to economic matters and social security measures. Some points in the programme referred to the rights of national minorities, generally guaranteed freedom of religion, speech and the press, and rejected official status for any doctrine, although the programme still contained certain ethnocentric and authoritarian elements.

2. The UPA encouraged the non-Russian prisoners-of-war who had been captured by the Germans and who later agreed to serve the Germans in various capacities, to desert from their units and join the UPA. Several detachments within the UPA were made up of non-Ukrainian personnel, of which the Uzbek legion, commanded by Tashkent (a pseudonym) was probably the best-known. Some sources claim that the personnel in these units fought bravely and were an important asset for the UPA (especially in view of their propaganda value); however, many (if not most) of the personnel in these detachments eventually deserted to the Soviet army.

3. In the late eighteenth and early nineteenth centuries many of the new settlers in the underpopulated Kuban (north-west Caucasus) area were Ukrainian Cossacks.

4. Andrii Bratun, who had been active in the Ukrainian SR (Socialist Revolutionary) Party during the Russian Civil War, was elected to the Polish Sejm in 1922 and was a member of the Socialist Faction within the Sejm's Ukrainian Club. After a split occurred in the Socialist Faction, Bratun became a founding member of the Selsoiuz. One of Andrii Bratun's sons, Rostyslav (short form—Rostia), born in 1927, is a well-known "regime poet" in Soviet Ukraine whose poetry depicts the "socialist transformation" of Western Ukraine after its incorporation into the Soviet Union. Rostyslav Bratun is also the author of books, articles and pamphlets directed against Ukrainian "bourgeois nationalists" and the Ukrainian Catholic (Uniate) Church.

5. Sosenko (real name Porfir Antoniuk) had been relieved of his command and was under surveillance. After the advance of the front, he found himself in a very difficult situation and began negotiations

with the command of the Sixteenth Division of the Fourth German Tank Army concerning co-operation against the advancing Soviet forces. By doing this, he disobeyed orders issued by the UPA-North Command in January 1944 forbidding such negotiations. The UPA Command was concerned about all such infractions, since in February and March 1944 the Soviet authorities had made statements attempting to explain the anti-German activities of the UPA and accusing the UPA of collaboration with the Germans. Thus on 7 March 1944 Sosenko was sentenced to death by a regional field court of the UPA.

6. After the February Revolution of 1917 a Central Rada (Council) was created in Kiev by the Society of Ukrainian Progressives and various Ukrainian socialists. This council soon became the leading advocate of political autonomy for Ukraine. It signed a separate peace with the Central Powers at Brest-Litovsk, and then resisted Bolshevik attempts to control Ukraine, but the Central Powers dispersed the Rada in April 1918 and established a new regime under Hetman Pavlo Skoropadsky.

7. At the turn of the century many Ukrainians who considered themselves distinct from the Russians but did not have a highly developed sense of Ukrainian national identity used the officially approved term "Little Russians" to identify themselves.

8. Mikhail Muravev (1880–1918): a lieutenant colonel in the tsarist army who transferred his allegiance to Lenin's regime after the Bolshevik Revolution and was appointed commander of the Petrograd Military District. At the beginning of 1918 Muravev commanded the military forces that opposed the Ukrainian Central Rada.

9. Mykhailo Hrushevsky (1866–1934): eminent Ukrainian historian and prominent political leader. In 1917 Hrushevsky became the president of the Central Rada, and after the fall of the Rada in April 1918 he emigrated to Vienna. Hrushevsky returned to Kiev in 1924 at the invitation of the Soviet government, and continued his scholarly work (he headed the historical section of the Ukrainian Academy of Sciences). In 1930 he was accused by the Soviet government of promoting "Ukrainian nationalism," and was arrested and exiled to Moscow.

10. Kanzo Uchimura (1861–1930): religious thinker and critic, and an important formative influence on many writers and intellectual leaders of modern Japan.

Chapter Eleven

1. Sydir Kovpak (1887–1967): a commander of pro-Soviet partisan units in 1918–19 and the Second World War. Kovpak formed a Soviet partisan detachment in the German rear in 1942, and in the summer of 1943 this detachment embarked on a lengthy raid which aimed at destroying oil installations in the Drohobych area of Western Ukraine. Kovpak's forces reached the Carpathian mountains, but they were dispersed by Ukrainian self-defence units and the remnants of Kovpak's forces became part of the Ukrainian Partisan Division headed by Vershyhora. Kovpak occupied a number of high-ranking (but symbolic) positions in the Soviet Ukrainian government after the Second World War, and was the author of a book entitled *From Putyvl to the Carpathians*.
2. According to Shankowsky, Mitla was actually the intelligence chief for the staff of UPA-North.
3. The reference here is probably to a major policy speech made by Khrushchev on 1 March 1944. An abridged version appeared in *Bolshevik*, no. 6 (March 1944) entitled "Liberation of Ukrainian Lands from the German Aggressors and the Immediate Tasks of Reconstructing the National Economy of Soviet Ukraine." Several pages of this article are devoted to an attack on Ukrainian nationalists and the UPA.

Chapter Twelve

1. According to Shankowsky, Shum, a prominent UPA commander in Volhynia, died in April 1944 in a skirmish with German forces (rather than with Soviet partisans).
2. At the end of February 1944, Marshal Nikolai Vatutin, the Soviet commander of the First Ukrainian Front, was ambushed by an UPA unit on the road between Korets and Rivne and was mortally wounded.
3. "Strybky" were members of so-called "extermination" or search-and-destroy battalions (*istrebitelnye batalony*), which were to collaborate with the Soviet ministry of internal affairs (MVD) in fighting the underground. Many *strybky* were local villagers who had been forced to serve in these battalions, and they were often less than enthusiastic about their duties. The *strybky* also included local party

and Komsomol activists, defectors from the underground, and demobilized Red Army soldiers.

## Chapter Thirteen

1. According to Wasyl Hryshko (the editor of the latest Ukrainian edition of the Shumuk memoirs, published in 1983), after the Soviet occupation of Western Ukraine in 1944 certain circles in the OUN underground considered changing the name of their organization to *Narodno-Vyzvolna Revoliutsiina Orhanizatsiia* (People's Liberation Revolutionary Organization). The NVRO was to adopt a new, more democratic platform. Shankowsky denies the existence of an organization called the NVRO and believes that Shumuk is referring to the First Founding Assembly of the UHVR. The social and political principles proclaimed by the UHVR represented further democratization within the Bandera faction of the OUN. Thus there was considerable emphasis in the UHVR resolutions on economic and social welfare and on the significance of individual rights, although nationalism remained the central point of the UHVR's ideology.
2. Melnykites (*Melnykivtsi* in Ukrainian) is the name given to the followers of the branch of the OUN headed by Andrii Melnyk (1890–1964) after the 1940 split in the OUN.
3. *Zahotsin*: state procurement agency for grain.
4. *Zahotskot*: state procurement agency for livestock.

## Chapter Fourteen

1. The Donbas (short form for the Donets coal basin) is a densely populated and highly industrialized region of Eastern Ukraine.

## Chapter Fifteen

1. Evno Azef (1869–1918): Social Revolutionary leader and police agent. Azev was the best-known representative of a series of double

agents who were active in the Russian revolutionary movement during the first decade of the twentieth century. He was exposed in 1909 by Vladimir Burtsev, a radical and a historian of the revolutionary movement, and the news of Azev's double career shocked and dismayed the entire revolutionary camp.

2. The Soviet military justice apparatus was greatly enlarged during the Second World War, and its sphere of jurisdiction was expanded. In the zone behind the front, military tribunals were often the only courts, and were responsible for trying "enemy agents" and other "hostile elements." The power of military tribunals was drastically curtailed in September 1953 as a result of the campaign, following Stalin's death, to promote "socialist legality."

## Chapter Seventeen

1. Trusties were prisoners (usually common criminals) whom the camp administration considered to be "trustworthy" and were thus allowed special privileges. They were given jobs within the camp compound as hospital orderlies, cooks or brigade leaders.

2. BOF is the Russian abbreviation for Bauxite Enrichment Plant (*Boksitno-Obogatitelnaia Fabrika*).

3. The original Russian word, *khokhly*, is a pejorative term used to 'denote stupidity and stubbornness in Ukrainians.

## Chapter Eighteen

1. In 1946, as a result of the redesignation of all the People's Commissariats as ministries, the NKVD became the MVD (ministry of internal affairs).

2. Andrei Vlasov (1900–1946): a lieutenant-general of the Red Army who surrendered to the Germans in June 1942 after commanding the Soviet Second Assault Army against them in the Volkhov area. Vlasov hoped to head an autonomous, indigenous anti-Stalinist movement, and agreed to set up a German-sponsored military force made up of Soviet prisoners-of-war and Soviet workers deported to Germany as forced labourers. However, the Germans did not permit him to hold any true military authority or command until 1945, and

many of the units under his control never saw combat. Vlasov was captured by Soviet forces near Prague in May 1945, and he and a number of his associates were executed after a summary trial and conviction. Those of his followers (often called Vlasovites) captured by Soviet forces or repatriated by the Allied forces were either executed or sentenced to lengthy terms of imprisonment as traitors.

## Chapter Nineteen

1. Some free employees in the camps were local residents; most, however, were ex-prisoners who had completed their sentences and were not allowed (or did not wish) to return to their homes.
2. Gorlag is the short form of *Gornyi lager*, or Mountain Camp.
3. The term *zek* is derived from the initials z/k, which were used as a short form for *zakliuchennye* (prisoners) in camp records and announcements.
4. KIP is the acronym in Russian for control and measuring instruments.

## Chapter Twenty

1. Iurii Levitan (b. 1914): radio announcer. Levitan became an announcer for the All-Union Radio of the USSR in 1931, and was well known for his deep, expressive voice and his broadcasts during the Second World War. After the war Levitan continued to deliver official news broadcasts on Radio Moscow, do dubs for motion pictures, and read reports from Red Square and the Kremlin Palace of Congresses.
2. Georgii Zhukov (1896–1974): Soviet military commander, marshal of the Soviet Union (1943). Zhukov was appointed first deputy people's commissar of defence of the USSR and deputy supreme commander-in-chief in August 1942. In March 1953 he was appointed first deputy minister of defence of the USSR and in February 1955 minister of defence, a post which he held until October 1957. In 1956–7 he was a candidate member and member of the Presidium of the Central Committee of the CPSU.
Kliment Voroshilov (1881–1969): Soviet statesman and party and

military leader, who occupied various important positions before, during and after the Second World War. From 1946 to 1953 he was deputy chairman of the Council of Ministers of the USSR; from March 1953 to May 1960 he was chairman of the Presidium of the Supreme Soviet of the USSR; and he was a member of the CPSU Politburo from 1926 to 1952.

3. A *subbotnik* is a period of "voluntary," collective, unpaid work in the performance of "socially useful" labour. The practice of promoting such "voluntary" work was initiated soon after the Bolshevik Revolution and was once performed on Saturdays (*subboty* in Russian); hence, the use of the term.

4. *Seksot* is the abbreviated form of *sekretnyi sotrudnik* (literally secret collaborator), a term of abuse for someone who collaborated with the authorities.

### Chapter Twenty-One

1. Gulag is the Russian abbreviation for the Main Administration of Corrective Labour Camps.

2. Lavrentii Beria (1899–1953): prominent politician and police chief under Joseph Stalin. Beria replaced Ezhov as head of the NKVD in December 1938 and was elevated to candidate membership in the Politburo in March 1939 (full membership followed in 1946). Beria exhibited arrogance and a lust for power after Stalin's death in 1953, and on 26 June 1953 his political colleagues forestalled any attempt on his part to carry out a possible coup d'état by having him arrested. He was denounced for "criminal anti-party and anti-state activities," and according to the Soviet press Beria and other police officials were tried on 23 December 1953 and shot by a firing squad on the same day.

3. *Bolshaia zemlia* (literally, "the big land") was the term used by Soviet partisans during the war to refer to that area of the Soviet Union not occupied by the Axis forces.

4. Ernst Thälmann (1886–1944): communist leader in interwar Germany and twice presidential candidate during the Weimar Republic (1919–33). Thälmann, who was chiefly responsible for moulding the German Communist Party, was arrested in 1933 and was eventually executed in the Buchenwald concentration camp.

### Chapter Twenty-Two

1. By June 1953 the post-Stalin changes in leadership and policy had created a public impression of indecision and weakness at the top, and several demonstrations of unrest occurred within a few weeks of each other in the satellites as well as in the USSR. On 16 June an increase of labour norms in East Germany provoked a protest that rapidly turned into a revolutionary general strike in Berlin and other East German cities. Soviet troops had to be brought in to crush the strike.

### Chapter Twenty-Three

1. Despite its remote location, Norilsk is still one of the Soviet Union's most important mining centres, and is often displayed to foreign visitors as an example of "innovative urban development" in the far north. In his memoirs (*Zapiski dissidenta*), Andrei Amalrik notes sarcastically that when Canadian Prime Minister Pierre Trudeau visited Norilsk during his tour of the Soviet Union in 1971 (Amalrik was imprisoned at the time), he praised the Soviet Union's "achievement" in constructing such a wonderful city, and expressed regret that there was no such urban centre in the Canadian far north.

2. Ievhen Hrytsiak (b. 1926): Ukrainian dissident. Hrytsiak was a member of a Ukrainian nationalist youth organization in Sniatyn, Western Ukraine, during the war. He was mobilized into the Red Army in 1944, and remained in its ranks until 1949. In 1949 he was "exposed" as a former member of a nationalist organization and received a death sentence which was later commuted to twenty-five years of imprisonment. Hrytsiak was freed during the post-Stalin "thaw," but was rearrested in 1959 and sentenced to five years of imprisonment. Since his release he has been continually harassed and persecuted by the KGB, and since 1976 he has demanded that he and his family be allowed to emigrate from the Soviet Union.

Chapter Twenty-Four

1. Taras Shevchenko (1814–61): Ukrainian poet, born a serf, whose poetry had a great impact on the Ukrainian national movement. Shevchenko was arrested by the tsarist authorities in 1847 for being a member of a radical group called the Brotherhood of SS. Cyril and Methodius, and died soon after returning from ten years of penal servitude in Central Asia. "Haidamaky," his longest poem, depicts the bloody insurrection of the Ukrainian peasantry and poor Cossacks against the Polish landlords who held sway over Right-Bank Ukraine in the eighteenth century. There were several such insurrections in that century, the most severe occurring in 1768.
2. Karl von Clausewitz (1780–1831): Prussian general and military historian. Clausewitz is considered to be the foremost modern theorist on land warfare, and his most significant single contribution to military theory is the doctrine of political direction in military matters. Thus he maintained that "war is nothing but a continuation of political intercourse with the admixture of different means."
3. According to Shankowsky the reference here is probably to Oleksander Kuts (not Kuts-Horbenko), who was the OUN Lutsk okruh leader before the Second World War. Oleksander Kuts was not a member of the OUN Provid.
4. According to Shankowsky the reference here is probably to the Moroz who was responsible for the OUN-UPA's economic direction in Volhynia.

Chapter Twenty-Five

1. Volodymyr Horbovy (1899–1984): lawyer, UVO and OUN activist. Horbovy was defence counsel in a number of political trials in Galicia during the thirties, and was himself imprisoned by the Polish authorities in Bereza Kartuzka. Horbovy was arrested in Czechoslovakia in 1947, extradited to Poland, and handed over to the Soviet authorities in 1948. In 1949 he was sentenced to twenty-five years of imprisonment under Articles 54–2 and 54–11 of the old Criminal Code of the Ukrainian SSR. Throughout the seventies Horbovy, then living in Western Ukraine, demanded that he be allowed to leave the Soviet Union and join his son in Czechoslovakia.
2. The reference here is to the trial which followed the assassination of

Bronisław Pieracki, the Polish minister of internal affairs, by an OUN member (see Chapter 4, note 1).

3. Ozerlag is the short form for *Ozerny lager,* or Lake Camp.

4. Lazar Kaganovich (1893– ): prominent Soviet statesman and CPSU official. Kaganovich, a loyal supporter of Stalin, joined the Bolshevik Party in 1911 and became a full member of the Politburo in 1930. After Stalin's death Kaganovich became a member of the Presidium of the Council of Ministers, first deputy premier, and a member of the Presidium of the Central Committee (CC) of the CPSU, but in 1957 he was demoted by Khrushchev, joined the "anti-party group," and lost all his government and party offices.

Mikhail Suslov (1902–82): prominent CPSU official and ideologist, known for his orthodoxy and opposition to liberalization. Suslov became a member of the Presidium (Politburo) of the CC of the CPSU in 1955, and remained a member until his death.

Georgii Malenkov (1902– ): prominent Soviet statesman and CPSU official. Malenkov, who had been deeply involved in the great party purges of the late 1930s, was one of Stalin's chief lieutenants in the postwar period. When Stalin died he assumed the post of senior party secretary as well as chairman of the Council of Ministers. In 1955 he was forced to resign as prime minister and, after participating in the "anti-party group's" unsuccessful effort to depose Khrushchev, he was expelled from both the Presidium and the Central Committee and removed from his ministerial position.

Nikolai Bulganin (1895– ): Soviet statesman and administrator. Bulganin occupied various important party and state positions under Stalin, and became a full member of the Politburo of the CC in 1948. After Stalin's death Bulganin became deputy premier and minister of defence, and replaced Malenkov as chairman of the Council of Ministers in 1955. In 1958, however, Bulganin was formally associated with the "anti-party group" and was forced to relinquish his posts as premier and member of the Presidium of the CC of the CPSU.

5. Andrii Patrus-Karpatsky (1917–80): Ukrainian poet, translator and journalist from Transcarpathia. Patrus-Karpatsky became a member of the Communist Party of Czechoslovakia in 1937 and emigrated to the Soviet Union in 1939. Some of his poetry was published in the Soviet Union during and immediately after the Second World War, but in the late forties he was imprisoned and was not released until 1956. Since 1958 several collections of his poetry have been published in the Soviet Union.

6. Hryhorii (Hryts) Pryshliak (b. 1912): OUN activist. Pryshliak was

arrested in 1946, sentenced to twenty-five years of imprisonment, and detained in camps in Taishet, Kazakhstan and Mordovia.

## Chapter Twenty-Six

1. There is some confusion here; although a general conference of the OUN-B[andera] called the "Second Great Congress of the OUN" was held in Cracow in 1941 (not 1940), no Melnykites participated.
2. The term *oprichniki* is derived from *oprichnina*, the private court or household created by Tsar Ivan IV. The *oprichniki* were the members of this new court, drawn primarily from the lower gentry, who joined an elite guard corps which was in effect the tsar's personal bodyguard. These *oprichniki* conducted a reign of terror until the *oprichnina* was abolished in 1572.

## Chapter Twenty-Seven

1. The Virgin Lands Campaign, begun by Nikita Khrushchev in 1954, involved bringing some seventy million acres of arid land in the Urals, Siberia and Central Asia under cultivation, and many young people from all parts of the Soviet Union were drafted to take part in this campaign.
2. The ROA (*Russkaia Osvoboditelnaia Armiia*, or Russian Liberation Army) was the military formation, composed of Soviet soldiers captured by the Germans or Soviet workers deported to Germany as forced labourers, which was headed by Andrei Vlasov.
3. After the German defeat at Stalingrad at the end of 1942 official German policies concerning the establishment of a Ukrainian military formation slowly began to change. On 28 April 1943 it was announced that an SS Volunteer Division "Galicia" was to be established, and despite German instructions that the Ukrainian nature of this formation be downplayed, almost 30,000 Ukrainians volunteered for service. After a disastrous defeat on the Eastern Front and action in the Balkans the "Galicia" Division surrendered to the British in 1945.
4. See endnote 3, Chapter 17.
5. This is probably a reference to the prudent fashion in which the

Swedes acceded to independence for the Norwegians in 1905, thereby possibly sparing themselves an "Irish problem."

6. By 1941 the Union of Armed Resistance emerged as the strongest of all the Polish underground military groups set up in occupied Poland. The next year the Union was renamed *Armia Krajowa* (AK), or the Home Army, and it tried, on the whole quite successfully, to unify the clandestine military forces of the various underground political parties into one single organization. However, the fighting units (*Gwardia Ludowa*) organized by the communist underground took exception to this action, and in 1944 these units became part of what was known as the People's Army (*Armia Ludowa*).

## Chapter Twenty-Eight

1. The KGB is the Russian acronym for the Committee of State Security. The name was created in March 1954, although the secret police organization in the USSR dates from December 1917 and has been retitled many times.

2. Władyslaw Gomułka (1905–82): first secretary of the CC of the Polish United Workers' Party (PUWP) from 1956 to 1970. Gomułka was active in the Polish underground during the Second World War, and occupied a number of important positions in postwar Poland; however, in 1949 he fell from grace and was removed from all offices. In 1951 he was arrested and held without trial until April 1956, but was rehabilitated by the party in August 1956 and became its first secretary in October of that year. He held this post for fourteen years but became increasingly unpopular and was deposed in December 1970 after food price riots. After 1970 he retired from public life.
Marian Spychalski (b. 1906): state and party official in Poland. Spychalski was one of the organizers of the Polish Workers' Party and People's Guard in 1942 and a prominent member of the PUWP in the immediate postwar period. Like Gomu ka, Spychalski was removed from his posts in 1949 and arrested in 1951, but he was rehabilitated in 1956 and was a member of the Politburo of the CC of the PUWP from 1956 to 1970.

3. Edward Ochab (b. 1906): Polish party and state official. Ochab occupied a number of important posts in postwar Poland before the death of Stalin, but despite his past toughness in pursuing Stalinist policies he supported reform measures in 1956. Ochab continued to

hold various party and state positions (he was a member of the PUWP Politburo 1954–68), but resigned from all posts in March 1968 during an anti-Semitic purge in the party.

Józef Cyrankiewicz (b. 1911): Polish party and state official. Before the Second World War, Cyrankiewicz was an activist of the Polish Socialist Party, and he presided over the purge of "reactionary" and "hostile" elements in this party as well as its formal union with the communists in 1948. Cyrankiewicz was a member of the Politburo of the CC of the PUWP 1948–71 and prime minister 1947–52 and 1954–70.

4. Mátyás Rákosi (1892–1971): first secretary of the Hungarian Workers' Party 1945–55. Rákosi was active in the Hungarian communist movement during the interwar period and spent the war years in Moscow. Upon returning to Hungary, Rákosi soon consolidated political power in his hands, and became a symbol of unbending Stalinism and subservience to Moscow. He was removed from all party offices in 1955 in order to placate Tito, whom Rákosi had offended, and during the unrest in Budapest in October 1956 he fled to the Soviet Union.

5. Imre Nagy (1896–1958): Hungarian communist leader and statesman. Nagy lived in Moscow between 1929 and 1944, and upon his return to Hungary helped establish the postwar government, holding several ministerial posts between 1944 and 1948. A steadfast supporter of peasant interests, Nagy was excluded from the government in 1949, readmitted after a public recantation, and forced out again in 1955. During the October 1956 revolution the anti-Soviet forces turned to Nagy for leadership, and he again became premier of Hungary. After the uprising had been crushed, Nagy sought refuge in the Yugoslav embassy. He later left this embassy under safe conduct; however, he was abducted by the Hungarian authorities, tried and executed.

6. There are a large number of "closed cities" in the Soviet Union. In Soviet usage a closed city is one where the authorities use the passport system and issue a *propiska* (a permit for permanent residence in the city) to select immigrants and limit population growth. This policy strongly discriminates against those wishing to move from the countryside to an urban centre.

7. The Pecherska Lavra is a complex of buildings (originally a monastery founded in the eleventh century) which was once the most important religious and cultural centre in Kiev and is the site of many architectural landmarks. Most of the buildings belonging to this complex are now used to house museums. The Cathedral of

St. Sophia is one of the oldest (construction began in 1037), largest and most striking Orthodox cathedrals in Ukraine (although services are no longer held here). The Golden Gates were built in 1037 during the reign of Iaroslav the Wise, and although only their ruins remain, they are an important historical monument and a major tourist attraction.

8. *Vesnianky* are ritual folk songs sung in the springtime, almost exclusively by young women. *Kupalo* songs are ritual songs connected with the celebration of the beginning of the harvest season, while *Petrivka* songs are sung during the period of the fast preceding the Orthodox church holiday honouring the apostles Peter and Paul.

## Chapter Twenty-Nine

1. Article 54 of the old Criminal Code of the Ukrainian SSR (Article 58 of the old Criminal Code of the RSFSR), which was in force during the period 1927–58, covered "especially dangerous crimes against the state." Under Article 54–1 an act was said to be "counter-revolutionary" if it was "directed toward the overthrow, subversion or weakening of the power of the worker-peasant Soviets."

## Chapter Thirty

1. Volodymyr Sosiura (1898–1965): popular Soviet Ukrainian lyrical poet. Over forty collections of his poetry have appeared in Soviet Ukraine, but at various points in his career Sosiura came under strong criticism for being "insufficiently party-minded." Thus in 1951 Sosiura was attacked in *Pravda* for his poem "Love Ukraine" (written in 1944), which was considered to be an "ideologically defective" work. This poem was "rehabilitated" in 1956.

2. Old burial mounds in Ukraine were often excavated by government-appointed archaeological commissions searching for historical antiquities. To Shevchenko, such excavations were symbolic of the general spoliation of Ukraine, and he addressed this issue in his well-known poem "The Desecrated Grave," written in 1843.

3. Oleksii Kyrychenko (b. 1908): Soviet party official from Ukraine. Kyrychenko started his career in the Ukrainian party apparatus in

1938, and from 1953 to 1957 he was first secretary of the Ukrainian party organization. He was a member of the Presidium of the CC of the CPSU, 1955–60, and a secretary of the CC of the CPSU, 1957–60. In 1960 he was relieved of his party duties.

4. Kolchyk is a well-known KGB investigator who interrogated and searched the quarters of a number of Ukrainian human-rights activists in the late sixties and early seventies. He was involved, for example, in the cases of Nina Strokata, Ivan Svitlychny, Valentyn Moroz and Ivan Dziuba.

5. Shumuk wrote this section of his memoirs before his third Soviet trial (1972), at which time he was sentenced to an additional ten years of imprisonment and five years of internal exile.

6. Ivan Franko (1856–1916): Ukrainian writer, scholar, critic, translator and journalist. Franko employs a wide range of themes and various genres in his prose, but is best known for his graphic descriptions of working-class life in Galicia.
Lesia Ukrainka—real name Larysa Petrivna Kosach-Kvitka (1871–1913): Ukrainian poet. Her early lyrical work dealt with the poet's loneliness and social alienation, and her later dramatic poems were inspired by various historical subjects.

### Chapter Thirty-One

1. Revolt Pimenov (b. 1931): mathematician. In 1958 Pimenov was sentenced in accordance with Article 58–10 and 58–11 of the Criminal Code of the RSFSR to ten years of imprisonment for establishing an "anti-Soviet organization." He was freed in 1963 after many Soviet scholars appealed for his release, but was arrested again in 1970 for preparing and distributing *samizdat* materials and was sentenced to five years of exile, which he spent in the Komi ASSR.

2. Lev Kamenev (1883–1936): revolutionary, Communist Party official. Kamenev, an Old Bolshevik and a prominent party and state official during the decade following the October Revolution, joined with Zinoviev and a former rival, Trotsky, in a united opposition against Stalin in 1926. Soon he was expelled from his party positions, and after a secret trial in 1934, at which he and Zinoviev were sentenced to five years of imprisonment, they were tried again in 1936, in the first public show trial of the Great Purge. After confessing to fabricated charges, Kamenev was shot.

Nikolai Bukharin (1888–1938): major Marxist theoretician, economist and protégé of Lenin. Bukharin published several important theoretical economic works after the October Revolution, and played an important role in party politics and the Comintern. However, he fell into disgrace in 1929, and never regained his earlier influence and power. He was secretly arrested in 1937 and in March 1938 he was a defendant in the last public purge trial, at which he was accused (falsely) of counter-revolutionary activities and espionage. He was declared guilty and executed.

3. One of the early show trials in the Soviet Union was that of the so-called "Industrial Party," headed by Professor Ramzin, in November-December 1930. Ramzin had been a Bolshevik in 1905–7, and was a loyal party supporter during the twenties, but had then, it was alleged, fallen into bad company and become a "wrecker." At the trial all the witnesses were prisoners, and no documentary evidence of any sort was produced. Five of the accused were sentenced to death, but all sentences were commuted. A few years later Ramzin was released and restored to his posts.

4. There is some confusion here, for Petro Duzhy was not a member of the OUN Provid, but his brother Mykola Duzhy (1902–55) was a Provid member and one of the organizers of the UHVR.

5. *Literaturna Ukraina* is the official organ of the Writers' Union of Ukraine. Since 1957 it has appeared twice weekly.

6. Ivan Dziuba (b. 1931): literary critic and journalist. Dziuba was an active participant in the literary ferment in Ukraine during the sixties. He is best known for his important work *Internationalism or Russification*, which was written in 1965 and copies of which were circulated among certain party leaders in Ukraine. Dziuba launched a public appeal following the arrests of Ukrainian intellectuals in 1965, and also made a bold speech at a gathering in 1966 to mark the twenty-fifth anniversary of the Babyn Iar massacres of Jews and Ukrainians in 1941. On 2 March 1972 Dziuba was expelled form the Writers' Union of Ukraine. He was arrested on 18 April 1972, and in mid-March 1973 he was sentenced at a closed trial to five years of imprisonment. Dziuba, who was seriously ill at the time, was released soon afterward after agreeing to engage in "self-criticism."

7. Vasyl Karkhut (b. 1905): doctor, Plast activist and writer. Karkhut was one of the editors of the monthly *Vohni* in the interwar period, and wrote many articles for this and other journals.

Chapter Thirty-Two

1. Vasyl Kuk succeeded Roman Shukhevych-Chuprynka as head of the UPA in 1950.


Chapter Thirty-Three

1. A work-day (*trudoden*) is a measure of work performed on a collective farm by an individual member and is used as the basis for the distribution of personal income. The system was first introduced in the USSR in 1931.

2. The Committees of Poor Peasants were the Ukrainian equivalent of the Committees of the Poor (known as *Kombedy*), which existed in the RSFSR from June 1918 until January 1919. The Committees of Poor Peasants were established in 1920 and played an important role in the collectivization of agriculture in Ukraine, with a membership of approximately 1.6 million in April 1930. These committees were abolished at the beginning of 1931, once it became clear that many of their members were reluctant to give up the land which they had acquired from the "kulaks" and were also resisting collectivization.

3. Sergei Kirov (1886–1934): Bolshevik revolutionary and prominent party leader. Kirov was a loyal supporter of Stalin during the twenties, and became a full member of the Politburo in 1930. On 1 December 1934 Kirov was assassinated by Nikolaev, a young party member. Subsequently Stalin, who has since fallen under suspicion of being responsible for the crime, claimed to have discovered a widespread conspiracy against the entire Soviet leadership and launched an intense purge which led to the show trials of 1936–8.


Epilogue

1. Immediately senior to the "Young Octobrists" youth organization (which caters to children between the ages of seven and nine), the Pioneer organization in the Soviet Union caters to young people aged 10–14/15 years. All schoolchildren of the appropriate age may join if accepted by their local Pioneer organizations (based upon school or residence), and virtually all who are eligible do so.

2. Ivan Svitlychny (b. 1929): literary critic, translator. Svitlychny, a leading figure in the Ukrainian national and human-rights movement of the sixties, was harassed and persecuted throughout this period for his activities. He was arrested on 14 January 1972, charged with "anti-Soviet agitation and propaganda," and sentenced, in April 1973, to seven years of imprisonment in a strict-regime labour camp and five years of internal exile.

3. Smoloskyp Ukrainian Information Service, Press Bulletin Y0403, 16 January 1981.

4. On Shumuk's arrest see *The Chronicle of Current Events* (referred to hereafter as *Chronicle*), nos. 24 (dated 5 March 1972), 123; and 25 (dated 20 May 1972), 178–9. According to the former source Shumuk was arrested in Kiev; according to the latter source he was arrested in a village in Volhynia. In Cronid Lubarsky's *List of Political Prisoners in the USSR* (1 May 1983), the date of Shumuk's arrest is given as 12 January 1972.

5. B. Nahaylo, "Ukrainian Dissent and Opposition After Shelest," in *Ukraine After Shelest*, ed. B. Krawchenko (Edmonton 1983), 31.

6. Milovan Djilas (b. 1911): author, political essayist and former communist official. Djilas was a prominent member of the Yugoslav Communist Party before and during the Second World War, and after the war he became one of Tito's leading cabinet ministers. In 1953, however, intensifying personal and political conflicts with other party leaders led to his removal from all party posts, and shortly afterward he became an outspoken critic of the regime. Since 1954 he has been harassed (and imprisoned on two occasions) for his political writings. *The New Class* (1957) portrayed the typical communist oligarchy as a new group of privileged tyrants, and other important works include *Conversations With Stalin* (1961) and *The Unperfect Society: Beyond the New Class* (1969).

7. On the trial, see *Chronicle*, no. 27 (dated 15 October 1972), 284.

8. Ibid., 334.

9. *Prisoners of Conscience in the USSR: Their Treatment and Conditions*, 2d. ed. (London 1980), 101. According to *Chronicle*, no. 45 (dated 25 May 1977), 247, eleven prisoners died in the Mordovian special-regime camp during 1976. One of the reasons for the high mortality rate is thought to be the harmful work conditions, as the air in the workshops is saturated with glass dust and dust from abrasives. According to Lubarsky's *List of Political Prisoners*, those prisoners who are held in strict-regime detention are allowed only one long visit (up to three days, in private) per year, one short visit (two to four hours, in the presence of a guard) per year, and can

send out only one letter every month. The number of parcels a strict-regime prisoner can receive is extremely limited, and as a punishment a prisoner may be deprived of his next parcel, of the right to buy supplies in the camp shop, or of a scheduled visit.

10. *Chronicle*, no. 36 (dated 31 May 1965), 210.

11. Ibid.

12. *Chronicle*, no. 35 (dated 31 March 1975), 131. For the full text of this document (in Russian) see the documentary series *Arkhiv Samizdata* (referred to hereafter as *AS*), no. 2091. See also E. Kuznetsov, "The Status of the Soviet Political Prisoner," *Crossroads*, no. 7 (Winter-Spring 1981): 183–211.

13. *Chronicle*, no. 48 (dated 14 March 1978), 67–8. For the full text of this document see *AS*, no. 3251.

14. *Chronicle*, no. 43 (dated 31 December 1976), 8 and *Chronicle*, no. 45 (dated 25 May 1977), 246.

15. *Chronicle*, no. 47 (dated 30 November 1977), 130. Vasyl Romaniuk (b. 1925): Orthodox priest. Romaniuk was originally sentenced in 1944 to ten years of imprisonment and exile for his "nationalist and religious activity," and a conviction for "anti-Soviet agitation and propaganda" was added in 1946. Romaniuk was rehabilitated in 1959, and after he was ordained as an Orthodox priest (1964) he criticized corruption in the Orthodox Church and state suppression of religion. He was arrested on 12 January 1972, charged with "anti-Soviet agitation and propaganda," and sentenced, in July 1972, to seven years of imprisonment and three years of internal exile. See *Vasyl Romanyuk: A Voice in the Wilderness*, ed. J. Dobczansky (Wheaton, Illinois 1980).

16. *Chronicle*, no. 48 (dated 14 March 1978), 50.

17. *Chronicle*, no. 47 (dated 30 November 1977), 107–108.

18. For the texts of these documents see: *Chronicle*, no. 41 (dated 3 August 1976), 153, and also *AS*, no. 2636; *Chronicle*, no. 47 (dated 30 November 1977), 126–7, and also *AS*, no. 3089; AS, no. 3759; and *AS*, no. 3761.

19. *Chronicle*, no. 45 (dated 25 May 1977), 247.

20. See, for example, *Svoboda*, 19 August 1977 and 18 November 1978.

21. *Chronicle*, no. 51 (dated 1 December 1978), 90.

22. *Svoboda*, 3 October 1978.

23. *House of Commons Debates* (Hansard), 30th Parliament, 4th Session, Vol. 122, no. 18, 3 November 1978, 777.

24. Further attacks on Shumuk were published in issue no. 16 (1981) of the Soviet mass-circulation weekly *Nedelia* and were broadcast on Moscow radio on 3 July 1981.

25. *Chronicle*, no. 57 (dated 3 August 1980), 86.
26. Letter to Ivan Shumuk from Danylo Shumuk, dated 2 March 1981.
27. *Prisoners of Conscience in the USSR*, 106–110.
28. Letter to Ivan Shumuk from Danylo Shumuk, dated 2 March 1981.
29. *Prisoners of Conscience in the USSR*, 101–103.
30. Letter to Ivan Shumuk from Danylo Shumuk, dated 3 March 1982.
31. Letter to Ivan Shumuk from Danylo Shumuk, dated 24 April 1982.